TURN ON YOUR MIND:

FOUR DECADES OF
GREAT PSYCHEDELIC ROCK

By Jim DeRogatis

HAL•LEONARD®
CORPORATION

781.66

11/05

18.95

B/T

Turn on your Mind
Four Decades of Great Psychedelic Rock

Library of Congress Cataloging-in-Publication Data

DeRogatis, Jim.
  Turn on your mind : four decades of great psychedelic rock / Jim DeRogatis.
    p. cm.

Originally published: Kaleidoscope eyes:
  psychedelic rock from the '60s to the '90s.
  Secaucus, N.J.: Carol Pub. Group, 1996.

Includes bibliographical references (p.) and index.
ISBN 0-634-05548-8
1. Psychedelic rock music--History and criticism. I. Title.
  ML3534.D47 2003
781.66--dc21   2003013273

Published by Hal Leonard Corporation
7777 West Bluemound Road
P. O. Box 13819
Milwaukee, WI 53213

Trade Book Division Editorial Offices
151 West 46th Street, 8th Floor
New York, NY 10036

Visit Hal Leonard online at **www.halleonard.com**

PRAISE FOR THE FIRST EDITION

Kaleidoscope Eyes does for psychedelic music what Jon Savage's *England's Dreaming* did for punk, and is an essential work in the significant world of rock writing.

—*Mid-Wales County Times & Express*

In this ambitious and fascinating book, Jim DeRogatis knowledgeably explores every facet of psychedelic rock—not merely the obvious tie-dyed, Day-Glo music that swirled around the Summer of Love, but every type of rock music with a theme of expanding the mind.

—Trudi Miller Rosenblum, *Billboard*

With all the media schlock about rock and roll in the '60s, a cynical twentysomething like me might think that psychedelic rock belongs to twirling Deadheads and Budweiser-sponsored concerts—music that investment bankers pop in the cassette player in the Volvo on the way to junior's soccer practice. I admit, I'm jaded; I think Jim Morrison was a lousy poet, and I don't "get" anything the Moody Blues sing...Enter *Kaleidoscope Eyes,* a refreshing and objective account of psychedelic rock over the last four decades.

—Gretchen Federlein, *Resonance*

Jim DeRogatis's *Kaleidoscope Eyes* is by no means the definitive book on psychedelic music, but its inclusiveness and flexibility expand the concept far beyond the standard canon of psychedelic masters like the Beatles, 13th Floor Elevators, Pink Floyd, the Grateful Dead, Jimi Hendrix, and Jefferson Airplane. It encompasses a myriad of musicians who also explore altered states of consciousness while coming out of cultural, artistic, political, and social contexts far removed from the youth explosion of the late '60s.

—Carlo McCormick, *High Times*

In his first book, *Kaleidoscope Eyes,* rock journalist, rabble-rouser, and *Chicago Sun-Times* pop music critic Jim DeRogatis persuasively argues that psychedelic music did not die in the '60s. Instead, DeRogatis draws the connection between Ken Kesey's acid tests and My Bloody Valentine's guitar tapestries, the Byrds' "Eight Miles High" and De La Soul's "3 Feet High and Rising," Pink Floyd and Portishead, Amon Düül II and Hüsker Dü.

—Greg Kot, *Chicago Tribune*

For music fans who want to explore the region where hippies, punks, hip-hoppers, and rave kids can sit down and share a spliff together, this is an indispensable guidebook.

—Will Hermes, *City Pages*

Kaleidoscope Eyes is a scholarly but opinionated chronicle/extended meditation that takes the reader from Dr. Albert Hoffman's discovery of LSD, through the early days of psych (Beatles, Beach Boys, the German krautrock bands) and onward, winding up in the modern era with analyses of pop, hip hop and rave culture, plus a pair of extended looks at contemporary avatars My Bloody Valentine and the Flaming Lips. Many, many bands and their significant recordings are mentioned along the way, from Pink Floyd to Pere Ubu to Plastikman.

—Fred Mills, *Magnet*

Jim DeRogatis is bound by neither time nor place; he follows psychedelic sound wherever it takes him, as the major or minor element in an array of styles. His concentration in *Kaleidoscope Eyes* is, as befits a rock critic, soundly on the music; personalities and scenes enter to elucidate musical points. Drug references are mainly confined to the impact of drugs on the creativity of the musicians and the ways in which the music attempts to simulate the psychedelic drug experience.

—Deena Dasein, *Illinois Entertainer*

ALSO BY JIM DeROGATIS

Let It Blurt: The Life and Times of Lester Bangs, America's Greatest Rock Critic

Milk It! Collected Musings on the Alternative Music Explosion of the '90s

"And wouldn't it be dumb /
If all their atrocities were just forgiven /
But she won't give that to them /
Until they learn how to love."

—*The Flaming Lips,*
"Kim's Watermelon Gun"

CONTENTS

INTRODUCTION

THE FIRST VERSION OF THE BOOK you hold in your hands was published in 1996, thirty years after the release of the first psychedelic rock masterpieces (*Revolver* by the Beatles, *Pet Sounds* by the Beach Boys, and *The Psychedelic Sounds of the 13th Floor Elevators*), and twenty-nine years after the much-vaunted but generally overrated Summer of Love. Since it was the only thing imposed upon me by my otherwise benevolent editor, Kevin McDonough, I accepted his title—*Kaleidoscope Eyes: Psychedelic Rock from the '60s to the '90s*—but I should have fought it. For one thing, it came from the wrong album; in the pages that follow, I posit *Sgt. Pepper's Lonely Hearts Club Band* as something of a mess and a letdown after the masterful *Revolver*. For another, it implies a certain self-delusion, as if looking at the world through rose-colored glasses, when the aspects of psychedelia that I want to champion are the crystalline clarity that comes the morning after a psychedelic experience, and those conveyed by the original Greek roots of the word, which mean "soul-revealing" or "mind-manifesting." Hence the return of my original name, with its nod to the Beatles' brilliant and enduring "Tomorrow Never Knows"—*Turn on Your Mind: Four Decades of Great Psychedelic Rock*.

In addition to nearly six more years of reading, listening, and writing, this edition benefits from the thousand-odd insertions, deletions, amendments, and edits that any writer would love to have the chance to make in order to improve his or her first book. It has been fully revised and updated since the original book published by Citadel Underground in the U.S. and Fourth Estate in the U.K.; includes the insights gleaned from dozens of additional interviews conducted with many of the key players in the story of this fascinating genre, and has been enriched incalculably by the hundreds of conversations and e-mail exchanges, pro and con, that I had with readers of the first book from around the world. (I cannot adequately thank everyone who took the time to share their thoughts with me.) Otherwise, the goals are exactly the same as they were the last time.

The first of these was to provide the sort of sweeping genre overview that psychedelic rock has always deserved but has never gotten. During the punk explosion of the mid-'70s, Lester Bangs drew a new line through rock history that connected the three-chord drive and amped-up attitude of "La Bamba" by Ritchie Valens to "Louie Louie" by the Kingsmen, "No Fun" by the Stooges, "Blitzkrieg Bop" by the Ramones, and—we could add today—"Smells Like Teen Spirit" by Nirvana. This book is not the definitive history of the genre; I doubt that any one tome ever could be. Instead, it is an attempt to draw a line from the hypnotic drone of the Velvet Underground to the disorienting swirl of My Bloody Valentine; from the artful experiments of *Pet Sounds* to the flowing, otherworldly samples of rappers P.M. Dawn; from the dementia of the 13th Floor Elevators to the grungy lunacy of the Flaming Lips; from the crazy psychedelic community of Amon Düül II to that of the Elephant 6 bands, and from the sounds and sights at Ken Kesey's '60s Acid Tests to those at '90s raves.

While trying to make those broad connections, I occasionally pause to zoom in and tell some of the most interesting stories along the way; trace some of the recurring themes and ideas (the white bicycle, the embrace of "happy accidents," or the use of the recording studio as an instrument); craft an aesthetic for evaluating the music that has been made and that which is yet to come (great psychedelic rock tries to transport the listener someplace that exists only in the space between the headphones, while never neglecting the drive, melody, and immediacy essential to all great rock 'n' roll), and offer my outline for the ideal psychedelic rock record collection. I hope that I can open the ears of more mature fans who think that the high point of psychedelic rock was the Haight-Ashbury scene of 1967, or that the music's evolution ended with *The Dark Side of the Moon* in 1973. At the same time I would like to enlighten the teenage raver and the twentysomething indie-rocker, give them a basic history, and provide them with a map for further exploring these sounds on their own. Thankfully, that is much easier now than when I first sat down to write this book, or at any other point in history, thanks not only to the proliferation of information on the Web, but to the ready availability of downloadable music. The industry's efforts be damned—curious listeners now have the ability to hear almost anything that intrigues them at a few clicks of the mouse (and that is a psychedelic concept if ever there was one!).

Though it starts with an account of the discovery of LSD, the drug that brought psychedelic consciousness into the mainstream of Western culture in the mid-'60s, *Turn on Your Mind* is a book about music, not drugs. As psychedelic rock evolved, it developed a code of sonic requirements—a distinctive sound produced according to certain conventions and including sonic, visual, and verbal clues that all mark a particular piece of music as a part of the genre. Many artists told me that they used drugs in the process of making those sounds, and many told me that they did not. In a review of the first edition for the Minneapolis weekly *City Pages*, then-music editor Will Hermes chided me for neglecting to mention my own psychedelic experiences, or to offer my own stance on whether or not psychedelic drugs are necessary for making great psychedelic rock. For what it's worth, two of the numerous experiments of my youth stand out. I recall one trip in the winter of 1984 during a house party thrown by the band Tiny Lights when I spent much of the evening jamming on congas as the Rolling Stones' "Sympathy for the Devil" boomed from the stereo. I had never heard or *been inside* music in quite the same way, and while I already held this opinion before that journey, I returned more convinced than ever that there is no more powerful artistic force in the universe than rock 'n' roll.

There was also the trip with my friend and spiritual brother, Anthony J. DiMurro, in the spring of '85, when he convinced me to drive from our native Jersey City, New Jersey, to a college in rural Redding, Pennsylvania. He had met a girl who went to school there, and upon arriving, he promptly ditched me at some frat house while he and his paramour went off to wrinkle the sheets in her dorm room. The small square of blotter acid that I'd taken during the drive came on hard around midnight, and I spent the next few hours playing *The Velvet Underground and Nico* over and over again on a beat-up record player while watching a TV set tuned to nothing but static and white noise. When A.J. had sated himself of love's sweet caress, we piled into my 1976 Ford Granada and started the drive back to Jersey, only we were both more than a little bit discombobulated. He had his sister's portable tape player perched between us on the front seat, and we were blasting a cassette of *Exile on Main Street* by the Rolling Stones (them again!). Transfixed by its celebratory sound and redemptive message, we kept rewinding and replaying "Shine a Light" as we drove. The sun was coming up, Mick was singing "May the good Lord / Shine a light on you / Make every song / Your favorite tune," and as we flew over rolling green hills and past verdant pastures (a landscape so unlike Jersey City), everything was beautiful and *everything made sense*. The only problem was we were driving south and west when we should have been traveling north and east, and we didn't realize our mistake until we reached the border of West Virginia. By then, it was hot, sticky, and too damn bright outside; we were desperately thirsty, and we looked and felt like Hunter S. Thompson and his attorney after their bender in *Fear and Loathing in Las Vegas*. We were exhausted but completely wired (you know the feeling), and I was freaked out because at some point we'd parked on the side of the road so we could get out and run through one of those verdant pastures—it seemed like a good idea at the time, but we emerged reeking of cow dung—and when we pulled off we must have driven over a rock or a stump, because something under the car had been punctured and all of the power steering fluid had leaked out. I only learned this later; at the time, I couldn't figure out why the Granada made the most horrifying *gggggrrrrrrccccccchhhhhh* sound whenever I turned the wheel, which felt like I was trying to roll a ten-ton slab of granite. When we finally turned around, the drive back home seemed to last for days. The batteries on the tape player had run out, and now the only soundtrack was the discomforting wail of a free-floating police siren, which I could physically sense hovering behind me just above my right shoulder, occasionally extending a very long tongue that rudely tickled my ear. I can feel it again right now, just thinking about it, lo these many years later.

Anyway, I never saw God and I never traveled toward the white light. In the end I have to say that I'm with Prince Be, Robyn Hitchcock, Wayne Coyne, and the many others who maintain that psychedelic drugs are not necessary for making or appreciating psychedelic rock—as the current title of this book suggests, it's all about opening your mind. While my psychedelic experiences may have been fun and illuminating, I have no burning desire to revisit them (though I never had the opportunity to try DMT, and I'll confess that I'm still curious about meeting Terence McKenna's elves who run the machinery of the cosmos). I generally prefer to attempt to break on through to the other side by musical, not chemical, means.

In addition to the power of the music, another thing I noticed under the influence of psychedelics was a severe impatience bordering on hatred for fellow travelers who resort to psychedelic clichés. Nothing bummed me out quicker than someone who wouldn't stop tediously rattling on about the "important" revelations they were having when they were really just contemplating their shoelaces for five hours. I also have little or no use for *bad* psychedelic rock, and there is plenty of it, just as there is a lot of self-indulgent or formulaic crap in any genre. Pop culture has a tendency to commodify any innovative sound and reduce it to its lowest common denominators and a marketing pose, and it is the critic's job to see through that.

Psychedelic rock has been particularly ill-served by the Baby Boomers, who have often elevated some of the least of its adherents to the pantheon while slighting or ignoring true giants. One of the challenges for my peers and the generation of critics who will follow is to offer alternative canons to the one that we've inherited. Fuck the Rock and Roll Hall of Fame and all that it implies—there is never only one way to look at history or at art. The story of Custer's Last Stand can be viewed from the perspectives of the arrogant general, the beleaguered horse soldiers, the Native American warriors, the wives and children that both teams of combatants left behind, the politicians who were pushing westward expansion, or the capitalist-industrialists who were driving it. Similarly there exists a generation for whom Kraftwerk is far more influential then the Beatles; there are listeners who think *Loveless* is more important than any other rock album ever made, and there are fans who saw God when Jimi Hendrix performed at Woodstock and don't believe that his performance will ever be matched. *Turn on Your Mind* is simply *my* version of the music's history, and my way of hearing it. Other books could be written emphasizing entirely different artists and other musical values, and I would enjoy reading them.

As is my style, this is a contentious book—if rock 'n' roll is our most immediate, vibrant, and honest art form, why on earth should rock critics mince their words or pull their punches? I cannot imagine the reader who will agree with everything that follows. Hell, I'm not even sure that I do! I double back on myself all the time, and never trust a critic who tells you that he or she doesn't. We are all constantly growing and evolving, and those of us who care passionately about music are forever gaining new insights and revising our opinions. My final goal is not to make you accept my vision of great psychedelic rock, but to prompt you to think about your own.

Once again, I'd like to thank all of those who were named in the first edition of this book for their help with listening, researching, and brainstorming, though I'd be remiss if I didn't single out Kevin McDonough, my original editor. Special thanks this time around are due to John Cerullo, Nicole Julius, Mary Vandenberg, Michael Messina, John J. O'Sullivan, and everyone at Hal Leonard, and to Ben Schafer, who originally brought this book to their attention. I'd also like to thank Gerry Howard, the editor of *Let It Blurt*; Chris Calhoun and Kassie Evashevski, my agents; Cynthia Taylor-Handrup, who helped me through some difficult times; my bandmates in Vortis, Chris Martiniano, Tony Tavano, and Michael Weinstein; my *Sound Opinions* cohorts, Shawn Campbell, Greg Kot, Jason Saldanha, Matt Spiegel, and Scott Taradesh; my parents, Helene and Harry Reynolds; my brother, his wife, and their son, Michael, Mary Ellen, and Ryan DeRogatis, and most of all the two Mels in my life—my daughter, Melody (how many stars would you give this, Mo?), and my beautiful love and soul mate, Carmél Carrillo.

Finally, thanks to you, the reader. If anything in the pages that follow sends you rushing to the CD player, the record store, or the Internet search engine, then I've succeeded at what I set out to do. Tune in, turn it up, and read on..

ONE

1

MY WHITE BICYCLE:
The Origins and Hallmarks of Psychedelic Rock

A psychedelic drug is one which, without causing physical addiction, craving, major physiological disturbances, delirium, disorientation, or amnesia, more or less reliably produces thought, mood, and perceptual changes otherwise rarely experienced except in dreams, contemplative and religious exaltations, flashes of vivid involuntary memory, and acute psychoses.

—Lester Grinspoon and James B. Bakalar
in Peter Stafford's *Psychedelics Encyclopedia*

SINCE PREHISTORIC TIMES, members of all societies have stumbled upon and ritualized the use of plants that enlarge the scope of the mind in ways that appear both healing and inspirational. In the nineteenth century, scientists began synthesizing chemicals with these same properties in the laboratory: mescaline, LSD, psilocybin,

Ecstasy. Musicians have sampled all of these drugs, and each has had some impact on rock 'n' roll. But it was the collision between rock and LSD that ushered in the genre of psychedelic rock and brought psychedelic thought into mainstream consciousness, so it is with a Swiss chemist's wild bicycle ride that this book must start.

In the spring of 1943, Albert Hofmann was a close-cropped, bespectacled professional and a thirty-seven-year-old father of three. He had been working as a research chemist at the Sandoz Company in Basel, Switzerland, for fourteen years, the last eight spent researching the medicinal properties of ergot, a fungus that grows on rye. During the Middle Ages, ergot-contaminated rye bread caused outbreaks of St. Anthony's Fire, a nasty disease that caused the fingers and toes to turn black and fall off, eventually resulting in death through violent convulsions. In the 1500s, mid-wives discovered that small amounts of ergot could help during childbirth by speeding uteral contractions and slowing the flow of blood. Hofmann's work involved synthesizing variations of lysergic acid, the key ingredient in the ergot alkaloid, in the hope that it could be used as a cure for migraines. The chemist produced his twenty-fifth synthesis, lysergic acid diethylamide or LSD-25, in 1938, but when it was first tested by Sandoz pharmacologists, they didn't notice anything special, and work moved on to other molecular combinations.

Five years later, Hofmann had an odd premonition that Sandoz staffers had overlooked something unique about LSD-25. In the '60s, hippies looking for cosmic coincidences would point out that this notion struck the good doctor only weeks after scientists first achieved nuclear fission under a football field at the University of

Chicago. New Age thinking holds that nature simultaneously gave humanity the tool to destroy itself (the atom bomb) and the key to open the door to a higher and more peaceful level of consciousness (LSD). Of course Hofmann couldn't have known about any of that. On April 16, 1943, he synthesized a new batch of LSD-25, and as he finished his work, he began to feel dizzy. Assuming he had a touch of the flu, he closed his lab for the weekend and went home, and there he embarked on the first acid trip. "I perceived an uninterrupted stream of fantastic pictures, extraordinary shapes with intense, kaleidoscopic play of colors," he wrote in his autobiography *LSD, My Problem Child*. "After some two hours, this condition faded away."

Reflecting on these gentle hallucinations over the weekend, Hoffmann decided that they had been caused by the drug, which he had handled without wearing gloves. Late on the afternoon of April 19 he tested his theory. The chemist dissolved 250 millionths of a gram of LSD in a glass of water and, in the name of science, drank it down. After forty minutes, he began to feel dizzy and anxious. He hopped on his beaten-up bicycle—the only form of transportation available in wartime Switzerland—and started the four-mile trip home. He felt as if he was barely moving, but the assistant who followed him on another bike reported that they pedaled at a furious pace. The road before him rose and fell like the swells of a turbulent sea, and the buildings that lined the streets bulged and contracted like objects thrust into a fun-house mirror. When Hofmann finally reached home, he was in the middle of the first *bad* acid trip. His world wouldn't stop spinning, the furniture took on grotesque forms, and the neighbor who offered him a glass of milk turned into a horrible witch. He only calmed down when his physician arrived. "Now, little by little I could begin to enjoy the unprecedented colors and shapes that persisted behind my closed eyes," he wrote. "Kaleidoscopic, fantastic images surged in on me...exploding in colored fountains."

Hofmann's bike ride would be commemorated (consciously or not) in several early psychedelic rock songs, including "I Just Wasn't Made for These Times" by the Beach Boys, "Bike" by Pink Floyd, and "My White Bicycle" by Tomorrow. But it took two decades for his surprising discovery to make its way from the laboratory to the recording studio.

The morning after his second LSD experience, Hofmann woke up clear and refreshed, and a sensation of well-being and renewed life flowed through him. Research to explain these odd experiences began almost immediately. Sandoz wanted to test the drug's toxicity on cats, mice, and chimpanzees, but Hofmann and members of his staff were impatient, and they began taking it themselves and recording their hallucinatory visions. Dr. Werner Stoll, the son of Hofmann's boss, took the drug and found himself swept away by images of Edgar Allan Poe's maelstrom. The experience convinced Stoll that LSD could be useful in psychotherapy, and he began studying its effects on schizophrenics at the University of Zurich psychiatry clinic. In 1947 he published some encouraging findings, and Sandoz started offering the drug to clinical psychiatrists around the world, "literature available on request."

British psychiatrist Humphry Osmond studied the effects of mescaline and LSD on alcoholics in Saskatchewan, Canada. In 1953 he published a paper stating that the drugs prompted a kind of artificial schizophrenia, mimicking the chemical reactions that happened in actual schizophrenics. Curious about mind-altering drugs—he had written about the fictional "soma" in his novel, *Brave New World*—English author Aldous Huxley corresponded with Osmond, and from these letters came a word to describe the drugs' effects. Huxley originally proposed "phanerothyme," from roots relating to "spirit" or "soul." He illustrated its use in a letter to Osmond that is quoted in Peter Stafford's *Psychedelics Encyclopedia*: "To make this trivial world sublime, take half a gram of phanerothyme." Osmond thought the word was too pretty—he wasn't convinced that every psychedelic experience was sublime—and he suggested a new one from the Greek *psyche* (soul or mind) and *delein* (to make manifest) or *deloun* (to show or reveal). "To fathom hell or soar angelic, just take a pinch of psychedelic," he wrote.

Under Osmond's supervision, Huxley took mescaline in 1953 at his home in Hollywood Hills, California. He described his beatific vision—a journey toward "the white light"—in *The Doors of Perception*. (The book's title was inspired by the eighteenth-century poet William Blake, who wrote that, "If the doors of perception were cleansed, everything would appear to man as it is—infinite.") Huxley went on to take LSD as part of a group of curious intellectuals that included Los Angeles psychiatrist Oscar Janiger and philosopher Alan Watts. Janiger had been interested in LSD since reading Stoll's first account. He started studying the drug in 1955, and his third subject was a painter who pronounced the experience the equal of four years in art school. Janiger began giving LSD to other artists, actors, and members of the Hollywood elite, including Anaïs Nin, Jack Nicholson, James Coburn, and conductor André

Previn. "All my life I've been searching for peace of mind," said Cary Grant, a particularly enthusiastic convert. "Nothing really seemed to give me what I wanted until this treatment."

LSD was starting to spread. "Captain" Al Hubbard was a Kentucky-born raconteur who served during World War II in the OSS, the predecessor to the CIA. In the early '50s, he bought four thousand vials of LSD from Sandoz and began distributing it with religious fervor on the West Coast and in Canada, an activity that earned him the sobriquet "the Johnny Appleseed of acid." Michael Hollingshead, a stylish Englishman with a similar mission, acquired ten thousand doses that he carried around in a mayonnaise jar. This stock launched the first trip by Harvard University professor Timothy Leary, who in turn became a devoted proselytizer. ("There is some possibility that my friends and I have illuminated more people than anyone else in history," Hollingshead is quoted as saying in *Psychedelics Encyclopedia*.) In 1957 LSD from the Sandoz plant in Hanover, New Jersey, began turning up in New York's underground scene of Beat poets, artists, and folk musicians. At the same time, curious artists such as novelist Ken Kesey lined up to take psychedelic drugs as part of clinical studies at West Coast universities. From there, it was only a short leap to California's burgeoning surf-music scene.

The Gamblers are remembered (when they're remembered at all) as the first rock band to mention LSD on record. "LSD 25" was the B side of "Moon Dawg," an unremarkable single released on the World Pacific label in 1960. The reference was little more than a hip, mysterious title, and there is nothing particularly psychedelic about the instrumental's twangy guitar and barrelhouse piano. The

The first mention of LSD on a rock recording: the Gamblers' 1960 surf instrumental, "LSD 25."

band broke up less than a year later, and drummer Sandy Nelson went on to a successful solo career. In an ironic twist, Gamblers key-boardist Bruce Johnston would replace Brian Wilson in the Beach Boys when Wilson broke down under the pressures of stardom, fam-ily, and too many psychedelic drugs. "I don't even remember the Gamblers," Johnston told me in 1994. "I was also a Hollywood Argyle for one day. I used to back up Ritchie Valens with Sandy Nelson, and Sandy, Phil Spector, and I were in the same band before that. The '60s surf scene was simplistic. It was a lot of people who didn't surf rec-ognizing that there was something out there. As far as the LSD, it's something I've never thought about and I've never done."

In the early '60s, LSD use was still so limited that it seemed as if everyone who had taken it knew everyone else. "Taking LSD was like being in a secret society," Charles Perry wrote in *The Haight Ashbury: A History.* "There was no way of knowing how many peo-ple might be messing with psychedelics. If you thought about it, you might conclude the only people taking LSD were Leary and the Harvard crowd, some Beats, and a few others, not many more than your own circle of insane friends." Or, as Byrds producer Jim Dickson put it in David Crosby's autobiography, "Everybody who got high knew each other then." More musical references popped up, often in the form of a wink and a nod between people in the know. New York folk musician Peter Stampfel claims to be the first person to use the word "psychedelic" in a song lyric, 1963's "Hesitation Blues." In 1964 Bob Dylan sang in "Mr. Tambourine Man" about what may or may not have been a psychedelic trip ("Take me for a trip upon your magic swirling ship..."). The next year, Dickson and the Byrds electrified the song; a former Chicago cop opened a rock club called The Trip on Sunset Strip, and Dylan sang about "Johnny in the basement mixing up the medicine" in "Subterranean Homesick Blues."

Meanwhile, a thirty-year-old chemist named Augustus Owsley Stanley was running the first major underground acid factory in the bathroom of a house in Berkeley. Stanley's potent LSD powered the Acid Tests hosted by Kesey and his band of Merry Pranksters. Flush from the success of his novel *One Flew Over the Cuckoo's Nest*, Kesey sponsored night-long multi-media "happenings" that featured films, strobe lights, taped messages, weird skits, and anything else that the Pranksters could come up with to jump-start the psychedelic experience. "It started off as a party, with movies flashed on the walls, and lights, and tapes, and the Pranksters providing the music themselves, not to mention the LSD," New Journalist Tom Wolfe wrote in *The Electric Kool-Aid Acid Test*, his account of his time with Kesey and his followers. "The Pranksters' strange atonal

Chinese music broadcast on all frequencies, a la John Cage."

Rechristened "Bear," Stanley became the sound wizard and resident chemist with the Grateful Dead, the house band at the Acid Tests. The group made its recorded debut in March 1967, after the major record companies descended on San Francisco in a rush to sign what were now regularly called "psychedelic" or "acid"-rock bands. But to the extent that it can be pinned down at all, the birth date of psychedelic rock is best listed as 1966.

Inspired by the soul-searching that followed Brian Wilson's first encounter with LSD, the Beach Boys' *Pet Sounds* was released in May of that year. Their competitors in studio innovations, the Beatles, followed in August with *Revolver*, which included "Tomorrow Never Knows," a song inspired by John Lennon's first profound acid trip. In Austin, Texas (of all places), a group called the 13th Floor Elevators was winning sometimes unwelcome attention for strange songs with lyrics that openly addressed the experience of taking psychedelic drugs. Although they maintained that it was about jet flight, the Byrds' otherworldly single, "Eight Miles High," was blacklisted by radio programmers because of its psychedelic subtext. The Rolling Stones scored a hit with the mysterious, Eastern-tinged "Paint It Black," and New York's Velvet Underground brought happenings to the heartland, touring the country with a sensory assault of swirling lights, underground films, whip-cracking dancers, and white-noise drones called Andy Warhol's Exploding Plastic Inevitable.

The psychedelic influence seemed to be everywhere. Conservative columnist Walter Winchell warned users that LSD would make them go blind. Some headlines claimed that the drug

killed the sex drive forever, while others asserted that it turned people into sex maniacs. (One rumor held that the initials stood for
"Let's Strip Down.") Prompted by lurid stories of acid excess and
mounting public pressure to protect their nations' youth, politicians in the U.S. and England started the process of outlawing LSD
at the end of 1966, but it was already too late. The drug that
Hofmann came to call his "problem child" continued to increase in
popularity. It peaked during 1967's Summer of Love, but following
a brief lull in the mid-'70s, LSD use by young people has been more
or less consistent ever since. (From the mid-'70s through the early
'90s, between 7 and 12 percent of high school seniors surveyed by
the federal government reported trying LSD at least once, according
to LSD: Still with Us After All These Years by sociologists Leigh
Henderson and William Glass. A February 2002 report by the Cox
News Service noted that the annual survey by the Partnership for a
Drug-Free America found that LSD use fell from 12 percent in 2000
to 10 percent in 2001, but Ecstasy use had increased.)

   Equally significant, LSD had captured the popular imagination
by 1966 to the point where people who never had a psychedelic
experience *thought* they had a fairly good idea of what one was like.
The drug became inextricably intertwined in the crazy quilt of
social, political, sexual, and racial issues raised by children of the
Baby Boom in what is now inevitably referred to in cultural short-
hand as The Sixties. As with most psychoactive drugs, a subculture
developed around the use of psychedelics, and it was brought to
mainstream attention by the fresh media outlets of FM radio, cool
new magazines such as *Rolling Stone* and *Crawdaddy!*, and hip young
writers like Wolfe and Joan Didion who struggled to explain the sea

change in older, more established publications. This drug subculture differed from others (say, heroin or methamphetamine users) in that the idea of "mind expansion" had spiritual and intellectual connotations that reached beyond the usual goal of "getting wasted" (though those didn't always translate to the mass audience). Psychedelics users were dubbed "hippies" in a snotty derivation of the Beat "hipsters," but even before that, the subculture's slang, fashions, and mannerisms were filtering into popular culture and key players such as Leary and Kesey became celebrities. Many of the bands that recorded psychedelic rock songs in the wake of the groundbreaking efforts of 1966 had never taken psychedelic drugs, but the subculture told them everything they needed to know to sound authentic or, as Kesey's Pranksters would say, to sound as if they were "on the bus." More importantly, the word "psychedelic" came to signal a set of sonic clues.

The psychedelic pioneers noted the unique effects of the drugs when listening to music, often referring to *synaesthesia*, or the sense that sounds could be seen as kaleidoscopic bursts of color. During the very first LSD trip, Hofmann noted that "every sound generated a vividly changing image with its own consistent form and color." Psychedelic drugs made inanimate objects buzz with energy as if they were alive. Describing an LSD experience in *The Joyous Cosmology*, Alan Watts wrote, "I am listening to the music of an organ; as leaves seemed to gesture, the organ seems quite literally to speak." The drugs caused a loss of ego ("depersonalization") and made users felt as if they were physically connected to everything they were seeing and hearing. "I *became* every musical instrument," Leary wrote in his autobiography, *Flashbacks*. Huxley and Beat poet and novelist William S. Burroughs added that music not only enhanced their psychedelic experiences, but the music they heard while tripping helped them to process and relive them long after the drugs wore off. Musicians couldn't specifically reproduce any of these sensations, but drug users also talked about a transfigured view of the everyday world and a sense that time was elastic. These feelings *could* be evoked—onstage, but even more effectively in the recording studio—with circular, mandala-like song structures; sustained or droning melodies; altered and effected instrumental sounds; reverb, echoes, and tape delays that created a sense of space, and layered mixes that rewarded repeated listening by revealing new and mysterious elements. The presence of all or any one of these sounds became enough to earn a piece of music the label "psychedelic."

Of course, the recording studio had been used before the onslaught of psychedelia to create rock 'n' roll with distinctive moods or atmospheres. Brian Eno, one of rock's most imaginative producers, said that as a young boy, he was fascinated by Elvis Presley's "Heartbreak Hotel" because of the way the echo created a feeling of loneliness. "Nobody in my family could tell me what that was," he's quoted as saying in Eric Tamm's *Brian Eno: His Music and the Vertical Color of Sound.* In the late '50s, record producers began making extensive use of reverb to create a feeling of creepiness, distance, or strange spaces—as on instrumental hits like Link Wray's "Rumble" (1958), Santo and Johnny's "Sleep Walk" (1959), Dick Dale's "Let's Go Trippin'" (1961), and the Tornadoes' "Telstar" (1962)—or to produce a larger-than-life, multi-layered effect, as on Phil Spector's fabled Wall of Sound productions, including "Then

ONE: MY WHITE BICYCLE   13

He Kissed Me" and "Be My Baby" (1963), "Walkin' in the Rain" (1964), and "River Deep—Mountain High" (1966). Outside the realm of rock 'n' roll, the "space-age bachelor pad music" recorded from the mid-'50s through the early '60s made maximum use of stereo gimmickry and studio effects (hello, Esquivel, Les Baxter, and Joe Meek). But the song that best predicted psychedelic rock was "I Put a Spell On You," recorded in 1956 by a twenty-seven-year-old singer from Cleveland. Over a slow and sinister R&B groove, Screamin' Jay Hawkins created a manic voodoo vibe by singing, shouting, and wailing like a man possessed, raging at the girl who walked out on him and at other demons far too sinister to name.

"Arnold Matson, who was the head of Columbia at the time, felt that we had to do something different in regards to the song," Hawkins told Nick Tosches in *Unsung Heroes of Rock 'n' Roll*. "So he brought in a case of Italian Swiss Colony muscatel, and we all got our heads bent! Ten days later, the record came out. I listened to it and I heard all those drunken screams and groans and yells, and I thought, 'Oh, my God!'" The record made bluenoses rail, charging that it evoked everything from devil worship to anal rape, but it was also a major hit.

Evoking the experience of becoming one with the universe through psychedelic drugs was considerably more difficult than duplicating a muscatel bender, but by 1966 musicians had more tools at their disposal. Like all of the '50s rockers, Hawkins and his band recorded live. The Beatles and the Beach Boys were among the first groups to utilize multitrack recording, allowing them to over-dub instruments one at a time without performing everything in one take. What's more, their phenomenal success earlier in the

The Ultimate Psychedelic Rock Library: Voodoo Jive: The Best of Screamin' Jay Hawkins *(Rhino) is proto-psychedelic insanity.*

decade gave them license and the means to explore the new technology at length over entire albums. On *Pet Sounds* and *Revolver*, they created worlds that existed only on tape and which couldn't necessarily be duplicated on stage, even with the help of an orchestra. In addition to familiar instruments such as organ, bass, and piano, "Tomorrow Never Knows" utilized radically compressed drums, backwards guitars, voices fed through a rotating Leslie speaker, double-speed guitar, tape loops, and percussive sounds played on wine glasses.

Because of its emphasis on sounds that fire the imagination, psychedelic rock has often been the first genre to embrace technological advances in music making. The recording studio itself has been its most effective instrument, and psychedelic rockers were at the forefront as the technology went from four tracks, to eight, to sixteen, to twenty-four, to the virtually limitless world of today's digital technology and Pro Tools-style computer programs. Starting in the late '60s, synthesizers offered musicians access to sound at its most basic physical level, allowing them to shape the actual wave forms. The instruments' potential was illustrated by Eno, Pink Floyd, Hawkwind, and a wave of adventurous bands in Germany in the early '70s. In the mid-'80s, digital samplers made it possible to record virtually any sound—a clap of thunder, a chirping cricket, or a rushing subway train—and turn it into a musical instrument. Groups such as De La Soul, PM Dawn, and the Orb did just that. But in all of these cases, the technology itself was less important than the imagination of its users and the music's listeners.

David Thomas of Pere Ubu calls psychedelic rock "the cinematic music of the imagination." Comparing psychedelics to poetry in his book, *Poetic Vision and the Psychedelic Experience*, scholar R. A. Durr wrote that every aspect of the drug experience really entails "the single fact of imaginative being: In imagination the Real Man knows ecstatically that he is That eternally…or, otherwise worded, to be awake in the present moment is to be in union with life, which is the Self, which is ecstasy." The quest to seize the moment is common to the psychedelic subculture, the Beat movement, and romanticism, while ecstasy—literally, "standing outside" routine ways of feeling, perceiving, and acting—is an experience fostered in many religions. Drugs can be a means to reaching these ends, but they aren't the only one, and as many psychedelic rockers say that they've taken them as say that they haven't. Psychedelic rock doesn't mean "drug rock," but rock that is inspired by a philosophical approach implied by the literal meanings of "psychedelic" as "mind-revealing" and "soul-manifesting."

Psychedelic rock offers something for the intellect as well as the body. Drug users are often called "heads," and the genre could just as easily be called "head rock." The early psychedelic rockers brought the lyrical sophistication of Dylan to rock 'n' roll, and, through him, they connected with the Beats and the romantics. They gave birth to the concept album, the musical equivalent of a novel (or at least a collection of short stories). But psychedelic lyrics are less political than those in folk rock, more playful than those in progressive rock, and more open-ended than either. Listeners are allowed to determine meaning for themselves, choosing between different interpretations—as in the case of the Byrds' "Eight Miles High" or the Beatles' "I Am the Walrus"—or searching for clues as if solving a puzzle. Witness the veiled reference to the psychedelic drug DMT in the 13th Floor Elevators' "Fire Engine," or the (perhaps unintentional) initials LSD in Lennon's "Lucy in the Sky with Diamonds."

The overwhelming majority of early psychedelic rockers were middle- to upper-middle-class college students, and many of them were art-school students. (This remained true into the '70s, though by the time the psychedelic punks appeared, it was no longer so easy to generalize.) They looked at rock 'n' roll as a romantic art form because it emphasized energy, originality, spontaneity, and emotional truth. Psychedelia became rock's most romantic genre because it was most devoted to shaking off emotional and intellectual repression. The romantics lionize children and madmen because they aren't bound by society's rules, hence they are, theoretically, the most open to creativity. Psychedelic rockers approach the recording studio with a spirit of playfulness and an open-minded attitude that isn't restricted by rules about the "right" or "sane" way to do things. "Since psychedelic drugs expose us to different levels of perception and experience, use of them is ultimately a philosophic enterprise, compelling us to confront the nature of reality and the nature of our fragile, subjective belief systems," Leary wrote in his autobiography, *Flashbacks*. "The contrast is what triggers the laughter, the terror. We discover abruptly that we have been programmed all these years, that everything we accept as reality is just social fabrication."

Living a psychedelic lifestyle or creating psychedelic art means accepting no rules, breaking down boundaries, and opening doors wherever possible. In their study of gender and sexuality in rock 'n' roll, *The Sex Revolts*, critics Simon Reynolds and Joy Press characterized male psychedelic rockers as mothers' boys longing to return to the womb. But a case can be made that male artists such as Lennon, Eno, Kevin Shields of My Bloody Valentine, and Elephant 6 auteur Robert Schneider are models of a more enlightened male sexuality, one that is in touch with the feminine (especially in terms of emotions) and open to sexual experimentation. Years before the glam movement, the English psychedelic scene embraced homosexuals and bisexuals. The invitation to a famous happening called the Spontaneous Underground read, "Who will be there? Poets, pop singers, hoods, Americans, homosexuals (because they make up 10 percent of the population), twenty clowns, jazz musicians, one murderer, sculptors, politicians, and some girls who defy description."

Psychedelia has also been at the forefront of breaking down gender roles. Women were accepted early on not just as lead singers (the Jefferson Airplane's Grace Slick), but as instrumentalists, such as the Velvet Underground's drummer Maureen Tucker, Sly and the

Family Stone's trumpeter Cynthia Robinson, or Christina "Licorice" McKechnie and Rose Simpson of the Incredible String Band. When riot grrrls were making "women in rock" an issue in the '90s, psychedelic guitar bands such as My Bloody Valentine, Spiritualized, Stereolab, Lush, the Feelies, and others had already gotten past the point where it was considered an issue. The women in these bands were equal, creative members—not "female rockers," but rockers, period.

Psychedelic drugs open people up to exploring other ways of living, and psychedelic rock circled the globe to incorporate the sounds of other cultures, including instruments such as the sitar, the gamelan, and the didgeridoo, which all produce tones that are considered to be conducive to meditating. Rhythmically, rock reconnected back through the blues to its African roots, and drummers turned to patterns that were more repetitive and trance-inducing. Since they were often part of religious rituals, these sounds could imply a mysterious spiritual dimension. "The modal progressions, the drone, the use of open tuning on guitars, and the improvising off one chord—those sounds became associated in people's minds with 'non-linear' and 'non-Western,'" Pink Floyd and Incredible String Band producer Joe Boyd told me. "In a way, that was what the drugs were accomplishing, getting out of that 'knocking back a scotch and soda' mentality to a more contemplative and agape mentality."

Peter Stafford, author of the *Psychedelics Encyclopedia*, suggested that psychedelia's second meaning as soul-manifesting is best understood in terms of contrast. "Just as 'empty' implies 'full,' so 'soul-manifesting' implies an enlargement or actualization of consciousness," he wrote. The impulse is not to escape the everyday, but to transcend it. Psychedelic rock is open to spirituality, whether it's in the form of Eastern religions, paganism / nature worship, or Christianity. "The major conceptual breakthrough of the '60s was its Romantic movement back toward nature, the awesome, star-studded panorama dwarfing social conventions and forms," punk scholar Camille Paglia wrote in *Vamps and Tramps*. The psychedelic reconnection with the natural world spawned the environmental activism that flourished in the '70s and continues today. But while psychedelic rock is full of images celebrating the beauty of nature, there are just as many cautionary tales about its power, which can't be harnessed or controlled. The list of psychedelic rockers who tempted fate and damaged their natural facilities by over-indulging in chemicals is a long one—including Brian Wilson, Roky Erickson, Syd Barrett, Skip Spence, and Robert Calvert—and their plight is often romanticized. Their abuse of drugs didn't make them vision-aries; it killed their visionary talents and removed them from the land of the living.

Many others who turned on and dropped out never came back, but their stories are less dramatic. "After a serious immersion in LSD, one couldn't go back to the 9-to-5 world of sales managers and upward mobility," Jay Stevens wrote in his definitive history of LSD, *Storming Heaven*. "Better to work for yourself, doing something simple and useful, which was why so many hippies became entre-preneurs, farmers, craftspeople." The quest to fill a spiritual void led some people astray, as in the case of Charles Manson's followers. Others went searching through the crystals and quackery of the New Age movement, or the cryptic conspiracies of cults like the

Illuminatis. Some returned to be born again in the Christian church. Christianity's emphasis on peace and love and the notion that being God-like is remembering what it is to be child-like neatly fit the psychedelic mind-set, and the early '70s witnessed the flowering of Christian rock in the form of vaguely psychedelic musicals such as *Jesus Christ Superstar* and *Godspell*. But unlike Christian rock, psychedelic rock doesn't preach, and its spiritual invocations are left open to interpretation. The references in Brian Wilson's "God Only Knows" and the Velvet Underground's "Jesus" are non-specific in that the sentiments could be addressed to *any* higher force, including one within ourselves.

Psychedelic rock is by definition polytheistic. When Lennon said in 1966 that the Beatles were more popular than Jesus, he was stating the obvious. Rock 'n' roll *is* a religion. Music is its sacrament, and the musicians are its god and saints. "Rock 'n' roll provides what the church provided for in other generations," Grateful Dead guitarist Jerry Garcia said. (Having been raised a Roman Catholic, he was certainly in the position to know.) To many people, it is just as important as any other form of organized worship and celebration, and just as life affirming. Like Lou Reed, psychedelic rockers believe in the possibility of a life that's saved by rock 'n' roll. Of course, the music isn't always capable of achieving this lofty goal.

There is no denying that the genre has resulted in some pointless indulgence. "*Sgt. Pepper's* was the thing that did it," psychedelic punk Julian Cope told me. "That was the kiss of death with people taking themselves way too seriously. I could sit down and say, 'Look, man, you've got to understand where I'm coming from, 'cause it's deadly important!' But the greatest artists have to accept that it has to be top entertainment. There's got to be that side to it, otherwise it's not rock 'n' roll."

A school of thought voiced by the Grateful Dead's Phil Lesh holds that psychedelic music is any music that's heard while tripping. But the best psychedelic *rock* never forgets the second half of the equation. It works first and foremost as rock 'n' roll, retaining the power, immediacy, and honesty of the music at its best. In Dionysian fashion, it celebrates the vital forces of life through all forms of ecstasy. But it also attempts the Apollonian goal of transcending the everyday and creating something pure, beautiful, artistic, and spiritual. These two drives can't be squared, but they aren't necessarily opposed. If God, however you define it, can indeed be found everywhere, why not in three chords and a backbeat?

Opening the Doors of Perception: The Road to Psychedelic Rock

2700 B.C.   *Shen Nung, one of the pioneers of Chinese medicines, makes the first written record of cannabis use in the pharmacopoeia.*

1430   *Jeanne d'Arc, better known as Saint Joan of Arc, is accused of using herbal "witch" drugs to facilitate her communiqués with heavenly voices.*

1484   *Pope Innocent VIII labels cannabis a sacrament of the Satanic mass and bans all medicinal uses via papal edict.*

1493   *During his second voyage, Columbus asks friar Ramon Pane to study the religion of the native inhabitants of Hispaniola (now Haiti). Pane notes their use of a psychoactive plant, cohoba-yopo (DMT), in shamanic rituals.*

1630s   *Several of the American colonies pass laws requiring farmers to grow cannabis hemp, a crop that is considered essential for the New World economy.*

1741   *A Jesuit missionary writes about cohoba use by natives in the area of Colombia and Venezuela.*

1794   *Mystic-poet William Blake publishes* Songs of Innocence.

1808   *Physician John Stearns publishes the first modern account of
                medicinal uses for ergot.*

1816   *English poet Samuel Taylor Coleridge publishes the image-filled
                "Kubla Khan."*

1816–1819   *Romantic poets Lord Byron and Percy Bysshe Shelley cavort like
                rock stars.*

1821   *Thomas De Quincey publishes* Confessions of an English
                Opium-Eater.

1839   *Opium enthusiast Edgar Allan Poe publishes* Tales of the
                Grotesque and Arabesque.

1844   *Writer Théophile Gautier opens Le Club des Haschischins in
                Paris, attracting regulars Charles Baudelaire, Honoré de Balzac,
                Alexandre Dumas, Gerard de Nerval, and Victor Hugo.*

1845   *French Dr. Jean-Jacques Moreau de Tours initiates the science of
                psycho-pharmacology.*

1855   *Von Bibra's* Die Narkotischen Genusmitteel unde der
                Mensch *identifies seventeen types of mind-altering plants.*

1857   *Baudelaire publishes* Les Fleurs du Mal.

1865   *English author Lewis Carroll publishes* Alice's Adventures in
                Wonderland.

1870s   *The soda fountain becomes a fixture in neighborhood pharma-
                cies across the U.S., selling "invigorating tonics" that are laced
                with cocaine.*

1871   *Arthur Rimbaud frequents the absinthe bars of Paris with his
                lover Paul Verlaine and achieves synaesthesia through "a sys-
                tematic derangement of all the senses."*

1876   *Visitors to the Centennial Exposition in Philadelphia visit the
                Turkish Hashish Exhibit and freely indulge. Hashish parlors
                soon appear throughout America; in 1883 police estimate some
                five hundred parlors in New York City alone.*

1884   *Sigmund Freud publishes* Über Coca, *which advocates the
                medicinal uses of cocaine.*

1894   *Surrealist Alfred Jarry writes "The Passion Considered as an
                Uphill Bicycle Race."*

1896   *Lewis Lewin and Arthur Heffter isolate the alkaloid mescaline
                from the Mexican cactus Lophophora williamsii, a.k.a. peyote.*

1918   *Arthur Stoll isolates ergotamine—the first pure ergot alkaloid—
            at the Sandoz Company in Basel, Switzerland.*

1919   *Ernst Späth produces the first synthetic mescaline in Germany.*

1924   *The Bureau of Surrealist Enquiries opens on the Rue de Grenelle
            in Paris.*

1926   *Ergot-contaminated rye causes the last great outbreak of St.
            Anthony's Fire in southern Russia.*

1928   *Spanish painter Salvador Dalí visits Paris and meets the French
            surrealists.*

1929   *Chemists at the Rockefeller Institute in New York isolate the
            nucleus common to all ergot alkaloids and name it lysergic acid.*

1931   *English novelist Aldous Huxley publishes* Brave New World.

            DMT is first synthesized by British chemist Richard Manske.

1935   *Albert Hofmann resumes the study of ergot alkaloids at Sandoz.*

1937   *Harry Ainslinger, commissioner of the U.S. Bureau of Narcotics,
            signals the start of the war on drugs with a harrowing article
            called "Marijuana: Assassin of Youth." By the end of the year,
            the Marijuana Tax Act is signed into law, prohibiting cannabis
            use in America.*

1938   *Hofmann produces his twenty-fifth synthesis, lysergic acid diethylamide.*

              French poet Anton Artaud travels to Mexico to participate in the peyote ritual with the Tarahumara Indians, the basis of his 1955 book, The Peyote Dance.

1942   *The U.S. Office of Strategic Services (OSS) experiments with various truth drugs, including a potent extract of marijuana and hashish oil.*

1943   *Scientists achieve nuclear fission at the University of Chicago.*

              Hofmann takes the first acid trip.

1944   *Mayor Fiorello LaGuardia asks the New York Academy of Medicine to study the pros and cons of marijuana. The academy contradicts almost all of Harry Ainslinger's alarmist warnings.*

1947   *Psychiatrist Werner Stoll publishes a study on LSD, and Sandoz issues a prospectus to researchers.*

              The U.S. Navy experiments with mescaline as a truth serum, drawing on the results of tests conducted by the Nazis on prisoners at the Dachau concentration camp.

1951   *The CIA , successor to the OSS, begins to experiment with LSD.*

            OSS veteran Al Hubbard takes LSD and has a visionary experience.

1952   *Humphry Osmond studies the effect of mescaline and LSD on alcoholics in Canada.*

1953   *Under Osmond's supervision, Huxley tries mescaline and writes* The Doors of Perception.

1955   *Oscar Janiger gives LSD to the Hollywood elite, including Cary Grant.*

            Hofmann and his Sandoz colleagues isolate and synthesize the key compounds of psilocybin and psilocin from psychedelic mushrooms.

1956   *Beat poet Allen Ginsberg publishes his book-length poem,* Howl.

1957   *Jack Kerouac publishes* On the Road.

            R. Gordon Wasson writes a seventeen-page article on psyche-delic mushrooms for Life *magazine.*

1960   *Timothy Leary and Richard Alpert begin researching psilocybin*
            at Harvard University.

            Ginsberg takes psilocybin at Leary's house, calls Kerouac, and
            identifies himself as God. Kerouac hangs up.

            Ken Kesey is paid $75 to take psilocybin at Stanford University.

1962   *Leary and Alpert drop acid with Michael Hollingshead and add*
            LSD to their research.

            American pharmacist Calvin Stevens first synthesizes ketamine
            in the Parke Davis Laboratories.

1963   *Leary and Alpert are expelled from Harvard.*

            On the day that President Kennedy is assassinated, Huxley dies
            at age seventy after his wife grants his last request: an intra-
            venous injection of LSD.

1964   *Kesey and his Merry Pranksters visit Leary and his researchers*
            at Millbrook, New York.

            Leary, Alpert, and Ralph Metzner publish The Psychedelic
            Experience: A Manual Based on the Tibetan Book of the
            Dead, *a guide for taking LSD.*

1965	Large batches of acid start to appear on big-city streets. Between March and December, psychiatrists at New York's Bellevue Hospital treat sixty-five people admitted during bad acid trips.
	Kesey holds the first Acid Test.
1966	Bill Graham opens the Fillmore in San Francisco. The city of San Francisco estimates that 15,000 "hippies" are living in the Haight.
	Sandoz terminates all research contracts and stops manufacturing LSD.
	A Texas court sentences Leary to thirty years and a $30,000 fine for possession of marijuana. Marshall McLuhan advises Leary to fight in the court of public opinion.
	Leary holds a press conference at the New York Advertising Club to announce the formation of the League for Spiritual Discovery (LSD). "Like every great religion of the past we seek to find the divinity within and to express this revelation in a life of glorification and the worship of God," he says. "These ancient goals we define in the metaphor of the present—turn on, tune in, drop out."

TWO

2

WHY DON'T WE SING THIS SONG ALL TOGETHER?
The Psychedelic Beach Boys, Beatles, and Rolling Stones

ALBERT HOFMANN'S "PROBLEM CHILD" had a profound impact on the three most influential bands of the 1960s. Like many of their smart, wealthy, curious, and slightly hedonistic peers, the members of the Beach Boys, the Beatles, and the Rolling Stones were game to try just about anything once. They were first exposed to LSD between 1964 and 1965. A few years later, the Beatles were particularly vocal in their endorsement, and their comments were quickly condemned as irresponsible. "When George Harrison once capriciously said he liked jelly beans, the Beatles spent three years performing in a perpetual hailstorm of them," Peter Brown and Steven Gaines wrote in their Beatles biography, *The Love You Make*. "If every jelly bean equaled a tab of LSD, there were going to be a lot of psychedelicized children around."

The charge was exaggerated, but it underscored the band's influential position, and the Beach Boys and the Stones were only a little less powerful. The psychedelic experience inspired radical changes in each band's music, and the music inspired fans and other musicians to follow in their psychedelic footsteps.

LET'S GO AWAY FOR AWHILE

> When Marilyn saw Brian the day after his first trip, he looked drained and exhausted. "I'll never do it again," he swore. "But what happened?" she asked him. "What was it like?" Tears welled in his eyes, and suddenly he was crying and hugging her. "I saw God," Brian told her. "I saw God and it just blew my mind."
>
> —Steven Gaines,
> *Heroes and Villains: The True Story of the Beach Boys*

STILL WEARING THEIR MATCHING STRIPED SHIRTS and neat, new cardigans, the happy harmonizers from Hawthorne, California, started 1965 with their last great albums about cars, girls, and fun in the sun. *Beach Boys Today* and *Summer Days (And Summer Nights!!)* yielded the hits "California Girls" and "Help Me, Rhonda." But the band members—especially songwriter Brian Wilson—were changing, and their Chuck Berry-style rock 'n' roll was about to be replaced by sounds that were much more complex, disturbing, and psychedelic.

Brian toured with his brothers and the rest of the band for the last time in December 1964. He was twenty-two and newly married, but he was still under the thumb of his abusive father and manager, Murry. Brian was feeling the strain of a relentless schedule of writing, recording, and performing. He broke down in public during a flight from Los Angeles to Houston, screaming hysterically that his new wife was falling for his cousin, singer Mike Love. Later, during tense meetings with the group and his father, he insisted that he wanted to stay home and concentrate on making albums. Murry and the band weren't happy, but in early 1965, they had no choice but to replace Brian in the touring group, first with guitarist Glen Campbell, then with former Gambler Bruce Johnston. (The Beach Boys had covered the A side of the Gamblers' "Moon Dawg" b/w "LSD-25" single, and they knew Johnston socially.)

Brian took LSD for the first time with his friend, Loren Schwartz, in mid-1965, dropping acid that came from the lab of Augustus Owsley Stanley. The experience had a profound impact on the way he heard music. "As I had been promised, music had never sounded so full and tangible, and it was denser and heavier than any music I'd ever heard," he wrote in his autobiography, *Wouldn't It Be Nice*. "I imagined wading through it like a river, until I felt consumed by it." He claimed that he tripped only twice after that, but the LSD contributed to an unraveling mental state that he called "psychedelicate." "My trips took me to the gates of consciousness, and then on to the other side," he wrote. "On acid, I saw myself stretched out from conception to death, the beginning to the end. Acid was everything I could ever be and anything I wouldn't be, and I had to come to grips with that....I opened the Pandora's box in my mind and saw things that scared the fucking daylights out of me, and I decided to hide."

Brian believed that the Beach Boys were in an intense competition with the Beatles, and each group was spurring the other on to better work. He first heard *Rubber Soul* while he was stoned on pot. "It flipped me out so much I said, 'I'm gonna try that, where a whole album becomes a gas!'" he recalled in his autobiography. The Beach Boys' last album in 1965 was a live disc that included three Beatles covers. It spawned a hit with the surf-style throwback, "Barbara Ann," and its success bought Brian some time with Capitol Records. He was standing at the edge of a frightening precipice—at the age of twenty-four, years of professional and personal stresses had combined with his LSD experiences to prompt an emotional crisis, but he was determined to make an album that bettered *Rubber Soul*. Sitting at the piano, he began writing bits of music that he called "feelings," each evoking a specific mood. Lyrics were written later in collaboration with Tony Asher, an advertising copy writer who had the ability to convey, simply and eloquently, the emotions that Brian wanted to express.

The resulting album, *Pet Sounds*, is a touching and tender plea for love and understanding. While psychedelic drugs inspired the Beatles to look at the problems in the world around them, they made Brian turn his attention inward and probe his emotional longings (as on "Caroline No" and "Wouldn't It Be Nice," a song of unrequited love for his sister-in-law) and his deep-seated self-doubts ("You Still Believe in Me" and "That's Not Me"). He yearned

The Ultimate Psychedelic Rock Library: The Beach Boys' Pet Sounds *(Capitol) was Brian Wilson's real "teenage symphony to God."*

to escape to some place safe and peaceful, a theme reflected in the instrumental "Let's Go Away for Awhile," a cover of the folk standard, "Sloop John B" (with the key line, "This is the worst trip I've ever been on"), and "Caroline No," which ends with the sounds of a departing train. ("Can't you just see me on the back of that train?" Wilson asked his wife. "I can. Just going away.") Despite their intensely personal nature, the songs touch a nerve with anyone facing difficult challenges, whether they're the standard trials of adolescence or something much more serious. (In the early '90s, "Doonesbury" cartoonist Garry Trudeau wrote a series of strips in which the album helps a character with AIDS find the strength to face his impending death.)

Although the Wilsons were raised as Christians, theirs wasn't a particularly religious household, so it's ironic that Brian is one of the first rock musician to use the word "God" in a single. "God Only Knows" is less of a prayer than a sensitive meditation about

moving forward in the face of loss. In the midst of emotional tur-
moil, Brian was aware that there are no easy answers, either in religion or in drugs. In "I Know There's an Answer," he expresses pity
for the uptight people who "trip through the day and waste all their
thoughts at night," but he doesn't try to tell them how to live. "I
know there's an answer, but I had to find out by myself," he sings.
While the lyrics are full of question marks, the music itself is optimistic, and its beauty suggests that somehow, everything is going to
work out.

Working with orchestral musicians and session players, Brian
created a sonic tapestry of organs, strings, acoustic guitars, banjos,
grand pianos, sleigh bells, and percussion that is so complex, it's
often hard to trace an individual instrumental line through an
entire song. Every tune is full of haunting and beautiful melodies
that continue to reveal themselves after dozens of listens, just as
previously unnoticed corners of the world reveal themselves during
the psychedelic experience. But when the Beach Boys came off the
road to add the vocal parts that Brian carefully prescribed, not everybody was impressed. "When we left the country, we were just a surfing group," Al Jardine is quoted as saying in Timothy White's *The
Nearest Faraway Place*. "This was a whole new thing." Love called the
new sounds "Brian's ego music," and he said he found the lyrics
"offensive" and "nauseating" in their psychedelic suggestiveness.

When it was released in May 1966, *Pet Sounds* sold half a million
copies, but it was a commercial disappointment compared to the
previous albums. Love felt vindicated by what he considered to be
Brian's failure, and he began an effort to seize control of the band so

that it could stick to the proven formula of the early hits. Brian held on to the reigns only long enough to complete one more single.

"Good Vibrations" is a three-and-a-half-minute "pocket symphony" that took six months to record, and its many melodic changes and complex vocal arrangements were worked out over ninety hours of tape. The distinctive swooping hook comes from a theremin, an early synthesizer played by moving your hand over an antenna. (Jimmy Page later used one on "Dazed and Confused," but before "Good Vibrations," it was most often featured on the soundtracks to '50s science-fiction movies.) Capitol executives were worried that the song was "too modern" and that the lyrics had sensual, druggy overtones. But while Brian said the production was inspired by LSD, the lyrics came from an offhand remark by his mother. "My mom told me dogs discriminate between people," he said. "They like some people because the people give off good vibrations....I have a feeling that this is a very spiritual song, and I want it to give off good vibrations."

The single turned out to be one of the Beach Boys' biggest hits—and the beginning of the end. The short version of the debacle that followed (most memorably traced in Domenic Priore's *Look, Listen, Vibrate, Smile—The Beach Boys*) is that Brian had his notorious meltdown in the midst of recording the group's tenth proper studio album. In late 1966, he began his ill-fated collaboration with Van Dyke Parks on *Smile*, an album that was originally called *Dumb Angel*. Brian described it as a "teenage symphony to God," adding a spiritual element to Phil Spector's description of his hit singles, and it was to have been an epic of baroque studio craft to top *Sgt. Pepper's Lonely Hearts Club Band*. But the sessions became legendary

for their indulgence. Brian was taking speed and smoking marijuana constantly, and he suffered bouts of depression and paranoia. He
built the infamous sandbox in his living room, and he refused to
leave his bed for long periods of time. The nadir came when he
tried to destroy the tapes of a track called "Fire" because he was convinced that the song caused several blazes around Los Angeles. In
May 1967, Capitol announced that *Smile* had been abandoned. The
group cancelled a headlining appearance at the Monterey Pop
Festival, and Jimi Hendrix told the crowd it had heard the last of
surf music. Brian withdrew further and further from music, his family, and the world, until, finally, he wasn't there at all.

On the Beach Boys albums that followed, the credits now point-
edly read, "Produced by the Beach Boys" instead of "Produced by
Brian Wilson." The band made a sharp U-turn away from its auteur's
complicated orchestrations back toward old-fashioned singing-in-
the-living room basics (presaging similar back-to-roots moves by the
Beatles circa "The White Album" and the Rolling Stones on *Beggars*

*The Ultimate Psychedelic Rock
Library: The Beach Boys'
Smiley Smile (Capitol) evokes a
"psychedelic barbershop quartet."*

Banquet). Some of the songs that had been on *Smile* were re-recorded for *Smiley Smile* in different, much less ambitious versions ("Heroes and Villains," "Wonderful," "Wind Chimes," and "Vegetables," which boasts a percussion track consisting of Paul McCartney chomping on celery and carrots), while a few new tunes were freshly recorded and tacked on (the best is Brian's "With Me Tonight" with brother Carl on lead vocals; the worst is the despicable Love's "She's Goin' Bald"). The harmony vocals hold the spotlight throughout, and the result is not unlike what Hendrix called "a psychedelic barbershop quartet" (he meant it as an insult, but it's an intriguing concept nonetheless). In the end, *Smiley Smile* was famously eulogized by brother Carl as "more of bunt than a grand slam"—certainly not the masterpiece that Brian originally envisioned.

From that point on, the Beach Boys began their long, sad decline into their current status as a state fair nostalgia act, with Brian only occasionally coming to the fore for underwhelming efforts such as 1977's *The Beach Boys Love You*. After he split from the group entirely, he launched a controversial solo career, initially with help from his much-vilified psychiatrist, Eugene Landy, then under the aegis of assorted other producers, handlers, and keepers. In the mid-'90s, the brilliance of *Pet Sounds* was rediscovered by a new generation of underground rockers, including Cardinal, the High Llamas, Yum-Yum, and members of the so-called Elephant 6 collective, and it became the central inspiration for a movement dubbed "ork pop" for "orchestral pop." In the midst of this, Brian returned to the stage with the core backing of the young Los Angeles psychedelic rock band the Wondermints, and on one tour, he performed *Pet Sounds* live in its entirety, proudly reclaiming his masterpiece.

A vulnerable, frightened man with a childlike openness, Brian today is a notoriously difficult interview subject. He adds little insight into the creations of his psychedelic era, but he comes across as a man who has survived a confrontation with his demons, only to continue in the struggle of coming to terms with his life and his art.

INTO THE VOID

> When the Beatles' work as a whole is viewed in retrospect, *Rubber Soul* and *Revolver* will stand as their major contributions. When the slicks and tricks of production on this new album no longer seem unusual, and the compositions are stripped to their musical and lyrical essentials, *Sgt. Pepper's* will be Beatles baroque—an elaboration without improvement.
> —Richard Goldstein,
> *The New York Times*, 1967

THE FAB FOUR ARE REMEMBERED as the Acid Apostles of the New Age, among many other things, but the Beatles' earliest psychedelic experiences were unfulfilling. John Lennon and George Harrison first tripped in 1964 after they were unknowingly dosed by their dentist during dinner at his flat. (The LSD came from Michael Hollingshead's notorious mayonnaise jar.) Though the dentist begged them to stay, the two Beatles were angry and stormed out. They made the mistake of speeding around London in Harrison's Aston-Martin, landing at several nightclubs where the crowds and the noise unnerved them further. They finally escaped to Harrison's house and unwound by playing music and drawing. Their second trip wasn't much better. In August 1965 they took LSD with members of the Byrds and others while they were staying in Los Angeles to perform at the Hollywood Bowl. This time, actor Peter Fonda wouldn't stop babbling about how he almost died on the operating table, until a freaked-out Lennon finally screamed at him to shut up.

Like the Beach Boys, the Beatles were struggling to meet a ridiculous schedule imposed by their label, EMI. *Help!*, the group's eighth U.S. album since early 1964, was released in August 1965, and a new album was expected by December. The band didn't start working on *Rubber Soul* until mid-October, but the Beatles finished writing and recording in little more than a month. They had started to escape the pressures of their relentless pace by smoking marijuana, and their carefully constructed image as lovable moptops was disintegrating. In its place was a cross between the wiseass rockers who played speed-crazed sets in Hamburg and the second-generation Beats who sat around in coffee shops dissecting Bob Dylan's electric turnarounds, *Bringing It All Back Home* and *Highway 61 Revisited*.

Rubber Soul is an album about change. The Beatles' worldview is expanding, their music is maturing, and the title and lyrics hint at concerns that are more spiritual than chasing and being chased by female fans. "It was the first album to present a new, growing Beatles to the world," producer George Martin said in Mark Lewisohn's *The Beatles Recording Sessions*. "For the first time, we

The Ultimate Psychedelic Rock Library: Rubber Soul *(Capitol) was the album where the moptops first let their hair down.*

began to think of albums as art on their own, as complete entities." Biographer Nicholas Schaffner described *Rubber Soul* as the moment in *The Wizard of Oz* when Dorothy's world goes from black and white to Technicolor. The relaxed rhythms are a surprising change, and Ringo Starr is as likely to play finger cymbals, tambourine, or maracas as drums. The instrumental textures are more elaborate, and Harrison plays sitar for the first time. (The guitarist was exposed to the twenty-one-stringed instrument on the set of *Help!* by Indian musicians who played during one of the chase scenes.) The lyrics bear an obvious Dylan influence. "In My Life" finds Lennon looking back wistfully at the people and places he's left behind, while "Girl," "I'm Looking Through You," and "Norwegian Wood" are cynical songs about relationships that are much more complicated than the one in "I Want to Hold Your Hand."

Like a lot of Baby Boomers in the mid-'60s, the Beatles were beginning to question authority and search for a way of living that was richer and fuller than what society offered. The A sides of the two singles that followed *Rubber Soul*—"Day Tripper" and "Paperback Writer"—both take a harsh view of people caught in the rat race. Lennon said the former was a critique of "weekend hippies" (though clearly it also works as an angry rant about a relationship gone bad), while the latter features a marijuana-inspired fascination with droning melody and lyrics that can be heard as sneering at the unbridled ambition of the young protagonist who so badly needs a job (though many note that McCartney himself displayed such overweening ambition). But it's the B side of "Paperback Writer" that is the Beatles' first great psychedelic rock song. "Rain" uses a stuttering rhythm and an expanding and contracting melody to evoke the sense of timelessness created by LSD, while the lyrics are inspired by Lennon's reading of philosopher Alan Watts, whose LSD experiences prompted him to question such basic assumptions as whether we can really say if it is raining or the sun is shining.

Lennon had his first profound psychedelic experience in December 1965, a month after the release of *Rubber Soul*. Sitting alone in his attic, armed with Timothy Leary and crew's how-to manual, *The Psychedelic Experience*, he traveled toward the "white light" described by Aldous Huxley. Three months later, he started work at Abbey Road on a song he called "The Void." The tune was eventually retitled "Tomorrow Never Knows," after one of Ringo's pet phrases. Inspired by Lennon's acid trip, it features several lines lifted directly from *The Psychedelic Experience*, which in turn had been adapted from *The Tibetan Book of the Dead*, ancient advice to a dying soul on how to reach heaven. "Turn off your mind, relax, and float downstream," Lennon sings. His voice is both intimate and

The Ultimate Psychedelic Rock Library: The Beatles' psychedelic masterpiece, Revolver *(Capitol).*

distant, as if he's whispering in your ear from somewhere over the horizon. An insistent drum beat folds in on itself again and again— a tribal trance groove—while an ominous organ drones in the back- ground and strange bird calls of backward guitars mock the mono- tone vocals, which Lennon intended to evoke the sound of a thou- sand chanting Tibetan monks.

Although it closes the album, "Tomorrow Never Knows" was the first song recorded for *Revolver*. It sets the tone for an album that is pregnant with possibilities. Released the month the Beatles played their last concert, it calls attention to the fact that it is a stu- dio creation. It opens with a voice counting off the intro to "Taxman," as if the Beatles are inviting the listener inside the recording process. The title is an in-joke referring to the revolving slab of vinyl that carried these new sounds in the days before CDs, while the cover art evokes the creative process with a collage of images flowing out of the musicians' heads. After his third LSD trip,

Lennon began taking the drug almost every day. McCartney, a swinging young bachelor, immersed himself in the London underground, while Harrison and Starr struggled to grow beyond the caricatures assigned to them at the height of Beatlemania. The four were starting to pull apart, but they still functioned as a group in the studio, and the joy they felt while working together is transmitted in their recordings.

Revolver shows each of the Beatles in their best light (especially the original British LP, which was initially cannibalized in America, but has been restored to the original running order on CD reissues). McCartney's "Here, There and Everywhere" is sweet and romantic without being saccharin, and his "Eleanor Rigby" makes a sharp social comment on isolation in the midst of community. (The lives of its subjects are centered around the church, where people gather to pray, but this religious community does nothing to quell their loneliness.) Melancholy in a good way, "For No One" boasts the single finest addition (and most *Pet Sounds*-like touch) that producer Martin ever gave a Beatles track via the regal French horn solo. "Good Day Sunshine" is as ebullient as a glorious sunrise (none other than Leonard Bernstein praised its musical sophistication), and "Got to Get You into My Life" is a soulful Motown homage with resplendent brass.

Harrison has often been mocked for whining about the bite from his paycheck on "Taxman," but this is the first Beatles song to openly question governmental authority. ("Don't ask me what I want it for" comes the bureaucratic reply.) "Love You To" is the best of his Eastern ragas because it's the most frantic, with the sitar chasing the vocals through the song. And the elastic guitar and bass interplay on "I Want to Tell You" nicely evokes the circular philosophy of karma that the guitarist had newly embraced, and which he adhered to through the end of his life in December 2001.

A dreamy tune about floating upstream, Lennon's "I'm Only Sleeping" foreshadows the full-blown psychedelic voyage of "Tomorrow Never Knows" and boasts more extraordinary backwards guitar by Harrison. With its underwater sound effects and sing-along chorus, "Yellow Submarine" is a whimsical children's ditty with a touch of perversity (if you believe Lennon biographer Albert Goldman's contention that it's about yellow, sub-shaped Nembutals). The soaring guitar, rolling drums, and flowing bass of "She Said, She Said" carry on a spirited discussion that recalls the non-stop babble of the L.A. acid trip, with lyrics inspired by Fonda's monologue. ("He said, 'I know what it's like to be dead.'") "Doctor Robert" may be a jaunty throwaway, but it's a great one, with a lyric that tackles New York's speed-dispensing Dr. Feelgood, as well as the carnival-barker shtick of the self-appointed acid apostle Leary. Finally the ringing acoustic guitars explode from the mix on "And Your Bird Can Sing," the best song left off *Rubber Soul*, with a lyric that's similar to "Rain" in its mocking of the limitations of analytical thought. ("Paperback Writer" b/w "Rain" was to have been included on *Revolver*, but it was rushed out as a 45 to satisfy the label. Ah, technology! We can now use our CD burners to restore it to its rightful place, making the Beatles' psychedelic masterpiece even more mind-blowing.)

While critics such as Richard Goldstein recognized the importance of *Revolver* when it was released, many fans didn't really catch up with the Beatles until the next album, ten months later.

The Ultimate Psychedelic Rock Library: Sgt. Pepper's Lonely Hearts Club Band *(Capitol) reeks of horns and harps, but it has its moments.*

Sgt. Pepper's Lonely Hearts Club Band is largely celebrated because of its timing: It's the album that was on the turntable during the Summer of Love, when psychedelic drugs went from being part of a small subculture to a media phenomenon. "The closest Western Civilization has come to unity since the Congress of Vienna in 1815 was the week *Sgt. Pepper's* was released," critic Langdon Winner wrote in *The Rolling Stone Illustrated History of Rock & Roll.* "In every city in Europe and America the stereo systems and the radio played...and everyone listened." But what they heard was not the Beatles' best. "Like an over-attended child, this album is spoiled," Goldstein wrote. The language he used would be repeated countless times in years to come whenever a punk attacked an art-rock album thick with pretensions: "It reeks of horns and harps, harmonica quartets, assorted animal noises, and a forty-one-piece orchestra."

The Beatles' Ten Best Psychedelic Rock Songs

1. "Tomorrow Never Knows"
2. "Rain"
3. "Hey Bulldog"
4. "She Said, She Said"
5. "A Day in The Life"
6. "Baby You're a Rich Man"
7. "Blue Jay Way"
8. "Paperback Writer"
9. "Strawberry Fields Forever"
10. "Flying"

The conceptual conceit is that the group is portraying a sentimental, old-time, Salvation Army-type band (as depicted on the famous cover) in an effort to free itself from the expectations of making "Beatles music." But the psychedelic rock on *Revolver* wasn't bound by any constrictions, and only three songs on *Sgt. Pepper's* transcend the boundaries the musicians set for themselves. "Lucy in the Sky with Diamonds" is a catchy but slight piece of escapism. McCartney drew hostile criticism for talking to the press about psychedelics—"LSD opened my eyes," he said in 1967. "It made me a better, more honest, more tolerant member of society, brought closer to God"—and Lennon's denial that the title was an acronym for LSD seemed coy and motivated by commercial concerns. "Being for the Benefit of Mr. Kite!" is notable primarily for the tape montage of calliope sounds that Martin created to realize Lennon's vision of a sinister circus. "A Day in the Life" succeeds in grafting half a McCartney song onto half a Lennon song, evoking an unexpected trip from the workaday to the cosmos, but its positioning at the end of *Sgt. Pepper's*—the slot held by "Tomorrow Never Knows" on *Revolver*—isn't enough to redeem the rest of the album.

Imaginative and influential psychedelic rock songs are scattered through the rest of the Beatles' releases. "Strawberry Fields Forever," one of the Beatles' greatest studio accomplishments, looks at some familiar terrain (the Liverpool orphanage near Lennon's childhood home) through the *idealist* and impressionistic eyes of a child. "Hey

The Ultimate Psychedelic Rock Library: Magical Mystery Tour *(Capitol) pays homage to Ken Kesey, his Merry Pranksters, and their famous bus.*

Bulldog" boasts the Beatles' best-ever psychedelic guitar riff. "I Am the Walrus" features Lennon flirting with the madness that is the flipside of the psychedelic ideal, something attempted less successfully by McCartney on "Maxwell's Silver Hammer," though the lyrical nod to surrealist Alfred Jarry is amusing. The rollicking "Magical Mystery Tour" was inspired by Ken Kesey, the Merry Pranksters, and their psychedelic bus, and "Baby, You're a Rich Man" commented on the English underground's first big happening, the 14-Hour Technicolour Dream, which was billed as a gathering of "beautiful people." Written while he was fog-bound in L.A., Harrison's "Blue Jay Way" captures an uneasy sense of dislocation, and Lennon's "Across the Universe" evokes the drained but optimistic feeling that comes with the dawn after a nightlong acid trip.

When the latter was recorded in 1968, the Beatles were in the process of shifting to a more stripped-down approach in the studio, though psychedelic touches still decorated otherwise straightforward rock songs such as "Glass Onion," "Everybody's Got Something to Hide, Except Me and My Monkey," and "Dear Prudence." The search for spiritual enlightenment sparked by psychedelic adventures had led to the group's famously silly dalliance with the Maharishi Mahesh Yogi and, in recoiling from the charlatan guru, the band members more or less abandoned cosmic concerns.

After the Beatles split, Lennon, the group's biggest user of psychedelic drugs, spent the rest of his career until his assassination in December 1980 distancing himself from psychedelic utopianism with cathartic and intensely personal songs that probed the everyday world instead of transcending it (though the chaotic guitars of *Live Peace in Toronto 1969* hinted at the "better living through noise" approach of psychedelic guitar bands in the '80s and '90s). McCartney became a consummate pop craftsman, and belated returns to mid-'60s experimentation via collaborations with ambient house DJ Youth as the fireman (1993's *strawberries oceans ships forest* and 1998's *Rushes*) and Welsh psychedelic-popsters the Super Furry Animals (2000's *Liverpool Sound Collage*) fell flat. Unable to sustain entire rock albums, Harrison produced his best solo effort with the instrumental soundscapes on 1968's *Wonderwall Music*. Ringo continues to be Ringo. The pieces were never as strong as the whole, and the whole was never stronger than during the recording of *Revolver* in the heady spring of 1966.

SOMETHING HAPPENED TO ME YESTERDAY

I don't know how Mick and Ronnie and little Mick moved so fast, but they disappeared, leaving me with Jo and Charlie Watts, the world's politest man. I tried to move him through the sea of sleeping bags, wine bottles, dogs, bodies, and hair....We were pushing through the crowd, stumbling, trying to avoid the big dogs. People were tossing us joints and things. Looking at a yellow-green LSD tab, Charlie asked, "D' you want it?" "I ain't too sure about this street acid," I said. "Maybe Keith will want it," Charlie replied.

—Stanley Booth
at Altamont in *The True Adventures of the Rolling Stones*

THE NOTORIOUS BAD BOYS of '60s rock came late to the psychedelic party, and with the exception of their blond, sleepy-eyed
founder Brian Jones, they never truly joined the festivities. During
the frantic days of the Rolling Stones' early tours, former econom-
ics student Mick Jagger and art-school dropout Keith Richards were
known to have people thrown out of their dressing rooms for smoking pot. This embarrassed bassist Bill Wyman and drummer Charlie
Watts, who, regardless of their own proclivities, were used to marijuana as part of the jazz scene. But by 1965, the Stones' attitudes
were changing.

The band started smoking a lot of pot while touring America,
and Jones and Richards dropped acid at a party thrown by Kesey. By
the end of the year, Jones and manager Andrew Loog Oldham were
tripping regularly. In his autobiography, *Stone Alone*, Wyman wrote
that "the effect of marijuana and LSD brought about a sea-change
in the outlooks, attitudes, and aspirations of thousands of musicians around the world," not the least of whom were the Stones.
Thanks largely to Jones, the band's music was growing more elaborate. In 1966, *Aftermath* added exotic textures such as dulcimer,
sitar, and marimba. Though he remained loyal to the blues that
inspired him to start the band, Jones' musical curiosity was insa-
tiable, and he was drawn to new electronic synthesizers, ancient
Eastern percussion, and the master musicians of Jajouka, who
drummed for hours in a drug-induced trance. The guitarist could
pick up any instrument and find the perfect way to incorporate it
into the Stones' music. "Charlie would recall how Brian sat for
hours learning to play sitar, put it on 'Paint It, Black,' and never
played it again," Booth wrote.

The Ultimate Psychedelic Rock Library: The Rolling Stones' Between the Buttons *(Abkco) finds the psychedelic fog rolling in.*

The drug influence was obvious in the titles and themes of the band's mid-'60s singles. The frantic "19th Nervous Breakdown" includes the line, "On our first trip I tried so hard to rearrange your mind." "Paint It, Black" has mysterious Eastern overtones, and "Mother's Little Helper" pokes fun at suburban moms on speed. The title of the 1966 best-of compilation, *Big Hits (High Tide and Green Grass),* winks at fellow potheads, but the psychedelic influence really comes to the forefront on 1967's *Between the Buttons.* The Stones peer at fans from the cover's blurry haze, and the songs include the swirling "Ruby Tuesday" and the jugband ditty "Something Happened to Me Yesterday," which critic Robert Christgau called "the most accurate LSD song ever." "He don't know if it's right of wrong / Maybe he should tell someone," Jagger and Richards sing. "He don't know just what it was / Or if it's against the law."

The Stones' Ten Best Psychedelic Rock Songs

1. "Paint It, Black"

2. "2000 Light Years from Home"

3. "Child of the Moon"

4. "She's a Rainbow"

5. "Rocks Off"

6. "Sister Morphine"

7. "Sway"

8. "Dandelion"

9. "Citadel"

10. "Lady Jane"

The Beatles were openly embracing LSD in 1967, but it was the Stones who were tagged as druggie outlaws. On February 5, the *News of the World* published a story charging that Jagger had attended an acid party at a house shared by members of the Moody Blues. (The reporters fingered the wrong Stone: It had really been Jones.) In private, Jagger praised the effects of LSD. According to biographer Chris Andersen, the singer told costume designer Cecil

Beaton, "You see yourself aglow. You see yourself beautiful and ugly, and other people as if for the first time." But Jagger wanted to keep the public guessing about his drug habits, and he filed a libel suit against the tabloid. A week later, he and Richards were busted during a raid on Redlands, Richards's country estate, that was generally considered a set-up. The weekend's guests included Jagger's girlfriend, Marianne Faithfull; gallery owner Robert Fraser; George and Patti Harrison (who ducked out before the bust), and a mysterious American nicknamed Acid King David, who dispensed LSD with the morning tea. Everyone was coming down from a day of tripping when the police arrived at 8 p.m.

To the delight of the tabloids, the officers found Faithfull nude except for a bearskin rug, and they collected marijuana residue and a vial of pills. As the property owner, Richards was charged with allowing marijuana to be smoked on the premises. Jagger took the rap for the vial of speed, though it actually belonged to Faithfull. The band's troubles continued mounting through the year. Jones' lover Anita Pallenberg left him for Richards, and Jones was devastated by the loss. He had been busted as well, and he was facing trial for possession of pot, methedrine, and cocaine. The group was in the process of an ugly split with its manager, Oldham, and it was coming under the influence of the American pitbull, Allen Klein. It was under these gray clouds that the band began to record its eleventh album, *Their Satanic Majesties Request*, a record that Jagger said was made "under the influence of bail."

*The Ultimate Psychedelic Rock
Library:* Their Satanic Majesties
Request *(Abkco) shows the flip
side of the psychedelic ideal.*

The title was the first time the Stones toyed with devilish imagery, and it reflects a shift in Jagger's reading habits from the Beats to stranger fare (including *The Master and Margarita*, the Russian novel that was one of the inspirations for "Sympathy for the Devil"). The album opens with "Sing This All Together," a hootenanny sing-along that wouldn't sound out of place at one of Kesey's Acid Tests. Over soundscapes that include theremins, synthesizers, shortwave radio static, and distinctive string arrangements by John Paul Jones, the Stones invite listeners to open their minds and "let the pictures come." The most colorful images include "Citadel," a candy-coated tune with a cheery Mellotron hook; "2000 Man," a song about alienation in familiar surroundings; "2000 Light Years from Home," which is just the opposite, a sort of space-age version of "Sloop John B"; the symbolic "Lantern"; and the beautiful "She's a Rainbow." But even at their spaciest, the Stones can't get away from their central obsession, sex. "She comes in colors everywhere," Jagger sings leeringly.

Wary of psychedelic drugs, Wyman parodied the band's current interest with "In Another Land," his first songwriting contribution. Originally titled "Acid in the Grass," the simple love song is decorated with psychedelic clichés such as tremeloed vocals and lyrics about "blue flowers." The chorus—"Then I awoke / Is this some kind of joke?"—predicts the return to basics that soon followed. The Stones' particular journey toward the white light was never too far removed from earthy concerns, and this may be the reason that *Their Satanic Majesties Request* was written off by critics. Consensus held it as a failed attempt to copy *Sgt. Pepper's*, a facile charge as deep as the observation that the 3-D cover was designed by the same artist, Peter Blake. "Despite moments of unquestionable brilliance, it puts the status of the Rolling Stones in jeopardy," critic Jon Landau wrote. *Rolling Stone* founder Jann Wenner added that it was "the prototype of junk masquerading as meaningful" (and he should certainly know).

The Stones themselves were soon dissing the album—even the unfailingly loyal Ian Stewart called it "that damn *Satanic Majesties*"—but Christgau maintained that "the tunes prove remarkably solid and the concept is legitimate in its tongue-in-cheekness." *Satanic Majesties* is the first psychedelic rock album to satirize the prevailing optimism about LSD and to hint that there could be a dark side to the psychedelic experience. The perception was that, like the brutish Hell's Angels at Kesey's acid tests, the Stones didn't understand the drug. But the reality was that they knew that it didn't guarantee peace and ecstasy, and it was foolish to pretend that it did. When the band followed *Their Satanic Majesties Request* with *Beggars Banquet* a year later, the songs were more sinister and streetwise ("Sympathy for the Devil," "Street Fighting Man"). "The short psychedelic dream had withered," Wyman wrote in his autobiography. The stripped-down sound took a turn toward country-blues—the music of factory girls and other salt of the earth—but there was a mysterious dimension that was amplified by Jones's death and the chaos at Altamont.

After *Their Satanic Majesties Request*, the Stones only occasionally made music that recalled its specific psychedelic sounds, as on the brilliant single, "Child of the Moon," and the dreamy break in "Rocks Off." But they carried the lantern along with all the other baggage they picked up. It could be glimpsed through the murk of their decadent masterpiece, 1972's *Exile on Main Street*, as they groped for spiritual salvation amid the insanity that they'd created. But with every passing year, the spark grew dimmer. "The group is still strong and together," critic Lillian Roxon wrote in 1969 in her celebrated *Rock Encyclopedia*. "But nothing is the same. How could it be?"

THREE

3

DRUGS, DEMENTIA, AND AMPLIFIED JUGS: Psychedelic Punk

I began to realize that it was all the same—my teenage-dis-solution lifestyle and the music of groups like the Troggs, Shadows of Knight, Music Machine, Seeds, Question Mark, Count Five. They were all full of shit and so was I. And none of us cared. We had all heard the Yardbirds' brilliant innovations, but since almost none of the above listed groups really knew how to play their instruments, all they could do was bang away in rackety imitation. Which was when I first realized that *quality* and *musicianship* and *taste* actually had nothing whatsoever to do with rock 'n' roll; in fact might be its worst enemies.

—Lester Bangs,
"The History of Garage Rock, Part 1,"
New Wave magazine No. 2, 1977

IN THE EARLY '60S, garages across America were filled with teenagers living out their rock-'n'-roll fantasies on cheap Sears, Roebuck instruments. At first, these acne-plagued legions imitated the surf bands, playing endless variations of "Wipe Out" that always fell apart during the drum solos. Later they pushed aside Dad's lawnmower and the folding chairs to bash through songs by the Byrds and the British Invasion bands. By late 1965, there was a new element in the mix. Some of these rock-star wannabes discovered psychedelic drugs, but most wrote about what they *imagined* the psychedelic experience to be. They were aided in their quest to freak out listeners by technical innovations such as fuzztone, electric twelve-string guitar, echo, and tape delay—tools that, as punk connoisseur Lester Bangs noted in another homage for *The Rolling Stone Illustrated History of Rock & Roll*, "put truly awesome sonic possibilities within the reach of the most limited musicians." At the same time, these hamfisted musicians were conscious of complying with the demands of AM radio for singles that were short, catchy, and devoid of instrumental displays that detracted from the tune at hand. The result was some of rock's most inventive and enduring one-hit wonders.

In 1972, barely five years after the trends shifted to more ponderous sounds, garage fan Lenny Kaye compiled some of the best psychedelic punks on *Nuggets: Original Artyfacts from the First Psychedelic Era, 1965–1968*. A rock archivist and writer, Kaye was working as a talent scout for Elektra Records when he compiled the album. (It was later reissued in the more familiar version on Sire in 1976, and once again as a box set on Rhino in 1998.) "These bands were more intoxicated by the Gibson fuzztone, the first fuzztone that came out, than by any drugs," Kaye told me. "Unless you lived in New York or San Francisco, I doubt you'd seen any LSD. A lot of it was just desire. That's what made these bands wonderful—there were millions of them, and if they were heard five blocks away, it kind of spoiled what they were doing." Nuggets spawned a legion of archeological imitators—*Pebbles, Boulders, Rubble* and the like— but it remains the definitive compilation. "What strikes me about *Nuggets* now is how unified it is when, at the time, it seemed to cover a lot of stylistic ground," Kaye said.

In sharp contrast to the whimsical psychedelia that became the rage in England, the sounds and visions of the American *Nuggets* bands were dark and ominous. "This was 'bad trip' psychedelia as opposed to the predominantly dreamy, optimistic feel of the U.K.," wrote Larry Grogan, editor of the psychedelic rock fanzine, *The Evil Eye.* "This might be due to extreme anti-drug paranoia in the U.S., or to real-world experiences with cheap street drugs (glue sniffing, bad acid, and/or speed)." Stories about people driven over the edge

The Ultimate Psychedelic Rock Library: Lenny Kaye compiled the first and best collection of psychedelic garage bands. In 1998, Rhino Records expanded the original Nuggets *double album into a four-CD box set.*

by marijuana use had been circulating since 1937, when U.S. narcotics commissioner Harry Ainslinger published a harrowing article
called "Marijuana: Assassin of Youth." A wave of media hysteria
and government propaganda followed, including the classic camp
film, *Reefer Madness*, until pot was firmly stereotyped as the drug of
choice for lowlifes and loonies. Hysteria about psychedelic drugs
built in similar fashion, fanned by anecdotal accounts of LSD users
going crazy, losing their eyesight, destroying their chromosomes, or
jumping out of windows in doomed attempts to fly. There were also
tales of horror from army veterans who learned that they had been
used as human guinea pigs in psychedelic experiments by government agencies, including the CIA. Then, too, there was the longstanding association by white, middle-class America of illegal drugs
with African Americans and "lower-class" lifestyles.

According to Peter Stafford's *Psychedelics Encyclopedia*, in early
1966, Dr. Huston Smith of MIT told an LSD conference that confusion about the drug was so great and genuine knowledge so small
"that there is no hope of telling the truth about it at this point." By
1967, LSD was outlawed across the United States. The flood of media
attention fixated on the idea that the drug caused psychosis in otherwise sane individuals. This notion convinced some initiates to fear
that they were losing their minds. "In any society whose culture
contains notions of sanity and insanity, the person who finds his
subjective state altered may think he has become insane," sociolo-
gist Howard Becker wrote in the *Journal of Health & Social Behavior* in
1967. "We learn at a young age that a person who 'acts funny,' 'sees
things,' 'hears things,' or has other bizarre and unusual experiences
may have become 'crazy.' The drug experience, perhaps originally as

The Ten Best Psychedelic Rock Songs from the American Garage

1.   The Standells, "Medication"
2.   The Electric Prunes, "I Had Too Much to Dream (Last Night)"
3.   The Seeds, "Pushin' Too Hard"
4.   The Count Five, "Psychotic Reaction"
5.   The Premiers, "Farmer John"
6.   The Music Machine, "Talk Talk"
7.   The Sonics, "The Witch"
8.   ? and the Mysterians, "96 Tears"
9.   The 13th Floor Elevators, "You're Gonna Miss Me"
10. The Strawberry Alarm Clock, "Incense and Peppermints"

a momentary entertainment, now looms as a momentous event which will disrupt one's life, possibly permanently. Faced with this conclusion, the person develops a full-blown anxiety attack, but it is an anxiety caused by his *reaction* to the drug experience rather than a direct consequence of the drug use itself."

Nineteenth-century romantics had equated the creative process with madness. As a romantic art form, rock 'n' roll was considered best when it was truly "out of control." Given all of these factors, it's not surprisingly that losing your mind became the topic of many psychedelic singles, including the Electric Prunes' rollicking "I Had Too Much to Dream (Last Night)," a cautionary tale of a psychedelic hangover, and the Count Five's "Psychotic Reaction," a shameless rip-off of the Yardbirds' "I'm a Man" with one of the most demented vocals since Screamin' Jay Hawkins' "I Put a Spell On You." Both songs were Top Ten hits, but most of the *Nuggets* bands settled for short-lived regional fame, and their marginality was part of their charm. The bands that stuck around inevitably showed their shortcomings—the Electric Prunes went on to record a pompous rock mass sung in Latin—but the groups that disappeared enabled fans to project their own fantasies on them.

The Count Five was never heard from again, but Bangs invented a long career for the group in his epic article "Psychotic Reactions and Carburetor Dung." Like the Count Five, the Chocolate Watchband hailed from San Jose, but it mixed Rolling Stones-style R&B with heavy-handed sitar playing. The Strawberry Alarm Clock scored a hit with the idyllic "Incense and Peppermints." The Sonics forged a path in Seattle for a new wave of grunge-rockers that would follow a generation later. The members of the Music Machine each wore one black glove, and they recorded the endearingly snotty "Talk Talk." ? and the Mysterians set a new standard for cheesy organ on "96 Tears," while the Standells sang about the River Charles and Boston University's frustrating curfew (despite the fact that they lived in L.A.) on "Dirty Water."

The Seeds were another L.A. band that talked a lot about flower power, but it was always clear exactly what kind of seeds their name referred to. "Pushin' Too Hard" was a minor hit that featured singer Sky Saxon railing against the forces that would keep him down (or bust him for smoking pot), while the band's second album included songs called "Tripmaker" and "Mr. Farmer," a tribute to marijuana growers. Most notorious of all in recent years have been the Monks, a band formed by a group of displaced American G.I.s stationed in Germany in the mid-'60s and devoted to playing furious, minimalist garage rock, a strange tale chronicled in bassist Eddie Shaw's memorable 1994 autobiography, *Black Monk Time*.

How many of these bands took any drug stronger than marijuana is open to debate. "By 1965 or '66, LSD was available in certain big-city communities, like Detroit, Chicago, L.A., and New York," Amboy Dukes singer John Drake told me. "But the suburbanite kids had no idea what it was. They were just singing about something that was in the air. And even later, you had to know

The Ultimate Psychedelic Rock Library: The Seeds' first two albums have been compiled on one must-own disc called The Seeds *(GNP Crescendo).*

somebody who knew somebody to get into it. The somebody *I* knew was John Sinclair." Fueled by acid provided by the radical journalist and leader of the White Panther Party, Drake and guitarist Steve Farmer helped craft a 1968 hit called "Journey to the Center of the Mind" that urged psychedelic experimentation over a riff adapted from the theme to the television Western series, *Bonanza*. The album of the same name was released with a cover showing an impressive array of pot pipes, but the band's third key member was opposed to drug use of any kind. "I didn't have the faintest idea what those pipes were all about," firebrand guitarist Ted Nugent, who eventually became a gun-toting conservative poster boy, said in Alan Vorda's *Psychedelic Psounds*. "Everybody else was getting stoned and trying every drug known to mankind. I was meeting women, playing rock 'n' roll, and meeting girls. I didn't know anything about this cosmic inner probe. I thought 'Journey to the Center of the Mind' meant look inside yourself, use your head, and move forward in life."

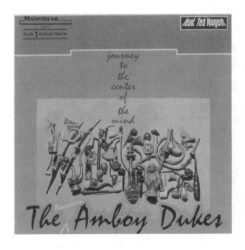

The Ultimate Psychedelic Rock Library: The Amboy Dukes flaunt an impressive collection of pot pipes on the cover of Journey to the Center of the Mind *(Repertoire). In case you didn't get the reference, the album included a track called "Down on Phillips Escalator" ("D-O-P-E").*

The most enduring of America's psychedelic-punk bands left no doubt about their positive stance on drugs. And unlike most of the *Nuggets* groups, their influence reached far beyond a few scattered tracks on archival compilations.

STEP INSIDE THIS HOUSE

> Dick Clark, self-described as "America's oldest living teenager," seemed thoroughly befuddled by the grungy band standing before him. The year was 1966, and the freaky quintet from Austin Texas, had just performed their Top 40 hit, "You're Gonna Miss Me," a stinging slice of lysergically fueled garage rock. Clark decided to try one of his surefire conversational gambits. "Who's the head of this band?" he asked. The long-haired guitarist with the piercing eyes and the unnaturally high voice smiled broadly. Said Roky Erickson: "We're all heads, Dick!"
>
> —The 13th Floor Elevators
> appear on *American Bandstand*

More than any other American group in the '60s, including the vaunted San Francisco bands that followed during the fabled Summer of Love, the 13th Floor Elevators proudly espoused the virtues of breaking on through to the other side via the use of psychedelic drugs. "Recently it has become possible for man to chemically alter his mental state," read the liner notes of their debut album, *The Psychedelic Sounds of the 13th Floor Elevators*. With their music, they intended to provide the soundtrack for this journey.

Born Roger Kynard Erickson (his first two names were truncated into "Roky," pronounced "rocky"), the youngest member of the group was kicked out of Austin's Travis High School in his junior year for growing his hair like the Rolling Stones. He'd already written "You're Gonna Miss Me," a minor hit for garage rockers the Spades, when he was approached in 1965 to join a sort of Texas supergroup. Guitarist Stacy Sutherland, bassist Benny Thurman, and drummer John Ike Walton had progressed from playing bluegrass to raunchy garage rock with Port Arthur's Lingsmen; their friend and neighbor, Janis Joplin, briefly considered joining the Elevators to sing alongside Erickson before setting off on her own. The musicians were introduced to Erickson by University of Texas undergrad Tommy Hall, who played the jug in another band called the Conqueroo.

Several years older than his band mates, Hall was a self-styled Beat poet who was already acquainted with psychedelic drugs and the writings of Timothy Leary and Aldous Huxley. Peyote had been widely available in Austin since 1961, and LSD started to circulate in 1965. The Elevators dropped acid together and set out to evoke the psychedelic experience in both music and lyrics. "When rock 'n' roll was happening and the music was coming on, it would piss you off that people would write really dumb lyrics," Hall told Bill Bentley in 1990 for an article in the *Austin Chronicle*. "You had Leary and the psychedelic concept, the beginning of that, and people didn't follow it. They'd just come out with the same old type of songs, so you'd think, 'Hey, you guys, talk about this. This is what we want to hear about.' It was really more of a brother-to-brother type of thing." The band's very name was meant to signify membership in a select group blessed with secret knowledge: The thirteenth floor doesn't exist in many high-rises, and the band was fond of pointing out that m (for marijuana) is the thirteenth letter of the alphabet.

Some of Erickson's friends charge that Hall manipulated the group and used drugs for control, but Erickson enthusiastically embraced psychedelics, describing tripping as an art. "I've always had the quest and want for something that would raise my consciousness up," he said in a 1984 article in *Third Coast* magazine by Doug Hanners, Joe Nick Patoski, and Kirby McDaniel. "People need to say more about what they're afraid to say, because that's how man discovers. That's science—being able to accept that there's something beyond." While Hall gave the band a philosophical backdrop, Erickson provided its musical focus. He had been born into a musical family; his mother sang at church and with a local opera group, and his younger brother, Sumner, would become a world-class symphonic tuba player. Roky favored different sounds, especially the powerful screaming of Little Richard and James Brown. "This is meant as a compliment," he's quoted as saying in *Psychedelic Psounds*. "[Rock 'n' roll] just *horrified* me." His own voice combined that kind of intensity with the plaintive emotion of another influence and fellow Texas native, the late Buddy Holly.

The Elevators built a reputation on powerful live shows and an independent single featuring a new version of "You're Gonna Miss Me," its sinister tone sharply contrasting with the prevailing sentiments of "I Want to Hold Your Hand" and "She Loves You."

Erickson's snarled warning to an errant lover is delivered over Sutherland's churning, Duane Eddy-gone-bad guitar and a classic E-D-A-G chord progression second in popularity only to "Louie Louie" in the annals of garage-rock history. Erickson's vocal veers between grief-filled pleading and psychotic threatening. "You're gonna wake up one morning as the sun greets the dawn / You're gonna look around and you'll find that I'm gone / You didn't realize / You're gonna miss me, baby!" he screams. Through it all runs the high-pitched burbling of Hall's "electric" jug. The jug had been a staple of the folk and bluegrass combos of the early '60s. Hall amplified his by holding a microphone close to the opening, but it's likely that as much of the sound came from his voice as the jug. According to Elevators lore, the jug was filled with Hall's pot stash, and Hall drew inspiration for his playing from John Coltrane. In retrospect, his random noises foreshadow the chaotic synthesizers of Roxy Music, the krautrock bands, and Pere Ubu.

The Ultimate Psychedelic Rock Library: The Psychedelic Sounds of the 13th Floor Elevators *(Collectables) is a call to arms for like-minded heads.*

Houston's International Artists label was run by Lelan Rogers, the brother of rocker-turned-country crooner Kenny Rogers (who scored his first big hit in 1968 with a transparently insincere psychedelic ditty, "Just Dropped In (To See What Condition My Condition Was In)"). By the end of the '60s, the company had a remarkable psychedelic roster including Lost & Found, the Golden Dawn, Bubble Puppy, and the Red Crayola, which debuted with an intriguing effort called *The Parable of Arable Land*, featuring a guest appearance by Erickson (though much of its music was static and self-consciously arty). International Artists signed the Elevators, but like many of their labelmates, the musicians soon had a long list of complaints about the label and Lelan Rogers, whose business practices helped doom them to obscurity. (For his part, Rogers told the *Washington Post* in 1991 that, "I didn't produce [the Elevators], I baby-sat them.") But despite the fact that it was recorded quickly on three tracks, *The Psychedelic Sounds of the 13th Floor Elevators* is one of rock's most powerful debuts, with sounds that viscerally evoke the lyrical topics at hand.

"The music makes you see things if you want to," Erickson said in *Third Coast*. Indeed, "Roller Coaster" careers like the amusement park ride. The chorus of "Reverberation (Doubt)" echoes as if bouncing off the walls of a dark cavern; "Splash 1" creates waves of sound like the ripples on a still pond, and "Fire Engine" is propelled by urgent, wailing sirens. These sounds didn't connect with a mass audience, but they did attract the attention of the band's peers. The Rolling Stones later rewrote the Elevators' "Monkey Island" as "Monkey Man," and Pink Floyd lifted the main theme for the *More* soundtrack from "Roller Coaster."

The Elevators' open attitude about psychedelic drug use was also inspiring. "Kingdom of Heaven" advances the notion that "the kingdom of heaven is within us," waiting to be accessed through psychedelic drugs, while "Fire Engine" pays tribute to DMT, a powerful drug that, when smoked, prompts an intense fifteen-minute trip. "'Let make take you to DMT place,'" Erickson said, quoting the lyrics. "It was like a fire engine without the calamity of a fire." With lyrics by Hall, "Roller Coaster" is even more explicit in its heralding of the psychedelic experience: "After you trip life opens up / You start doing what you want to do / No one can ever hurt you / But you know more than you thought you knew."

Not surprisingly, the band attracted the attention of Texas law enforcement. "It was sort of like being in Jesse James's gang," said bassist Danny Galindo, who joined the group in 1967. "We had the cops after us wherever we went." The harassment began to take its toll, but the band recorded a second brilliant release before fracturing. *Easter Everywhere* opens with the eight-minute "Slip Inside This House." Unlike similar efforts by the San Francisco bands, the rhythm and melody never flag as the epic lyric unfolds. "If your limbs begin dissolving / In the water that you tread / All surroundings are evolving / In the stream that clears your head / Find yourself a caravan / Like Noah must have led / And slip inside this house as you pass by," Erickson sings. As on the first album, the psychedelic sounds of songs such as "Slide Machine," "Levitation," and "Earthquake" perfectly match the lyrics, but there is also a strong soul influence, and the album includes a cover of Bob Dylan's "It's All Over Now, Baby Blue" that's as impressive as any of the Byrds' reworkings.

The Ultimate Psychedelic Rock Library: Easter Everywhere *(Collectables) kicks off with the brilliant "Slip Inside This House."*

Shortly after the second album's release, Erickson was busted for pot for the second time. In court, his lawyers called a psychiatrist who said that the singer had taken three hundred LSD trips that had "messed up" his mind, but the strategy backfired. Erickson was acquitted of possession, but the jury declared him insane and the judge sentenced him to Rusk State Mental Hospital, where he was prodded by shock therapy and kept fully stoked on mood-altering drugs. "I was going to jail and so I said, 'Hey, man, I'm seeing things on the wall and I'm hearing voices. I'm crazy, put me away.' So they said, 'Alright, he's crazy,'" Erickson recalled in *Third Coast.* "I was such a good actor. When you put your mind to it, you can really convince people, but you gotta be careful. 'Cause at the end of three years, I'm sitting there and they said, 'Hmm, so you're still hearing voices.' And I said, 'No, man, I lied.' And they said, 'Yeah, sure, you lied.'"

Without Erickson, the band fell apart, but that didn't stop International Artists from releasing two more albums. *Bull of the*

Woods is comprised of unremarkable Sutherland tunes and three old Erickson songs, while *The 13th Floor Elevators Live* is made up of studio outtakes with crowd noise dubbed in. Sutherland kept playing, but he was shot to death by his wife during a fight in 1978. Hall moved to San Francisco, and when writer and Elevators fan Bill Bentley tracked him down in 1990, he was still taking LSD weekly.

Bearded, bulkier, and no longer the teenaged rock star, Erickson emerged from Rusk in 1972 after a jury declared him legally sane. In 1975 he reappeared on record with the single "Starry Eyes," a touching, romantic piece of Buddy Holly-style pop, and "Red Temple Prayer (Two Headed Dog)," which pairs driving guitar rock with vivid horror-movie imagery. Erickson was now obsessed with monster movies. "The horror of Rusk sort of made fantasy easier to deal with," said his mom, Evelyn.

From the mid-'70s through the mid-'80s, Erickson shuffled between Austin and San Francisco. At one point he declared himself an alien and had his statement legally notarized. On the cover of his first book, *Openers*, he appointed himself a reverend and presented poems such as "Jesus Is Not a Hallucinogenic Mushroom." Through it all, he played with a succession of bands that appear on a lengthy list of bootlegs and independent releases. The best of these, *Roky Erickson and the Aliens*, was produced by former Creedence Clearwater Revival bassist Stu Cook and released in 1980 by CBS International after the label's U.S. branch passed. The intensity of Erickson's vocals on tunes such as "I Think of Demons," "Don't Shake Me Lucifer," "Bloody Hammer," and "If You Have Ghosts" contrasts with the campiness of the lyrics. "When you're working with Roky, you're basically living B-grade horror movies all

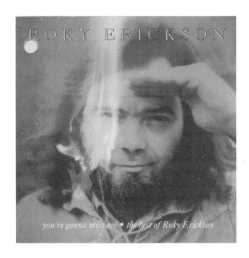

*The Ultimate Psychedelic Rock
Library:* You're Gonna Miss Me:
The Best of Roky Erickson
*(Restless) features twenty-one prime
nuggets of solo Roky.*

day," Cook told me. But the fact is, Roky *believed.* "In his fashion,
he had come to know the devil the way that Robert Johnson knew
the devil, by carrying on daily conversations with him," critic John
Morthland wrote in the liner notes to the 1991 compilation, *You're
Gonna Miss Me: The Best of Roky Erickson.*

By 1986 Erickson was reluctant to talk about "the real world" at
all. When I spoke to him by phone shortly after the release of *Don't
Slander Me,* which was supposed to have been his second release for
CBS International, he chatted amiably about horror films such as
Halloween, The Evil Dead, and *Friday the 13th,* but he dodged every
question about music. At one point, he said that "his lady" had just
been hit by a car and wanted to say hello. He disappeared and there
was a long stretch of silence before he returned. "Lady just said
'hi,'" he said. It dawned on me that Lady was Roky's dog. Trying to
sound nonplussed, I asked what kind of canine she was. "Black," he
said. (Of course.) Finally, he thanked me for calling, invited me to

visit anytime, and indicated that he shared Brian Wilson's belief about dogs picking up good vibrations. "You're a really nice guy," he said. "And Lady liked you."

A short time later, Erickson moved into federally subsidized housing outside Austin and officially retired from the music scene. He spent his days surrounded by countless TVs turned up full volume, sometimes with nothing on but static, and waited enthusiastically for each day's mail. In late 1989 he got a little too enthusiastic and was arrested for collecting his neighbors' mail; he was found unfit to stand trial and briefly hospitalized with a diagnosis of organic brain damage and schizophrenia. For years, a large circle in Austin's tight-knit music community provided Erickson with support and companionship—after the mail trouble, Bentley, an executive at Warner Bros. Records, put together a classic tribute album, *Where the Pyramid Meets the Eye*, with contributions from fans such as R.E.M., the Jesus and Mary Chain, and Julian Cope. In 1995 Texas music booster Casey Monahan compiled the book *Openers II* for punk poet Henry Rollins's 2.13.61 imprint, and he and musician Speedy Sparks midwifed *All That May Do My Rhyme* for the Butthole Surfers' Trance Syndicate label. Half of the songs date from aborted sessions a decade earlier, and all of them were written before the early '80s.

Erickson tends to burn out the people who are kind enough to help tend to his health and welfare. Having finally exhausted Austin's good will, he relocated a few years ago to Pennsylvania, where he lives with his brother Sumner, the principal tuba player with the Pittsburgh Symphony Orchestra. Roky has either lost the ability or the desire to write new material. As with Syd Barrett and

The Ultimate Psychedelic Rock Library: A collection of psychedelic- and alternative-rock greats appear on 1990's Where the Pyramid Meets the Eye: A Tribute to Roky Erickson *(Sire).*

Brian Wilson, the words "acid casualty" follow his name in most rock histories, but this angers people who know him. His art speaks for itself, they say, and it's wrong for any fan to hang expectations on him. On the other hand, Erickson clearly isn't what anyone would call a productive member of society. "Roky's crazy, but he's also smart enough to kind of use the craziness," his friend, journalist Rob Patterson, told me. "It's a real chicken or the egg thing. He works with it, and he's been able to use it in a way where he just gets to sit around and relax and watch TV." Added Monahan: "Roky is one of the funniest—and the laziest—people you ever want to meet. He doesn't talk about music, but he knows what he's doing."

"I couldn't really care less what people think, and that puts them in a place where they don't have any kind of say-so or control over anything I do," Erickson wrote in 1984. In the classic Elevators tune "I Had to Tell You," he sang, "If you fear I'll lose my spirit / Like a drunkard's wasted wine / Don't you even think about it / I'm feeling fine." And who are we to second-guess him?

AND THEN MY MIND SPLIT OPEN

> Coming here on a trip is bound to make a tremendous dif-
> ference. But we're here to stimulate a different kind of
> intoxication. The sounds, the visual stuff—all this bom-
> barding of the senses—it can be very heady in itself, if
> you're geared to it.
>
> —John Cale on the Exploding Plastic Inevitable,
> *New York* magazine, 1966

HOW ON EARTH CAN YOU CONSIDER the Velvet Underground psychedelic? This was one of the most frequent questions I got following the publication of the first edition of this book. That the band was hugely influential was taken as a given; I had joked that the name should officially be changed to "the Seminal Velvet Underground," and many agreed. Yet critics and fans tend to honor the band as "godfathers of punk," which is true enough, but it ignores the context in which the group emerged (the first album in particular was *perceived* as psychedelic at the time, though not in the utopian sense of the West Coast bands), and it certainly isn't *all* that the Velvets were. It overlooks other parts of their legacy and seizes upon select aspects of a complicated sound, privileging the street reportage of some of Lou Reed's lyrics over the unedited stream of consciousness of others; favoring the concise, churning rhythm guitars over the disorienting blasts of feedback and white noise, and emphasizing the desperate, primal aggression over the quiet, painful introspection and soul-searching. The Velvet Underground was a schizophrenic band, and from its most schizophrenic moments come its psychedelic legacy and its brilliant debut, an enduring psychedelic-rock masterpiece.

The Velvets' best work resulted from the collision of two radically different sensibilities. Reed grew up in a middle-class family on Long Island, and he fell in love with rock 'n' roll as a teenager. Concerned about his fondness for the devil's music and his homosexual tendencies, his parents subjected him to electroshock therapy at age seventeen. At Syracuse University, Reed studied poetry, imitated the excessive ways of his mentor, Delmore Schwartz, and cultivated a snotty punk persona. When he was finally kicked out, he wound up back at home, commuting to work as a staff writer at Pickwick Records and churning out imitation Motown and surf singles. In contrast, John Cale was born in Wales and became a child prodigy on the piano. He studied music in London in the early '60s, but instead of the blues that captivated so many of his peers, he was fascinated with the electronic experiments of Karlheinz Stockhausen and John Cage. (The German composer Stockhausen would be an especially significant influence on many psychedelic rockers, who related to the intuitive and often very noisy approach to synthesizers and recording technology in his early '60s work.) In 1963 Cale moved to New York to work with Cage and wound up playing with avant-garde musicians and composers Tony Conrad and La Monte Young in the Dream Syndicate, a group whose use of long, trance-inducing drones predated any rock band's embrace of Eastern sounds.

The Velvets' Ten Best Psychedelic Rock Songs

1. "The Black Angel's Death Song"
2. "European Son"
3. "I Heard Her Call My Name"
4. "Sister Ray"
5. "All Tomorrow's Parties"
6. "The Murder Mystery"
7. "Ocean"
8. "Foggy Notion"
9. "Hey Mr. Rain"
10. "Run Run Run"

Reed met Cale and Conrad at a party, and he recruited them to play a few gigs as the Primitives, the *nom de rock* behind a quickie Pickwick single called "The Ostrich." The record flopped, but a friendship grew. "It seemed like a very powerful encounter in a sense, each of them moving in a direction which was daring and audacious for the other as well as themselves," Conrad said in *Up-Tight: The Velvet Underground Story* by Victor Bockris and Gerard Malanga. "John was moving at a very, very fast pace away from a classical training background through the avant-garde and into performance art and then rock. It was phenomenal for Lou, considering his interest in what would be referred to today as punk—somebody who is really living rock and is interested in an extremely aggressive, assertive position—to discover that classical musicians and avant-garde artists were also engaged in that."

The group slowly came together in an apartment on the Lower East Side. Sterling Morrison was a guitarist that Reed knew from Syracuse. Original drummer Angus MacLise brought Eastern percussion into the mix, but he disliked demands such as having to show up at gigs on time. Maureen Tucker, the sister of another Syracuse buddy, was a last-minute replacement whose powerful backbeat became a key element in the band's sound. (Her tom-heavy approach came from favorites Bo Diddley and African drummer Olatunji.) The band name was borrowed from the title of a paperback about sado-masochism.

The Velvet Underground was already playing much of what would become its first album when it linked up with Andy Warhol. The pop artist was at the height of his popularity, and expanding into music seemed like a natural move. "The pop idea, after all, was that anybody could do anything, so naturally we were all trying to do it all," Warhol is quoted as saying in *Up-Tight*. "Nobody wanted to stay in one category, we all wanted to branch out into every creative thing we could." He convinced the band to add the platinum blonde ice princess Nico, and the Velvets began to perform as part of Andy Warhol, Up-Tight, a multimedia show that featured lights, films, and dancing by Factory regulars Gerard Malanga and Edie Sedgwick. The show went on tour as Andy Warhol's Exploding

Plastic Inevitable, a swirling psychedelic circus much like Ken Kesey's Acid Tests or the disorienting shows that were starting to be held in the San Francisco ballrooms.

With the exception of the Byrds—Reed praised "Eight Miles High"—the Velvets despised the California rock scene. "People like the Jefferson Airplane and the Grateful Dead are the most untalented bores that ever came up," Reed was quoted as saying in *Up-Tight*. Added Morrison: "San Francisco was rigged. It was like shooting fish in a barrel, the fish being the innocent heads prowling around Haight-Ashbury." As part of Warhol's inner circle, the Velvets certainly had access to LSD, but perhaps because of the drugs' association with the West Coast, the musicians distanced themselves from psychedelics even as the Exploding Plastic Inevitable played off people's curiosity about tripping. While the members of the Velvets may have personally preferred recreational use of other drugs (including speed and heroin), rumor held that the peelable Warhol banana on the cover of the group's first album was laced with acid.

By all accounts, Warhol did little to earn his producer's credit on the band's first album, but the connection brought notoriety, the blessing of unhampered creative freedom, and a sense that what the band was doing was *art*. Released in March 1967, almost a year after it was completed, *The Velvet Underground & Nico* was like *Pet Sounds* or *Revolver* in that it used the studio to transport listeners to worlds that they had never visited. But the Velvets moved through much darker universes than the Beatles or The Beach Boys: Over the course of these eleven songs, we visit a drug dealer's street corner in Harlem ("I'm Waiting for the Man"); the inner sanctum

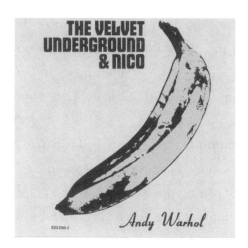

The Ultimate Psychedelic Rock Library: Rumor held that Warhol's peelable banana on the cover of The Velvet Underground & Nico *(Verve/MGM) was steeped in LSD.*

of a sado-masochistic couple ("Venus in Furs"); the crime-ridden New York subway system ("Run Run Run"), and the decadent world of the rich and bored ("All Tomorrow's Parties").

Melodically, the songs are divided between short, catchy "pop" songs and noisy, experimental "art" songs. Contrary to their image as defiant anticommercial revolutionaries, the Velvets were aware of AM radio and tailored the pop songs to its specifications, though usually with some twist. The calm and quiet of "Sunday Morning" begs questions about the excesses of Saturday night. Nico's vocals add mystery to "Femme Fatale" and "I'll Be Your Mirror," fragile tunes that she sings "in perfect mellow ovals, like a cello getting up in the morning," in the words of critic Richard Goldstein. On the surface, "There She Goes Again" is a simple rock rewrite of Marvin Gaye's "Hitchhike," but Reed portrays a brutal misogynist whose response to his lover's actions is "better hit her."

The art songs are even more explicit in their depiction of the dark side. Upping the ante on the Byrds and even the 13th Floor Elevators, "Heroin" addresses the experience of shooting up in language that is crystal clear as surging waves of sound evoke the opiate high. Punctuated by Cale's droning viola, "The Black Angel's Death Song" is a powerful evocation of the ultimate bad trip, while the waves of feedback and explosions of noise in "European Son" convey the sheer exhilaration of tearing things down. At one point, Cale scrapes a chair across the floor and shatters a glass. To fathom hell or soar angelic, indeed.

The first album contains the roots of all of the Velvets' future innovations; the group equaled but never topped it, and it was never quite as psychedelic again. The first post-Warhol effort, *White Light/White Heat*, extends the noisy experimentation of "The Black Angel's Death Song" and "European Son" to its logical conclusion with the epic cataclysm of "Sister Ray" and the controlled fury of "I Heard Her Call My Name," which features Reed screaming about his mind splitting open before launching into one of rock's most explosive guitar solos. (When it was released, the album title was widely believed to refer to an acid trip instead of the amphetamine rush that Reed intended.) After the album's release, Reed was no longer willing to share the creative reigns, and he succeeded in pushing Cale out of the band. The Velvets' self-titled third album further explored the quiet intimacy of "Sunday Morning," including a touching plea for redemption in "Jesus," while the fourth delivered more straightforward rock in the style of "There She Goes Again." The title was *Loaded* because the band hoped it was loaded with hits, but it was also a dope pun, and the cover art showed a cloud of smoke wafting up from a subway entrance.

The Velvets' greatest talent was striking a balance between the polished beauty of great art and the raw spontaneity of great rock 'n' roll, between the Apollonian and the Dionysian. That balance is something that Reed never really got quite right again, though his lengthy discography boasts such game attempts as the dramatic 1973 concept album *Berlin* (his most psychedelic solo album, if not in the jazzy grooves, than in the sense of creating a very vivid aural universe); the extreme white-noise fuck-you *Metal Machine Music* (1975), and the driven collaboration with Robert Quine, *The Blue Mask* (1982). Cale came closer to psychedelia on grand, stylized efforts such as *Paris 1919* (1973) and a trio of albums for Island in the mid-'70s (*Fear*, *Slow Dazzle*, and *Helen of Troy*). Nico's efforts hold up as spectacularly curious footnotes, though the Cale-Reed contributions to *Chelsea Girl* (1968) explore some of the terrain left behind after parting with Warhol, and *The Marble Index* (1969) is a masterpiece of purged misery and minimalist, bad-trip psychedelia.

"Everybody assumes that mind and body are opposed," Lester Bangs wrote in one of his many attempts at the ultimate Velvets eulogy/tribute. "The trog vs. the cerebrite. How boring. But we still buy it, all of us. The Velvet Underground were the greatest band that ever existed because they began to suggest that such was not so."

FOUR

4

EIGHT MILES HIGH:
Folk Rock Turns Psychedelic

BOB DYLAN'S ENORMOUS INFLUENCE on mid-'60s rock not only led directly to the birth of folk rock but also inspired the psychedelic rockers who followed. "For all that he had effectively renounced conventional politics, the notion that Dylan embodied—that what he and his expanding coterie believed, what they did, what they were, was immeasurably superior to the orthodox culture surrounding them—was a profoundly political and prescient idea," critic Geoffrey Stokes wrote in *Rock of Ages: The Rolling Stone History of Rock & Roll*. "It informed the Buffalo Springfield's seminal 'For What It's Worth' and would be at the core of virtually all the important San Francisco music." But while echoes of Dylan's ambitious, literary style of lyric-writing could be heard in rock, and while rock in turn inspired him to go electric, the Minnesota native never turned toward crafting any sounds that could rightly be considered psychedelic. Nor did the other members of New York's folk scene.

The Lovin' Spoonful was at heart an insipid jug band. Though the Fugs eventually recorded acid-inspired odes to poets William Blake and Algernon Swinburne, they are best remembered as later-day Beats howling about sex and speed on primitive masterpieces such as "Coca-Cola Douche" and "New Amphetamine Shriek." Even more primitive and cacophonous were the Fugs' neighbors and ESP label mates the Godz (not to be confused with the Midwest metal band that followed a decade and a half later). Led by guitarist Jim McCarthy, the group outdid the most raucous American garage bands in terms of its primitive musical abilities, though the scene it conjured on efforts such as 1966's *Contact High with the Godz* and 1967's *Godz 2* was of a bunch of cynical yet idealistic hippies having a hootenanny in a Lower East Side tenement while stoned out of their minds and horny as hell. Yet as intriguing as that may sound, the merger of folk rock and psychedelia made its most lasting impacts elsewhere—in Los Angeles, San Francisco, and London.

I'D BE SAFE AND WARM IF I WAS IN L.A.

The sound of the airplane in the '40s was a 'Roaaah!' sound, and Sinatra and other people sang like that with those sorts of overtones. Now we've got the 'Krishhh' jet sound, and all the kids are singing up in there now. It's the mechanical sounds of the era: The sounds are different and so the music is different.

—James (Roger) McGuinn, 1965, as quoted in *The Byrds* by Bud Scoppa

LIKE A LOT OF GROUPS IN THE '60s, the Byrds could pinpoint the exact moment that changed their musical styles, careers, and lives. As a teenager in his native Chicago, McGuinn studied at the Old Town School of Folk Music. After touring with the Limelighters and the Chad Mitchell Trio, he moved to the folk capital of the world, Greenwich Village, but he soon found the New York folk scene too rigid. In late 1963 he moved to Los Angeles and started playing at the Troubadour folk club, where he met Gene Clark and David Crosby. A native of rural Missouri, Clark had been a member of the New Christy Minstrels. Crosby belonged to a Hollywood film family—his father was the cinematographer on *High Noon*—and he had done time in Les Baxter's Balladeers. On an off night, the three went to see *A Hard Day's Night*, and the staid folk world suddenly seemed a lot less appealing.

Sharp and cynical, McGuinn has always admitted that the Byrds were formed to ape the Beatles and achieve rock stardom, in that order. "The Beatles came out and changed the whole game for me," he said in the liner notes to *The Byrds* box set (1990). "I saw a definite niche where the folk sensibility and rock 'n' roll energy blended together. If you took John Lennon and Bob Dylan and mixed them together, that was something that hadn't been done before." The group was completed by Chris Hillman, a bluegrass guitarist and mandolin player who bought his first bass for thirty-five dollars, and Crosby's friend, conga player Michael Clarke. Clarke had never sat behind a real drum set, but he did have a shaggy blond haircut that mirrored Brian Jones', and that was enough.

The Byrds spent much of 1964 woodshedding at World Pacific Studios with producer and benefactor Jim Dickson, best known for his work with the bluegrass group the Dillards. "We were rehearsing eight hours a day for months and months in this old Hollywood studio and we just developed that sound and style from nothing," Hillman recalled in the box set's liner notes, but he wasn't entirely correct. McGuinn acquired an electric twelve-string Rickenbacker because George Harrison used one in *A Hard Day's Night*. (Played with a combination of finger- and flat-picking, the strings he didn't play resonated in sympathy, adding the distinctive harmonic drone or "jangle.") Crosby crafted the band's harmonies, reaching back past the Beatles to one of their inspirations, the Everly Brothers. And the song that became the Byrds' first hit came not from the group's three songwriters but from Dylan.

The Byrds weren't thrilled by the idea of covering "Mr. Tambourine Man." McGuinn had known Dylan in the Village and was turned off by what he called his "mind games." But Dickson had stirred interest at Columbia Records; he insisted that the band needed a strong single, and the fact that Dylan was signed to Columbia couldn't hurt. The group was beginning to get a taste of stardom courtesy of a regular gig at Ciro's, and they weren't about to derail Dickson's plans. They didn't even complain when most of them were replaced in the studio by session musicians, a common practice at the time. In the hands of the studio Byrds, Dylan's sarcasm disappears and "Mr. Tambourine Man" becomes an invitation to a party. "On the heels of his 'don't follow leaders' message, the song assumes an ironic glow: Dylan is himself the 'Mr. Tambourine Man' whom people are looking to follow," critic Tim Riley wrote in *Hard Rain: A Dylan Commentary*. "Like a Day-Glo painting dipped in glitter, the Byrds' version seduces you into the Tambourine Man's con and misses the art of the con in the process."

Dickson was replaced by Columbia staff producer Terry Melcher on the Byrds' first two albums, *Mr. Tambourine Man* and *Turn! Turn! Turn!*. "They remain the definitive folk-rock albums, charged with a giddy effervescence," critic David Fricke wrote in an essay for the box set. They also remain faithful to the formula of the Byrds' first hit. More chart successes followed, but in their rapid ascent, the Byrds were starting to fly too high. They were using speed to keep up with their schedule and marijuana to chill out in the off moments. "A connoisseur of grass, Crosby was the first man in any-one's experience who could hold forth on weed the way oenophiles go on about wine," wrote biographer Carl Gottlieb.

Always the Beatest Byrd, Crosby was the first to try LSD, and he shared his enthusiasm with his band mates. He was also fascinated with Indian culture, an interest that may have started when he played with Les Baxter, an ethnomusicologist who wrote some of Martin Denny's best cocktail-lounge exotica. Dickson later intro-duced Crosby to sitar master Ravi Shankar, and Crosby came to consider Shankar and free jazz saxophonist John Coltrane "the finest musicians on the planet." He bombarded his fellow Byrds with Shankar and Coltrane music as the group toured the south in a van in late 1965, and the influences are obvious on the band's fifth single. "Eight miles high, and when you touch down / You'll find that it's stranger than known," the group sings. McGuinn maintained that the tune wasn't about drugs, but about a 1965 flight to London on which Clark nearly had a nervous breakdown because of his acute fear of flying. (A devoted fan of jets and airplanes, McGuinn couldn't have been less sympathetic.) The song was banned by radio regardless. The lyrics may be ambiguous, but there is no denying the psychedelic sound. After an introduction by an ominous, throbbing bass line, McGuinn launches into an explosive free-form solo while Clarke plays fast and loose with the beat. The song's only anchor is the reassuring three-part harmony, but the friendly naïveté of earlier Byrds songs is replaced with a sarcastic sneer. On "Eight Miles High," the Byrds finally capture the tone of Dylan's original "Mr. Tambourine Man."

The group continued exploring varied psychedelic sounds. Ornate and orchestrated, 1966's *Fifth Dimension* is the album that included "Eight Miles High." It stands as the Byrds' most psychedelic effort, with other tunes including the enchanting and trippy ballad "I See You," McGuinn's country-flavored science-fiction novelty, "Mr. Spaceman," and "I Come and Stand at Every Door," a haunting, droning tune by McGuinn about a child who was a victim of the atomic bombing at Hiroshima. Released in 1967, *Younger*

The Ultimate Psychedelic Rock Library: Fifth Dimension *(Columbia) stands as the Byrds' most psychedelic album.*

Than Yesterday is a sparer effort noteworthy for the driving raga "Why?", Hillman's mysterious "Thoughts and Words," and McGuinn's effects-laden "CTA-102," another tale of life on other planets. But the creative forces in the Byrds were pulling apart. Clark left the group in 1966. The tension between songwriters continued, and Crosby was fired after *Younger Than Yesterday*. The Byrds shifted gears as the group fell firmly into the control of Roger McGuinn. (In late 1966, McGuinn converted to the Indonesian religion of Subud and changed his first name. He converted again to Christianity in 1969 but kept the name Roger.)

Many critics perceived the jangly but bitter "So You Want to Be a Rock 'n' Roll Star" as McGuinn's farewell to rock. Released in 1968 and 1969, *The Notorious Byrd Brothers*, *Sweetheart of the Rodeo*, *Dr. Byrds and Mr. Hyde*, and *The Ballad of Easy Rider* paved the way for the country-rock explosion of the early '70s. "The Byrds were the first acid rockers, the first head rockers, the first message rockers, and, of course, the first outer space rockers," critic Lillian Roxon wrote in her groundbreaking *Rock Encyclopedia*. "It's no wonder that by the time everyone else caught up with it all, they lapsed happily back into the country sound that had been in their music all along." McGuinn finally disbanded the group in 1973. After a fourteen-year break from recording, he released a strong and very Byrdsy solo album in 1991, *Back from Rio*, but it was his last real rock effort, and he has returned to working in the margins of the folk world. "You still need the hair, you still need the pants, and you still need the guitar," McGuinn told David Sprague in *Request* magazine in 1991, paraphrasing his famous recipe for rock stardom. "Just different hair, different pants, and a different guitar."

The Byrds' early success prompted a wave of folk rock on the L.A. scene, including Sonny and Cher, the Turtles, and the Left Banke. Barry McGuire had played with Clark in the New Christy Minstrels, and he copied Dylan's lyrics and the Byrds' sound on the creepy, pseudo-psychedelic single "Eve of Destruction." The Mamas and the Papas released the cheerfully transcendent "California Dreamin'" and after relocating from Portland, Paul Revere and the Raiders scored a hit with the anti-drug tune "Kicks." The members of the American Kaleidoscope were genuine folkies and talented multi-instrumentalists who pioneered an early blend of psychedelia and world beat, and the Peanut Butter Conspiracy debuted in 1967 with a sound that was similar to the San Francisco bands' but more focused and melodic. Tim Buckley remained in the folk realm, though his image-filled excursions were clearly influenced by the burgeoning psychedelic subculture (as well as by his heroin addiction). The Buffalo Springfield came closest to psychedelic rock on Stephen Stills's eerie "For What It's Worth," which was inspired by a police riot on the Sunset Strip, and Neil Young's fuzz-driven "Mr. Soul." But after the Byrds, the most ambitious L.A. band to put a psychedelic twist on the folk-rock sound was Love.

Love thrived on the combination of two mismatched songwriters. Born in Memphis, singer Arthur Lee was raised in L.A.'s tough Crenshaw neighborhood. Strongly influenced by Mick Jagger, he presented what critic Lillian Roxon called "an amusing paradox," an African American singing like a white Englishman singing like an old African American. His partner Bryan MacLean was the son of a Hollywood architect, and he swam in Elizabeth Taylor's pool. His first girlfriend was Liza Minelli, and he was raised on classical music and Broadway standards. "You hear more of my influence on Arthur than his influence on me," MacLean told journalist Alan Vorda in *Psychedelic Psounds*. "What you have [in Love] is a black guy from L.A. writing show tunes." There was also a heaping dose of the Beatles circa *Rubber Soul*, folk rock via the Byrds (Lee originally linked up with MacLean because MacLean was a Byrds roadie and Lee thought he was likely to draw their crowd), and the lush, orchestrated soundscapes of Hollywood film scores. (The band's use of beautiful orchestral flourishes is the most influential element of its sound today, with Love standing second only to the Beach Boys' *Pet Sounds* as the biggest inspiration for the so-called "ork-pop" or orchestral-pop movement.)

Love debuted in 1966 with a memorable self-titled album that opens with a snarling, speed-freak version of "My Little Red Book," a Burt Bacharach-Hal David tune from the soundtrack to *What's New Pussycat?*. Several songs are steeped in druggie imagery, including "Signed D.C.," a warning against heroin use, the foreboding

The Ultimate Psychedelic Rock Library: The members of Love hang out at Bela's place on the cover of their self-titled debut for Elektra.

"Mushroom Clouds," and the expansive "Colored Balls Falling." The album also boasts a cover of "Hey Joe" inspired by the Byrds' rendition on *Fifth Dimension*, but much punkier in its execution. (Garage rockers the Leaves later copied Love's version and scored a major hit.) Like the Byrds, Love worked hard to present a hipper-than-thou image, and the album cover features the quintet scowling like angry young poets posing before a broken-down chimney in a fire-gutted mansion that was said to have belonged to Hollywood's Dracula, Bela Lugosi.

The cover of *Da Capo*, released in 1967, shows the expanded sextet back at the same site, but the baroque sounds are a major leap forward. "7 and 7 Is" builds on an even more rollicking version of the beat that propelled "My Little Red Book." MacLean contributes the timeless "Orange Skies," and Lee delivers his best vocal. The title of the ballad "She Comes in Colors" was borrowed by the Stones in "She's a Rainbow," but Lee wasn't being metaphoric. (He said the tune is about making love to a woman who has her peri-

The Ultimate Psychedelic Rock Library: Love, back at Bela's place again on the cover of 1967's Da Capo *(Elektra).*

od.) Lee's raunchy side also comes through on the epic "Revelation," which was produced by an uncredited Neil Young. At the time, the bluesy, nineteen-minute jam was the longest rock track ever released. "I believe we did that long tune out of laziness," MacLean told Vorda. "But Arthur claims it was an innovation."

Hip to the streets, Lee never fully bought into the hippie ideal. MacLean said that Lee made taking LSD a religious experience, but while the band was making gentle, idyllic music, Lee's impressionistic lyrics were often lampooning psychedelic culture. ("The snot has caked against my pants," is a memorable line from the band's third album.) Lee managed the group himself, but his tactics were far from egalitarian. "He was the tough guy from the neighborhood; that was the only reason he was the leader," MacLean said in *Psychedelic Psounds*. Lee's decisions not to tour or play certain gigs cost the band dearly. "When we didn't do Monterey Pop, that was when we missed the train."

By 1968 Love was starting to suffer from drug problems, turning from psychedelics to heroin. Lee contends that prejudice also kept the band from the heights achieved by some of its labelmates. "I wasn't gonna go eat garbage like the Doors did," Lee told *The Bob* magazine in 1994. "And then, too, I wasn't white. The cold fact of the matter is birds of a feather flock together." When Love recorded *Forever Changes*, Lee was convinced that his life and his career were coming to an end. (The back cover shows the singer standing with a cracked vase full of dead flowers.) But although the album is the last collaboration between Lee and MacLean, it's their most cohesive effort. The group recorded acoustically, sitting in a circle as if jamming in the living room, and the tracks were augmented

The Ultimate Psychedelic Rock
Library: Love's masterpiece,
Forever Changes (Elektra).

later with tasteful orchestrations. MacLean presents two quiet and beautiful tunes, "Alone Again Or" and "Old Man," and Lee explores his psyche on "The Red Telephone," which builds from a quiet ballad to a paranoid nursery rhyme. "They're locking him up today / They're throwing away the key / I wonder who it will be tomorrow / You or me?" he chants. "We're all normal and we want our freedom," another voice responds.

Lee's failure to produce much worthwhile music after 1968 has prompted some critics to put him in a class with cracked psychedelic geniuses Syd Barrett, Brian Wilson, and Roky Erickson. But while he emerged from the '60s bitter about the business and as eccentric as ever, Lee wasn't crazy or permanently damaged. After MacLean left the band, Lee made several more albums with a new version of Love, including 1969's *Four Sail* and 1970's *False Start*, which is noteworthy primarily for a guest appearance by Jimi Hendrix. He largely dropped out of sight after 1972's *Vindicator*; and though he and MacLean both became born-again Christians in the years that followed, that didn't bring them back together. MacLean continued to write songs for the likes of Debbie Boone, Patty Loveless, and his sister, Maria McKee, until he died of an apparent heart attack on Christmas Day, 1998. Lee toured the U.S. in 1994, playing Love's old songs for a new generation of fans, but a short time later, he was sentenced to a twelve-year prison term thanks to California's "three strikes you're out" legislation and a string of stupid incidents that qualified as felonies.

Freed after six years behind bars, Lee returned to touring the rock underground in 2002, backed by a group of L.A. psychedelic-popsters called Baby Lemonade, but which he billed as "Arthur Lee's Love." He is said to be gearing up to record new music, but Love's third album will likely remain his crowning achievement, something that even he readily acknowledges. *"Forever Changes* were my last words of Love," Lee told Dave DiMartino of *Creem* magazine in 1981. "My last words to the world, only I've been here ever since. Just like a guy saying goodbye, and you look out your front door and he's still there fifteen years later."

IF YOU'RE GOING TO SAN FRANCISCO BE SURE TO WEAR FLOWERS IN YOUR HAIR

> You who stand, sit, and crawl around and about the floor,
> about you and above you, on the ceiling—that madness
> that's running in color is your brain!
>
> —Ken Kesey
> at the San Francisco State Trips Festival, 1966

LIKE THE MUSICIANS IN L.A., the players who drew national attention to San Francisco in 1966 and 1967 all had roots in the folk scene. Jerome Garcia played bluegrass banjo in Palo Alto coffee houses, Paul Kantner sang at hootenannies, and Marty Balin owned the Matrix, a Fillmore Street folk club. The Jefferson Airplane's first manager tried to coin the word "fojazz" from "folk" and "jazz" to describe their sound. "Most of the rock musicians in San Francisco were basically folkies learning how to play electrified instruments," Charles Perry wrote in his definitive history, *The Haight-Ashbury*. "They had a tentative sound at first and played a lot of solemn, chiming chords on the beat. When it came time for the guitarist to take a solo break, he often noodled up and down the notes of the scale in a way that might owe as much to inexperience in improvisation as it did to the influence of Indian ragas."

Scenesters were quick to emphasize the distinctions between the bands, but the San Francisco groups did have some common traits. One was the absence of driving rock beats. Bill Kreutzmann of the Grateful Dead was one of the few genuine drummers—most of the other groups had former folk guitarists or conga players in the percussion seat—and the rhythms tended to shuffle or percolate rather than propel. The bands shared a fondness for Chicago blues via the Rolling Stones, and they embraced the Paul Butterfield Blues Band when it came to town for a three-night stand in March 1966. (Many drew inspiration from the epic "East-West," a raga-inspired piece that guitarist Mike Bloomfield wrote while listening to Ravi Shankar during an LSD trip.) Of course, there was also a common fascination with LSD, which flooded the scene courtesy of Augustus Owsley Stanley. "The San Francisco 'sound' was less a musical phenomenon than a manner," Perry wrote. "It was premised on the simple and straightforward assumption that this was trip music being played by dopers for other dopers."

These dopers were essentially a new class of rich Beatniks. The first-generation Beats coined the word "hippies" as a derisive term to describe kids who were living on the parents' money or cash from dealing pot. "Dealing wasn't work, really, and by doing what came naturally to them, hippies found money raining down upon them," Perry wrote. "They spent it on mod or antique or handmade clothes, or on toys or Navajo jewelry or Persian rugs." They backed a new class of stores on Haight Street—*their* stores—but mostly they supported the bands at dances in old ballrooms such as the Avalon and the Fillmore. By 1967 these places were as famous as any of the bands, and so were some of the characters behind the scenes. Bill Graham was the prototype for the frantic, bullying promoter who was also obsessed with good sound and great music. Chet Helms and the Family Dog sponsored dances with fanciful names such as "A Tribute to Dr. Strange," and Ken Kesey and the Merry Pranksters moved the Acid Tests down from the hills into the city. Stanley

Mouse, Rick Griffin, Victor Moscoso, and others defined a style of psychedelic poster art, and by 1968, there were five hundred people working with psychedelic light shows such as Bill Ham's, Roy's Audioptics, and the Holy See.

"The important thing about San Francisco rock 'n' roll is that the bands here all sing and play live and not for recordings," wrote Ralph Gleason, the jazz-turned-rock critic for the *San Francisco Chronicle*. "You get a different sound at a dance; it's harder and more direct." In other words, you really had to be there; the recorded legacy simply doesn't support the scene's vaunted reputation. Plenty of readers took issue with this assessment in the first edition of this book, but while there was plenty of psychedelic filigree, and the impact of the scene as a pop-culture phenomenon was indeed significant, much of the music doesn't really hold up as psychedelic *rock*—the critical focus of this book.

Most of the musical histories of San Francisco in the '60s start with the Charlatans, a group whose stretched-out blues tunes were as old-timey as their Western costumes. Though they were the first band on the scene, they didn't release their self-titled debut until 1969, and by then, founder George Hunter and much of the spirit were gone. The first band to make an impact outside San Francisco was Sopwith Camel, a campy folk outfit that scored a hit in 1967 with "Hello Hello," but the band was quickly and justly forgotten.

Looking to fill the bill at his folk club, Balin put together a band in 1965 with guitarist and vocalist Kantner, lead guitarist Jorma Kaukonen, and singer Signe Anderson. After moving through a series of musicians (including Skip Spence, a guitarist and songwriter who filled in on drums for the first album), the rhythm section solidified around drummer Spencer Dryden and bassist Jack Casady, whose fluid, loping lines provided the perfect compliment for Kaukonen's flittery, jazzy leads. The band's name came from a joke by Kaukonen: The musicians had been riffing on the monikers of fictional blues players, and he suggested "Blind Lemon Jefferson Airplane." Its shortened version proved to be wonderfully evocative, hinting at both old-fashioned roots and modern technological power.

Jefferson Airplane Takes Off (1966) was dominated by Balin's simple folk ballads, which were tarted up by Anderson's fetching harmonies and the dexterous playing of Casady and Kaukonen. It had only limited commercial success, but when Anderson quit the group, the band found the missing piece of the puzzle. Born in Chicago, Grace Barnett Wing was a child of privilege who attended expensive private schools in New York and spent time as a model in Los Angeles before moving to San Francisco, marrying musician Jerry Slick, and joining him in his band, the Great Society. She'd seen the Airplane and been impressed, and when she was invited to join the group, she readily left her first outfit (and eventually her husband) behind.

Slick arrived bearing two songs that would become the biggest hits from the Airplane's second album. "Somebody to Love" was written by her brother-in-law, the Great Society's Darby Slick, during a depressing LSD trip while he waited for his girlfriend to come home. She wrote "White Rabbit" as a musical tribute to "Bolero" and a lyrical homage to Lewis Carroll's surreal children's book, *Alice's Adventures in Wonderland*. "The adults were saying, 'Why are you taking all these drugs? This is bad,'" Slick recalls in the liner notes to the Airplane's box set. "But they had read us these books,

*The Ultimate Psychedelic Rock
Library: Jerry Garcia named the
Jefferson Airplane's second album
(RCA) because he said it was
"surrealistic as a pillow."*

like *Alice in Wonderland*, where she gets high, tall, takes mushrooms,
a hookah, pills, alcohol. I was saying, 'You read us all this stuff
when we're little and then you wonder why we do it?'"

When the band entered the studio again, Slick's powerful, soaring vocals on these two tunes and her fluid, sexy scat singing
behind Balin and Kantner's lead vocals on the other numbers was
the most striking element of the Airplane's sound. The album was
recorded on four tracks by an RCA staff producer in a little less than
two weeks. The band's friend, Jerry Garcia, appeared uncredited as
guest guitarist, though he did receive a nod on the cover as "musical and spiritual adviser," and he suggested the disc's name:
Surrealistic Pillow. Once again, the title is apt—there is a gentle,
lulling, somnambulant feel to much of the album, with the notable
exceptions of Slick's two turns at the mike. Spence contributed the
old-timey, clip-clopping "My Best Friend"; "Today" and "How Do
You Feel" are gorgeous ballads, with the harmonies on the latter
owing a debt to the Mamas and the Papas; the idyllic "Comin' Back

to Me" features Garcia and Casady on intertwining guitars and Slick on medieval recorder, and "Embryonic Journey" is an enigmatic instrumental and solo acoustic showcase for Kaukonen.

Musically and lyrically, parts of the disc are very much tethered to the times. "She Has Funny Cars" is notable primarily for the pounding drums and repetitive, mantra-like guitar and bass riffs, while "3/5 of a Mile in 10 Seconds" is a groovy slice of psychedelic pop with exceptionally goofy lyrics ("Do away with people laughing at my hair / Do away with people climbing on my precious prayers / Take me to a circus tent where I can easily pay my rent / And all the other freaks can share my cares"). Elsewhere, the Airplane still sounds ahead of its time and remarkably current. Bathed in reverb and propelled by an insistent beat, "Plastic Fantastic Lover" is a nicely barbed critique of the insidious powers of television. Then of course there's "Somebody to Love." The Airplane's masterpiece and the ultimate anthem of the Summer of Love boasts a relentless four-on-the-floor rhythm, great sweeping waves of reverb that make the massive guitar riff and nimble solo sound larger than life, and a slippery bass line that weaves in and out of the mix throughout. But the most breathtaking aspect is Slick's voice. Even if you didn't know that she was stunningly pretty, with intense, piercing eyes and a brilliant, sarcastic wit, her singing brings into vivid focus a strong, self-assertive, and utterly confident woman who is introducing a new role model to rock, replacing the meek waifs who dominated much of the pop scene, and perfectly summing up the attitude of a generation unafraid to seize what it wants from life. The chorus is rightly posed as a question, but in Slick's hands, it becomes an emphatic declaration.

The Airplane followed with two albums of failed experiments. *After Bathing at Baxter's* (1967) is a pastiche of song fragments and long, unfocused "suites," including the tedious "Ballad of You and Me and Pooneil." *Crown of Creation* (1968) introduces Kantner's lyrical obsession with science fiction, but the only standout is Slick's version of David Crosby's homage to threesomes, "Triad." More noteworthy is 1969's *Volunteers*. Critic Paul Evans described it as "a summing up of psychedelia," a rousing call to political activism in the face of failed utopianism ("Got a revolution!"). Balin left after *Volunteers*, and the feuding factions—Kantner and Slick versus Casady and Kaukonen—fought for control. Eventually the Airplane became the Starship, a group committed only to commercialism. Cynics said the seeds were there ever since the Airplane recorded a commercial for Levi's jeans in 1967.

The Grateful Dead had been a fixture on the scene since it performed under its earlier guise as the Warlocks at Kesey's Acid Tests. In its early incarnation, on material that is memorably compiled on the 2001 box set, *The Golden Road (1965–1973)*, it was a hard-rocking psychedelic garage band that wouldn't have sounded out of place on *Nuggets*. By the time the band changed its name and made its recorded debut for Warner Bros. in 1967, many Haight residents were sporting buttons that read, "Good Ol' Grateful Dead." Recorded in a three-day amphetamine blur, *The Grateful Dead* is a bluesy folk effort that tries unsuccessfully to impose structure on the band's live improvisations. "They didn't, as might be expected, play what we now call acid or psychedelic rock, but instead produced fine, strong, straightforward traditional blues," Roxon wrote in her *Rock Encyclopedia*.

The band expanded in 1968 with the addition of second drummer Mickey Hart, a player well-versed in ethnic rhythms, and keyboardist Tom Constanten, an avant-garde musician inspired by John Cage and Karlheinz Stockhausen. Owsley knew as much about sound as chemistry, and he and Dan Healy recorded the band at every stop on a Northwest tour. The result was *Anthem of the Sun*, a fascinating if flawed album that was compiled from hundreds of edits from fourteen different performances. The sprawling, improvised collage has moments of hypnotic beauty, but it's ultimately a compromise, neither a spontaneous live document nor a consistent studio creation.

Aoxomoxoa (1969) returned to more familiar song structures and marked the Dead's first collaboration with Beat poet and lyricist Robert Hunter, a friend of Garcia's from the folkie days in Palo Alto. "St. Stephen" is a shuffling hippie anthem with a pretty psychedelic bridge, and "Rosemary" is a delicate ballad with a creepy phased vocal. But the Dead didn't really come into its own on album until a trio of 1970 releases. *Live Dead* introduced the moody jazz excursion, "Dark Star," while *Workingman's Dead* and *American Beauty* are melodic, stripped-down efforts with harmonies crafted by Crosby and lyrics that try to find common ground between the reality of life in America and the fantasies of the psychedelic ideal. The albums boast some of the Dead's best tunes—"Sugar Magnolia," "Uncle John's Band," "Casey Jones," and "Truckin'"—but they are modern folk music, not psychedelic rock.

Of the other San Francisco bands, Big Brother and the Holding Company played clunky blues elevated by the soulful voice of Texan Janis Joplin. (Joplin moved to San Francisco from Austin after a plan to join the 13th Floor Elevators fell through.) Downing Southern Comfort, she fashioned herself after blues belters like Bessie Smith and Willie Mae Thornton, and she joked that her music was "alkydelic." Country Joe and the Fish were a jug band best remembered for their antiwar songs ("Feel-Like-I'm-Fixin'-to-Die Rag") and the "F-U-C-K" cheer. Quicksilver Messenger Service was long on meandering jams featuring fluid lead guitarist John Cipollina, and short on solid rhythmic drive and strong songwriting; its most impressive numbers, live and on record, were borrowed from Bo Diddley ("Mona" and "Who Do You Love") and Buffy Sainte-Marie (the addict's lament, "Codine"). Santana initially attacked its trademark South American rhythms with a garage-rock edge; in the years that followed, bandleader Carlos Santana would occasionally deliver some wonderfully elegiac and psychedelic guitarwork in the heart of a great rock song (as on the wonderfully witchy "Black Magic Woman"), but there was even more jazz-fusion wanking in the band's diverse mix. The Steve Miller Band used psychedelic sound effects to decorate its blues before shifting toward a slicker and sleaker sound.

With tight harmonies, a layered three-guitar sound, and an exuberant spirit, Moby Grape rocked harder than its peers, but the band members were victims of too much hype, over indulgence, bad management, and bad luck. The quintet's self-titled debut might have scored a hit with the rollicking "Omaha" if Columbia Records hadn't seized on the gimmick of releasing five singles at once. Rock fans resented this and other crass promotional stunts, and the company started resenting the band after three members were busted with underage girls the morning after their record release party. The band's second album, *Wow*, was recorded in New York using strings and horns to mask a lack of inspiration and a deteriorating situation. Guitarist-vocalist Skip Spence, a graduate of the Jefferson Airplane, was living with a practicing witch and ingesting too much acid, and he was committed to Bellevue mental hospital after attacking Grape drummer Don Stevenson with an ax. "He was a visionary," Stevenson said in the liner notes to *Vintage: The Very Best of Moby Grape*. "And what happened was he broke through."

The group stumbled on without its best songwriter until splitting up in 1969, while Spence went on to make a fabulously strange psychedelic country record in Nashville. *Oar* (1969) has been revered by collectors and lovers of alternative country in recent years mostly because of its obscurity; indulgent sonic explorations such as the nearly ten-minute "Grey/Afro" and bizarre novelties such as "Lawrence of Euphoria" don't necessarily hold up to repeated listenings. Spence dropped out of sight after the disc's release, joining the list of legendary '60s casualties. When Johnny Angel tracked him down for the *L.A. Weekly* in 1994, he was a diagnosed schizophrenic living in a residential care facility in San Jose, scraping by on an allowance of a dollar a day provided by Santa Clara county.

After a visit in 1967, New York critic Richard Goldstein wrote that it would "be interesting to visit the Bay Area when the breadmen have gutted every artery; to watch the Fillmore become the Radio City Music Hall of pop music, to take a Greyhound sightseeing tour through the Haight." All of these things came to pass, but even more problematic was the flood of heroin and an increase in violent crime that started shortly after the Summer of Love. Like the residents of Seattle in the early '90s, San Franciscans blamed the media and big business for ruining their scene, but the roots of its undoing were there from the beginning. Novelist Bill Craddock joked that the unspoken conclusion of Timothy Leary's "Turn on, tune in, drop out" was "Freak out, fuck up, crawl back." The same week in December 1969 that a free concert at the Altamont Raceway ended in murder, a grand jury in L.A. was investigating former Haight resident Charles Manson for a series of ritualistic killings committed by the young followers whom he brainwashed with psychedelic drugs and messianic preaching. "The real dead end," Perry wrote, "was the dream that this was a blessed generation, immune to the darkness of the heart that has always caused violence and oppression."

Debating the Merits of the Dead

For some, the Grateful Dead is a religion, and its basic tenets are not to be questioned. Many Deadheads strongly disagreed with my take on the group in the first edition of this book, among them the band's long-time publicist and biographer, Dennis McNally. To his credit, McNally is always up for a spirited debate. The following conversation occurred shortly before the release of the 2001 box set, *The Golden Road (1965–1973)*, and not long before the publication of McNally's definitive account of the band, *A Long Strange Trip: The Inside History of the Grateful Dead*.

J.D.: *I know I'm being contrary here, but I think that for the first ten years of their career, the Grateful Dead made very good albums, while the live performances—at least what I've heard on the innumerable bootlegs—were always overrated. There's that whole Deadhead thing of, "One in three shows is magic!" But that's a bad batting average, because it means two shows fell short. For me the Dead has always felt like an exclusive club requiring all of this arcane knowledge of ponderous trivia. To borrow Ken Kesey's line, "You're either on the bus or off the bus."*

McNally: Right. The Grateful Dead is an experiential thing. Either you do or you don't. It's a quasi-spiritual thing. Either you are mentally and emotionally acceptable to a certain zeitgeist—you're either open to a certain approach to playing music which involves randomness—or you're not. Not many people like John Cage, either, and there's a healthy dose of Cage in the Grateful Dead. Either you're open to what I call magic—or the potential for magic—or you're not. Now sometimes it's just the potential for a grand train wreck. But let's go back three thousand or four thousand years—there are Apollonians or Dionysians. Critics tend to be Apollonians. They want order, even when music is at its craziest.

J.D.: *Not at all! I think rock 'n' roll is a visceral experience that is Dionysian to the core.*

McNally: But the point is the Grateful Dead is not a rock 'n' roll band. They use rock modalities, but to evaluate them purely as a rock 'n' roll band, they're not. They are a twenty-first century American electronic string band.

J.D.: *Yeah, yeah, I've heard it all before. But I like rock 'n' roll, and what I'm saying is that on occasion, on album, the Dead made good rock 'n' roll. I wish there was more Warlocks—the early stuff on this box set—and less pretentious faux-Cage and Coltrane in what followed.*

McNally: You and [former Sire Records chief] Howie Klein both. He'll still tell you the first album was the best because it was the crudest and the funkiest. But the fact is the Grateful Dead grew up and assimilated a whole lot more music. They were using bop chords that nobody in rock 'n' roll had ever heard of.

J.D.: *Oh, come on. The Velvet Underground during the same period was incorporating Karlheinz Stockhausen and LaMonte Young and Ornette Coleman.*

McNally: But they were so God-awful depressing, singing about "Heroin"...

J.D.: *In the end, Jerry Garcia died as a junkie, despite preaching psychedelic transcendence, while Lou Reed is still alive, like a cockroach after the nuclear holocaust. So who was more depressing?*

McNally: The Velvets' whole thing was they were dark and wrestling with the demons. The thing that has always pissed off critics about the Grateful Dead was that they were deliberately happy, despite the fact that they were wrestling individually with their own demons. The problem with the Grateful Dead is that, A.) Critics would be pissed off because of the fanaticism of their audience, and B.) There was the general notion that they were the frontmen for whatever happened in San Francisco in the '60s. But their attitude always was a fairly consistent, "Hey, I'm just a musician."

J.D.: *I was born in 1964; I missed the '60s, but I saw a dozen Dead shows. To me, the best thing was the audience. The Dead threw a great party in the parking lot, but unfortunately, they played this pointless, meandering music during it. I have to insist: The 13th Floor Elevators were a better band than the Grateful Dead.*

McNally: Oh, kiss my ass! For God's sake! What a typical thing for a critic to say!

J.D.: *More critics kiss up to the Dead than don't.*

McNally: Most critics never actually listened to the show that was in front of them. They came, but they'd already written the review in their head, good or bad.

J.D.: *Hey, if I added up all the time I wasted listening to different versions of "Drums In Space"—I want those seven hours of my life back!*

McNally: There *are* five or ten critics that I can list that ripped us when we sucked and said, "Wow, that was a good one" when they heard a good one. The problem is that the party and the colorfulness of the parking lot obscured whatever was going on musically. Very few people approached them on anything like fair terms. Too much had already been written.

J.D.: *Again, I'd be a rich man if I had a dime for every Deadhead who told me, "One in three is magic." Now if I saw the two shows in Chicago, and they were both rotten, should I have driven seven hours to Minneapolis to hear the good one?*

McNally: It depends on what you wanted to do. I will certainly concede that the last five years of the Grateful Dead, as Garcia's health failed, were not the peak of Grateful Dead playing. By then it had become distinctly erratic, no question about it. And yeah, there was a lot of bumptiousness the last few years in our audience. The worst thing that ever happened to the Grateful Dead was that damn hit record ["Touch of Grey"]. Until then, kids became Deadheads in an organic, logical way: Somebody turned them on. It was a human way—they became interested and they went to the show and they had their little epiphany of recognition. In 1987, suddenly we're on the radio and you've got people going down to find out what all the buzz is about and when they get there they discover a parking lot full of beer and girls to hit on, and the end result is thousands of people who are there for all the wrong reasons who haven't got that sort of training in basic good-visitor manners.

J.D.: *Don't you think a band gets the audience it deserves to some extent?*

McNally: To the point where we had that damn hit record, we did. Whatever you want to say about that audience, it was benign. We were able to get through towns with five thousand people without tickets with no trouble. Then we were suddenly exposed on MTV and radio and we had no business being there. The Grateful Dead fell victim to their own unwillingness to be cops. There's no question. Jerry's laissez-faire anarchy worked beautifully at a certain size and scale, but by the time we were done it was out of hand.

J.D.: *They were also making more money than ever when they were refusing to be cops. Sure, there was this hippie-community thing, but there was also a lust for lucre. They wanted to play to stadiums full of people.*

McNally: That's absolutely not true. You can take a pound of salt, you can believe it or not, but I will tell you flatly: Nobody liked playing stadiums. We played stadiums because we couldn't figure out a way to tour in the summertime with people out of school unless we did play stadiums. The conversation and the tone in the room when we said, "Well, I guess we've got to step up to stadiums" was not, "Oh, wow, we're gonna make more money." The fact of the matter is Garcia complained endlessly that the band's playing became almost like a cartoon in the stadiums because you have to make the broad strokes both musically and visually. At that point we were victims of our own popularity.

J.D.: *Do you see the other guys and yourself and all of the various and sundry people associated with the Grateful Dead machine just continuing to put out product until you all die off?*

McNally: It's not a machine, it's a bunch of people! Your dislike of the Grateful Dead is showing.

J.D.: *I'm sorry. It's just that I've lived in the shadow of the Dead for thirty-eight years, and I'm wondering if I'm going to have to live with it for the rest of my life.*

McNally: Who says you have to pay attention to it? Just ignore it!

J.D.: *It's an inescapable part of popular culture; it's constantly in my face. And I'm a critic: I have to deal with the Dead! I've been grappling with the music for my entire professional life, and I have to confess: I still don't get it.*

McNally: The answer is it will go as long as the audience wants to hear that music. We've put out—I'm guessing, and discounting this big box set—forty or fifty shows so far. If you'll give me the "one in three" rule, there's three hundred good shows to choose from. We're certainly not going to put out eight hundred shows in my lifetime, but as long as the audience wants it—well, poor Jim, he's just gonna have to suffer with the Grateful Dead.

MJNOTAUR SONGS
JN THE SEASON OF THE WJTCH

Earth water fire and air / Met together in a garden fair /
Put in a basket bound with skin / If you answer this riddle,
you'll never begin.
                —The Incredible String Band, "Koeeoaddi There"

IN BRITAIN, BERT JANSCH AND JOHN RENBOURN were the urban
folkies who paved the way for the first wave of English folk rock.
Like Dylan, they provided a link between folk, the Beats, and the
blues, and they eventually went electric with the jazzy quintet
Pentangle. But there was an added dimension in their music, a
whimsical style in the storytelling and a timelessness in the gentle
melodies. America had musical traditions that went back generations, but the folklore of the British Isles was measured in centuries.

Born in Glasgow, Scotland, Donovan Leitch had an abiding fascination with his Celtic heritage, though he was actually raised in
Hatfield, England. When he first won attention in 1965 with
appearances on the TV show *Ready Steady Go*, he was positioned as
the British Dylan. Dylan laid waste to that idea when the two met,
a moment captured in D.A. Pennebaker's film *Don't Look Back*, but
it was never a fair match. Dylan was sharp, cynical, and serious
where Donovan was carefree, naïve, and happy to deliver his jolly
melodies. Early on, he was an earnest folkie, wearing sweaters,
denim, and a railroad brakeman's cap; he aimed for Woody Guthrie
but sounded more like Woody Woodpecker. Sure, the charming
roundelay of "There Is A Mountain" is fun in a gather-round-the-

The Ultimate Psychedelic Rock Library: Sure, there's some twee drivel, but you need Donovan—Troubadour: The Definitive Collection / 1964–1976 *(Epic/Legacy) for the great psychedelic singles.*

campfire-girls way, but a little bit of "Epistle to Dippy" or "Wear Your Love Like Heaven" goes a very long way indeed.

After he sampled some of Michael Hollingshead's LSD in 1966, Donovan was transformed into a patchouli and pot-scented love child—in his hippie heyday, he even *looked* like an elf—and the psychedelic experience inspired his most lovable work. On his mid-'60s singles, his flowery lyrics and simple melodicism are nicely paired with the studio sophistication of imaginative collaborators such as producer Mickey Most and arranger John Paul Jones. "Sunshine Superman" is a jazzed-up skiffle tune that perfectly captures the stoned teen's sense of indomitably ("Superman and Green Lantern ain't got nothing on me"), while the moving "Bert's Blues" is a tribute to Jansch. "Season of the Witch" is a cheerfully creepy delight, and the brassy Summer of Love single "Mellow Yellow" features a whispered chorus by Paul McCartney and a mysterious lyric that students of psychedelic arcana are still parsing today. Donovan's evocation of an "electrical banana" is sometimes linked to the urban legend, initiated by the *Berkeley Barb*, that you could get high smoking dried banana peels, but the song actually preceded the beginning of that hoax by several months. (Others have suggested that Donovan was actually crooning about a yellow vibrator, though the tune also notes that he's "just mad about saffron," another of the many plant substances that tireless heads tried to snort in an effort to get high.)

More erroneous information is linked to 1968's "Hurdy Gurdy Man," Donovan's wonderful, rhythmically shifting answer to "Mr. Tambourine Man." According to Jones, the single does not feature the playing of Jimmy Page and John Bonham, as is often stated, and the soon-to-be Led Zeppelin bassist didn't even arrange that tune.

The peak of Donovan's psychedelic accomplishments is the masterful "Atlantis," a hypnotic, circular tribute to the lost continent with an unintentionally hilarious spoken-word intro and an irresistible sing-along chorus. (All together now: "Way down, below the ocean / Where she may be, I may be.") The singer-songwriter began to lose it after his 1969 collaboration with the Jeff Beck Group, *Barabajagal*; he really was a creature of the '60s, and he just didn't fit in the Me Decade. He took up with the Maharishi, moved to the Irish countryside, ran out of memorable melodies, and, in the words of critic Paul Nelson, "floated away into the lilac mist" to be mentioned in a new millennium primarily as the father of two pleasant-to-look-at Gen X actors, Ione Skye and Donovan Leitch, Jr. (The less said about the 1993 Rick Rubin-helmed comeback effort, *Sutras*, the better.)

More influential were the folk rock sounds recorded by transplanted American Joe Boyd. A talent scout for Elektra Records and the promoter of the psychedelic rock club UFO, Boyd came to England from Harvard University, where he knew Richard Alpert and followed the work of Timothy Leary. "It's important to remember that both in the early '60s and in the '80s, taking acid did not necessarily mean that you liked things in Day-Glo and paisley," Boyd told me. "It was an awareness of a social context more than anything else, and it linked you to certain types of people who were interested in certain types of things." Boyd produced Fairport Convention's 1968 debut after he saw guitarist Richard Thompson deliver a mindblowing version of "East-West" at the UFO Club. Drawing heavily on the Byrds, Fairport added a Scottish-Irish accent and Sandy Denny's voice, a powerful instrument that surpassed even Grace Slick's. But the band never really embraced psychedelia, and Boyd described the musicians as "seventeen-year-old kids from Muswell Hill who had hardly ever seen a cigarette."

The otherworldly vibe in the music of another Boyd protégé, Nick Drake, came from deep within the artist himself. An awkward, lonely college student, Drake expressed himself freely only when he was playing his songs around Cambridge. His first album, *Five Leaves Left* (1969), is the tentative work of a twenty-year-old musician, but Boyd called 1970's *Bryter Layter* the one perfect album he's produced. The songs feature a jazzy, R&B feel similar to *Astral Weeks*, Van Morrison's spiritual masterpiece, and they boast fine playing by Thompson, Dave Mattacks, and Dave Pegg of Fairport as well as John Cale, who had recently left the Velvet Underground. Drake sank into a deep depression after *Bryter Layter* and was barely able to speak when he recorded *Pink Moon* in 1972, but the album stands as his best. The songs offer an intimate look into the soul of a deeply troubled individual struggling to find a reason for living. Shortly after their release, Drake died of a drug overdose, but the title track was given new life three decades later when it was used as the soundtrack for a Volkswagen commercial.

The most psychedelic of the artists on Boyd's roster or anywhere else on the English folk scene were the members of the Incredible String Band. The group was formed in 1965 by three Scottish musicians, guitarist-vocalists Clive Palmer, Robin Williamson, and Mike Heron. Their self-titled 1966 debut hints at the promise of things to come, but it's hesitant in embracing the ethnic sounds that later became a staple of the band's mix. "I started off doing Scottish and Irish music," Williamson told *Washington Post* writer Geoffrey Himes in 1987. "But I also liked the visionary writing of Americans like Walt Whitman and Jack Kerouac, and those two opposites caused me to go and search for a common root to world music. I went to North Africa in 1963 to learn more about the music there, and I got interested in Indian music from the tremendous wave of immigrants entering Britain at that time. The notion of fusion music wasn't a word used in 1963 when we started doing it. We just thought it would be a good idea."

Williamson was the folkie and Heron the rocker. The two forces were balanced by Palmer, but between the first and second albums, Palmer went off to Morocco and didn't return. "Mike and Robin were each friends of Clive but not of each other," Boyd told Himes. "It was like they'd both come to Clive's party and he'd left. There they were with each other, and they didn't like each other. They hated each other." The rivalry wasn't even quelled by a shared enthusiasm for LSD, but somehow, the pair produced beautiful,

*The Ultimate Psychedelic Rock
Library: We're a happy
(psychedelic) family—the Incredible
String Band,* The Hangman's
Beautiful Daughter *(Hannibal).*

pastoral music. Williamson's slippery vocals take some getting used
to—they slither and slide around a melody like an eel swimming
through the reeds—but the duo's overdubbed orchestrations are
truly impressive. (Together, Williamson and Heron played some
forty instruments.) Their tunes sink into your subconscious, and
the whimsy of the lyrics approaches Whitman's sunny optimism
without being laughable.

Released in 1967, *The 5000 Spirits or The Layers of the Onion*
features a psychedelic cover painted by The Fool—the artists who
decorated John Lennon's flamboyantly colored Rolls-Royce—and a
lusher, more mysterious sound than the debut. But *The Hangman's
Beautiful Daughter* is the band's finest moment. The lyrics of "The
Minotaur's Song" and "Koeeoaddi There" evoke classical myths and
pagan rituals, while the mini-symphony "A Very Cellular Song"
deals with the acid-trip revelation that all living beings are inter-
connected. Even more than the lyrics, it's the quality of the strange
and exotic sounds that creates what Paul Evans called "a freeform

spiritual buzz." "Initially, we were just having fun discovering what you could do with a multi-track machine," Boyd said. "Of course, each one had to impose their personality on the other one's songs. They wouldn't allow a song to join the repertoire unless they could make it their own—Mike playing sitar on Robin's songs, and Robin singing harmonies on Mike's songs."

After *Hangman's*, Williamson and Heron were joined by their girlfriends, Christina "Licorice" McKechnie and Rose Simpson. (This electrified lineup played a little-remembered set at Woodstock.) The two songwriters continued trying to outdo each other with wilder and more elaborate arrangements on the double album, *Wee Tam and the Big Huge*, but over the next few releases, invention gave way to indulgence. "One of the reasons for the decline was that they stopped hating each other," Boyd claimed. "They all became Scientologists, and Scientology taught them to like each other." The band forged ahead through various permutations, outliving Williamson's and Heron's relationships with Licorice and Rose, until calling it quits in 1974. Heron made several solo albums, including *Smiling Men With Bad Reputations*, which features backing by most of the Who. Williamson continues to tour as a folk artist and Celtic storyteller. Both agree that the first four of the Incredible String Band's nine years were the best.

"There was an inspired amateurism in those days, a feeling that anybody could play music, that anybody could play a lot of different instruments," Williamson told Himes. "Mike and I were radically different characters, and I think that inspired the creativity of the band. Mike was inspired by rock 'n' roll music, and I was interested in folk music and poetry. Now we have both reverted to type."

FIVE

5

PIPERS AT THE GATES OF DAWN: The Pink Floyd

Sudden and magnificent, the sun's broad golden disc showed itself over the horizon facing them, and the first rays, shooting across the level water-meadows, took the animals full in the eyes and dazzled them. When they were able to look once more, the Vision had vanished, and the air was full of the carol of birds that hailed the dawn.

—Kenneth Grahame,
The Wind in the Willows

IN 1964 THE FOUNDING MEMBERS of the longest-running English psychedelic rock band were four of the 120,000 middle-class art students in fifty-nine colleges spread across Great Britain. Rick Wright, Roger Waters, and Nick Mason met while studying architecture at Regent Street Polytechnic. They played together in a succession of bad R&B bands with awful names (the T-Set, the Meggadeaths, and the Architectural Abdabs) before linking up with Roger "Syd" Barrett, a nineteen-year-old painter who lived in the same apartment building as Waters. Both grew up in Cambridge, where Barrett learned to play guitar with his future replacement, David Gilmour. Barrett named the band after two blues heroes, Pink Anderson and Floyd Council, and the group played its first gig in late 1965.

Pink Floyd biographer Nicholas Schaffner noted that the band members were different from earlier art students-turned-rockers (including John Lennon, Pete Townshend, and Eric Clapton) because they were members of rock's third generation, "just young enough to have been drawn into rock 'n' roll as much by the Beatles and the Rolling Stones as by first-generation stars like Buddy Holly or Elvis Presley." When the Floyd started, the Byrds had already scored a hit with "Mr. Tambourine Man" and the Beatles were recording *Rubber Soul*. "A new sophistication and self-consciousness was already well-established in pop music," Schaffner wrote. "Unlike previous art school rock 'n' rollers, the band Syd made famous conceived their music as *art* virtually from day one."

Like many of the early British psychedelic bands, Pink Floyd started out playing R&B to audiences of drunken college students who wanted to dance. "We were interested in the R&B revival but we never had the abilities along those lines," Mason told me three decades later. "In fact, if the Summer of Love and the Underground never would have happened, I don't think we would have passed the starting point." The psychedelic rock of the Beatles, the Byrds, and Love inspired the Floyd to expand its horizons. "I was trying to tell Syd about this Arthur Lee song I couldn't remember the title of, so I just hummed the main riff," the group's first manager, Peter Jenner, recalled in the liner notes to the *Syd Barrett: Crazy Diamond* box set. "Syd picked up his guitar, followed what I was humming, and went on to use the chord pattern he worked out for 'Interstellar Overdrive.'"

Starting in the spring of 1966, the Floyd's outer-space excursions were launched from its slot as house band at Spontaneous Underground, mixed-media events at the Marquee Club that were similar to the happenings in San Francisco. "Initially, I never saw the Floyd as individuals. I saw them as part of an avant-garde movement that was happening in London," Barry Miles, founder of the underground newspaper *International Times*, told Schaffner. Among the movement's catalysts was the now readily available LSD. The psychedelic influence became apparent in the Floyd's music as songs were extended into lengthy explorations of feedback and echoed effects, and the band took up a residency at UFO, the new psychedelic rock club booked by Joe Boyd. The British psychedelic rock scene coalesced there around regular performances by Tomorrow, the Crazy World of Arthur Brown, and the Soft Machine, but the Floyd was always the crowd's favorite. Elektra Records passed when Boyd suggested that the company sign the band, but it secured a contract with EMI, and Boyd produced its first single in early 1967.

Hesitant to tailor the band's onstage jams to fit the single format, Barrett responded to the opportunity by crafting a brilliant pop song, "Arnold Layne," perhaps the catchiest song ever about transvestism. Over a driving bass and upbeat organ, Barrett's soaring vocals tell the story of a lad with a penchant for stealing women's underwear from Cambridge clotheslines. English bluenoses attacked it as smut, and some rock critics dismiss it as judgmental because it ends with Arnold in jail, admonished not to do it again. But the song's most effective hook is the line, "It takes two to know," and Barrett certainly sings with empathy. In colorful finery from the Granny Takes A Trip boutique, the members of the Floyd didn't look much different than Arnold when he was all dolled up. "Arnold Layne just happens to dig dressing up in women's clothing," Schaffner quotes Barrett as saying. "A lot of people do, so let's face up to reality." The BBC wasn't appeased, and the song was banned, but it became a hit anyway. There was just as much controversy over the single's B side, a jaunty throwaway called "Let's Roll Another One" that was retitled "Candy and a Currant Bun" when censors objected to the obvious marijuana reference.

For subsequent projects, EMI insisted that Pink Floyd work with staff producer Norman Smith, a career engineer who won the nickname "Normal" when he was working with George Martin and the Beatles. (He adopted the more flattering "Hurricane" when he became a pop star in his own right.) The Floyd's second single, "See Emily Play" b/w "Scarecrow," was released shortly after an all-night happening called the 14-Hour Technicolour Dream in June 1967. Though these songs were less provocative lyrically, the dominant instruments of Barrett's voice and Wright's organ were no less effective melodically. Still, the band members considered the single a step backward. They believed they had grown beyond three-minute pop novelties, and with the release of *The Piper at the Gates of Dawn*, they showed that they were right.

The Floyd used Abbey Road studios with the same glee as label-mates the Beatles, working with the white-coated technicians to

The Ultimate Psychedelic Rock Library: The Pink Floyd's brilliant debut album, The Piper at the Gates of Dawn *(Capitol).*

craft new and imaginative sounds. "A lot of the best sounds were developed by some of the dullest people," Mason told me. "Some of the engineers at Abbey Road were enormously clever and devised some very weird sounds, and they'd never had more than a glass of beer." (This was also true of the crew that worked with the Beatles, including George Martin.) The Floyd's debut opens with radio noise and a high-pitched electronic signal cueing the start of "Astronomy Dominé," a frightening tour of the cosmos that also evokes the chill of "icy waters underground." "Pow R. Toc H." and "Interstellar Overdrive" are the first of many evocative Floyd instrumentals, and it's hard to hear them without thinking of the swirling light shows and gyrating dancers at UFO. "The Scarecrow" shows that Barrett had listened to the Incredible String Band, while "Chapter 24" is as effective as any of George Harrison's Eastern meditations. (The lyrics were inspired by the *I Ching*, an ancient Chinese system for assessing a situation and divining the best course of action.) But it's the closing track that comes closest to matching the Beatles' bril-

liant studio accomplishments. "Bike" builds in intensity as Barrett
tries to impress his heartthrob with an array of fanciful gifts, including a bicycle, a clan of gingerbread men, and a pet mouse named
Gerald. We never know whether or not he gets the girl, since the
last gift is a mysterious room of "musical tunes" that swallows the
singer whole in an impressive explosion of sound effects.

The Piper at the Gates of Dawn was clearly Barrett's album. He
wrote eight of the eleven songs, and he chose the title from a chapter in his favorite book, Kenneth Grahame's *The Wind in the
Willows*. The singer had also become the center of attention during
live shows, raising his arms in dramatic gestures and wringing
increasingly amazing sounds from his Telecaster, which was covered with mirrors to reflect the swirling light show. Considering his
importance to the group, it's not hard to imagine his bandmates'
concern when he started to lose his grip on reality. Barrett was over-
indulging in the sex and the drugs that were so readily available to
young rock stars. He had been smoking huge amounts of marijuana since the age of seventeen, and after his first LSD experience at
nineteen, he began dropping acid almost daily. The rock-star
lifestyle seemed to aggravate a manic-depressive nature, and he
could veer instantly from lucid conversation to a blank stare or an
evil, mocking laugh.

What Schaffner called "the classic Barrett episode" came during
a gig in late 1967 following the Floyd's tour opening for Jimi
Hendrix. "While Syd lingered before the dressing room mirror,
primping up a luxuriant Afro modeled after the American guitar
hero's—'the obligatory Hendrix perm,' as Roger Waters would call
it twelve years later in *The Wall*—his exasperated colleagues finally

hit the stage without him. This apparently prodded Barrett to take decisive measures. Impulsively crushing the contents of a jar of his beloved Mandrax tablets (a powerful barbiturate marketed until the late '70s in the United States under the brand name Quaalude), he ground the fragments into his hair along with a full tube of Brylcreem. Syd then joined the group on stage, where the heat of the spotlights soon turned his unique beauty treatment into a dribbling mess that left the Pink Floyd's star looking, in the eyes of their dumbstruck lighting director, 'like a guttered candle.'"

The band's response to this deteriorating situation was to recruit Barrett's pal Gilmour as a fifth member to fill in on guitar and vocals. It was thought that Barrett could keep contributing new songs, like Brian Wilson in the Beach Boys. The story goes that the rest of the Floyd decided while en route to a gig that picking Barrett up was more trouble than it was worth. Behind the scenes, tensions with management played into this "spur of the moment" decision. Jenner and Andrew King of Blackhill Enterprises were adamant that Barrett *was* Pink Floyd, and Pink Floyd was eager to prove otherwise. In unguarded moments, the band members still wonder if they did the right thing. "Could we have saved the day? Could we have prevented Syd from going off the rail? I suppose this is the issue exercising me the most," Mason told me in 1995. "We are not really talking about four loveable moptops, we are talking about a bunch of poised individuals who were so busy pursuing their own ends that they weren't even capable of looking after each other."

Released a year after *The Piper at the Gates of Dawn*, the Floyd's second album contains guitar work by both Barrett and Gilmour but only one Barrett original. (Two other Barrett-Floyd tunes from this era, "Scream Thy Last Scream" and "Vegetable Man," have been heavily bootlegged but remain officially unreleased.) "Jugband Blues" seems to be Barrett's sarcastic farewell to his bandmates: "I'm most obliged to you for making it clear that I'm not here," he sings. Yet his influence weighs heavily throughout *A Saucerful of Secrets*. The ominous "Set the Controls for the Heart of the Sun" is a staple from his time in the band, and two delightfully silly pop songs— Wright's "See Saw" and Waters's "Corporal Clegg"—are clearly in the style of the Syd songbook. Only the instrumental title track points to a new direction. "'A Saucerful of Secrets' was the first thing we'd done without Syd that we thought was any good," Waters is quoted as saying in *Pink Floyd: Bricks in the Wall* by Karl Dallas. The psychedelic instrumental summons images of a battle in the heavens between angry Greek gods, moving from an uneasy vamp with fluttering organ chords and layers of weird cymbal overtones to a section titled "Syncopated Pandemonium." The hypnotic Mason drum loop yields to discordant clashing until the song is resolved with the majestic melody and wordless vocals of "Celestial Voices." It's all a bit pretentious, but the song succeeds because of the lush, made-for-headphones production and the powerful hooks.

"The title track strikes me as being the first of a line of ideas that led on into what Pink Floyd later became," Gilmour told me. "That sort of half a side of strange sections joined together with sound effects and things. That theme was followed in the four pieces on *Ummagumma*, the title track on *Atom Heart Mother*, and 'Echoes' on the *Meddle* album, and it developed into becoming a whole album by the time we got to *The Dark Side of the Moon*."

THE AMAZING PUDDING

> I still think most people think of us as a very drug orien-
> tated group. [Pause, smile.] Of course, we're not. You can
> trust us.
>
> —David Gilmour
> in *Pink Floyd Live at Pompeii*, 1972

NEVER LET IT BE SAID that the Floyd didn't stick with a winning formula. The band's midperiod albums are strikingly similar, but each
includes a handful of memorable tunes in addition to a lot of pot-
smoking background music. Taking its title from a slang phrase for
screwing, 1969's *Ummagumma* contains one album of old songs from
a prime live set and another of very dismissible solo suites by each of
the band members. The title track of 1970's *Atom Heart Mother*—formerly titled "The Amazing Pudding"—is another catchy side-long
suite, this one beefed up by Scottish composer Ron Geesin's over-the-
top orchestrations and choral arrangements. The album is fleshed out
with the beautiful Waters ballad "If," which may have been the first
of many recollections about the band's departed leader, Barrett ("And
if I go insane / Will you still let me join in with the game"), Wright's
typically idyllic, pastoral, and Beach Boys-flavored "Summer '68,"
Gilmour's Kinks-styled "Fat Old Sun," and the goofy sound collage-
instrumental "Alan's Psychedelic Breakfast". The disc stands as the
band's best effort in this era.

The central piece on 1971's *Meddle* grows from a single piano
note driven through an echo box on its maximum setting.
"Echoes" proceeds to add vocals to the mix, with Gilmour and

Wright singing hippie-dippy lyrics about a motionless albatross, a dangerous image to evoke. But while "One of These Days" is one of the band's most driving instrumentals, the rest of the album is relatively weak.

The Floyd's music was tailor-made for soundtracks, and the group did more than its share. *More* was recorded for the Barbet Schroeder film of the same name and released in 1969. It includes "Cymbaline," which muses on the mundane life of a rock star ("Your manager and agent are both busy on the phone / Selling colored photographs to magazines back home"), and "The Nile Song," a furious stomper that's the closest the Floyd got to heavy metal before "Run Like Hell" from *The Wall*. The band contributed three tracks to Michelangelo Antonioni's *Zabriskie Point*, sharing space on the 1970 soundtrack album with the Grateful Dead, while *Obscured By Clouds* was recorded in 1972 for another Schroeder film, *La Vallée*. The latter is the only sub-par offering, but the band has dismissed all of its soundtracks as "contract work," and they were

The Ultimate Psychedelic Rock Library: Don't have a cow— Atom Heart Mother *(Capitol) is the strongest offering from the midperiod Floyd.*

excluded—along with *Atom Heart Mother*— from the 1992 box set, *Shine On*.

One of the best tunes from this period didn't make it onto any of the band's albums. "Point Me at the Sky" was the group's only single between 1968 and "Another Brick in the Wall, Part Two" eleven years later. The song is clearly influenced by the Beatles' "Lucy in the Sky with Diamonds," but it's one of Waters's best science-fiction lyrics, painting an old-fashioned picture of Jules Verne-style space travel. The verses display the bassist's increasingly sharp and nasty wit. "If you survive to 2005 / I hope you're exceedingly thin," he sings. "For if you are stout you will have to breathe out / While the people around you breathe in."

The rap during the early '70s was that, like the Dead, the Floyd was best experienced live. The 1972 concert film *Pink Floyd Live at Pompeii* has its share of silliness. The group plays in the ancient ruins, traipses over fields of volcanic ash, and says incredibly dopey things in "off-the-cuff" interviews. But the movie is a valuable document of four guys seducing fantastic sounds from a relatively small and primitive collection of instruments, pre-samplers, digital synthesizers, or sequencers. "A Saucerful of Secrets" is especially inspiring as Wright plays the grand piano with his elbows and Gilmour fools with his Strat and an echo box while sitting cross-legged in the dirt. By the late '80s, the Floyd was using a small army onstage and off to duplicate such sounds.

While many fans claimed that midperiod Floyd sonically replicated many of the sensations of an acid trip, the band members claimed that they never took a lot of psychedelic drugs. Waters said he only used psychedelics twice. "None of us were tripping except for Syd," Mason told me. "We surfed on the psychedelic movement. We used it more than we played a part in it." "The post-Barrett Floyd inherited that "acid generation" image almost by default, and were often mystified by it," said a longtime friend quoted by Schaffner. "They were a bit too balanced to go the whole way, and seeing Syd so greatly affected by all the chemicals he pumped into himself was a lesson to be learned. Their attitude was, 'Fair enough—they may *think* we're doing it, and we're very happy they think so, but we'll just carry on in our own normal way.'"

Unlike the progressive-rock bands that they were sometimes wrongly grouped with, the Floyd stayed grounded in rock conventions. Wright's organ and Waters's trademark swooping bass never failed to provide big, beefy hooks, and Gilmour's solos invited you to hum along. Mason's wonderfully ham-fisted drumming kept even the wildest interstellar overdrives from careering out of control. Although they were sometimes stretched a bit thin over entire album sides, the Floyd always emphasized the importance of *songs*. "That came from Syd, mostly, because he was a songwriter," Mason said. "Syd was a natural; he was the romantic who spinned it off in a stream of consciousness. Whereas Roger had to work to become a songwriter, and he worked at it like mad. Much of what passed for psychedelic rock was blues, because people weren't songwriters and they just had a repertoire of classic blues pieces that they wrote their own versions of."

When the Floyd and Barrett parted ways, Blackhill Enterprises stood by Syd. Jenner produced the first tentative Barrett solo sessions in May 1968, but the recordings soon broke down. When the sessions resumed a year later, production chores fell by default to

The Ultimate Psychedelic Rock
Library: Syd's solo debut,
The Madcap Laughs *(Capitol).*

Malcolm Jones, the new head of EMI's Harvest subsidiary. Gilmour and Waters expressed interest halfway through the project, and Jones was happy to let them finish it. The moonlighting Floyds added a few touches, but most of the backing music was provided by Humble Pie drummer Jerry Shirley, bassist Willie Wilson, and special guests the Soft Machine. They often had to add their contributions to guitar and vocal tracks that Syd had recorded in one take, matching his mistakes and tempo changes. Released in January 1970, *The Madcap Laughs*—with its haunting title, eerie cover art of Barrett crouching in an empty apartment, and a strange inside photo of a baby that's apparently snorting something off a spoon and floating amid the clouds—would seem to be about alienation and isolation. Yet the disc is often beguiling, upbeat, and carefree—even if unsettling hints of Barrett's mental state *do* creep out. "Terrapin" is a stark acoustic love song that borders on a stalker's obsessiveness. The fuzz-driven "No Man's Land" is a statement about entropy ("When I live I die") that dissolves into babble and a meandering instrumental, and "Dark Globe" features the singer cracking on the telling lines, "With Eskimo chain I tattooed my brain all the way / Won't you miss me? / Wouldn't you miss me at all?"

A second, equally strong Barrett solo album produced by Gilmour and Wright followed less than a year later. Criticism of *Barrett* holds that the songwriter is unraveling on tape, but that's melodramatic nonsense. While the acoustic tunes are even sparer and less focused, "Baby Lemonade," "Gigolo Aunt," and "Wined and Dined" are pop songs every bit as memorable as "Arnold Layne." The album contains several skiffle throwaways, but "Dominoes" is an idiosyncratic tune that seems to be moving forward and reverse at the same time, and "Rats" is a creepy rant that evokes paranoid visions of insects on the walls, the image that Barrett chose for the cover.

Aside from a short and quickly aborted session in 1974, *Barrett* was the singer's last interaction with the world of rock 'n' roll. (The 1988 collection, *Opel*, features unreleased material from the Jenner sessions—including unsettling oddities such as "The Word Song," a

The Ultimate Psychedelic Rock Library: Barrett *(Capitol) may have found its auteur unraveling, but Syd could still craft strong pop tunes.*

seemingly random spewing of verbiage—and alternate versions of songs that appear on the albums.). But Barrett wasn't about to be forgotten. "Make your name like a ghost," he sang on "Baby Lemonade," and a cult of celebrity sprang up in his absence. Rock archivists, Floyd scholars, and obsessive collectors continue to mine the vaults for any scrap of music he ever committed to tape, and Internet newsgroups faithfully chart and discuss his doings, past and present; the most active of these (http://groups.yahoo.com/group/LaughingMadcaps) has sponsored an ambitious tape and CD-trading tree that has issued a dozen volumes of Barrett esoterica.

"I'm not really surprised by it. He's a very charismatic figure, and he did write some wonderful songs," Gilmour told me. "But you can say this of anyone whose career is cut off in its prime and died young—James Dean or anyone else—they are considered wonderful because they never grew old and showed us all their weaknesses." Rock scholar Deena Weinstein contends that the canonization of the drug-addled madman is in the romantic tradition of worshipping the idiot savant. "In part, it's the whole conflation of creativity and non-rationality," Weinstein said. "And in part it is the far more ancient notion of 'the innocent' and the brain-damaged as speakers of the Truth—Dostoevsky's *Idiot*, Faulkner's Benjy in *The Sound and the Fury*—a variation on *in vino veritas*."

The only truth Barrett found in LSD was that he couldn't handle a daily dose of it. His recorded output displays an inventive guitar style, an intuitive melodic talent, and a flair for sharp wordplay that owes more to a perceptive reading of James Joyce and William Blake than random stoner babbling. Drugs didn't create these talents, and romanticizing Barrett's abuse of them clouds the tragedy of his decline. "Certainly acid had *something* to do with it," Wright told Schaffner. "The point is, you don't know whether the acid accelerated this process that was happening in his brain or was the cause of it." The Floyd spent the next four albums partially wondering about "the cause of it"—fame, money, drugs, or plain old lunacy—and asking how they fit into the society that Syd dropped out of.

MONEY CHANGES EVERYTHING

> "He came into the studio," recalls Rick Wright, "And no one recognized this person." Andrew King tried to break the ice by asking his former star client how he'd put on so much weight. "I've got a very large fridge in the kitchen," Syd explained, "and I've been eating a lot of pork chops."
> —Schaffner on Barrett visiting his old mates during the recording of *Wish You Were Here,* 1975

PINK FLOYD WROTE MOST of its eighth album in late 1971. Unlike previous efforts, *The Dark Side of the Moon* evolved in live performances before recording started. It was premiered as part of the set in February 1972, at London's Rainbow Theatre. The Floyd entered Abbey Road in June, wrapped up in January, and the album was released in March 1973. Ubiquitous on classic-rock radio ever since, it's difficult to listen to *The Dark Side of the Moon* today with fresh ears. Subtly reworking melodies that had been almost-but-not-quite-there on earlier albums, it is the Floyd's catchiest record. The power of the hooks can't be underestimated, as *Dark Side* became one of the best-selling albums of all time. But there are additional reasons for its success. Years of knob-twirling practice, a strong partnership with engineer Alan Parsons (who used his connection with the band to launch his own progressive-rock group, the Alan Parson Project), and Abbey Road's new twenty-four-track tape machines produced a luxurious psychedelic sound that deserves its vaunted reputation. (Not for nothing is *Dark Side* the favorite of stereo salesmen everywhere.) Gilmour and Wright never sang better than on "Time" and "Us and Them"; the guitar and synthesizer solos are extraordinary, and Mason's drumming is musical and creative, especially on "Time" and "Money."

The Ultimate Psychedelic Rock Library: The Dark Side of the Moon *(Capitol), the favorite album of stereo salesmen everywhere.*

Writing in *Melody Maker*, critic Chris Charlesworth offered that *Dark Side* is "a *great* record to fuck to," especially side one, which climaxes with Clare Torry's orgasmic vocals on "The Great Gig in the Sky." Dick Parry's saxophone and a quartet of backing singers give the album a stronger and more sensual R&B feel than anything the Floyd recorded earlier. *Dark Side* also betters earlier concept albums because it is much more intriguing and open-ended. Shifting into the role of the band's primary lyricist, Waters reveals himself as a romantic *and* a pessimist. He believes that the need to care for and be cared for by others is what makes life meaningful, but it is difficult if not impossible to attain authentic interpersonal communications. The songs explore the factors that drive people apart, resulting in isolation and, ultimately, madness. Rather than contrived lyrical bridges, thematic links are provided by sound effects and snippets of interviews in which people respond to questions such as, "When was the last time you were violent?" and "What do you think of death?" (Abbey Road doorman Jerry Driscoll provides the memorable closing, "There is no dark side of the moon, really. Matter of fact, it's all dark.")

In an interview with me nineteen years after *Dark Side's* release, Gilmour reflected on the album's success. "All the things we'd been doing before had been pointing toward it, but it was the first time all the elements came together really well," he said. "The words were brilliant, it had a lovely cover, and it was just at that point in our career where we were moving to becoming quite popular. There was something to appeal to everyone in the world in at least one of the songs." The problem with perfection is that it's hard to top. "At that point," Schaffner quotes Waters as saying, "all our ambitions were realized." The group had become a money-making megalith, enabling the musicians to buy holiday villas in the Greek Islands and indulge passions for collecting guitars (Gilmour), antiques (Wright), cars (Mason), and French Impressionist paintings (Waters). The cocoon of creature comforts slowly smothered their creativity, but in the mid-'70s, the musicians hadn't yet lost that playful psychedelic spirit.

In the autumn of 1973, the Floyd started work on the aborted *Household Objects* album. The group spent several months recording the sounds of stretched rubber bands, cardboard boxes, and an assortment of wine glasses filled with different amounts of water. "We tried to make all the sounds without using real instruments," Gilmour recalled in our conversation. "Of course, it's a dead easy thing to do today with samplers, but then, we abandoned it without having made any real tracks. It just got too difficult—and pointless. I mean, in the end, after you've spent weeks trying to make

The Ultimate Psychedelic Rock Library: Wish You Were Here *(Capitol), the masterpiece of the Floyd's "classic-rock" era.*

cardboard boxes sound like bass drums and snare drums, you think, 'Well, why the fuck don't I use a bass drum and snare drum?'"

When the band finally went back to using real instruments, there were three originals that had been tightened, like the songs on *Dark Side*, through live performances. Gilmour wanted to put "Shine On" on one side of an album and "Raving and Drooling" and "You Gotta Be Crazy" on the other and be done with it. But touring commitments kept interrupting the sessions, and the musicians succumbed to a general ennui as the recording grew labored and torturous. Waters felt that the only way the Floyd could rise above its artistic malaise was to cut "Shine On" in two and complete the album with new material that drew on the emotions the band was experiencing at the moment. It's revealing that the new songs include two that are superficially about the evils of the music business while in a broader sense addressing false promises and a failure to communicate.

Released in September 1975, *Wish You Were* Here stands as the best of the Floyd's four "classic-rock" efforts. The title track is a touching and tender acoustic folk song, and the subject of distance and longing is underscored by the sound of the introduction, which is mixed to create the effect of tuning in on a crappy transistor radio. (Waters commented that the song could just as well have been called "Wish *We* Were Here.") "Welcome to the Machine" is a state-of-the-art exposition of what could be done with a synthesizer, and the repetitive throb perfectly evokes the machine in the title. "Have a Cigar" is a funky throwaway, the sort of tune that used to serve as filler on Floyd soundtracks, but its very ordinariness compliments the sarcastic lyrics. Guest vocalist Roy

Harper plays a smug but clueless music executive who utters the immortal line, "Oh, by the way, which one's Pink?" (Another Jenner-King client, Harper was a ubiquitous figure on the English underground.) The album's crowning achievement is "Shine on You Crazy Diamond," a tribute to that "painter, piper, prisoner, and martyr," Barrett. More gripping and graceful than any of the Floyd's other long suites, it has a symphonic elegance while retaining a rock 'n' roll grit, thanks in part once again to Mason, master of the slow-motion drum fill. The tension between the plodding rhythm and the soaring keyboards and guitar evoke an injured bird struggling to fly. The music perfectly complements Waters's lyrics—the idea that Barrett "wore out his welcome with random precision" is a thoughtful assessment of his decline—but the fact that the bassist thought the long, wonderfully psychedelic instrumentals distracted from the lyrical concept is evidence of the rift that would eventually divide the band.

Seven months after the release of *Wish You Were Here*, the Floyd returned to the studio. "Raving and Drooling" became "Sheep" and "You Gotta Be Crazy" became "Dogs" as the band got downright nasty with the allegorical *Animals*. "It was the moment of high punk over here in England, where everyone sort of hated everything," Gilmour told me. "I'm sure that had an influence on us making a bit of a tougher, starker, more aggressive album—as close as we ever got to a punk album, if you like." There's still the matter of Floydian tempos and song lengths, but the album *is* full of jagged edges and harsh instrumental textures. Lyrically, Waters takes dead aim at the mind-numbing constraints of society, attacking the pigs (which include the "bus-stop ratbag" Lumpenproletariat, the

The Ultimate Psychedelic Rock Library: The Floyd got downright nasty with the allegorical Animals *(Capitol).*

"house-proud town mouse" bourgeoisie, and the "well-heeled big wheel" wealthy); the sheep who unthinkingly accept religion as panacea, and the ruthless yuppie dogs who prey upon them, as Weinstein noted in her book, *Serious Rock.* This cynical vision was very much in line with the punks', even as Johnny Rotten was making headlines for sporting a Pink Floyd T-shirt with the words "I Hate" scrawled on it.

In many ways the Floyd had fallen into the trap that Waters despised. Wright told Schaffner that *Animals* was "the beginning of where Roger wanted to do everything." Despite his pleas for inter-personal communications, Waters didn't really want to hear from his musical partners anymore, even though the band's best moments had always been the result of four individuals working together. The solo suites on *Ummagumma* were flops; the Gilmour, Mason, and Wright solo albums released between *Animals* and *The Wall* were interesting primarily for the way they illuminated the individual players' strengths and weaknesses, and Waters' solo collaboration with Geesin, *Music from The Body*, was a way-too-clever novelty. The bassist's new self-image as the Floyd's primary auteur simply wasn't based in fact, and *The Wall* suffers from its creator's delusion and the exclusion of his bandmates.

Released in November 1979, *The Wall* mixes elements from Waters's and Barrett's life stories, but its primary themes had all been covered before with more subtlety and artistry. Waters wrote about the tragedy of war in "Corporal Clegg" and "Us and Them"; the cruelness of society in *The Dark Side of the Moon* and *Animals*; the machinations of the music business in "Cymbaline," "Have a Cigar," and "Welcome to the Machine," and the self-constructed wall of insanity in "If," "Brain Damage," and "Shine on You Crazy Diamond." Some of the instrumental settings are familiar— "Mother" recalls the idyllic vibe of *More*, and "Comfortably Numb" has a patented, brilliant Gilmour guitar solo—but there's no evidence of the Floyd playing together as a band. *The Wall* could have been recorded by anybody, and in fact, the roster of unlikely session contributors includes lounge chanteuse Toni Tennile, Beach Boy Bruce Johnston, and Toto drummer Jeff Porcaro.

The Floyd's subsequent output nosedives quicker than the spitfire that crashed into the wall during the band's overwrought stage shows. Nobody but Waters showed up for *The Final Cut*, a relatively tune-free album released in 1983 and inspired by the war in the Falklands. Afterward Waters and the rest of the band parted ways in an ugly burst of lawsuits and bitter slurs. It was a tawdry end for a group that had previously avoided public rock-star embarrassments. Gilmour, Wright, and Mason continued as a Floyd devoid of intellectual structure (*A Momentary Lapse of Reason*, *The Division*

Bell), while Waters continued as a songwriter devoid of musical inspiration (*The Pros and Cons of Hitch Hiking*, *Radio K.A.O.S.*, and *Amused to Death*). Even if the remaining members of the band settle their differences with Waters (which those in the know say is unlikely), they will probably never recapture the "no-boundaries" psychedelic spirit of their very best work.

"In the beginning, you think that you can do anything you like, but as time goes by, it narrows down," Mason told me with welcomed frankness in 1995. "So your breadth of vision in 1967 is like one-hundred feet, but thirty years later, you have learned so much that you have found the areas where you operate best. It's not laziness, but now you operate within three feet. One has to make a very conscious effort to break those boundaries. I think, also, that when you get more successful, it gives you increased responsibility. You carry the baggage of your history, and every record is judged against all the other things that you have done, and that can be quite onerous. You feel like you are limited to what you can do."

Barrett has avoided this dilemma by simply doing nothing at all. Gilmour said he checks in with his former mate's family from time to time to make sure that he's getting his royalty checks (which are considerable in the age of CD reissues), but the band hasn't seen Syd since he showed up unexpectedly at Gilmour's wedding during a break in the recording of *Wish You Were Here* in 1975. "Syd Barrett, or Roger as everyone now calls him, is today the antithesis of the colorful '60s rock star that so many fans remember," wrote biographers Mike Watkinson and Pete Anderson. "A balding, rather heavyset figure who lives alone in his Cambridge flat, he seldom ventures into the center of town. His brother-in-law,

Paul Breen, says of his current lifestyle: 'He's improving with age, like good wine, and is happy to get on with his life. He doesn't really see anyone, apart from his sister, and clearly enjoys his own company. He does not really show much emotion but certainly gives the impression that he is comfortably settled into his way of life.'"

It's tempting to think of the madcap sitting at home and laughing—about the cost of opening the doors of perception, about the way his life has been romanticized, and about how he still figures in the story of his former band after a quarter of a century. (The Floyd's 1994 tour featured a film of a group of men struggling to carry an enormous bust of someone who looked very much like Syd.) But it's more likely that Barrett concentrates on his favorite diversions—TV, painting, and the occasional bike ride through town—and in that way, he's not much different from Gilmour, Mason, Waters, Wright, or many of the rest of us.

The Artist As Critic

In 1992, Pink Floyd released the *Shine On* box set, consisting of eight complete albums newly remastered for CD, plus a bonus disc collecting all of the group's early singles. In an interview to promote the project, I asked David Gilmour to play "autodiscography," giving me his assessments of his own albums. Here are his comments.

A Saucerful of Secrets (1968)

"The title track strikes me as being the first of a line of ideas that led on into what Pink Floyd later became, that sort of half a side of strange sections joined together with sound effects and things....And I particularly like Syd's 'Jugband Blues.'"

Meddle (1971)

"I still love 'Echoes'—it's brilliant. 'One of These Days' stands up great. *Meddle* was the first album after *Saucerful* that was really getting to grips with where we were going."

The Dark Side of the Moon (1973)

"Everything gelled perfectly at that one moment."

Wish You Were Here (1975)

"I think it's probably my favorite album. There were a lot of difficult times during it, but maybe they helped. I think what we achieved with it is a really good, balanced album, musically and lyrically."

Animals (1977)

"The remastering has shown it up brighter and better than it's ever been. It's definitely the one that's improved the most."

The Wall (1979)

"The shows made it make sense, and doing the shows was great fun for about the first thirty performances. Then it finally got dull because there was no place to stretch out and just play music. Everything had to be rigidly routined, and that has its upside and its downside."

A Momentary Lapse of Reason (1987)

"That is part of the ongoing Pink Floyd, and we want to convince people of that. You might want to use it to confirm that we're still going and it's still part of what we do."

The Pink Floyd Early Singles (1992)

"One of my builders working on doing up the house here suggested to me that we put these things out, so we threw that in as an extra freebie. We've gone back to the originals, and they're all remastered in glorious mono."

6

THE U.K.'S
TECHNICOLOUR DREAM

ON APRIL 29, 1967, an all-night happening called the 14-Hour Technicolour Dream overran London's stately Alexandra Palace, a Victorian exhibition hall atop Muswell Hill. Ostensibly a benefit to raise cash for the *International Times*, an underground newspaper whose offices had been raided by the police, the event became a coming-out party for England's psychedelic underground. Clad in brightly colored caftans, long lace scarves, and flowing robes and beads, some ten thousand people roamed the grounds. They were entertained by a troupe of mimes, underground films, a full-sized fairground helter-skelter, a giant jelly mold, an igloo dispensing free but ineffectual banana-peel joints, and poetry and performance art by Ron Geesin, Yoko Ono, and her husband at the time, Tony Cox. But the main attraction was the music.

Tomorrow took the stage just as the party was starting to swing. Twink, the group's lunatic drummer, bashed his set in an anarchic flurry while his bandmates fiddled with their effects boxes and amplifiers. Wearing a red velvet suit from Granny Takes a Trip, a young guitar prodigy named Steve Howe played a droning raga that was just on the verge of feeding back. (He had customized one of the pickups on his Japanese Guyatone guitar so that the D string fed back automatically whenever he stepped on his volume pedal.) As usual, bassist John "Junior" Wood was dressed only in a loincloth. He and Twink fell into a quick eight-beat rhythm that rushed past like the posts on a picket fence during a brisk bike ride through the country. Singer Keith West held the microphone stand as if to steady himself. "The lamp post hangs his head in disgrace / Shines no light upon my face," he sang. "Through the darkness we still see/My white bicycle and me." Most of the lyrics were a blur, but three words leaped out of the mix, repeated in the choruses and echoed by the other band members. *"My white bicycle."*

Twenty-seven years later, Howe told me that he and the other members of Tomorrow hadn't been aware of Albert Hofmann's famous acid-powered bike ride. He recalled "My White Bicycle" as a song about the Provos, a sect of anarchist hippies in Holland who shared communal bicycles. "It was, on the other hand, a pretty druggy kind of song," he added with a chuckle. "This was definitely a record that challenged the establishment to ride the white bicycle."

Tomorrow certainly wasn't alone in issuing such a challenge. The bill at the 14-Hour Technicolour Dream was indicative of the diversity of the English psychedelic rock scene in the wake of *Rubber Soul* and *Revolver*. In addition to Tomorrow and Pink Floyd, the Crazy World of Arthur Brown, the Soft Machine, the Pretty Things, and the Creation all delivered transcendent sets.

Brown was an operatic singer with a flair for the dramatic. He went on to score a hit in 1968 with "Fire," an urgent tune that he performed while wearing a flaming crown; the band also played a riveting version of "I Put a Spell on You." Produced by Pete Townshend, the Crazy World's debut album went gold and the band appeared on the British music show *Top of the Pops*, but Brown was suspicious of the starmaking machine, and he decided to release future recordings independently. "We represented a different sort of music and a different approach altogether to what the [pop] music thing was about," he told *Your Flesh* magazine in 1993. Relocating to a communal farm, the group recorded a more ethereal album called *Strange Lands* that wasn't released until 1988. The Crazy World ended when organist Vincent Crane and drummer Carl Palmer left to form Atomic Rooster. Brown subsequently recorded three albums of Hawkwind-style space rock with Kingdom Come; painted houses with former Mothers of Invention guitarist Jimmy Carl Black in his new hometown of Austin, Texas; released two techno albums, and formed a new version of his old band for odd gigs in England and the United States.

Leaders of the active scene in Canterbury, the Soft Machine took its name from a novel by William S. Burroughs. The group was formed by bassist-vocalist Kevin Ayers, drummer-vocalist Robert Wyatt, organist Mike Ratledge, and guitarist Daevid Allen, but Allen quit before the first album. Produced by Chas Chandler of the Animals and released in 1968, *The Soft Machine* attempts to cross the Beatles' psychedelic rock and Ornette Coleman's harmelodic jams. On tracks such as the joyful "Hope for Happiness" and "Why Are We Sleeping?" (a political call to arms), it nearly succeeds. Ayers

The Ultimate Psychedelic Rock Library: The Soft Machine Volumes One and Two *(Big Beat) combines the psychedelic jazz-rockers' first and second albums.*

soon left to craft moody, hypnotic, and oh-so-romantic solo albums such as *Joy of a Toy* and *The Confessions of Dr. Dream and Other Stories*, while the Soft Machine moved toward a more peculiar and less rocking brand of jazz fusion. Wyatt later collaborated with David Sinclair of the jam-happy Canterbury bands Caravan and Camel in the tuneful Matching Mole, but in 1973, he was paralyzed from the waist down after falling out of a third-story window while partying a bit too enthusiastically. He mined the depths of his painful experience to produce the most beautiful and enduring album by any member of the Canterbury mafia, 1974's *Rock Bottom*, produced by Nick Mason of Pink Floyd.

Meanwhile the Australian ex-patriate Allen had relocated to Paris with his wife, singer Gilli Smyth, and formed an ever-shifting commune and rock band that eventually became known as Gong. (Other members who came and went included drummer Pierre Moerlen, guitarist Steve Hillage, synthesizer player Tim Blake, and—after the band lost its initial gonzo tilt—soon-to-be-jazz-fusion giant Alan Holdsworth.) Allen had been strongly influenced by Syd Barrett's guitar style, but Gong incorporated many other elements—notably free jazz and avant-garde classical music—to become the key band in a subgenre that some have called space rock, thanks as much to the lyrics as the music. Gong was devoted to exploring the mythology of Planet Gong, a science-fiction fantasy world populated by Radio Gnomes, Pothead Pixies, and Octave Doctors. This strange terrain was throughly charted on a series of albums known as "the Radio Gnome Invisible Trilogy"—*Flying Teapot* (1972), *Angels Egg* (1973), and *You* (1975)—which mix moments of trippy inspiration with bursts of pointless indulgence.

Back in England, the Pretty Things were one of the many bands that were inspired by psychedelic drugs to shift from R&B to more expansive sounds, starting with the heavily orchestrated *Emotions* in 1967. Like Brian Wilson, Phil May and his bandmates tried to evoke a different emotion on each song, but the result was much less successful than *Pet Sounds*. The group fared better with a pair of 1968 discs recorded by Pink Floyd producer Norman Smith, *Parachute* and *S.F. Sorrow*, a concept album that stands as the group's finest moment. Like *Tommy* by the Who, the story of the title character is a bit convoluted and silly—spiraling off a short story that band member Phil May wrote about World War I, it charts various phases in the life of the title character, climaxing with disaster aboard a dirigible—but the album succeeds on the strength of the melodies and the inventiveness of the soundscapes in songs such as "Death" and "Baron Saturday." Unfortunately, the band devolved into a proto-grunge hard-rock parody shortly thereafter.

The Ultimate Psychedelic Rock Library: S.F. Sorrow *(Sony) is a complex but tuneful concept album.*

Declaring that its music was "red with purple flashes," the Creation first came together in Middlesex in 1966 from the remains of a mod combo called the Mark Four. Signed to a label started by Shel Talmy, the producer of the Who and the Kinks, the quartet made its recorded debut with a noisy three-minute epiphany called "Making Time" that featured guitarist Eddie Phillips soloing with a violin bow. (Jimmy Page was a fan, and he later borrowed the trick on "Dazed and Confused.") An amazingly creative player—legend holds that Townshend offered him the lead guitar slot in the Who but he declined—Phillips was a master at creating layers of disorienting feedback, and he stands beside Jimi Hendrix as one of the genre's most inventive guitarists.

"For me, that all started around about '62 or '63," Phillips told me in 2002. "I'd always used a solid-body guitar, but I saw this cherry-red Gibson 335 looking at me through a shop window and I thought, 'I want to give that a go!' Being a semi-acoustic, the tone was different, and there was this feedback. I thought, 'This is going

The Ultimate Psychedelic Rock Library: The Creation's strongest tunes are collected on Our music is red—with purple flashes *(Diablo), an English compilation from 1998.*

to be a problem if I can't play loud enough without getting that noise.' Then I realized, 'Why I don't try and make it work?' It was really good at that time, because we were coming out of playing rock 'n' roll covers into more of our own beat—the guitar solo that would start and never finish. It was more freeform, and I got the hang of hitting a chord and making the feedback ring on the note instead of just being an out of control racket. Then I had this idea that I'd really like to get a big sustain. Before the bow, I used a hacksaw, took the blade out of it, and put a guitar string in. Unfortunately, it sort of wrecked the guitar a bit—and let's face it, a Gibson 335 in 1963 was a lot of money in comparison to other guitars, like three grand! So I went down to the local shop, which sold everything from piano accordions to double basses, and I saw this violin bow and thought, 'Why don't I try that?' At first it wouldn't work, then someone told me you've got to put this rosin on the bow. So it came along in stages, and pretty soon I could get a note out of it. It turned out to be a unique sound, and it was a great, great visual thing as well."

Following the pop-art template, the Creation tried to make every performance "a happening." Its second single, "Painter Man", was a humorous tale of art-school pretensions, and singer Kenny Pickett splashed paint Jackson Pollock-style on a giant canvas as the group performed. Topping the Who's onstage demolitions, he sometimes set his work alight to end the show. "We always considered ourselves the world's first graffiti artists," Phillips said with a chuckle. "We were able to sort of do the pop-art thing live while we were doing the stuff on stage; that's how we got into the painting thing. That was just really, really different at the time. Our thing was always trying to look forward and trying to be just a bit ahead of things. It's so easy to get on the stage and stand still and play guitar, but we always wanted to take it further."

Indeed, the Creation's legacy is that it was a band that was radically ahead of its time. While the group scored several hits in the U.K. in the mid-'60s, its managers chose to focus on introducing the band to continental Europe rather than attempting to conquer America a la the rest of the British Invasion. The strategy backfired, and the group started to fall apart in 1968. (For a time after Phillips quit, the guitar slot was filled by Ron Wood, now famously a Rolling Stone.) By '69 the band was no more. In the years that followed, Pickett landed a job on Led Zeppelin's road crew, and Phillips went to work for London Transport. The two later reteamed to write "Teacher Teacher" for Rockpile.

Feeling that they'd never properly put the Creation to rest, the members reunited in 1993 for a surprisingly vital live album called

Lay the Ghost. By that time, echoes of the group could be heard in a new wave of British psychedelic rock bands. The Jesus and Mary Chain and Oasis shamelessly stole elements of its sound, Ride covered "How Does It Feel to Feel," and Creation Records founder Alan McGee paid homage to the band with the monikers of his label and his own group (Biff! Bang! Pow! was named for one of the Creation's jauntier mod tunes). Not long after the '93 reunion, Pickett passed away, but surviving members Phillips and bassist Bob Garner recruited some young blood and toured the United States for the first time in 2002, finally capitalizing on their cult stardom. (The group reached a new audience when several of its songs were featured in Wes Anderson's 1998 film, *Rushmore.*) The songs still sounded remarkably fresh.

"If you had said to me in 1966 that, 'In the year 2002, you'll be traveling to play these songs in America, and people from seventeen to fifty-seven will be singing along with all the words,' I'd have said, 'Are you daft? You must be smoking some good stuff!'" Phillips told me. While some artists might be bitter that they came close without ever grabbing the brass ring, he was philosophical. "You look at Oasis and all that and you say, 'Hmmm....' But we're forty years down the line, and people still remember us. They still remember our songs, and that's as good as it gets. Some people get really bitter and twisted by the whole thing, but I'm okay with all that. It's just nice that in our time we can stand up and travel all that distance and play to people that like the songs. That never gets old."

As for Tomorrow, "My White Bicycle" became a hit when it appeared on the group's only album in 1968. The self-titled disc boasts such highlights as "Real Life Permanent Dream" and

The Ultimate Psychedelic Rock Library: Tomorrow's self-titled debut (See For Miles) is a flawed effort, but the high points are very high indeed.

"Revolution," a scary tune commemorating the night police raided a Pink Floyd gig at UFO and turned their dogs on a crowd of stoned freaks. But it also includes slight, whimsical ditties such as "Three Jolly Little Dwarfs" and "Auntie Mary's Dress Shop" (like "Arnold Layne," a song that looked kindly on transvestites). *Tomorrow* is awfully derivative of the Beatles, right down to the unremarkable cover of "Strawberry Fields Forever," but the band's story is worth telling because it's so typical of the first wave of English psychedelic rock.

Howe and West first came together in 1965 in a group called the In Crowd. The band wore modish striped polo shirts and tapered jeans and played revved-up soul and R&B. By 1966 things were starting to change. "We were starting to 'psychedelic' things up," Howe told me. "It came from the Byrds, really. We were looking at more obscure music than Beatles, but of course, they were in there, too." The change was partly due to the London social scene—the exchange of ideas as musicians gathered in the clubs—but LSD also played a role. "The idea that you could go beyond normality was somehow so incredibly irresistible," Howe said. "Humanity had gone through two world wars and one needed—I don't think you can avoid the word—*escape*, whether it was a blind, useless escape or actually a very therapeutic and beautiful experience. Although it was against mainstream thinking, in a way, it became a mainstream of people who were on to something, and it became very fashionable and trendy to be part of that thing."

Tomorrow broke up in 1968 when West quit to concentrate on a concept album called *Teenage Opera*. In 1970 Howe joined Yes, where he was united with Chris Squire, another veteran of a one-hit-wonder from the psychedelic rock scene. The Syn scored a hit in 1967 with the catchy single "Grounded," which rewrote the Beatles' "Rain" and added lyrics about a truly awful trip ("I'm high and I'm dry and I'm grounded"). For Squire, psychedelic drugs and psychedelic rock were inextricably linked. "There was a lot of LSD around," he told me in 2002. "Of course, the Beatles were leading the charge in the recording studio from *Sgt. Pepper*, really—everyone wanted to be part of that experience. But I think the drugs were just as much a part of it; I doubt there were very many people who didn't take drugs who were involved in that movement."

Ten Great English
Psychedelic Rock Songs

1. The Syn, "Grounded"
2. The Small Faces, "Afterglow"
3. The Eyes, "When the Night Falls"
4. The Crazy World of Arthur Brown, "Fire"
5. Status Quo, "Pictures of Matchstick Men"
6. The Yardbirds, "Shapes of Things"
7. The Small Faces, "Itchycoo Park"
8. The Eyes, "I'm Rowed Out"
9. The Move, "Fire Brigade"
10. John's Children, "Desdemona"

Among the other U.K. bands involved in the movement were Apple, the Koobas, the Open Mind, Nirvana (who recorded one of the first concept albums, *The Story of Simon Simopath*), and the English Kaleidoscope. (In 2001 Rhino released a second *Nuggets* box set, *Nuggets II: Original Artyfacts from the British Empire and Beyond*, rounding up sample recordings from many of these English groups, as well as psychedelic rock bands from the continent in the same era.) Most of these bands were quickly forgotten, but a few deserve at least a footnote. The Birds (not to be confused with that

American group) played over-amped R&B and first introduced Wood to the rock scene. Hailing from Birmingham, the Move also one-upped the Who's instrument-smashing by wrecking TV sets and pianos while playing gentle psychedelic pop songs such as "Fire Brigade" and "Flowers in the Rain." (The group later morphed into the Electric Light Orchestra.) The Action started out as a conventional mod band, notable primarily for the fact that it was produced by George Martin. It broke up after a series of singles, but a posthumous compilation of demos called *Rolled Gold* chronicles a more intriguing turn toward lilting psychedelia before the band's demise. Status Quo scored a hit with the timeless single "Pictures of Matchstick Men," and John's Children recorded the infamous *Legendary Orgasm Album*, a "live" record with crowd noise dubbed in from other discs. When the group split up, guitarist Marc Bolan went on to form Tyrannosaurus Rex with conga player Steve Peregrine-Took. Before the group went electric, began crafting indelible glam-rock hits, and shortened its name to T. Rex, the acid-dropping flower child Bolan worked with Blackhill Enterprises, Syd Barrett's management firm, and sang fetching and whimsical psychedelic-folk songs about elves, witches, and magicians on albums such as *My people were fair and had sky in their hair...but now they're content to wear stars on their brows* and *Prophets, Seers, and Sages, the Angels of The Ages*.

As with the American *Nuggets* groups, many of the first-wave English psychedelic rock bands embraced the musical style without ever having had a psychedelic experience. "There were English working-class guys, as opposed to the Pink Floyd, the Incredible String Band, and the Soft Machine, who were all very middle class," promoter and record producer Joe Boyd told me. "Twink and the guys from the Move would have been on a building site if they hadn't been working in a band. The Move learned psychedelia while drinking beer. They copied the musical ethos, and they copied it almost better than the people who invented it."

Other groups that took a sharp left turn into psychedelia were better known. The Yardbirds formed in late 1963 from the remains of the Metropolis Blues Quartet, and they followed the Rolling Stones into the Crawdaddy Club as the house band. By 1965 they had progressed from relatively straight covers of Bo Diddley, the Isley Brothers, and Muddy Waters to extended blues-based raveups, wild improvisations that allowed guitarist Eric Clapton to jam for as long as thirty minutes. Clapton quit in disgust when the group moved into the pop mainstream with the 1965 hit "For Your Love." He was replaced by Jeff Beck, who started to experiment with fuzzboxes, sitar-like drones, and other exotic colors on captivating singles such as "Heart Full of Soul," "Shapes of Things," and "The Train Kept A-Rollin'." Beck also presided over the Yardbirds' most psychedelic album, *Over Under Sideways Down*, which climaxed with the brilliant title track. Jimmy Page joined the group as bassist and eventually replaced Beck on lead guitar before the band finally morphed into Led Zeppelin in 1968.

Steve Marriot, Ronnie Lane, Kenny Jones, and Ian McLagan were fresh-faced young mods ("faces") who came together as the Small Faces in 1966. The band members maintained their R&B influence and a cockney sense of humor while coloring their sound with flower-power lyrics (as on the early single "Itchycoo Park") and trippy, ever-shifting productions (as on their second and last album, *Ogden's Nut Gone Flake*, a post-*Sgt. Pepper's* conceptual curiosity that came packaged in a round album cover that resembled a tobacco tin). Marriot left in 1969 for Humble Pie, and Wood and Rod Stewart joined. The band became the Faces, and the substance of favor turned from psychedelic drugs to lager.

The first incarnation of Traffic was strongly influenced by the psychedelic sounds of 1967, as evidenced by the singles "Paper Sun" and "Hole in My Shoe" and the debut album, *Mr. Fantasy*, but the band soon shifted into a less cosmic merger of jazz, rock, and folk. After the original R&B Animals split, singer Eric Burdon relocated to San Francisco, put together the New Animals, and recorded an acid-tinged testament to the times called *Winds of Change*. Burdon also wrote a tune paying homage to the original manufacturers of LSD, "A Girl Named Sandoz," and effectively captured a drunk and psychedelically disoriented vibe on "Spill the Wine."

The less substantive British Invasion bands were mostly history by 1967, but two other groups from that earlier era tried to reinvent themselves by drawing on psychedelic sounds. With their swirling organ, the Zombies already had a spooky undertone on singles such as "She's Not There," but 1968's masterful *Odyssey and Oracle*, released shortly after the band broke up, stands as a fascinating aural tapestry, if not quite "the British *Pet Sounds*" that its boosters sometimes proclaim. Rod Argent's piano, organ, harpsichord, harmonium, and Mellotron merge with Colin Blunstone's gorgeous harmony vocals to create a sort of melancholy musing on England's lost innocence; standout tracks include the lovely "A Rose for Emily" (the same girl from Pink Floyd's "See Emily Play"?), the haunting World War I reminiscence, "Butchers Tale (Western Front

The Ultimate Psychedelic Rock Library: The Zombies' Odyssey and Oracle *(Big Beat) is a melancholy look at England's lost innocence.*

1914)," and the amazing album-closer, "Time of the Season," a song that captures the underlying tensions of the day almost as well as "For What It's Worth."

The Hollies were less successful. They had emerged in 1965 with simple harmony-driven pop hits such as "Bus Stop," but they explored more elaborate instrumental backings and orchestration on the 1967 album *Dear Eloise/King Midas In Reverse*, a spectacular flop. Graham Nash eventually left to link up with David Crosby and Stephen Stills and form the supergroup of Crosby, Stills and Nash.

While the Zombies and the Hollies symbolize the shift of one era of British rock into another—the beat groups of the British Invasion to psychedelic rock—Procul Harum, the Moody Blues, the Nice, and King Crimson herald the move from psychedelia to progressive rock. The new genre emerged as a direct outgrowth of the psychedelic explosion: The doors of perception that were thrown open by the first wave of psychedelic rockers encouraged wide-ranging stylistic explorations by the bands that followed. Suddenly rock was incorporating elements of classical music, jazz, the avant garde, world beat, and ancient Celtic folk music. As Howe told me several decades later, "Yes couldn't have played the kind of music it made without having the experience of developing the freedom and total noncon-formist approach that came from the psychedelic bands."

Procul Harum took its name from the Latin phrase for "beyond these things" and scored its biggest hit by paraphrasing a Bach can-tata, Suite no. 3 in D Major. The pretensions are thick even without hallucinatory lyrics about vestal virgins, flying ceilings, and light fandangos. Nevertheless, "A Whiter Shade of Pale" remains a hauntingly effective single. The band plays as if it is barely restrain-ing an emotional outburst: The group could be a hippie version of the lounge band on the *Titanic*, dutifully playing as the ship sinks into the icy depths. The quintet's first three albums explored increasingly less interesting variations of this theme, until the band finally lapsed into a fatal coma in 1970 after the departure of gui-tarist Robin Trower.

The Moody Blues first surfaced as a modish second-tier British Invasion band, scoring a 1965 hit with "Go Now." The group fell apart in 1966 when singer Denny Laine quit, but keyboardist Mike Pinder recruited new members and moved everyone to Belgium so that they could "find themselves." They reappeared in 1968 with *Days of Future Passed*. The Moodies recorded some catchy if melo-dramatic tunes, including "Nights in White Satin," "Forever Afternoon (Tuesday)," and "Legend of a Mind," which paid tribute to Timothy Leary. But their albums bogged down with long, snooze-inducing instrumentals and dramatic poetry readings, and like many in the art-rock class of 1968, they never learned when to

The Ultimate Psychedelic Rock Library: The orchestra and the conceptual conceit of the phases of the day grow a bit tiresome, but at its best, the Moody Blues' Days of Future Passed *(Polygram) is trippy and tuneful.*

call it quits. After a brief lull in the mid-'70s, they came back reinvigorated but softer, more self-indulgent, and far less interesting than before.

Managed by the post-Stones Andrew Loog Oldham, the Nice certainly knew how to get attention. "At their New York debut at Steve Paul's Scene in 1968, they stripped to the waist and whipped each other," critic Lillian Roxon wrote. "In England, they stabbed an American flag with knives, stomped on it, and burned it onstage, and organ player Keith Emerson has been known to tap-dance on the keys with remarkably musical results." Unfortunately, the group's albums are fairly flaccid. *The Thoughts of Emerlist Davjack* (1968) and *Ars Longa Vita Brevis* (1969) are clumsy beasts that stomp with equal disdain on jazz, blues, Tchaikovsky, Sibelius, and *West Side Story*. When the group split up, Keith Emerson joined with King Crimson bassist and vocalist John Wetton and drummer Carl Palmer from the Crazy World of Arthur Brown to form the progressive-rock supergroup Emerson, Lake and Palmer.

Of all these bands, King Crimson provides the most direct link between psychedelia and progressive rock, and it was by far the most influential group of the nascent genre. Its 1969 debut, *In the Court of the Crimson King*, suffers at times from instrumental excess and pointless displays of virtuosity, but "21st Century Schizoid Man" is a concise rock song driven by a killer riff, sinister vocals, and Beat-poetic lyrics that evoke the panic of a bad acid trip, "The Court of the Crimson King" is a fanciful medieval epic decorated with lovely flute work, and "I Talk to the Wind" is a beautiful, idyllic psychedelic folk song. Bandleader Robert Fripp did more interesting things with feedback and odd harmonics than any guitarist since Hendrix, and drummer Michael Giles added control and chops to Keith Moon's chaos, inspiring Phil Collins, Bill Bruford, and many others who followed.

THE PROGRESSIVE-ROCK EXPLOSION

PROGRESSIVE ROCK IS A GENRE that has been largely reviled by critics, and not always for sound musical reasons. "Why British bands feel compelled to quote the classics, however tongue-in-cheek, leads into the murky waters of class and nation analysis," John Rockwell wrote in *The Rolling Stone Illustrated History of Rock & Roll*. "In comparison with the British, Americans tend to be happy apes. Most American rockers wouldn't know a Beethoven symphony if they were run down by one in the middle of a freeway. One result of such ignorance is that American art (music, painting, poetry, films, etc.) can develop untroubled by lame affectations of a cultured sensibility. In Britain, the lower classes enjoy no such isolation. The class divisions and the crushing weight of high culture flourish essentially untrammeled. Rockers seem far more eager to 'dignify' their work, to make it acceptable for upper-class approbation."

It's true that the progressive movement was in part a self-conscious attempt to elevate rock 'n' roll by embracing high-culture values such as technical virtuosity and conceptual density. Many musicians in the first wave of British psychedelia were upper-middle-class kids who discovered rock, drugs, and the London nightlife and dropped out of college or art school. *Sgt. Pepper's Lonely Hearts Club Band* convinced them that they could make music that was just as serious as the art they'd been studying before they tuned in, turned on, and dropped out—and maybe it could even be respectable enough to please Mum and Dad. But more than any genre besides heavy metal, "prog" (as aficionados call it) has gotten a bum rap. "Pompous," "self-indulgent," "bloated," and "pretentious" are just a few of the critics' favorite slurs. What is sorely lacking in this limited discourse is any sort of workable aesthetic for evaluating the music's golden era.

In his book *Listening to the Future: The Time of Progressive Rock 1968-1978* (a genre study similar to this one), Bill Martin pinpoints five traits that define the movement: 1) It is visionary and experimental. 2) It is played, at least in part, on instruments typically associated with rock. 3) It is made by musicians who have consummate instrumental and compositional skills. 4) At its core it is a very English phenomenon. 5) It is expressive of some longstanding romantic and prophetic aspects of British culture. Point one is pretty much up to the listener: One man's breakthrough or innovation might be another's failed experiment. Point three is where many critics had problems: It seemed to eliminate any rocker who didn't have the chops to keep up, and rock is supposed to be a democratic art form. But just because punk made it clear that you didn't have to know how to play your instrument in order to make great rock 'n' roll, that didn't make the converse false. Who said you *couldn't* make great rock if you *did* know how to play? As for the charge of pretensions, it's unfair to say that prog-rockers had any more of them than the artists in any other genre. What musician doesn't aspire to accomplish *something* when picking up a guitar to write a song?

Martin further argues that critics seem to be daunted by the vision of the prog bands. He maintains that what some have dismissed as drug-addled sci-fi ramblings—all that talk of brain salad surgery and the return of the fire witch—is in fact a utopian vision, a glimpse of a perfect world based on English traditions of romantic poetry and mythmaking about idyllic and entirely invented lands. ("In and around the lake, mountains come out of the sky and they stand there," as Yes sang in "Roundabout.") Well, why *not* celebrate the sunny possibilities of the imagination? There are more than enough bad trips and mundane landscapes in everyday life.

In my view, prog is best judged by the same standards used to determine good psychedelic rock from bad psychedelic rock. It has to work first and foremost as *rock*—it must have the immediacy, drive, basic hummability, and visceral kick of all good rock 'n' roll. Only then can it strive for the added goals of impressing the listener with technical virtuosity, or of transporting him or her to a place that exists only in the imagination and in the space between the headphones.

As with any rock movement, prog can be divided over the course of its long history into countless subgenres. The best-known groups are the "symphonic" bands that emerged in 1970: groups such as Yes, Emerson, Lake and Palmer, and Jethro Tull. Later variations of the sound came from the "pomp" or "pop-prog" bands (Styx and Kansas), "prog metal" (starting with Rush and flourishing today with Dream Theatre), the jazzy "Canterbury sound" (which began with the Soft Machine but continued with groups such as Caravan, Gentle Giant, and Happy the Man), "neo-prog" (which started when Marillion picked up where early Genesis left off), "Dutch rock" (which begins with the happy yodelers Focus of "Hocus Pocus" fame), "Euro rock" (Nektar, Message, Analogy, and perhaps the Danish psychedelic-pop/pseudo-prog band Savage Rose), the "French-theatrical" bands (Mona Lisa, Angipatch), Italian and Japanese prog, "Zeuhl" music (bizarro jazz fusion a la France's Magma), and "rock in opposition" (avant-gardists such as Henry Cow, the Art Bears, and Thinking Plague).

Diving into this confusing tangle of complex musical styles is beyond the scope of this book, and as prog continued to mutate and evolve, its connection to psychedelia (and to rock) grew ever more tenuous. The sidebar offers my choices for the ten most psychedelic (and I would say best) progressive-rock albums; discussions of the rest are best left to books devoted entirely to the genre. But before this tome departs from the murky waters of those fabled topographic oceans, it's worth taking a closer look at two other artists.

PLUS... TUBULAR... BELLS!

SOMETIMES WRONGLY LUMPED INTO the New Age genre, Mike Oldfield's music is more like instrumental surf-rock given a psyche-delic twist and taken to its ultimate conclusion via symphonic instrumentation and studio wizardry. An introspective child subject to fits of depression, Oldfield turned to the guitar for solace from a troubled family life. He was influenced by the baroque folk of John Renbourn and Bert Jansch, and he started his career in 1967 as part of a folk duo with his sister, Sally. In 1970, at age seventeen, he linked up with former Soft Machine bassist Kevin Ayers in a group called the Whole World, and he started to turn heads as a soloist. "I would do an electric guitar solo and, depending on how pissed I was, I used to let it feed back and do somersaults all over the floor," he said in the liner notes to the 1993 box set, *Mike Oldfield: Elements.*

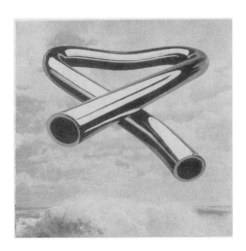

The Ultimate Psychedelic Rock Library: Mike Oldfield's astounding one-man debut, Tubular Bells *(Virgin).*

Oldfield lived with members of the band, and he recorded the demos for what would become *Tubular Bells* in his bedroom. Using a tape recorder borrowed from Ayers, he found that he could over-dub more than one instrument if he masked the erase head with a piece of cardboard. Virgin Records founders Simon Draper and Richard Branson heard Oldfield's tape and agreed to front him some time at a sixteen-track studio. The guitarist recorded some twenty-eight instrumental parts—including everything from Spanish guitar to Lowrey organ to glockenspiel—saturating the master tape with some two-thousand overdubs. The result was the first half of *Tubular Bells*, a sprawling, psychedelic instrumental full of hum-along melodies that serves as a sort of a soundtrack for an imaginary film. (Four minutes of the piece would later be used on the soundtrack of *The Exorcist*.) This is classical music for people who wouldn't other-wise touch the stuff, or rock 'n' roll that rejects conventional song structure, vocals, and instrumentation. (And who ever said you couldn't rock out with a glockenspiel?) A masterpiece of headphone rock, the lulling tour of Oldfield's bedroom world is interrupted only when Vivian Stanshall of the Bonzo Dog Doo-Dah Band makes his grand entrance to introduce each of the instruments: "Double speed guitar...one slightly distorted guitar...plus...tubular...bells!" The dramatic voice-over caused more than a few tranced-out potheads to jerk awake and spill the bongwater.

Released in 1973, *Tubular Bells* sold sixteen million copies. Virgin was established as a major record company, and Oldfield was signed to a lengthy contract, a situation he came to regret. ("It was a horrible situation to be in, just like serving a prison sentence," he told me years later.) The artist followed his spectacular debut with two more albums adhering to the formula of one long instrumental per vinyl album side, and *Hergest Ridge* and *Ommadawn* are only slightly less engaging than the debut. The first live performance of *Tubular Bells* drew together an all-star ensemble featuring Ayers, Mick Taylor of the Rolling Stones, Steve Hillage and Pierre Moerlen of Gong, and Fred Frith of Henry Cow. Oldfield also popped up alongside Ayers, Nico, John Cale, and Brian Eno in the ultimate art-rock supergroup, recorded on the album, *June 1, 1974*. Later, he toured with a fifty-member band captured on the excellent 1979 live album, *Mike Oldfield Exposed*. But the rest of Oldfield's discography is spottier.

In the early '80s the guitarist formed the Mike Oldfield Group, a sextet featuring powerful vocalist Maggie Reilly. The group recorded *QE2* (1980), which introduced shorter, poppier songs, and *Five Miles Out* (1982), which scored two European hits with the title track and "Family Man," which later became a hit for Daryl Hall and John Oates. Despite the success of these albums, Oldfield said

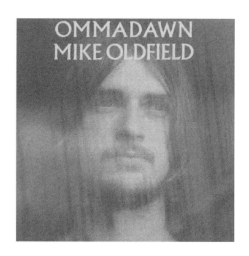

The Ultimate Psychedelic Rock Library: Ommadawn *(Virgin) is an even more tuneful psychedelic soundscape than* Tubular Bells. *This time the solitary auteur gets some help from the African percussion group Jabula and Paddy Moloney of the Chieftains on uilleann pipes.*

he found writing pop songs "limiting and boring." In 1984 he returned to instrumental soundtracks, recording the moving score to *The Killing Fields*. Finally freed from his original label, he made a sequel to *Tubular Bells* for Warner Bros. in 1992, working with producer Trevor Horn (briefly a member of later-day Yes). "All these years I've avoided sounding like *Tubular Bells* while a lot of people have been doing the opposite," he told me at the time. "You hear it on adverts and film soundtracks. Apparently the film soundtrack world will say, 'I want a piece of *Tubular Bells*-type music here.' It's become integrated into the culture. So I was talking to this guy from the record company and I said, 'Maybe I should start sounding like myself.'" A slicker, digital version of the original, *Tubular Bells 2* is still full of hooks, unencumbered by dumb lyrics, and fueled by a healthy sense of humor. (The strait-laced announcer this time is everyone's favorite screen villain, Alan Rickman. "We did try and get Viv Stanshall to do this new one, but the day that we turned up to pick him up for the session, he was asleep in the bath covered by a pot plant and wouldn't respond to proddings to get up," Oldfield said.)

While his instrumental visions aren't nearly as unique as they once were, Oldfield's work stands with Brian Eno's ambient albums as psychedelic rock's version of respectable background music. "I think my music is what rock 'n' roll would have become if it hadn't been for punk rock and it hadn't been for sampling," he told me. "But I suppose if punk and sampling hadn't happened, it would have been rather pompous. You just have to listen to it and watch the performance to see that when people play *Tubular Bells 2*, there's a lot of fun in there, a lot of laughs and a lot of enjoyment.

It's not like 'I'm a genius' stuff. You'll find *that* if you look at the Guns N' Roses video with the orchestra. Now *that's* pompous."

WATCHERS OF THE SKIES

> The visual sense, the kind of landscape of another world—
> it's definitely a secret world on *Us* where there are a lot of
> psychedelic references. Psychedelia is definitely a period
> that interests me. It was one of the few periods where
> experimentation *was* the style.
>
> —Peter Gabriel, 1993

IN THE BEGINNING there was Genesis the art-rock band, the oh-so-serious quintet of polite, proper, upper-middle-class boys' school students. Tony Banks and Peter Gabriel met as teens attending the Charterhouse school near Godalming, Surrey, and they struck up a friendship based on playing songs by the Beatles, Otis Redding, and Screamin' Jay Hawkins. Their music-room jams attracted several classmates, including Mike Rutherford. In late 1968 this loose-knit group recorded a demo that Gabriel slipped to Charterhouse graduate Jonathan King, who had scored a sub-Donovan novelty hit in 1965 with "Everyone's Gone to the Moon." He liked the band's gentle, Beatles-inspired melodies, and he produced its first album, *From Genesis to Revelation*, released on the Decca label in March 1969. The album sold only six hundred copies and the band was dropped, but the eighteen-year-old musicians weren't easily discouraged.

Genesis moved into an isolated cottage in Dorking. The musicians set up in a circle and jammed for hours every day for six months, forging the flowing, pastoral sound that would characterize their best early work. Former Creation manager Tony Stratton-Smith heard one of their rare gigs and signed them to his new label, Charisma Records, fostering their development on 1970's *Trespass* and 1971's *Nursery Cryme*. On the latter, Gabriel, Banks, and Rutherford were joined by two new members, guitarist Steve Hackett and drummer Phil Collins. "Genesis was full of charm and weakness," Hackett told biographer Armando Gallo in *Genesis: I Know What I Like*. "Feminine, you know. Very pastel shades. 'Stagnation' is a very impressionist sort of thing, very evocative of branches and leaves. It conjures up feelings of scenery to me."

The romantic sound that attracted Hackett gelled for the first time on record on 1972's *Foxtrot*. Unlike Yes or ELP, Genesis was more interested in sounds and textures than virtuosic solos, and its long, ever-shifting songs keep the focus on melody and storytelling.

The Ultimate Psychedelic Rock Library: Genesis's Foxtrot *(Atlantic) builds to a climax with the epic "Supper's Ready."*

Banks' regal organ introduces "Watcher of the Skies," which includes a bravura Gabriel vocal about aliens and the end of the world. Twelve-string guitars create a folkie backdrop for "Time Table," a dramatic tune that couches anti-war sentiments in a medieval setting, and Gabriel plays several different roles in "Get 'Em Out by Friday," a tune that satirizes greedy slumlords. But the album's centerpiece is the side-long, hook-filled epic, "Supper's Ready," a song disguised as a screenplay (or vice versa). The tune deals with no less than the balance between good and evil and man's place in the universe, and it was inspired by an odd experience that Gabriel had with his first wife Jill at her parents' house in Kensington. "We just stared at each other, and strange things began to happen," the singer told Gallo. "We saw other faces in each other, and I was very frightened. It was almost as if something had come into us and was using us as a meeting point. It was late at night, and we were tired and all the rest, so it was quite easy for us to hallucinate, [though] we hadn't been drinking or drugging."

After *Foxtrot*, Gabriel's performances started to get more theatrical. He donned masks, robes, and giant bat wings to act out the characters in different songs, and he became the center of attention (not surprising, considering that the other members played sitting down and staring at their feet). The band followed with 1973's *Selling England by the Pound*, but its most effective merger of theater and musical invention is *The Lamb Lies Down on Broadway*. The double album was written in 1974 at a time when Gabriel was pulling away from the group. The singer argued for the opportunity to write the lyrics alone as part of a unified story, and he added his vocals to music that the band had already recorded. *The Lamb* sounds a bit

The Ultimate Psychedelic Rock Library: The Lamb Lies Down on Broadway *(Atlantic) is a masterful if somewhat befuddled psychedelic concept album.*

disjointed at points, and the science-fiction tale of a Puerto Rican graffiti artist swept into a hallucinatory underworld of Lamia and Slippermen is a bit hard to fathom. But the album is full of twisted but memorable melodies and unique sounds, including Banks' exotic synthesizer textures and Hackett's conversational guitar lines.

The Lamb inspired the band's most elaborate stage show yet, and the group performed the album in its entirety more than one hundred times. When Gabriel announced that he would be leaving Genesis at the end of the tour, the musicians didn't try to dissuade him. "They didn't like what I was becoming," he told Gallo. "I felt that my hands were beginning to feel tied within the group because the publicity thing was getting worse rather than better; the jealousy." He launched his solo career in 1976 with the first of three self-titled albums. Produced by Bob Ezrin, the high point of the first is the celebratory single, "Solsbury Hill," a messianic fantasy with an indelible melody that some saw as his comment about leaving Genesis. The 1978 follow-up was produced by Robert Fripp, and it's a darker, sparer effort that pays tribute to the punk aesthetic on the tune "D.I.Y." But the singer's best post-Genesis album is the third *Peter Gabriel*, produced by Steve Lillywhite and released in 1980. Working with Kate Bush, XTC's Dave Gregory, Fripp, and bassist Tony Levin, among others, Gabriel focused on the rhythms (he was a former drummer) and his vocals, using the other instruments to add color, texture, or the odd instrumental hook. Over tribal, cymbal-less, pseudo-African grooves, he delivers ten vignettes that explore the minds of a presidential assassin ("Family Snapshot"), a burglar-home invader ("Intruder"), and an imprisoned mental patient ("Lead a Normal Life"). In "Biko," he pays heartfelt tribute to the slain South African activist, and in "Games Without Frontiers," he creates one of the catchiest singles ever about the stupidity of war.

Gabriel's subsequent efforts offer variations on these formulas, incorporating ethnic instruments and more elaborate beats, or streamlining the production for MTV-friendly dance tunes. Hits such as "Sledgehammer" and "Steam" changed his status from

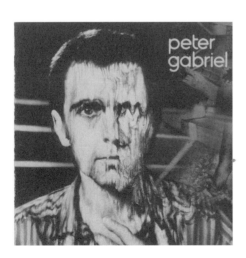

The Ultimate Psychedelic Rock Library: Peter Gabriel's third self-titled solo album (Mercury) stands as his masterpiece.

art-rocker to pop celebrity, but he continued to experiment with more ethereal sounds on soundtracks such as *Birdy* and *The Last Temptation of Christ*. He championed worthy artists from around the world, his live shows consistently set new standards for what was possible in the enormodomes, and he made a welcomed return to art-rock form after a ten-year wait with 2002's *Up*. In contrast, after Collins came out from behind the drum set to lead the band as vocalist on two strong progressive-rock albums (1976's rollicking *A Trick of the Tail* and 1977's pastoral *Wind & Wuthering*), Genesis followed a slow but steady decline into stultifying mediocrity. After Hackett left the group, it increasingly became a vehicle for platinum-selling easy-listening hits such as "Misunderstanding," "Mama," "Invisible Touch," and "Land of Confusion."

Sitting in the presidential suite at New York's haughty Peninsula Hotel in 1991, I talked with the three remaining members of Genesis about their seventeenth album, a declaration of pride in dinosaurdom called *We Can't Dance*. Did they ever wish they could record under a different name, I asked, lock themselves in their studio, get really stoned, and cut loose to make another album as willfully weird as *The Lamb Lies Down on Broadway?* "I suppose if one was doing that, one would probably try to be more off the wall," Banks said wistfully, transformed for a moment into the teenage musician jamming in the cottage in Dorking. "I think the sheer reason for doing it would surely be to try to do a few things that might be disastrous."

"At the same time, it might be nice to do something like we've just done and call it a different name and see how it's received," Collins added with more than a touch of annoyance. "By saying that, you're playing into—what's your name?—Jim's hands, because you're admitting that, because we're going in and calling it a different band, we actually have confines within Genesis that we want to stick to."

"Well that's a fair enough comment to make," Banks said, scowling at his partner. "Because there's probably some truth in it."

A Dozen Progressive-Rock Albums That Stand As Great Psychedelic Rock

1. King Crimson, *In the Court of the Crimson King* (Caroline)
The album that got the progressive ball rolling: Symphonic arrangements meet poetic lyrics and the influential guitar playing of Robert Fripp, who, depending on your perspective, is either the genre's biggest hero, its most insufferable boor, or both. One thing's for sure: He never rocked harder than he does on the metal-edged "21st Century Schizoid Man."

2. Yes, *The Yes Album* (Atlantic)

More than any other group, Yes epito-
mizes progressive rock, hence its dominating presence on this list. But it also
rocked harder than many of its peers,
maintaining a vital pulse and delivering
memorable riffs in between the showy solos. Its third album
boasts three brilliant tracks: the anthemic "Yours Is No
Disgrace," the epic "Starship Trooper" (inspired by Robert A.
Heinlein's novel), and "Your Move"/"(I've Seen) All Good
People," which, in classic prog-geek style, uses a chess game as
a metaphor for romantic relations.

3. Yes, *Fragile* (Atlantic)

This is still the prog album most often
celebrated by FM-rock radio, thanks to
the relatively concise and catchy but
still fantastically evocative epics
"Roundabout," "Long Distance
Runaround," and "Heart of the Sunrise."
A treat, for sure, but the least of the Yes albums on this list.

4. Jethro Tull, *Aqualung* **(Capitol)**

With half an album devoted to portraying
forgotten faces from the urban underground and half a bitter, sustained attack
on the hypocrisy of the Church of
England, you'd think this was a punk
record instead of Jethro Tull's premiere concept album. In fact,
the band rocks harder than it's often given credit for (especially on the title track, "Cross-Eyed Mary," and "Locomotive
Breath"), as well as incorporating elements of free jazz (via
Rahsaan Roland Kirk) and traditional Celtic music (as filtered
through the folk-rock of Fairport Convention), all while flamboyant frontman Ian Anderson reinvents himself as a medieval
Merlin in a modern-rock world.

5. Yes, *Close to the Edge* **(Atlantic)**

Generally hailed by fans as the band's
finest moment, this sweeping double
album combines Jon Anderson's helium-
voiced singing and space-age hippie
visions with the almost absurd ambition
of the musicians. Yet even as they frantically work their way
up and down fret- and keyboards, they never fail to lose sight
of the mission: conducting a cinematic tour of the sort of
strange and otherworldly landscapes famously evoked in
Roger Dean's watercolor cover art.

6. Jethro Tull, *Thick As a Brick* (Capitol)

Even more than *Aqualung*, this album is the most "prog" that Jethro Tull ever got. Consisting of one very long song, it's a satirical concept album about the jour-ney from adolescence to manhood, full of medieval melodies, symphonic swells, classical rips, frenetic flute, and the sadly under-rated guitar playing of the ever-tasteful Martin Barre.

7. Emerson, Lake and Palmer, *Brain Salad Surgery* (Atlantic)

The dark, creepy, some would say gothic ambiance of this album is established by the H.R. Giger cover. The music is no less somber, from the opening hymn, "Jerusalem," an Old Testament anthem based on William Blake's poem, through the eerie but seductive "Still...You Turn Me On," and from Emerson's flashy reinterpretation of Argentine composer Alberto Ginastera's first piano concerto, fourth movement (retitled "Toccata"), through the nearly thir-ty-minute closing epic, "Karn Evil 9" ("Welcome back my friends to the show that never ends"—nor, for that matter, does the song).

8. Magma, *Mekanik Destruktiw Kommandoh* (Phantom)

Led by the extraordinary drummer Christian Vander, this French "Zeuhl" band veered wildly between ultra-repetitive, percussive minimalism and ultra-bombastic, choir- and horn-driven maximalism. This is the group's magnum opus, a blatant rip-off of "Carmina Burana," and an increasingly tense portrait of a totalitarian invasion. At least that's what I *think* it's about—the group sang entirely in "Kobaian," a language that Vander invented as the native tongue of a fictional universe.

9. Yes, *Going for the One* (Atlantic)

The punk explosion of 1976 inspired a new vitality in several of the first-generation prog bands, prompting a return to shorter and catchier songs and more driving rhythms. This is the last start-to-finish great Yes album. Recorded in Montreux, Switzerland, complete with cathedral organs and lap steel guitar, it boasts a focus, coherence, and sheer visceral kick that the group has rarely matched since, especially on songs like the title track and the enchanting "Wondrous Stories."

10. Gentle Giant,
Giant for a Day (1978)

Hardcore prog fans tend to prefer earlier Gentle Giant efforts such as *Acquiring the Taste* (1971) and *Octopus* (1973), but just as punk kicked Yes into high gear one last time, it inspired these long-running classical-symphonic-Canterbury favorites to veer toward inspired pop songs, albeit ones that clocked in at eight minutes or longer.

11. King Crimson, *Discipline*
(EG, 1981)

Crimson maniacs (the sort of people who indulge in 50,000-word debates on Robert Fripp news groups) might place other efforts on the list before this one— say, 1973's *Larks' Tongues in Aspic*. But the debut by the reinvigorated quartet of Fripp, Adrian Belew, Tony Levin, and Bill Bruford illustrates that prog did not die after its first golden era, and that its vocabulary could be expanded to include everything from Talking Heads-style New Wave ("Elephant Talk," with its nifty, roaring-pachyderm guitar) to polyrhythmic world beats ("Thela Hun Ginjeet").

12. Marillion, *Misplaced Childhood* (Sanctuary)

The best of the second-wave progressive or "neo-prog" bands, Marillion had its finest moment with lead singer Fish on this concept album about youthful inno-cence lost and regained. Taking its cues from early Genesis, the quintet stripped down the basic prog sound ever so slight-ly and scored English pop hits with "Kayleigh" and "Lavender," tunes that are undeniably effective.

SEVEN

7

JUST SAY YES:
Psychedelia Stretches Out

Jimi Hendrix was the flower generation's electric nigger dandy—its king stud and golden calf, its maker of mighty dope music, its most outrageously visible force—super-spade, in the argot of the day. Though his music still sounds resonant today—even his most faddish stuff, some-how—his image remains a troubling one. For Hendrix was a revolutionary musician—perhaps the only one, in the end, to come out of the whole mid-'60s psychedelic explo-sion. Yet this has often been obscured, both by the rather degrading image and by the freakishly flamboyant veneer that helped make his art so popular.

—John Morthland,
The Rolling Stone Illustrated History of Rock & Roll

STARTING IN THE LATE '60s and continuing into the '70s, the influence of psychedelic drugs and the rock 'n' roll they inspired could clearly be heard in other musical genres, including soul, jazz, and blues. The most influential artists synthesized sounds in ways that hadn't been heard before, and the first and most influential synthesist was a guitarist from Seattle.

Critic John Morthland wrote the words quoted above in the mid-'70s. Through the '80s, yuppie nostalgia for the halcyon '60s obscured Hendrix's contributions even more, at least in the minds of post-Baby Boomers. Today, record store bins are filled with dozens of pieces of Hendrix product, despite the fact that he sanctioned the release of only three studio albums and one live disc in his lifetime. It's difficult if not impossible for new listeners to assess his legacy when the meaningless notion that he was "the greatest electric guitarist who ever lived" is carved in granite on the base of his statue in the rock pantheon. "The 'authorized version' of the Jimi Hendrix experience (*sic*) is that Hendrix was a crazy black man who did funny things with a guitar, had thousands of women, and eventually died of drugs, which was a shame because he was a really good guitarist, and he could play it with his teeth, too," Charles Shaar Murray wrote in *Crosstown Traffic*, the best guide to appreciating Hendrix's music. The problem with the "authorized version" is that it doesn't tally with the facts.

He was born John Allen Hendrix in Seattle in 1942 (when he was three, his father legally changed his name to James Marshall Hendrix), and he turned to the guitar at age thirteen as refuge from a troubled home life. He dropped out of high school, joined the 101st Airborne, and was discharged in 1962 when he injured his back. For the next three years, Hendrix worked as a freelance R&B sideman on the Southern chitlin' circuit, playing with Little Richard, the Isley Brothers, and Curtis Knight, among others. In 1966 he struck out on his own, leading Jimmy James and the Blue Flames in an extended run at the Café Wha? in Greenwich Village. If Hendrix hadn't been exposed to LSD before—and the biographies are sketchy on this point—he certainly sampled it when he began hanging out with Ed Sanders and the Fugs. By this time, he'd become a devotee of John Coltrane, Ornette Coleman, and Roland Kirk, and echoes of free jazz could be heard in his extended onstage jams. These soon attracted the rock cognoscenti. Animals bassist Chas Chandler presented himself as manager and brought Hendrix to London in September 1966. The guitarist was immersed in the nascent psychedelic rock scene, and he was paired with the Experience: Englishmen Noel Redding, a guitarist turned bassist, and Mitch Mitchell, a jazzy drummer heavily influenced by Elvin Jones.

Over the next four years—until he choked on his own vomit in September 1970—Hendrix produced four albums. *Are You Experienced* (1967) and the singles that preceded it are raw, focused psychedelic rock that wouldn't sound out of place on *Nuggets*. Much of *Axis: Bold as Love* was recorded at the same Chandler-produced sessions, but it's looser, jazzier, and more expansive. *Electric Ladyland* (1968) is the only album Hendrix produced himself, and it's a sprawling exploration of the studio as a place to create what he called "sound paintings." Finally, there's *Band of Gypsys*, recorded live at New York's Fillmore East with army buddy Billy Cox and drummer Buddy Miles on New Year's Eve, 1969. With the exception

The Ultimate Psychedelic Rock Library: Are You Experienced *(MCA) remains Hendrix's rawest (and best) recording.*

of "Machine Gun," it's a sloppy throwaway released to pay off the claims of an earlier manager.

Those who worked with Hendrix talk about his high standards in the studio, but those standards were trashed soon after his death. *The Cry of Love* and *Soundtrack from Rainbow Bridge* (1971) cannibalized the double album in progress when he died at age twenty-seven. In the years that followed, jams, demos, and studio experiments were packaged and sold with the justification that every note played by the greatest guitarist who ever lived was something to be cherished. But the albums that Hendrix himself sanctioned show that his accomplishment was crafting songs, sounds, and stylistic syntheses—not solos. "Hendrix was a composer and lyricist of considerable gifts, but his songwriting talents have been largely overshadowed by his achievements as a showman and an instrumentalist," Murray wrote. His three studio albums succeed because of the emotions conveyed by the melodies and lyrics on songs such as "Manic Depression," "Purple Haze," "Spanish Castle Magic,"

"Rainy Day, Dream Away," and "1983...(A Merman I Should Turn to Be)." These songs didn't exist just so Hendrix could solo over them. On all of these tracks, Hendrix is more interested in creating moods with the sound of his guitar than impressing people with the notes that he's playing.

Hendrix's time as an R&B sideman taught him that rhythm guitar was as important as lead. His style was based on playing both at once, as well as employing the psychedelic rocker's arsenal of effects (feedback, wah-wah, fuzz and distortion, variable tape speed, and the rotating Leslie speaker). "It's the most psychedelic experience I ever had, going to see Hendrix play," Pete Townshend told Murray. "When he started to play, something changed: colors changed, everything changed." In a famous dis of his appearance at the Monterey Pop Festival, critic Robert Christgau called Hendrix "a psychedelic Uncle Tom." Unlike many of his peers, his songs didn't directly address political or racial issues. But as Murray and others pointed out, Hendrix's whole public life was a political act—a chal-

The Ultimate Psychedelic Rock Library: Axis: Bold as Love *(MCA) further stretched the boundaries of what could be done in a four-track recording studio.*

lenge to conformity among both whites and blacks—and he did have a political vision, albeit a utopian one. Hendrix was fascinated with science fiction (the exploration of outer space) and psychedelic drugs (the exploration of inner space), not because he wanted to escape but because he wanted to create an ideal world. He had a dream, and he called it the Electric or Sky Church. Murray described it as "a context for participatory worship, learning and communion without regard for denomination or demeanor."

Hendrix himself rejected the label "psychedelic" for his music. "It's a mixture of rock, blues, and jazz, a music that's still developing, that's just now coming, a music of the future," he is quoted as saying in the liner notes to MCA's 1993 reissue of *Are You Experienced*. "We just happened to be playing freak-out and psychedelic things, but it does bother us because 'psychedelic' only means mind expansion anyway. There's so many other types of music." Wrote Murray: "His unique musical formulation—that 'jazz,' 'blues,' 'rock,' and 'soul' were not distinct musics which needed to be combined through fusions and hyphenations, but one music seen from different perspectives—was utterly his own."

This originality shines forth on Hendrix's most enduring psychedelic anthems. "Third Stone from the Sun" and "Manic Depression" synthesize free jazz and psychedelic garage rock. "Red House" and "Voodoo Chile" fuse psychedelic rock and blues, complete with the ancient black-magic mysteries. ("Hendrix played Delta blues for sure—only the Delta may have been on Mars," bluesman and critic Tony Glover once wrote.) As for soul, it was there in the rhythms and in the way that Hendrix arranged tunes for his bands. "Jimi Hendrix's music could not have existed with-

The Ultimate Psychedelic Rock Library: Electric Ladyland *(MCA) was the only album Hendrix produced himself.*

out soul music, and modern soul music would have been inconceivable without his," Murray wrote.

One of the saddest aspects of Hendrix's legacy is that the syntheses he created were never extended in jazz or blues. The jazz fusion that followed was arid and vapid, full of indulgent instrumental displays and devoid of rock 'n' roll grit or punch. (Miles Davis hinted at what his aborted collaboration with Hendrix could have sounded like on *Agharta,* but it was only an approximation.) Plenty of blues musicians invoke Hendrix's tones and notes while remaining hopelessly earthbound in their vision. But things were different in the realms of soul and funk.

COSMIC CONTRIVANCES AND PSYCHEDELIC SOUL

"Mommy, what's a Funkadelic?"
"Someone from Carolina who encountered eternity on
LSD and vowed to contain it in a groove."
                              —George Clinton, 1970

THE EXPERIENCE FOLLOWED Sly and the Family Stone at
Woodstock, but it was the other way around on the pop charts.
Hendrix's success paved the way for Texas-born Sylvester Stewart, a
former Bay Area record producer and deejay whose radio show mixed
Bob Dylan, the psychedelic Beatles, and R&B. Stewart/Stone took the
same approach with his own band, adding a slippery bass and snap-
py backbeat that took prominence over everything else in the mix.

Like Hendrix, Stone had a vision of a psychedelic utopia. His
band was a microcosm of this ideal world: men and women, blacks

*The Ultimate Psychedelic Rock
Library: Sly and the Family Stone's*
There's a Riot Goin' On *(Epic)—
the aural equivalent of*
Naked Lunch.

and whites, working together, shifting roles, and sharing the spotlight. He urged the rest of America to do the same on songs such as
"Everyday People," "Everybody Is a Star," and "I Want to Take You
Higher." But like many idealists, his optimism was drained by the end
of the '60s. Critic Dave Marsh called 1971's *There's a Riot Goin' On* the
aural equivalent of William Burroughs's *Naked Lunch.* "Sly's utopia
had revealed its other face: hell," he wrote in *The Rolling Stone
Illustrated History of Rock & Roll.* As the '70s progressed, Stone was
increasingly lost in a druggy haze and his albums turned to uninspired disco, until he finally withdrew from music completely.

Others picked up where he left off. Curtis Mayfield and War
blended elements of Hendrix's guitar sound and Stone's rhythms
into soul and pop classics. Hendrix pals the Chambers Brothers created a brilliant psychedelic single with 1968's "Time Has Come
Today." Stevie Wonder adopted psychedelia's open-ended approach
to synthesizers and the recording studio, using it to talk with God,
deride superstition, and rail against living in the city. Working with
producer Norman Whitfield, Wonder's Motown labelmates the
Temptations produced a string of uplifting psychedelic singles,
including "I Can't Get Next to You," "Cloud Nine," "Psychedelic
Shack," and "Ball of Confusion." Comedian Bill Cosby parodied
this outbreak of psychedelic soul on a 1968 single called "Hooray
for the Salvation Army Band." Like many members of his generation, he dismissed the music as escapism, but this was before he or
anyone else had heard Parliament-Funkadelic.

George Clinton was born in Kannapolis, North Carolina, in
1941, and he likes to say his momma delivered him in an outhouse.
In 1952 his family moved north to Newark, New Jersey. He found

The Ultimate Psychedelic Rock Library: The Temptations' Psychedelic Shack *(Motown) is the perfect soundtrack for a psychedelic house party.*

escape from the spiritless urban sprawl in doo-wop music, and he formed his first group at age fourteen, taking the name from a brand of cigarettes. The Parliaments recorded for two small labels based in Detroit, and Clinton was intrigued by groups such as the Amboy Dukes, the Stooges, and the MC5. He was also a fan of the Beatles and Sly Stone, and he was impressed by what they had accomplished in the studio. Taking the PATH train from Newark to Manhattan after a day's work at the Uptown Tonsorial Parlor, the young barber and musician immersed himself in the psychedelic subculture at clubs like the Cheetah, and he soon convinced his group to adopt its colorful fashions.

The band traveled regularly to Boston and indulged in LSD courtesy of the test program at Harvard University. "We weren't even supposed to be there, but the kids were giving it to us," Clinton told me. "We met Tim Leary, but we didn't know who the hell he was and he didn't know who we were. We were older, so we thought they were all crazy. We were just having a ball with the free love, and we just thought we were getting over. But it just kind of changed us. The LSD thing and traveling around really opened us up and got us out of the whole ghetto thing."

Another turning point came when the Parliaments opened for the Vanilla Fudge and used that band's massive Marshall stacks. "Now we knew what that sound was about," Clinton said. The band dropped the "s" from its name and started honing a new and weirder sound, extending soul, R&B, and psychedelic rock into a new brand of funk. Motown passed, but another Detroit label called Westbound was interested. For a while, it wasn't clear that Clinton had rights to the name, so the same band started recording as the Funkadelics. When Clinton recovered the Parliament moniker, the group started using that name to record for Casablanca. Thus Clinton pulled off the rare feat of signing the same band to two labels at once.

The ParliaFunkadelicment family came to include several veterans of James Brown's band—Fred Wesley, Maceo Parker, Rick Gardner, and William "Bootsy" Collins—as well as Hendrix-inspired guitarists Eddie Hazel, Glenn Goins, and Dewayne "Blackbird" McKnight. Parliament was the more focused, accessible, horn-driven group; Funkadelic, the trippier, guitar-happy, experimental outfit. Albums were released at the frantic pace of two or three a year into the early '80s, when the bands fell apart amid mounting financial and drug problems. Funkadelic's swan song was 1981's pioneering electronic effort, *The Electric Spanking of War Babies*, which briefly coaxed Sly Stone out of retirement.

Most Clinton albums are equal parts brilliance and bullshit, but the music is bearable even at its most indulgent because the emphasis is always on the hypnotic groove. The bands were never really about songs, so they are ill-served by "greatest hits" collections. Listeners tend to wind up owning either all or none of the thirty-odd releases, not counting offshoots such as Bootsy's Rubber Band, a side project that spun out of the bassist's ability to improvise long cosmic monologues in the style of Hendrix. At the core of every effort is the rhythm section, harmony group vocals, and trademark chanting, but at any given time, these can be augmented by bagpipes, steel guitars, synthesizers, early drum machines, cartoony Alvin-and-the-Chipmunks vocals, and countless other weird overdubs, most of them done on the fly.

One of the best of the early albums, 1970's acid-drenched *Free Your Mind and Your Ass Will Follow,* was recorded and mixed in one day. "I had just learned about panning," Clinton says in a piece entitled "Brothers from Another Planet," a fascinating essay reprinted in critic John Corbett's collection, *Extended Play.* "I still don't know about the board. I don't wanna know nothin' about the

The Ultimate Psychedelic Rock Library: Funkadelic's Free Your Mind and Your Ass Will Follow *(Westbound) stands as one of the funky family's strongest albums.*

board... Sly said, 'Hey, man, don't learn no better.' I said, 'What do you mean?' He said, 'If you knew better, you wouldn't do that!' It takes you a long time to think about what that means: If you knew better, you wouldn't make those *nice mistakes*."

Clinton's lyrics can be scatological or nonsensical, but a central message emerges loud and clear on every album. Christgau described this recurring theme as "the forces of life—autonomous intelligence, a childlike openness, sexual energy, and humor—defeat those of death: by seduction if possible, by force if necessary." In the mid-'70s Clinton began couching this idea in elaborate outer-space fantasies in concept albums modeled after *Tommy* and *Sgt. Pepper's Lonely Hearts Club Band*. In 1977 Parliament toured with an outrageous spaceship stage set. "The idea was putting blacks in places where you weren't supposed to see them at," Clinton told me. "I thought, 'Space!' The only black person you saw in space was Uhura on *Star Trek*. A nigger on a space ship was probably a real cool dude, especially if it was leaving."

Corbett linked Clinton's "Afronauts" and "space madness" to the work of two other influential African-Americans: jazz composer Sun Ra and reggae producer Lee "Scratch" Perry. All three men were innovators. Clinton's use of drum machines and raps paved the way for hip hop, Sun Ra was among the first musicians to use synthesizers, and Perry championed the production technique known as dub in effects-laden instrumental remixes. All three worked under various aliases; sported outlandish, colorful costumes, and favored wild and sometimes incomprehensible wordplay. And all three were dismissed as loony after claiming to be aliens.

*The Ultimate Psychedelic Rock
Library: The searing title track
of Funkadelic's* Maggot Brain
*(Westbound) is the group's
psychedelic pinnacle.*

After Clinton, Perry has had the most influence in the world of psychedelic rock. Rainford Hugh Perry was born in 1936 in Kendal, a small town in northwest Jamaica. He adopted the name Lee when he gravitated to Kingston in the late '50s and started his musical career as an apprentice of Clement "Coxsone" Dodd, working as a gofer at Dodd's famous Studio One, and looking after the portable sound systems that carried the new hybrid ska music to the streets. In the years that followed, he became a recording artist himself and scored a hit with 1965's "Chicken Scratch," which spawned his nickname. He was one of several key musicians who instigated the shift from upbeat ska to slower and more sinister rock steady and finally to reggae; he ran his own label, Upsetter Records, from 1968 to 1974, and he recorded the early efforts of a young Bob Marley and the Wailers. Through it all, he constantly complained about being screwed out of money and recognition by other producers. Two of his best-known early recordings, "I Am the Upsetter" and "People Funny Boy," are vicious diatribes aimed at Dodd and Joe Gibbs, another former employer.

Perry was no happier in 1975 after he signed to Island Records, whose founder Chris Blackwell he called "a vampire sucking the blood of the sufferer." In 1973 he had purchased a house in the Kingston suburb of Washington Gardens and built himself a concrete recording studio in the backyard, christening it with a sign over the front door reading "Black Ark." Here he recorded his own music with the Upsetters (a band comprised of whatever session players were sitting around the studio at any given time); produced the work of artists such as Max Romeo, Junior Murvin, and the pioneering female reggae singer Susan Cadogan, and extended the dub experiments of the ground-breaking King Tubby. Perry didn't invent dub, as has often been stated, but he certainly embraced it. The word is thought to refer to the practice of "dubbing out" various tracks on the master tape, putting a sudden and unexpected emphasis on sounds that are usually in the background—say, the rhythmic interplay of the hi-hat

The Ultimate Psychedelic Rock Library: Open the Gate *(Trojan) is the best overview and introduction to the trippy dub productions of the inimitable Lee "Scratch" Perry.*

and bass. On the island of Jamaica, the word "dub" closely resembles the patois word "dup," which means "ghost." Perry's dub productions are marked by a haze of reverb and sound effects such as pistol shots, crying babies, and falling rain that jump out at you like ghosts in the machine. "It was only four [tracks] written on the machine," he has said. "But I was picking up twenty from the extra-terrestrial squad."

Listeners in search of one handy package compiling Perry's freakiest and most influential dub productions are well served by Trojan's two-disc collection, *Open the Gate*. The secrets of his success on legendary tracks such as "Talk About It," "Bionic Rats," "Bad Weed," and "Vampire" were good taste in choosing the right collaborators and the ability to create a vibe that encouraged artists to use their imaginations to transcend the ordinary. In order to summon the ghosts, he would blow ganja smoke on the master tape as it rolled, and the feeling of druggy disorientation permeates his work to such an extent that you can get a pot hangover just by listening to too much of it. This places him firmly in the continuum of psychedelic rock: He wasn't reinventing the use of the recording studio or abandoning conventional song structure as much as he was trying to capture the experience of being stoned, plain and simple. But like psychedelic avatars such as Syd Barrett and Roky Erickson, he eventually flew too high for his own good. He overindulged in rum and ganja, split with his wife and children, angered his business partners, unwisely ignored the thugs who shook him down for protection money, and finally saw Black Ark destroyed in 1979 by a fire that many people believe he started himself. He's been playing the role of the mad genius ever since, granting colorful interviews in which rambles about outer space, aliens, sex, Rastafarianism, and being ripped off by the "bald head" white man, all while living with his second wife and manager in a house overlooking Lake Zurich in Switzerland.

As Corbett pointed out, an obsession with aliens was something that Clinton, Perry, and Sun Ra all shared. "While this E.T. metaphor—if it can be considered a metaphor—may indicate the insanity of its maker, it also cuts back the other direction, suggesting the fundamental unreality of existence for people imported into New World servitude and then disenfranchised into poverty," he wrote. He included Sun Ra's *Cosmic Tones for Mental Therapy*, Funkadelic's "Back In Our Minds," and Perry's "I Am a Madman" in a long line of African-American songs that talk about "madness" not only in terms of the intoxicating effect of drugs, but as a way of shaking off inhibitions and escaping social oppression. These artists weren't trying to run away to outer space; like Hendrix, they were hoping to build a new society there. "Tradition = earth; innovation = outer space," Corbett wrote. "In the language of black music, madness and extraterrestriality go hand in hand." Of course, space wasn't restricted only to the funky.

PSYCHEDELIC WARLORDS

> Originally, we just wanted to freak people out. We used to portray different trips, and because of our own experiences, we knew exactly how to get through to people.
>
> —Dave Brock
> quoted in Dave Thompson's *Space Daze*

While many groups in the initial wave of psychedelic rock proceeded to hone a more genteel brand of art rock, the freedom
inspired by the original movements' mix of drugs, radical politics,
and a more freewheeling approach to rock 'n' roll prompted music
with a much harder edge from several likeminded camps in
England and the United States. Beyond helping to inspire its origins, there are fewer connections between psychedelic rock and
heavy metal than there are between psychedelia and the genre of
progressive rock, but they deserve some consideration.

A Dozen Heavy- or Proto-Metal Albums Deeply Rooted in Psychedelic Rock

1. Blue Cheer, *Vincebus Eruptum* (Polygram)

2. The Stooges, *The Stooges* (Elektra)

3. Deep Purple, *Shades of Deep Purple* (Spitfire)

4. The Stooges, *Funhouse* (Elektra)

5. Iron Butterfly, *In-A-Gadda-Da-Vida* (Rhino)

6. Cream, *Disraeli Gears* (Polygram)

7. The MC5, *Kick Out the Jams* (Elektra)

8. Blue Öyster Cult, *Agents of Fortune* (Columbia)

9. Steppenwolf, *Steppenwolf the Second* (MCA)

10. Black Sabbath, *Master of Reality* (Warner Bros.)

11. Judas Priest, *Rocka Rolla* (Koch)

12. UFO, *Unidentified Flying Object* (Disky)

The same druggy Detroit scene that spawned the Amboy Dukes produced punk and metal forbearers the MC5. The band combined John Sinclair's White Panther Party politics with ferocious two-guitar assaults that drew inspiration from Ornette Coleman, John Coltrane, and Sun Ra, whose "Starship" it covered as the closing track on its debut album. In an effort to capture the excitement of the group's performances, *Kick Out the Jams* was recorded live at Detroit's Grande Ballroom on the night of October 30, 1968. The title track stands as one of rock's most indelible anthems, and one of the group's catchiest and most concise tunes. The MC5 was at heart a great jam band—the songs spiraled off in new directions each time they were played—but it never lost the crucial drive, energy, and focus essential to great rock. Tracks such as "Ramblin' Rose" and "Rocket Reducer No. 62 (Rama Lama Fa Fa Fa)" are like James Brown at double-speed. These maniacal groovers zoom past on sheer energy and with unexpected detours into insane explosions of guitar noise, making it possible to ignore the sometimes naïve politics that Sinclair ascribed to the group.

"I think [the music connects] with all of those who are addicted to the sound of Marshall amplifiers, blistering drumbeats, and lyrics that have some sense of political consciousness," guitarist Wayne Kramer told me in 1995. "If not overtly, they tell the truth on some level. And the truth is always more interesting than anything you could make up."

Often portrayed as the MC5's "baby brothers," Ann Arbor's Psychedelic Stooges were signed to Elektra at the same time, but they had a much more primitive—and, early on, psychedelic—sound. By the time the group recorded its 1969 debut with producer John Cale, it had shortened its name to the Stooges, but the acid influence lived on in Ron Asheton's fuzz-, feedback-, and wah-wah-drenched guitar, Iggy Pop's howling banshee vocals, and the epic droning raga of "We Will Fall," more than ten minutes of frightening bad-trip psychedelia. In 1970 the group offered its own take on free jazz with *Fun House*; the title track and "L.A. Blues" evoke Albert Ayler doused with LSD and locked in a garage that has been set on fire. The lineup shifted after this album to include James Williamson, a more accomplished blues-based guitarist. Iggy grabbed more of the spotlight, and the band veered away from psychedelic rock toward the proto-punk for which it is now most famous.

Renowned as "the thinking man's heavy-metal group," Blue Öyster Cult boasted one rock critic as manager (Sandy Pearlman) and another as lyrical contributor (Richard Meltzer). It formed at Stony Brook College on Long Island from the ashes of a psychedelic rock band called the Soft White Underbelly, and it retained touches of the lysergic influence on many of its recordings, including its 1976 masterpiece, "Don't Fear the Reaper," which put Byrdsy guitar jangle in a new, echo-laden, and much more sinister context.

On the West Coast, Iron Butterfly came together in the San Diego area in 1966 around vocalist-organist Doug Ingle, and it proceeded to tour with the Doors and the Jefferson Airplane, overpowering both with sheer volume and bombast. The group will always be best remembered for the seventeen-minute "In-A-Gadda-Da-Vida" (said to be a stoned slurring of a utopian vision "in the garden of Eden"), which can be lauded for its massive guitar riff and intriguing Eastern influence, and cursed for introducing the extended drum solo. Led by German immigrant John Kay (the former Joachim Krauledat), Steppenwolf made its name on the West Coast as the ultimate biker band, thanks to the anthemic hit, "Born to Be Wild." But touches of psychedelia could also be heard on songs such as "Magic Carpet Ride," "Jupiter's Child," and "Monster/Suicide/America," an ambitious attempt to weave the history of America into a call for political action. One of the best American power trios, Blue Cheer formed in San Francisco in the late '60s. The band was managed by Augustus Owsley Stanley, who was still pursuing his primary career as a master chemist, and he brewed up a special batch of his finest in honor of the group. On its classic debut, *Vincebus Eruptum*, the band mangled Eddie Cochran and Mose Allison with gleefully noisy psychedelic abandon, but its career was derailed after a powerful second effort—*Outsideinside*— by a series of personnel changes.

Across the ocean, a more self-indulgent, less trippy vision of the power trio was offered by one of rock's first supergroups. "Epic solos were the order of the day, often extended far beyond the bounds of discipline or taste," critic Dave Marsh wrote in *The Rolling Stone Illustrated History of Rock & Roll*. "While the group spawned a seemingly infinite flock of imitators—boogie bands, power trios, heavy metal groups—it is only as an influence that most of Cream's music, so widely hailed at the time, will last." I disagree, in part— while the band's instrumental flatulence is indeed ridiculously overrated, the band also recorded some enduring psychedelic rock in the form of truncated singles that were considered concessions to commercialism at the time. Yet "Badge," "Sunshine of Your Love," and "White Room" stand as the group's finest moments.

Emerging from London's psychedelic underground, singer, poet, rock critic, science-fiction writer, and UFO club doorman Mick Farren led a group called the Social Deviants (later just the Deviants) who urged anti-authoritarian action over raw, bluesy, psychedelic rock that has elements of both metal and punk. *Ptoof!* (1967) was the first and best of the group's three albums, proudly flaunting both its freakishness and its incompetence (the group's former manager dubbed it "the worst record in the history of man"). In addition to the standard lysergic blues ("I'm Coming Home") and pastoral acoustic folk music ("Child of the Sky," "Bun") so common to the era, the album included a bizarre and inspired tape collage of treated percussion, electronic noise, and poetry called "Nothing Man," the catchy psychedelic pop song "Deviation Street," and the stomping "Garbage," which includes the sound of a Deviant vomiting on record after the chanted chorus, "Won't you buy / Buy some garbage?" In 1969 the Deviants mutated into the Pink Fairies and continued making strange noises through shifting lineups that included Pretty Things drummer Twink and guitarist Larry Wallis of UFO, a band that took its name from the psychedelic rock club.

Now considered heavy-metal pioneers, UFO, Judas Priest, Deep Purple, and Black Sabbath all started as bluesy psychedelic rock bands complete with trippy effects and lighting. "Acid rock was aimed not at one's legs or crotch, but at one's head," rock scholar Deena Weinstein wrote in her definitive genre history, *Heavy Metal.* "It wasn't dance music. Getting lost in the music was 'getting' the music. This ecstatic use of music was taken up by heavy metal in a Dionysian key, for heavy metal revels in the powers of life." Metal

The Ultimate Psychedelic Rock Library: The Deviants' Ptooff! *(Alive) pays homage to garbage but is actually an inspired if amateurish freak-out.*

was born when these bands shifted modes from mind-bending to head-banging, but one group managed both at once.

Guitarist Dave Brock, free-jazz saxophonist Nik Turner, and electronics wizard Dikmik first came together as Group X in London's Ladbroke Grove hippie community, which was also home to the Pink Fairies. In late 1969 Group X became Hawkwind, and in 1970 it signed to Liberty/United Artists, which was also home to several adventurous German bands. Hawkwind built its early reputation by playing long jams at free shows and festivals such as the Glastonbury Fayre. Produced by the Pretty Things' Dick Taylor, its 1970 debut is typical, bluesy proto-metal with occasional nods to Pink Floyd.

Before returning to the studio, the group added several key ingredients: the more elaborate synthesizers of Del Dettmar (perhaps the only dwarf to ever play in a rock band), a more assertive style of bass playing, courtesy of Dave Anderson from the German group Amon Düül II, and imaginative lyrics penned by Robert

*The Ultimate Psychedelic Rock
Library: Space rock takes flight on
Hawkwind's* In Search of Space
(One Way).

Calvert, a talented South African poet and science-fiction writer. Pink Floyd and Hendrix had flirted with science fiction on tunes such as "Interstellar Overdrive" and "Third Stone from the Sun," but 1971's *In Search of Space* was a double-album-length voyage into the cosmos, and Hawkwind never really returned. Not coincidentally, the album arrived in the middle of the United States' six lunar expeditions. "There was the exploration of the moon and all of that, and we seem to have caught the public's attention by doing that sort of stuff at the same time," Brock said in *The Illustrated Collector's Guide to Hawkwind.*

Like many Hawkwind albums, *In Search of Space* was recorded live in the studio without the benefit of overdubs or retakes. "We were taking a lot of LSD at the time," Turner told space-rock biographer Thompson. "It helped." The random synthesizer sounds and saxophone bleats verge on the chaotic, and the lyrics can be laughable for anyone who doesn't appreciate science fiction. But the group is saved from pointless indulgence by a love of pounding

The Ultimate Psychedelic Rock Library: Hawkwind's Space Ritual *(One Way)—recorded live, fueled by LSD.*

backbeats and catchy riffs—hallmarks of the best heavy metal. Not for nothing was Hawkwind adopted by bikers on both sides of the Atlantic.

The pinnacle of Hawkwind's psychedelic-metal-science-fiction synthesis is the anthemic single "Silver Machine." The song features a driving bass line and vocals courtesy of former Hendrix roadie Lemmy Kilmister, who spent five years with the band before he was kicked out for taking too much of the wrong drug. (The speed-happy Lemmy went on to form the punk-metal Motörhead, which took its name from a Hawkwind song.) A bona fide hit, "Silver Machine" funded the band's ambitious Space Ritual tour in 1973. The traveling group consisted of seven band members, six roadies, five lighting technicians, three go-go dancers (including the legendary Stacia), and DJ Andy Dunkley, who spun records backward before and during the set in a primitive precursor to scratching and sampling.

"It was a very communal thing," Turner told me, but members joined and left the community at a dizzying pace. Calvert had started performing with the group in 1972, singing, reading poetry, and acting out characters in the songs by swinging a giant broadsword or donning an aviator's helmet and goggles. He quit in 1974 and was replaced by his friend, science-fiction writer Michael Moorcock. "Periodically, [Calvert] would have to be carted off by the men in white coats," Moorcock told Thompson. "He was certifiably crazy, whatever that means." On his own, Calvert made two extraordinary concept albums with Brian Eno, *Captain Lockheed and the Starfighters* (1974) and *Lucky Lief and the Longships* (1975). He rejoined Hawkwind in 1976 as the group switched labels from United Artists to Charisma, quit again a few years later, and was reportedly considering another return when he died of a heart attack in 1988.

Turner left the group following *Astounding Sounds Amazing Music* in 1976, and by this time, its "all-aboard" collaborative spirit was long gone. "Throughout the history of Hawkwind, Dave is the guy who hired and fired everybody," Turner told me. "Everybody thought it was their band until they suddenly got the sack." Re-energized by interest from the ambient and techno communities, Brock is the sole original member leading Hawkwind into the '90s. Turner is going strong as well, and in 1994, he toured with Dettmar and San Francisco guitarist Helios Creed as "Nik Turner's Space Ritual '94." Both camps still provide wonderful live experiences. "Personally, I'm surprised we've gotten so far," Turner said in 1971. "I never thought our music would appeal to anybody, simply because we've never pandered to public taste, never compromised, and just played

exactly what we wanted. By a happy accident, people seem to dig
it." His words still ring true a quarter-century later.

TITS! TITS! THE BLIMP! THE BLIMP!

> I had the rare good fortune to talk to the Captain recently
> about his music, and noted that I hadn't really understood
> *Trout Mask Replica*. "That's okay," he said, "just put it on
> and then go back to doing whatever it was you were doing
> and it'll come to you." Well, what I was doing was sweep-
> ing the floor, so I had my doubts, but I did it anyhow.
> Damned if it didn't push the broom.
>
> —Ed Ward,
> *The Rolling Stone Record Review Volume II,* 1970

THOUGH FEW SERIOUS CONTENDERS EMERGED to extend the
specific fusions that Hendrix pioneered, some bands did incorporate
elements of jazz, blues, and psychedelic rock in other distinctive
syntheses. England's Soft Machine toured with Hendrix and readily
swapped free-jazz influences, while Georgia's Allman Brothers
honed a merger of bluesy vocals, jazzy polyrhythms, and intricate
twin guitar parts that recalled a more structured Grateful Dead. The
Allmans also incorporated psychedelic mushrooms into their
mythology the same way the Dead incorporated Owsley's acid.

A more focused and melodic version of Southern-fried psychedelia was explored by the Memphis band Big Star on its third

album. The band's first two efforts combined a love of British pop with soulful Stax/Volt roots. Much of the magic came from the interplay between former teen sensation Alex Chilton, a veteran of the Box Tops, and band founder Chris Bell, who quit early into the making of 1974's *Radio City*. Bell went on to craft a transcendent album called *I Am the Cosmos* with strings, marimbas, synthesizers, and backward guitars floating in and out of the mix, but it was not released until long after his death in 1978. Burned out, bitter, and abusing drugs and alcohol, Chilton purged his demons on *Third* (a.k.a. *Sister Lovers*), a haunting, soul-searching disc that contorted the band's influences into strange and often psychedelic shapes. Chilton never matched its power again.

The psychedelic influence was also spreading around the globe. In South America, the Brazilian scene was especially intriguing. Though the influence filtered north only in the form of the infectious bossa nova hit "The Girl from Ipanema," in his native country, Tom Zé was combining elements of rock with traditional Latin

The Ultimate Psychedelic Rock Library: On songs such as "Panis et Circenses (Bread and Circuses)," included on the 1999 compilation Everything Is Possible!: The Best of Os Mutantes *(Luaka Bop), the Brazilian tropicalia group pairs a lush sound to rival the psychedelic Beach Boys with a lyrical cynicism to match Bob Dylan.*

American rhythms and touches of psychedelia (three decades later, his work would experience a revival in the United States when he toured with backing from the Chicago "post-rock"/new progressive band, Tortoise). Caetano Veloso, "the Brazilian Bob Dylan," also dabbled with otherworldly productions. But the kings of South American psychedelia were Os Mutantes (the Mutants), who performed dressed in plastic or shiny reflective costumes and mixed subversive politics with acid rock and exotica/lounge music to become the most adventurous proponents of a sound called "tropicalia." "We took pleasure in knowing that we struck a nerve," guitarist Sergio Dias Baptista told Greg Kot of the *Chicago Tribune* in 1999. "The idea was to destroy all formulas....We hated all that was established, and we mocked all."

Psychedelia was also embraced by Japan's rock underground via the "GS bands" (for "group sounds," or Japanese beat combos). The emphasis was not on drugs—Japanese musicians such as Kosugi Takehisa, Haino Keiji, Nanjo Asahito all spoke out against drug use—but on music that produced an altered state of conscious, a tradition that was centuries old in the East. Inspired by English and American psychedelic rockers, groups such as the Dynamites, the Golden Cups, and the Mops first emerged in the late '60s, but while they were inspired by Western rock, one of the factors that united them was a hatred of capitalism and polices such as the U.S.-Japan Joint Securities treaty, and the music had a pronounced political edge. Keiji's recordings were especially dark, with hints of Albert Ayler in his group Lost Aaraaff. Other bands of note included Stomu Yamash'ta and the Horizon, the Taj Mahal Travelers, the East Bionic Symphonia, the Rallizes, and Acid Seven. Some of the best of these groups are included on the 2000 compilation *Love, Peace & Poetry, Vol. 4: Japanese Psychedelic.*

The Japanese psychedelic-rock tradition was carried into the new millennium most enthusiastically by Acid Mothers Temple, a testament to the better aspects of globalization—in an ever-shrinking world, it is now possible for the American underground rock scene to embrace an obscure band from Japan that has recorded soundtracks for Russian films and is dedicated to recapturing the creative spirit of German krautrock, which was itself originally inspired by American and English psychedelia. Formed by veteran rocker Kawabata Makoto in 1996 as "a freak-out group for the twenty-first century," the Acid Mothers Temple & the Melting Paraiso UFO—to use the group's full name—functions in Japan as a collective with some thirty members, including musicians, artists, dancers, and farmers, though when it tours, it strips down to a core group of five. The band's best recordings include the soundtrack for *Wild Gals a Go-Go* by Russian filmmaker Ivan Piskov, which puts a gonzo psychedelic spin on typically cheesy porno soundtrack music; *Troubadours from Another Heavenly World*, which consists of three long, improvised tracks entitled "Heroin Heroine's Heritage," "She Is a Rainbow in Curved Air," and "Acid Heart Mother," and *In C*, which starts with a cover of the classical minimalist composition by Terry Riley, then adds the originals "In E" and "In D." The collective well understands the importance of maintaining the rock drive in its hairiest freak-outs. "We play trip music and rock 'n' roll, and we all want to continue being rockers," Makoto told me. "When I was younger, I tried every drug I could get my hands on. I realized that drugs can provide you with a hint but they can't give you an answer. I was able to find my way to the door with the help of drugs, but for going beyond that door drugs were useless. Being high on drugs is only a fake experience—it can only give you a hint of what you can do without them. I don't need any drugs now because I learned a way to trip over to the next stage without them."

Behind the Iron Curtain in Czechoslovakia, the Plastic People of the Universe were inspired not only by psychedelic rock, but by the '60s ideal that music can change the world. Building on the uncompromising sounds of the Velvet Underground, Captain Beefheart, and the Mothers of Invention, the band came together in 1968, the same year Soviet tanks rolled into Prague. The Plastic People paid the price for politically and musically challenging efforts such as 1973's *Egon Bondy's Happy Hearts Clubs Band*. "There was a special movement that we called the second culture or parallel culture or the underground," saxophonist Vratislav Brabenec told me in 1999. "That was especially if you were not just making music, but if it was part of your whole philosophy, what you are doing and how are you living. If you used the rock 'n' roll here in the socialist countries of the Eastern Bloc twenty years ago not just as fashion music, you were an enemy of the state—a political enemy." The band was outlawed by the Soviet regime, and in 1976 Brabenec and the group's artistic director, Ivan Jirous, were imprisoned. The jailings spurred a political group called Charter 77 to compose an urgent document demanding human rights, and this manifesto was so inspiring that it coalesced the Czech opposition and eventually led to independence. The power of the words was not be surprising: They were written by a poet, Vaclav Havel, a major fan of the Velvets and the Plastic People who eventually became the elected leader of the new democracy after the so-called "Velvet Revolution." Brabenec and some his old bandmates regrouped as Pulnoc, and they even secured an American record deal; later, at the new president's urging, the Plastic People reunited. (Who can say "no" to a presidential request?)

Meanwhile, back in the West, the other heavies of psychedelic synthesis were two teenage buddies from the Mojave Desert town of Lancaster, California. Frank Zappa and Don Van Vliet attended Antelope Valley High School together in the late '50s. They shared a fondness for raw blues, R&B, and doo-wop, and played in a number of unrecorded bands before drifting apart. Zappa moved to Los Angeles in the early '60s and linked up with a five-piece R&B band called the Soul Giants, which became the Mothers of Invention. Under Zappa's direction, the Mothers progressed from standard bar-band fare such as "Louie Louie" and "Gloria" to compositions that combined modern classical music, jazz, R&B, and rock.

The Mothers were signed to MGM/Verve by producer Tom Wilson, who also worked with the Velvet Underground. Four times more expensive to record than most rock albums at the time, *Freak Out!* was released in 1966 and featured the Mothers plus a seventeen-piece orchestra. While some of the songs allude to modern composers Igor Stravinsky, Edgard Varèse, and Karlheinz Stockhausen, much of the album is raw, fuzz-driven, *Nuggets*-style rock. At the time it was perceived as a druggy, scatological effort in the style of the Fugs, but in fact, Zappa was positioning freaks (genuinely weird and creative people) against hippies (whom he considered sheep), and he was strongly antidrug. "We are here to turn you loose, not turn you on," he's quoted as saying in Ben Watson's *Frank Zappa: The Negative Dialectics of Poodle Play.* "Turn *yourself* on."

The band continued railing against conformity in similar fashion on 1967's *Absolutely Free.* Later the same year, Zappa took a detour along with some of the Mothers and a fifty-piece orchestra to experiment with electronics and *musique concrète* on *Lumpy Gravy* before gearing up for his ultimate assault on plastic people, psychedelia, and idealism. The cover of 1968's *We're Only In It for the Money* parodied *Sgt. Pepper's Lonely Hearts Club Band*; its lyrics mercilessly lampooned the hippies, and its music was the most intricate from Zappa or rock in general to date. "Whether it is the best is a moot point—how would you compare it with, for instance, Otis Redding?" wrote *Rolling Stone* reviewer Barret Hansen. Actually, it wasn't a moot point, and comparisons show that—regardless of his accomplishments in the unique genre best described as Zappa music—Uncle Frank was never an especially great *rocker.* "In the end, the most pertinent thing to be said about Frank Zappa is prob-

The Ultimate Psychedelic Rock Library: We're Only In It for the Money *(Rykodisc) was the Mothers of Invention's bitter parody of psychedelic idealism.*

ably that for all he knows about music, he lacks the talent to write a song like 'Louie Louie,'" Lester Bangs wrote in *Rolling Stone*. While Zappa was conning rock audiences into thinking that his arrogance and condescension were warranted by his horizon-broadening sounds, Bangs contended, Captain Beefheart was making statements that were much more far-reaching.

Rechristened by his old pal Zappa, Van Vliet/Beefheart had a much harder time getting his musical career off the ground. In the mid-'60s he won a Vox battle of the bands contest and got to record two singles for A&M Records. The first, a garagey version of "Diddy Wah Diddy," was a regional hit, but A&M rejected a debut album as "too negative." Beefheart formed a new band and recorded *Safe As Milk* for Kama Sutra in 1967. It was straightforward garage-band blues distinguished by the captain's remarkable vocals, which were strongly influenced by Howlin' Wolf and Little Richard. But when the music took a turn for the weirder on tour, guitarist Ry Cooder quit just in time to force the cancellation of an appearance at the Monterey Pop Festival.

Released in 1968, *Strictly Personal* started to focus on Beefheart's new sound, a music that was as carefully planned and orchestrated as Zappa's, but as raw as the rawest Delta blues and as unrestricted as the most adventurous free jazz. Unfortunately, the album was mixed without Beefheart's participation, and the Captain was disgusted by the addition of superfluous psychedelic effects. (The music was strange enough as it was.) Beefheart was beginning to think he'd never get it right on tape when Zappa reappeared and offered him the chance to record for his new label, Straight Records. Zappa gave Beefheart the same sort of freedom that Andy Warhol gave the Velvet Underground. "When we did the album with him, Frank said, 'Hey, let's go into the studio and you rehearse the group and we'll put down exactly what you want,"' Zappa's manager, Herb Cohen, told biographer Ben Watson. "It was the first album he ever made where he had total control of everything that went down." Zappa's level of involvement is hard to pin down; Beefheart later complained that he just fell asleep at the console, but Watson believes that Zappa gave Beefheart the necessary grounding so that his brand of surrealism wouldn't devolve into irrationality. Zappa's bitter cynicism balanced Beefheart's childlike charm.

The mix on 1970's *Trout Mask Replica* highlights the recording in progress, including false beginnings, shouted cues, and flubbed vocal lines. The feeling of inspired improvisation contrasts with the knowledge that Beefheart obsessed over every note, carefully prescribing the intertwining guitar parts and preparing the drums by muting them with bits of cardboard to make the polyrhythms even harder to get a grip on. The influence of Delta blues and free-jazzer

The Ultimate Psychedelic Rock Library: On Trout Mask Replica *(Reprise), Captain Beefheart finally had the freedom (and the talented sidemen) to realize his twisted vision.*

Albert Ayler are clear, but the album retains an essential rock 'n' roll drive, and the Magic Band plays with a deliberate, primitive force. The music may or may not have been influenced by psychedelic drugs—"I can paint better than that," Beefheart said about LSD— but the swirl of guitars, drums, clarinets, and saxophones creates its own reality, and it's as disorienting as plunging into a sudden hallucination. The lyrics prompted Bangs to call Beefheart "the only true Dadaist in rock," and they are a delight for anyone who savors the way words *sound*. "Children stop yer nursin' unless yer renderin' fun / The mother ship the mother ship / The mother ship's the one / The blimp the blimp / The tape's uh trip it's uh trailin' tail / It's traipse'n along behind the blimp the blimp," goes one memorable passage from "The Blimp (mousetrapreplica)."

Trout Mask Replica stands as Beefheart's masterpiece, but that's not to slight the albums that followed. *Lick My Decals Off, Baby* (1970) hones the sound of its predecessor, adds marimba, and reflects the influence of African music. *The Spotlight Kid* (1971) is simpler and bluesier, while *Clear Spot* (1972) has a harder rock edge. *Unconditionally Guaranteed* and *Bluejeans & Moonbeams* (1974) are both watered-down attempts to penetrate the mainstream, but Beefheart returns to his own idiosyncratic backwaters on *Shiny Beast (Bat Chain Puller)* (1978), *Doc at the Radar Station* (1980), and *Ice Cream for Crow* (1982). Always at odds with the business of making music and sensing that he had stopped breaking ground, Beefheart retired in 1983 to concentrate on sculpture and painting. His artwork now sells in the range of $40,000 per piece, and he rarely discusses his earlier adventures, making him one of the very few rockers who actually shut up once he said what he'd had to say.

EIGHT

8

BROKEN HEAD
(Quiet, Super Genius at Work)

Use "unqualified" people...Give way to your worst impulse...A line has two sides...Do we need holes?...Is it finished?

—Oblique Strategies

Standing in the shadows, just out of a view but always part of the action, Brian Eno has been present at the back-alley births of some of the most adventurous musical movements since the early 1970s. Through the different phases of his career—from synthesizer player in Roxy Music, to solo artist, to producer and artistic instigator—the sounds he has made and the ideas he has expressed have inspired others in such diverse genres as punk, noise rock, and ambient music. The common thread in all of his work has been an extremely psychedelic approach to the recording studio. Eno has never been at a loss to explain his methodology, and while some of his music ranks with the best psychedelic rock ever made, in the end, he earns a place of honor in this book as the music's great philosopher.

Given his reputation as the ultimate "ideas man," it's ironic that Eno first gained attention as a supporting player in a project planned to the last detail by another artist. Eno and Bryan Ferry both attended art school in the mid-'60s, but they emerged with radically different philosophies. The son of a miner from County Durham, Ferry studied at Newcastle University with pop artist Richard Hamilton. "Both the surrealists and the Dada people were interesting to me because they shook things up so much without being so serious," Ferry told me. "But with pop art and Richard, suddenly there was a whole new world that was relevant, and that was sexier and more potent because it had to do with everyday life."

Born in 1948 to upper-middle-class parents in Woodbridge, Suffolk, Eno enrolled in Ipswich Art School in 1964. The school was run by Roy Ascott, a visionary teacher who had earlier taught Pete Townshend at Ealing Art College. After lunch one day, Ascott and the other teachers directed Eno and his classmates to assemble in the courtyard. The teachers locked them in and left them there for an hour, looking down at them from a rooftop but refusing to answer their questions. "All kinds of odd things began to happen," Eno recalled in the book *More Dark Than Shark*. "Guys tried to scale the walls, others banded together into ad hoc revolutionary committees, some said this was the last straw, others cried or formed conga chains and walked round chanting abuse at the staff." Finally, a taped voice announced, "You are worse than chickens....You have drawn with your own hands the formula, and now

you look at it instead of reality." Eno came away with an object lesson in creative thinking and the tension that can arise from being
plunged into a novel situation.

While he was in college, Ferry gigged with a horn-driven R&B
band called the Gas Board, singing songs by Otis Redding, Sam and
Dave, Screamin' Jay Hawkins, and Wilson Pickett. After graduation,
he moved to London and taught ceramics at a girls' school in
Hammersmith, but his interest in music remained. "When I started
writing music, I found it was like pop art," he said in the book *Bryan
Ferry & Roxy Music*. "I was using images—like in the lyrics—throwaway clichés and amusing phrases that you found in magazines or
used in everyday speech." By late 1970, he was talking with former
Gas Board mate Graham Simpson about forming a band that would
be a total pop-art concept expressed in music. Ferry wanted a synthesizer player, and he heard that Andy Mackay was his man.
Mackay was actually a classically trained woodwinds player, but he
was interested, and he knew someone who *did* play synthesizer.

Mackay and Eno had been drawn together in college by a mutu-
al interest in John Cage, Karlheinz Stockhausen, and electronic
music pioneer Morton Subotnick. Eno had fooled around with tape
recorders, signal generators, and synthesizers in two improvisation-
al bands, Merchant Taylor's Simultaneous Cabinet and Maxwell's
Demon. The notion of mixing things up in a rock band appealed to
him. "I'd been working with avant-garde music, but had just
become interested in the many sides of rock music—not least the
audience/performer relationship," he recalled in *Bryan Ferry & Roxy
Music*. "There's a whole lot of physical excitement in it which
appealed to me." Eno called this physical excitement "idiot ener-

gy." Growing up in the shadows of two American air bases, he had become addicted to it while listening to Armed Forces Radio. The psychedelic rock of the '60s—especially the Beatles, Jimi Hendrix, and the Velvet Underground—convinced him that the music was unlimited and could even be expanded to include more "serious" ideas from the electronic avant-garde.

Electronic music-making had evolved from early, primitive instruments such as the theremin, through the limited and enormous synthesizers of the mid-'60s (including the one that Walter / Wendy Carlos used on the celebrated *Switched On Bach*), to relatively portable and reliable "performance" models such as the Moogs favored by most rockers. Synthesizers crept into rock slowly through the late '60s and early '70s, and snatches of Moog could be heard on the Beatles' *Abbey Road*, but more significant and psychedelic was their use by a new wave of purely or primarily electronic bands.

Led by ethnomusicologist Joseph Byrd, the United States of America mixed classical instruments, ethnic percussion, primitive synthesizers and oscillators, and the gorgeous vocals of Dorothy Moskowitz on a tuneful self-titled 1967 debut. Tonto's Expanding Headband was formed by the West Coast duo of Robert Margouleff and Malcolm Cecil and named for a jury-rigged combination of seven Moogs that they claimed was the world's first polyphonic synthesizer ("Tonto" was their acronym for "The Original New Timbral Orchestra"). The group's 1972 debut, *Zero Time,* is trippy instrumental Muzak. Colorado garage-rockers Lothar and the Hand People also took their name from an electronic instrument—"Lothar" was the group's theremin—and their 1968 debut, *Presenting...Lothar and the*

Hand People, is a mix of *Nuggets*-style rock, psychedelic playfulness, and electronic tomfoolery. Much more serious and self-important were San Franciscans Paul Beaver and Bernard Krause, who created synthetic environmental soundscapes on albums such as *In a Wild Sanctuary* and *Gandharva,* paving the way for New Age music, and synthesist Tim Blake, who left Gong and recorded grandiose sci-fi synthesizer epics such as *New Jerusalem.*

The legendary New York duo Silver Apples emerged in 1968 with a stunning self-titled album consisting of synthesizer buzzes and bleeps, relentlessly straightforward drumming, and occasional monotone vocals—in other words, electronica long before its time. As depicted on the LP's memorable gatefold cover, Simeon played a homemade synthesizer consisting of a plywood box with thirteen oscillators controlled by eighty-six telegraph keys (a machine he dubbed "the Simeon"), while his partner Danny Taylor added metronomic drumming on a huge drum set. Both men sang typically stoned hippie lyrics ("Life is full of big machines / And there

The Ultimate Psychedelic Rock Library: The self-titled debut by the United States of America (Sony) opens with a track called "The American Metaphysical Circus," which aptly describes the band's sound.

ain't no room for the little things") and though their debut spent
ten weeks at the bottom of *Billboard's* Top 100 albums chart, they
were largely written off as a novelty act. "Even when Silver Apples
was at its peak, very few people gave us credit for being musicians,"
Simeon told me. "Freaks? Yes. Something amusing to behold? Yes.
Something unusual to write about? Yes. An integral part of the
whole hippie-revolutionary thing? Yes. But respect or acknowledg-
ment in the field of music? Never." The group broke up after a second album, 1969's *Contact*, which offered more of the same but
with a slightly nastier edge (one tune was called "A Pox On You"),
and Simeon relocated to Virginia to paint. Inspired by a 1995
album of covers by modern-day inheritors, *Electronic Evocations: A
Tribute to Silver Apples*, he formed a new version of the group minus
Taylor and returned to live performance in 1997.

   By the early '70s every progressive rock band had to have a synthesizer, but classically-trained keyboardists such as Yes's Rick
Wakeman and ELP's Keith Emerson treated them like souped-up

*The Ultimate Psychedelic Rock
Library: The 1997 reissue* Silver
Apples *(MCA) combines the band's
self-titled debut and the 1969 follow-up* Contact *on one handy disc.*

organs. Eno prized them as purely electronic instruments, and he favored sounds that didn't mimic the instruments of the orchestra. He used them to throw an element of alien noise and random chaos into rock, the way psychedelic guitarists used feedback and the 13th Floor Elevators used their amplified jug. Twirling any one of the dozens of knobs and dials on a Mini-Moog could produce fantastic results that no one could predict, least of all Eno, and he further heightened the unpredictability of his keyboards by refusing to have them serviced when they developed glitches.

Ferry had already chosen a name for his group when Eno and Mackay joined. A press release noted that Roxy Music "was intended to convey a slightly old-style glamour with a pun on rock." Ferry had also designed the band's look as a cross between '50s greasers and futuristic, glitzy aliens. The band was completed by two final recruits, drummer Paul Thompson and guitarist Phil Manzanera. (Originally the band's soundman, Manzanera replaced Ferry's first choice on guitar, Davey O'List of the Nice.) Ferry knew that pop art is half marketing and half art. A well-orchestrated campaign spread the word about Roxy through the *Melody Maker* and a session with BBC DJ John Peel recorded while O'List was still in the group. The band's popularity exploded almost overnight, and with only half a dozen gigs to its credit, the group was signed to Island Records.

Roxy Music was recorded in March 1972. King Crimson guitarist Robert Fripp had been pegged as producer, but he had scheduling conflicts, so the band settled for former Crimson lyricist Peter Sinfield. Naturally, Ferry designed the art. The nostalgic Vargas-style pinup on the front cover fit perfectly, but the inside shots of the band in their retro/futuristic outfits backfired. More than one

*Contains
1 Bonus Song

*The Ultimate Psychedelic Rock
Library: Roxy Music's self-titled
debut (Reprise) remains one of
rock's most inventive stylistic
pastiches.*

reviewer dismissed the group as "Sha Na Na with a synthesizer,"
which was a horrible injustice. *Roxy Music* draws on rock's past and
twists it thoroughly, as evidenced by the crazy-quilt construction of
"Re-make / Re-Model." The tune could be a love song to a girl, a car,
or both. (Its driving beat builds to a shouted chorus based on the
English license plate number CPL 593A.) The band's four lead
instruments—Mackay's '50s-style sax, Manzanera's fluid guitar,
Eno's synthesizer, and Ferry's sexy, theatrical singing—fight a constant battle for dominance. At one point, each player is given a solo
spot, and the musicians draw attention to the influences at work.
Simpson plays the bass lick from the Beatles' "Day Tripper," Eno
whooshes and bleeps like a passing UFO, Mackay samples "The Ride
of the Valkyries," Manzanera churns through some classic garage-
band chords, and Ferry pounds his piano in Cage-style discord.

The rest of the album is equally inventive. The first wave of psychedelic rock had been adventurous in embracing different musical
genres and world beats, but Roxy was going even further, and—in

pop-art fashion—it was drawing attention to the creative process as it went. As publicist Simon Puxley wrote in the album's Beat-poetic liner notes, "Fantasising: phantomising: echoes of magic-golden moments become real presences…dreamworld & realworld loaded with images." Onstage, Ferry was a captivating frontman with a matinee idol looks and a voice to match, but Eno was just as hard to ignore. Blond hair flying and ostrich feathers flapping, he played the role of mad scientist, coaxing strange noises from his Mini-Moog and warping the sounds being made by Manzanera and Mackay by feeding them through an EMS modular synthesizer. Much was made in the early '70s of Eno's status as a "nonmusician." He never had any formal musical training and he couldn't read music, but he certainly had an ear for melody, harmonizing with Ferry, and later layering vocals on his own albums. Eventually, he learned to play chords on keyboard, guitar, and bass, but the instrument he loved best was the studio itself. With childlike naïveté, Eno simply refused to believe that there were things that *couldn't* be done.

Rock was primed for such fresh thinking in 1972. Along with Marc Bolan and David Bowie, Roxy was fighting boring pub rock on one front and pompous art rock on the other. The glam movement's weapons of choice were sex, drugs, and good, old-fashioned rock-'n'-roll energy, but in Roxy, the sex and energy were always more evident than the drugs. Eno, in particular, thought that the "view of the musician or artist as an impulsive, drug-taking romantic" had become a cliché. He challenged convention in other ways, too, proudly proclaiming his love for women's clothing. "I don't like masculine clothing," critic Brian Tamm quotes him as saying in *Brian Eno: His Music and the Vertical Color of Sound.* "The Western version of masculinity opposes rational man against intuitive woman. The part of my being that interests me has always been my intuition."

Before its second album, Roxy underwent a series of personnel changes. Ferry fired his old chum Simpson for missing rehearsals. He was replaced by Rik Kenton, who, in turn, was canned for thinking that the group should record some of *his* songs. The cover of *For Your Pleasure* reminded everyone who was boss. Ferry is the only band member pictured, posing as a limo driver waiting to chauffeur a glamorous model who is walking a black panther on a chain. The album polishes the formulas established on the debut, but it still boasts a freewheeling creativity that the musicians said came directly from the tradition of psychedelic rock. "I think it was this desire by all of us to do something different, something new, and to push the boundaries," Manzanera told me in 2001. "If you heard some-

The Ultimate Psychedelic Rock Library: The cover of For Your Pleasure *(Reprise) hints at the dark and somewhat deviant treats contained within.*

thing that you thought you'd heard before, well, that was rejected. You're out there in the same way as free-form jazz and all the psychedelic experiments. The idea of being free to do what you want—that's one of the problems now with the control of groups by record companies. They don't have enough opportunities just to be free and to go way out there, unless they do it themselves. Which is why all the independent labels are potentially great, because it's a liberating factor if you can sort of exist and do what you do and make a living out of it. It's important to maintain one's freedom as a musician."

For Your Pleasure was even more successful critically and commercially than Roxy's debut, but tensions in the band erupted during the group's first headlining tour. "Basically, the problems stemmed from the fact that we're too similar," Eno said of Ferry in *Bryan Ferry & Roxy Music*. "We're both from almost identical backgrounds, with a very similar approach to music in the sense that we're both non-musicians, working from an ideas angle rather than musical material." Eno was derailing Ferry's concepts simply by being Eno. "I was cramping Eno's style," Ferry said in the official press statement about Eno's departure. "Two non-musicians in a band is one too many. I think he'll do very well by himself."

Ferry didn't do badly, either. He replaced Eno with violinist Eddie Jobson of progressive rockers Curved Air, and the other band members were only temporarily peeved that they weren't consulted. The group took a break and Ferry recorded his first solo album, *These Foolish Things*, but it returned with *Stranded* in 1973, *Country Life* in 1974, and *Siren* in 1975. The rough edges of Ferry's increasingly romantic pop songs gradually smoothed out, but Manzanera and Mackay powered occasional psychedelic rockers such as "Amazona," "Street Life," and "The Thrill of It All" with bursts of frenzied energy. Roxy Music took a four-year hiatus after *Siren* but returned at the height of the New Wave with *Manifesto*. Where before Ferry's suave crooning was one of several elements in a unique mix, it was now the focus. The band continued until 1982, disbanding after the pleasant background music of *Avalon*, its biggest U.S. hit. (Eno sat out a 2001 reunion tour and, in his place, rather than injecting someone to add his signature random twists, the band had a session player faithfully replicate all of his parts.)

Since the mid '80s Ferry has been at his best recording other people's songs (from "Eight Miles High" by the Byrds to "Jealous Guy" by John Lennon to "I Put a Spell on You" by Screamin' Jay Hawkins). In the spirit of surrealist artist Marcel Duchamp, he prefers the term "readymades" to "covers." "A lot of people have this strange prejudice against singers doing other people's songs," he told me. "Elvis and Sinatra, the biggest singers or our century, they weren't songwriters. I think there's room for an interpretative role." Unlike Eno, Ferry chose his role and settled into it.

THE POP ALBUMS

> Repetition is a form of change...Honor thy error as a hidden intention...Ask people to work against their better judgment...Turn it upside down.
>
> —Oblique Strategies

FREED FROM ROXY MUSIC but with plenty of idiot energy left to burn, Eno embarked on his solo career. Between 1973 and 1977, he produced four extraordinary efforts that are often referred to as his "pop albums." Rock 'n' roll continued to fascinate him, and now he was free to tackle it on his own terms. "What [*Stranded*] lacks for me is one of the most important elements of my musical life, which is insanity," Tamm quoted him as saying. "I'm interested in things being absurd."

One of Eno's central ideas was juxtaposing styles that were normally at odds. He provided a diverse group of musicians with a "central issue"—a basic groove, a melody, or a chord progression—then directed them through body language and the use of visual images. They often took his skeletal tunes in directions he'd never anticipated. The idea of "happy accidents" in the studio has a Zen beauty: You accept whatever fate has in store. But it also acknowledges the immediacy and spontaneity of all great rock 'n' roll. "Early rock music was, in a lot of cases, the product of incompetence, not competence," Eno says in Tamm's book. "There's a misconception that these people were brilliant musicians, and they weren't. They had terrific ideas and a lot of balls."

The Ultimate Psychedelic Rock
Library: Eno's solo debut
Here Come the Warm Jets
(EG) is a golden shower of
smart psychedelic pop.

Eno recorded *Here Come the Warm Jets* during twelve days at London's Majestic Studios. He played "simplistic keyboards, snake guitar, electric larynx, and synthesizer" and electronically treated the other musicians' parts by feeding them through his synthesizers and racks of effects. The ten tunes are rock songs with identifiable verses, choruses, and solos, but everything is a bit left of center. Sometimes the drums provide the hook, the solos are deliberate "nonevents," or the vocals are buried in the mix. In many cases, all of the instruments are used in rhythmic roles.

During his college fascination with the avant-garde, Eno performed a piece by La Monte Young that required him to hit the same cluster of notes on the piano at one-second intervals for an hour. This exercise taught him that repetition is a form of change—with slight variations in a repeating pattern taking on tremendous importance. In rock he found similar ideas in Sly and the Family Stone—who placed the snare and bass as the dominant instruments in the mix—and the Velvets. "The Velvet Underground used all of their instruments in the rhythm role and the singing in a deliberate monotone, which is a deliberate non-surprise," Eno said in *More Dark Than Shark*. "When you listen to the music, your focus is shifting all the time because there's no ranking."

Here Come the Warm Jets opens with the prominent, pounding rhythms of "Needles in the Camel's Eye." The title was inspired by the discordant "needle-like" guitar sound, which Eno achieved by rhythmically "playing" the tremolo bar on Phil Manzanera's guitar. Equally inventive are "Driving Me Backwards," a tune with an unwavering 4/4 rhythm that creates the feeling of swimming against a strong current; "Blank Frank," a song based on an Ipswich gangster who spoke only in the "incomprehensible proverbs" of a Benzedrine head; "Baby's on Fire," which climaxes with one of the most frightening psychedelic guitar solos ever, and the title track, which recalls Mike Oldfield's regal instrumentals. (Eno said the phrase refers to urinating, but the feel of the song has more in common with the tides rolling in.) The singing that begins late in the song never becomes fully audible and one of the only lines that can be made out is about "words that mean nothing to me."

At Ipswich, Eno was impressed with the phonetic recordings of Dadaist poets Hugo Ball and Kurt Schwitters. In the studio, he often added his vocals after the instruments were recorded, developing melodies by scat-singing nonsense syllables. Eno was more interested in letting sounds rather than lyrics dictate what a song was "about." "I don't want to hear [lyrics] most of the time," Tamm quoted him as saying. "They always impose something that is so unmysterious compared to the sound of the music that they debase the music for me." Nevertheless, Eno could be a smart and funny lyricist. His tunes are full of evocative, poetic images. As Tamm noted, "Eno's lyrics stand directly in the tradition of painting with words in rock music that begins with Dylan and runs through the psychedelic songwriters of the late 1960s and early 1970s." "Send for an ambulance or an accident investigator / He's breathing like a furnace / So I'll see you later, alligator / He'll set the sheets on fire / Mmm, quite a burning lover," Eno sings in "The Paw Paw Negro Blowtorch," a song inspired by a Michigan man whose breath supposedly caused things to ignite.

On his second album, Eno worked with a core band of Manzanera, Brian Turrington and Freddie Smith (the rhythm section of the Winkies), and former Soft Machine vocalist Robert Wyatt. He found the title on a set of postcards depicting scenes from a Chinese opera. Some journalists probed the implications of *Taking Tiger Mountain (By Strategy)*—was Eno a Maoist?—but as always, the artist shied away from directly addressing his politics.

The Ultimate Psychedelic Rock Library: There was nothing oblique about the appeal of Eno's hard-rocking sophomore effort, Taking Tiger Mountain (By Strategy) *(EG).*

"To require of art that it gives political direction strikes me as rather like asking Albert Einstein to tell you the four times table," he said in *More Dark Than Shark*. It's likely that Eno meant the phrase as an obscure reference to his own creative process and a set of cards called Oblique Strategies. The origins of the strategies can be traced to index cards that Eno left lying around the studio to challenge his band mates in Roxy Music. By *Tiger Mountain*, he had formalized sixty-four "worthwhile dilemmas" in collaboration with his painter friend, Peter Schmidt. The cards were intended to be used like the *I Ching:* Artists would choose a card and follow its advice absolutely whenever a problem presented itself in a creative endeavor. Their purpose, Eno said, was to bring the consciousness of an objective listener to one's consciousness as a composer.

It's impossible to say exactly how the Oblique Strategies were used on *Tiger Mountain*, but the disc is full of abrupt left turns. Manzanera told me that making the album was one of the most enjoyable experiences he ever had in the studio. "On *Taking Tiger Mountain (By Strategy)*, we were just doing anything we felt like doing at the time. The engineer we used, Rhett Davies, also did *Diamond Head* and *801 Live* and *Quiet Sun*, so it was like family. There was a lot of experimenting and a lot of hours spent with Brian Eno, me, and Rhett in the control room doing all the things that eventually evolved into those cards, the Oblique Strategies, and it was just a lot of fun."

Overall, the album is bouncier and more upbeat than Eno's first effort, but the rollicking rhythms and strong melodies mask sinister subject matter. Behind the cheerful doo-wop vocals of "Burning Airlines Give You So Much More" is a lyric inspired by the 1974 explosion of a Turkish DC-10, at the time the worst air disaster in history. "The Fat Lady of Limbourg" is one of several of what Eno calls "Burroughs-type" songs. It could be the soundtrack to a spy film set in the Interzone, but it's actually about a town in Belgium where the inmates of a famous asylum outnumber the townsfolk. As with slightly older peers such as Roger Waters, World War II loomed large during Eno's childhood, and a distinctly British wartime spirit is echoed in "Back in Judy's Jungle" and "Mother Whale Eyeless." But the most striking tune—and the one that predicts Eno's next move—is "The Great Pretender." The song depicts the rape of a suburban housewife by a crazed machine, and it fades into an electronic chorus of chirping crickets that evoke natural forces as evil as the unnatural acts in the lyrics.

The "crickets" were evidence of Eno's growing interest in the texture of sounds. "To a great extent, Eno's music is concerned with the sheer color of sound, rather than with the linear, horizontal growth of melodies," Tamm wrote. Eno began to think song structure was

The Ultimate Psychedelic Rock Library: Another Green World *(EG) is the best of Eno's four brilliant "pop" albums.*

irrelevant. He wanted it to seem as if his songs existed before he turned on the tape recorder and continued after he stopped. Lyrics were becoming less important than ever, and nine of the fourteen pieces on *Another Green World* are instrumentals. Using a Hammond organ, synthetic percussion, and "electric elements and unnatural sounds," Eno conjures dinosaurs dancing on the edge of the tar pit on "Sombre Reptiles." "Little Fishes" takes the listener inside Eno's aquarium; the title track paints a picture of a womb-like Garden of Eden, and "In Dark Trees" is full of lurking menace.

Less forceful than its predecessors, *Another Green World* stands as the best of Eno's pop albums. He was aware that he had reached a pinnacle, and the pressure of crafting a follow-up weighed heavily. He spent nearly three years recording some one hundred pieces, and after months of indecision, he finally settled on ten tracks that were released as *Before and After Science*. In keeping with the futuristic themes of several songs, the album is the coldest and most clinical of Eno's pop efforts. "Energy Fools the Magician" could be a sample

The Ultimate Psychedelic Rock Library: Eno more or less bid farewell to rock with 1977's Before and After Science *(EG).*

*The Ultimate Psychedelic Rock
Library:*
801 Live *(EG) captures a
psychedelic/prog-rock
supergroup onstage.*

of the Muzak playing in Dr. Frankenstein's lab. Several songs are in
a similar mold, and only "King's Lead Hat" and "Kurt's Rejoinder"
rock out. (The former is a tribute to Talking Heads—the title is an
anagram—and the latter samples Eno's old hero, Kurt Schwitters.)

After leaving Roxy Music, Eno played live on only a few occasions. In 1974 he taped a session for the BBC backed by the
Winkies, playing a set that climaxed in a psychotic version of
"Fever." With Manzanera and bassist Bill MacCormick, he was a
member of the all-star progressive-rock band 801, which was
captured on a live album released in 1976. An earlier live effort,
June 1,1974, features former Velvets John Cale and Nico, Kevin
Ayers of the Soft Machine, and Mike Oldfield. The standouts on
both albums are songs from the first psychedelic era. 801 covers the
Beatles' "Tomorrow Never Knows," and the *June 1, 1974* group takes
on "The End" by the Doors.

Eno wasn't interested in touring, and he didn't care about
recording hits. With *Before and After Science*, he concluded that he

had accomplished as much as he could in the rock idiom. "Effectively, what I've done is abandoned rock music," he said in the early '80s. "For me, rock isn't capable of producing that spiritual quality anymore...Despite all the criticism that's been made of psychedelic music, it certainly was committed to the production of an expanded awareness."

AMBIENT ALBUMS AND PRODUCTIONS

> Take a break...Listen in total darkness, or in a very large
> room, very quietly...Ghost echoes...Give the game away.
> —Oblique Strategies

ENO ABANDONED ROCK, but he didn't abandon the psychedelic goal of transporting listeners to unexplored (and sometimes non-existent) places. He began a series of albums that lacked vocals and obvious rhythmic drive and which boasted only simple, minimal hooks, when there were any at all. What Eno called his "ambient" efforts were albums that were designed to subliminally enhance the thousand tasks of everyday life; he said they rewarded close listening but didn't demand it. Something similar would be claimed by another genre that started gaining popularity at roughly the same time in the late '70s and early'80s. New Age music is the soundtrack to what *The New Rolling Stone Encyclopedia of Rock & Roll* called a "loosely defined metaphysical movement that incorporates Jungian

psychology, ecological concern, and nontraditional spirituality."
But while these sounds appeal to some veterans of psychedelic
exploration, diverse New Age practitioners (such as synthesizer
players Vangelis and Jean-Michel Jarre, harpist Andres
Vollenweider, guitarist Kitaro, and virtually the entire Windham
Hill roster) were obsessed with such decidedly nonrock musical values as virtuosity and good taste. They had as their antecedent the
impressionistic composer Claude Debussy, who tried to find musical equivalents for natural sounds. In contrast, ambient music is
rather "punk" in its technical demands (there are none), and its
techniques come from psychedelic rock (via its approach to the
recording studio) and *musique concrète* (which used natural sounds
themselves as music).

Eno's methods on his ambient albums were similar to the ones
on his rock albums. Still no virtuoso, he simply set up systems that
allowed the recordings to generate themselves. "I tend towards the
roles of planner and programmer and then become an audience to
the results," he said. Anyone who had a digital synthesizer (the
Yamaha DX7 was Eno's new weapon of choice), an echo unit, and
two tape recorders could make similar pieces at home. Eno's albums
were available for those who didn't want to bother.

Recorded in September 1975, the thirty-minute title track on
Discreet Music was intended to serve as the background for a live performance by frequent collaborator Robert Fripp. ("Perhaps in the
spirit of Satie, who wanted to make music that could mingle with
the sound of the knives and forks at dinner," Eno wrote in the liner
notes.) "Discreet Music" is perfect for writing, reading, drifting off to
sleep, gentle afternoon lovemaking—or giving birth. "There are

maternity hospitals that have this record around to play in the background because pregnant mothers like it a lot," Eno told me. "That's one of the nicest things to me, to think that I've made something that people actually can use and like to have in their lives."

Music for Films followed in 1978. A compilation of eighteen instrumentals recorded during the sessions for the pop albums, it features regular contributors such as Fripp, Collins, MacCormick, Cale, and Fred Frith. The uninspired quality of many of the fragments makes it clear why they originally wound up as outtakes. *Music for Airports* was released in 1979, and to Eno's joy, it was actually pumped into New York's LaGuardia Airport. Unfortunately, the music is less evocative of flight than of waiting around in a sterile public place. *The Plateaux of Mirrors* and *Days of Radiance* are unremarkable collaborations with, respectively, pianist Harold Budd and the hammer-dulcimer player Laraaji. *On Land* (1982) is more involving; in addition to recording frogs and insects, Eno reworked sounds from some of his earlier albums. ("Some earlier pieces I worked on became digested by later ones," he wrote in the liner notes. "This technique is like composting: converting what would otherwise have been waste into nourishment.") The best of any of the ambient albums came relatively late in the game with 1985's tuneful and pleasant *Thursday Afternoon.*

While his solo career was turning toward ambient instrumentals, Eno was also becoming known as a rock producer. At first, his production work resulted from personal relationships with other musicians. Later, artists began seeking him out because of his novel and well-publicized ideas. In the studio he was part guru, part guilty conscience, and part childhood troublemaker, prodding the other kids to misbehave. "I often take extreme positions in the studio," he told *Musician* magazine in 1993. "I try to push opinions as far as I can, even to the point of saying, 'This is potentially the best piece of music I've ever heard in my life! And here, next to it, is possibly the worst.' It gets people's blood going, gets them fighting to defend something." Eno's early productions included John Cale's *Fear*, Robert Calvert's *Lucky Lief and the Longships*, and the debut by a beguiling instrumental group called the Penguin Cafe Orchestra. Eno made two albums with the German group Cluster, and he contributed soundscapes and songs to projects by Manzanera, Genesis (*The Lamb Lies Down on Broadway*), and Wyatt. (Cluster's *Old Land* includes the Eno tune "Broken Head," a throwback to the pop albums and a song its author said was autobiographical. "I was just a broken head / I stole the world that others punctured," Eno sings. "Now I stumble through the garbage / Slide and tumble, slide and tumble.")

A year older than Eno, David Bowie had a similar background and many of the same interests, but his personal style was a sharp contrast. Bowie was fascinated with playing the star, and he had an obsessive desire to continually reinvent his musical persona. He had flirted with psychedelic rock on "Space Oddity" and a cover of Pink Floyd's "See Emily Play," but by the mid-'70s, he had also played at being a mod, a Dylanesque troubadour, an ambi-sexual glam-rock alien, and a Philadelphia soul man. His biggest talent was orchestrating these strange ch-ch-ch-changes at precisely the right times. But with *Station to Station* in 1976, he began to distance himself from his various poses by embracing new technology and deconstructing some of his earlier sounds. Bowie had been impressed with *Another Green World*, and he viewed Eno as a bottomless well of new ideas. Eno had admired *Station to Station* and saw in Bowie a willing vehicle for taking some of his ideas into the pop mainstream. Their three collaborations—the so-called "Berlin trilogy" of *Low*, *"Heroes,"* and *Lodger*—gave Eno a new notoriety and Bowie the most psychedelic albums of his career, mixing ambient instrumentals with rock songs turned inside-out and upside-down. The middle installment, 1977's *"Heroes,"* stands as the strongest of these discs.

When the album was released, the Berlin Wall had been standing for sixteen years. Erected by the Soviet Union to stop the exodus of people fleeing toward the West to escape a harsh and repressive life in the Communist bloc, this imposing structure loomed even larger as an image than it did as reality; it captured people's imaginations. *"Ich bin ein Berliner"* President John F. Kennedy had declared. *"Heroes"* was Bowie's version of that same statement. Ably abetted by Eno and his longtime producer, Tony Visconti, the Great Chameleon also drew on the contributions of two extremely

The Ultimate Psychedelic Rock Library: "Heroes" *(Rykodisc) is the best (and most psychedelic) of Bowie and Eno's Berlin collaborations.*

different but phenomenally inventive guitarists: the soulful Carlos Alomar and the progressive-rock hero Robert Fripp. This diverse ensemble bunkered down at Hansa Studio ("by the wall," as Bowie sang) and crated a record that is very much a relic of the vinyl era, when albums had two distinct sides. The result can be neatly divided between the vocal- and guitar-driven music of the first half and the more meandering instrumental music of the second, but in its best moments, especially during the phenomenal title track, the ambient ideas are intertwined with great, catchy rock music.

Driven by an infectious, tubular Fripp guitar riff and a steady, metronomic drum beat, and subtly decorated by Eno's synthesizer squeals and bleeps, "Heroes" is a futuristic take on a Velvet Underground drone, a mysterious, enigmatic-sounding backing track for an apocalyptic scene whose drama is conveyed by the emotion of Bowie's vocals, even if it is never specifically addressed in the lyrics. (Rising to his theatrical best, the singer spits out the words as if dictating an urgent telegram: "I...I remember...standing...by the wall / The guns...shot about our heads...and we kissed...as though nothing could fall.") Slightly less complex, the other proper songs are only marginally less powerful. "Beauty and the Beast" and "Joe the Lion" are hard-hitting if somewhat twisted psychedelic rockers with prime Bowie vocal turns; "Sons of the Silent Age" harkens back to his "Space Oddity"-era solo work with less obvious, more oblique production twists; "The Secret Life of Arabia" is a nice little snake-charmer mood piece; "Blackout" expands on the dance-groove funkiness of "Young Americans," and "Station to Station," adds a sort of distant android coldness to the mix. The instrumentals are primarily comprised of Eno's synths, a stringed Japanese instrument called a samisen, and Bowie's heavily treated saxophone. There are moments of static beauty, haunting sparseness, and pointless wankery, sometimes all in the same tune. (The best of these, "V-2 Schneider," name-checks the Nazi rockets that fell on the World War II England of Bowie's youth as well as Florian Schneider, one of the two driving forces of the ground-breaking German electronic band, Kraftwerk.)

After completing *Lodger* the following year, Bowie spun off into increasingly vapid dance-pop, and then begin revisiting earlier accomplishments with lesser results and a lack of fresh inspiration. "Artistically, 1977 to '81 were absolutely dynamic," he said from the safe distance of the '90s in Scott Cohen's *Yakety Yak: The Midnight Confessions and Revelations of Thirty-Seven Rock Stars and Legends*. "Brian Eno treats studios the way no other person has. He works with it like an instrument, which is actually quite the thing now, especially in dance music, but at the particular time, there was

The Ultimate Psychedelic Rock Library: Eno and David Byrne's My Life in the Bush of Ghosts *(Sire) is a pioneering mix of ambient/psychedelic instrumentals and "found" or sampled vocals.*

The Ultimate Psychedelic Rock Library: Eno's influence is clearly felt on Achtung Baby *(Island), U2's most inventive and psychedelic album.*

no one else doing that, except for a couple of Germans. He really hipped me to the potential of arranging musical accidents."

Eno did the same for many others. He was at the controls as Talking Heads expanded their sound far beyond their early minimalism by embracing African and Funkadelic-style rhythms and mandala-like melodies. Eno also recorded 1981's *My Life in the Bush of Ghosts* with head Head David Byrne, taking the title from Nigerian novelist Amos Tutuola and using snippets of sound from talk radio, chanting Algerian Moslems, and Egyptian pop music, thereby prompting an early controversy over would later be called sampling. "Like most 'found' art, *My Life in the Bush of Ghosts* raises stubborn questions about context, manipulation and cultural imperialism," critic Jon Pareles wrote. Even more notorious was Eno's work with U2. After helping the echo-happy Irish rockers strike a balance between ambience and earnestness on *The Unforgettable Fire* and *The Joshua Tree,* he prodded the group into crafting a distinctly '90s brand of psychedelic rock on *Achtung Baby* and *Zooropa*—the perfect soundtracks for slipping on the virtual reality helmet or flipping through three hundred channels of satellite TV while waiting for the Ecstasy to kick in. Eno accomplished this by dropping in on the *Achtung Baby* sessions every few weeks and erasing anything that sounded too much like U2.

"There were some occasions where Brian was practically physically restrained from erasing," the Edge told me. Said Eno: "It's much easier to encourage something that you recognize, so people from the company and the people they work with will come along and say, 'That sounds great,' because it sounds like the U2 they know and love. I'm part of the small contingent that redress that by coming along and hearing things that I don't recognize and saying, 'Wow, now that sounds really exciting. Let's follow that for a while.'"

THE PERFECT CIRCLE

> Trust in the you of now...Don't be frightened to display
> your talents...Use an old idea...Just carry on.
> —Oblique Strategies

IN THE FALL OF 1990, Eno and I sat in a suite in Minneapolis' most luxurious hotel as he prepared to give a lecture at the Walker Art Institute on high art versus low art. Perhaps because he has always straddled that line himself, he was in the mood to reflect. "*The Joshua Tree* sold more copies in the first morning than all of the records I've made put together, but I don't mind that," he said. "I think you can see certain things as a kind of research, things that are made for other artists in a way. It's what other artists take and use, like a single strong spice that then forms part of their work."

A few months later, Eno made the surprising move of singing again on a new pop album with John Cale. His only vocal appearance between *Before and After Science* and *Wrong Way Up* was a moving rendition of the spiritual "You Don't Miss Your Water," included on the soundtrack to Jonathan Demme's 1988 film, *Married to the Mob.* The following year, he went to Moscow to record *Words for the Dying*, an album of Cale compositions performed by the Orchestra of Symphonic and Popular Music of Gosteleradio. Almost as an afterthought, Cale and Eno tacked on a catchy sing-along called "The Soul of Carmen Miranda," and that prompted them to record a full album.

Wrong Way Up was not an easy album to make. Evidence of the tension is seen in cover art of the two players exchanging daggers.

The Ultimate Psychedelic Rock Library: Eno's last "rock" effort was his 1990 collaboration with John Cale, Wrong Way Up *(Warner Bros.).*

Eno would only say that he and Cale weren't likely to work together again. Cale offered that Eno had attempted to do too much, acting as producer, writer, engineer, and host at his home studio in Woodbridge, England. He added that Eno has a nasty habit of erasing his partners' work. Despite these problems, *Wrong Way Up* is an optimistic album full of catchy, upbeat rock songs built around newly streamlined computer rhythms and Cale and Eno's familiar keyboard styles. The two clearly enjoyed trading lead vocals and building "harmonic stacks" of backing vocals, but Eno seemed surprised by the positive reaction. "I like the way I sing, but I never really expected anyone else to like it," he told me.

Eno continued to incorporate vocals on 1992's *Nerve Net*, which was recorded with a variety of musicians as he crossed the United States on his 1990 lecture tour. He had become convinced that the most innovative work in the studio was being done in the dance genre, and he was impressed by techno musicians such as Moby and the Orb, who were incorporating some of his ambient ideas. *Nerve Net* and *The Shutov Assembly* (a collection of "robot instrumentals" recorded during the *Nerve Net* sessions) pay tribute to the dance musicians who paid tribute to Eno, but they aren't nearly as inspired as *Wrong Way Up*.

After decades of trailblazing, Eno seems to finally be repeating himself. *Neroli* (1993) was inspired by his new hobby of crafting his own perfumes; *The Drop* (1997) had a pronounced techno edge, and *Drawn from Life* (2001) was a collaboration with German DJ and percussionist Peter Schwalm, but the ambient music on each of these efforts was really nothing special. In 1994 Eno contributed unremarkable synthesizer playing to *Mamouna*, a solo album by

Ferry and in 1995, he worked with another figure from his past, Bowie, on an embarrassingly bad concept album called *Outside*. He also crafted another mediocre volume of music for films with members of U2 under the *nom de rock*, Passengers. Eno claims he is becoming increasingly less interested in music because it is increasingly less important as a cultural force, but it could just as well be said that his music is increasingly less vital because making music is increasingly less important to him. Nevertheless, his ideas remain inspirational.

"For me, it's all about passion," he told me. "One of the challenges of being alive and staying alive is knowing how to use these different styles: to be sometimes passionate, sometimes analytical, and sometimes a gardener around the house. People are sometimes disappointed to hear that. They say, 'Fuck, he's just like me.' Either that, or sometimes they're very pleased, because they realize the potential is there for them as well."

NINE

9

YOO DOO RIGHT:
The Krautrock Blitzkrieg

Some skeezix from one of the local dailies was up here the other day to do a "human interest" story, and naturally our beneficent publisher hauled me into his office to answer this fish's edition of the perennial: "Where is rock going?" "It's being taken over by the Germans and the machines," I unhesitatingly answered. And this I believe to my funky soul.

—Lester Bangs,
"Kraftwerkfeature," *Creem* magazine, 1975

THE PSYCHEDELIC ROCK made in England and the United States in 1966 and 1967 didn't go unheard in mainland Europe, but with few exceptions, contemporary European bands were content to play covers or thinly-veiled rewrites of songs by British and American groups. "Perhaps because of the lack of musical role models, the European student movements took on serious political overtones," critic Pascal Bussy wrote in *Kraftwerk: Man, Machine and Music*. "They were unwilling to merely sit around with flowers in their hair listening to rock music, thus avoiding the hedonistic excesses produced by the London, San Francisco, and New York hippie 'scenes.'" European student activism climaxed with the Paris riots of 1968, in which left-wing students nearly toppled the French government.

This anarchic energy was also felt in West Germany, where a generation of young people was searching for an identity amid the cold war tensions, the lingering consciousness of Nazism and World War II, and the same experimentation with alternative lifestyles, sex, and psychedelic drugs that was happening in the West. From this milieu came a generation of artists dedicated to challenging the mainstream and establishing a new German cultural identity, including performance artist Joseph Beuys, filmmakers Rainer Werner Fassbinder and Wim Wenders, and the bands that the English music press dubbed krautrock. (The Germans themselves initially preferred the far more psychedelic *kosmische musick*, or cosmic music, though they came to embrace the term krautrock with several song and album titles.)

The krautrock/cosmic music bands occasionally shared the same stage or producer—notably Conrad (Conny) Plank or Dieter Dierks—or recorded for the same label, especially the adventurous independents, Brain and Ohr. But most prided themselves on their self-sufficiency, funding their own recordings and building their own home studios. "Krautrock wasn't a movement, but a moment, a final thrust of the psychedelic project to gobble up every kind of music—and every kind of non-musical noise, too—in order to excrete the outermost sound conceivable," critic Simon Reynolds wrote in 1992. The press release for Faust's 1971 debut described the goals in even grander terms: "Unlike rock musicians in other countries, this new breed of German musicians is not interested in imitating what's gone before them. They're looking for new sounds and new forms of expression. Their music is no hand-me-down Beatles or Stones or the white man's idea of R&B. It's their own, building as much on the immense tradition of German music as on the Anglo-Saxon dominated traditions of current pop."

Like the psychedelic bands in England and America, the German groups never believed that rock had to be limited to tidy three-minute packages. They embraced long Eastern drones and hypnotic percussion. The work of Terry Riley and La Monte Young taught them the power of repeating simple melodic patterns. From *musique concrète* and avant-garde composer Karlheinz Stockhausen, they got the idea of music based on the sounds of industry, and from the Velvet Underground came the raw rock aggression of "Sister Ray." These influences were combined with a Teutonic fascination with technology, especially synthesizers and the recording studio itself. "In a studio you make a concert for machines," Holger Czukay said in *The Can Book*. "And machines really like to listen."

That Can, Kraftwerk, and Neu! were the most important krautrock bands is evidenced to some degree by their commercial success, but even more by their enduring influence. Can's worldbeat experiments inspired Public Image and the Talking Heads of *Remain in Light*, while their earlier, noisier sounds influenced the bands on England's Too Pure label in the '90s. Time has revealed the members of Kraftwerk to be forefathers of synthesizer groups such as Depeche Mode, Gary Numan, and the Human League, as well as pioneers in a new way of making music based on rhythms and samples. Neu!'s rhythmic trance-rock was echoed in the '80s in the Feelies and Sonic Youth (whose alter egos Ciccone Youth paid tribute with a song called "Two Cool Rock Chicks Listening to Neu!"), and in the '90s by Stereolab, LaBradford, and the ever-tasteful Julian Cope. But this isn't to say that the other krautrock bands aren't interesting footnotes.

"If Can and Neu!'s sometime minimalist approach was indicative of a harsh, spare German outlook, then Amon Düül may represent all that was grand and eloquent," krautrock chronicler Armstrong Whitworth wrote in the fanzine *Strange Things Are Happening*. The group was the musical arm of an anarchist/libertarian commune formed in 1968 near Munich. The band and its would-be utopia shared the same name, taking the "Amon" from the Egyptian sun god Amen-Ra and the "Düül" from the Turkish god of music. But it wasn't always fun and games in this ideal community, and the group splintered after performing with the Fugs

The Ultimate Psychedelic Rock Library: Eastern drones meet Western acid-rock freak-outs on Amon Düül II's epic Phallus Dei *(Mantra).*

The Ultimate Psychedelic Rock Library: Krautrock fan Julian Cope has noted that Amon Düül II's Yeti *(Mantra) was such a hit among heads in his native Tamworth that they referred to each other as "yeti's."*

and the Mothers of Invention at Essen's Song Days Festival in late 1968. The best musicians left to form Amon Düül II, while Amon Düül I made a joyous cacophony in the style of the free-form sounds at Ken Kesey's Acid Tests. Its first three albums all date from one twenty-four-hour recording session/freak-out.

Amon Düül II mixed spacey, free-flowing jams with expressionist lyrics, the classical violin of Chris Karrer, and the sensual vocals of Bavarian earth mother Renate Knaup-Krötenschwanz. Englishman Dave Anderson played bass on the band's best efforts, 1969's *Phallus Dei* ("God's Cock") and 1970's *Yeti*, a double album featuring a tribute to the original manufacturers of LSD called "Sandoz in the Rain." Anderson left in 1970 to join Hawkwind, but the group continued to make wonderfully trippy rock on *Dance of the Lemmings* (1971) and *Wolf City* (1972) before starting a long, slow decline into schlocky, sub-cabaret jazz.

With a name inspired by John Lennon's vision of "tangerine trees and marmalade skies," Tangerine Dream progressed from imi-

tating Pink Floyd to delivering snooze-inducing synthesizer instrumentals. The band was formed in 1967 by Edgar Froese, a sculptor
who studied under Salvador Dalí. Its first album, *Electronic
Meditation*, was released on Ohr in 1970. Featuring Froese on guitar,
Klaus Schulze on drums, and Conrad Schnitzler ("the mad genius
from Berlin") on organ, it borrows liberally from *A Saucerful of
Secrets*. Schulze and Schnitzler departed a short time later, and the
faint but distinctive rock heartbeat went with them. Leading a new,
three-synthesizer lineup, Froese recorded several mildly engaging
albums, including *Alpha Centauri*, dedicated to "all people who feel
obliged to space," and 1975's *Rubycon*. But it was all downhill into
bland New Age music after 1975's *Rubycon*, a depressing fact when
you consider that the group's discography contains some forty
more albums (including the soundtrack to *Risky Business*).

Before striking out on his own, Schulze did a brief stint with
Ash Ra Tempel, whose members were the most overt acidheads of
any of the krautrockers. The cover of the group's self-titled debut

*The Ultimate Psychedelic Rock
Library: Cleopatra's 1998 CD
combines Ash Ra Tempel's*
Schwingungen *and* Seven Up
in one trippy package.

The Ultimate Psychedelic Rock Library: The back cover of Popol Vuh's delightfully droney Affenstunde (Spalax) pictures the three band members jamming on tabla, djembe, and modular Moog.

features a portrait of a psychedelicized Egyptian pharaoh, and nuggets of Eastern philosophy are tossed in among the exotic electronic drones. Acid guru Timothy Leary can be heard howling horny improvised blues lyrics under the psychedelic cacophony of the band's sophomore effort, *Seven Up*; recorded live in Switzerland when Leary was on the lam after escaping from an American prison, it was named after the brand of soda pop that the good doctor spiked with LSD before the show. The band's driving force, guitarist Matt Gottsching, eventually abandoned his freakier impulses and went on to record genteel New Age instrumentals under the trimmed-down name of Ashra.

Synthesists Dieter Moebius and Hans Joachim Roedelius of Cluster did their best work in collaboration with others, either with Brian Eno, or with guitarist Michael Rother as part of Harmonia. On their own the pair produced pleasant but unmemorable ambient drones. Revolving around the gothic-sounding, minor-chord moodiness of its synthesist and primary auteur, Florian Fricke,

Popol Vuh (named after the Mayan *Book of the Dead*) is best remembered for crafting the Pink Floyd-style soundtracks to most of Werner Herzog's films, including *Nosferatu the Vampyre, Fitzcarraldo,* and *Aguirre: The Wrath of God.* But the group's first two albums, 1970's *Affenstunde* ("Ape Hour") and 1971's *In Den Garten Pharoas* ("In the Garden of Pharaoh") include some of the best and most psychedelic krautrock. "We have an old expression in Germany, " Fricke said in Dave Thompson's *Space Daze.* "'To have one's feet in the sky.' Isn't that what it's all about?"

The krautrock list goes on. Floh De Cologne recorded a rock opera called *Profitgeier* as a sarcastic response to the Who's *Tommy.* Guru Guru started out as a trio recording hard-rock instrumentals such as "Der LSD-Marsch" and wound up making bad cabaret music. The only other band with anywhere near the influence of Can, Kraftwerk, and Neu! is Faust. Formed in 1971 at the instigation of producer and former journalist Uwe Nettlebeck, the quintet lived in a converted schoolhouse in Wümme in the countryside between Hamburg and Bremen. "Devoted to the spirit of the May 1968 revolts," to quote their press release, they believed that each musician should make his own instruments. Clanging metal, tumbling bricks, and resounding sledgehammers powered Faust's music a decade before Throbbing Gristle or Einstürzende Neubauten used such techniques. The quintet was determined to tear down rock 'n' roll and romp in the debris, a point driven home by snippets of "All You Need Is Love" and "Satisfaction" buried in the murky mix of its first album.

"We were naïve and arrogant," Jean-Hervé Peron told Greg Kot of the *Chicago Tribune* in 1994. "We took some drugs, took a few

The Ultimate Psychedelic Rock Library: Collector's Choice paired Faust *and* So Far *on one post-psychedelic, proto-industrial disc.*

trips, but we never played on trips. We would stand on the rooftop of the farm, staring out at the stars, and shout until we were empty. That would be a high. Or we would dig a hole for hours in the yard. We were our own drugs....We wanted to break everything, not just the rules." Like Can, the members of Faust simply let the tapes roll while they experimented, and albums were compiled later from the diverse results. *Faust* (1971) featured three long suites that critic Simon Reynolds described as a mix of "acid-rock hoo-ha, zany chorale, found sounds, synth-gibberish, freeform jazz, nonsense incantations, mock-Muzak, [and] animal noises (genuine and falsified)." The follow-up, 1972's *So Fa*r, was more accessible and featured several genuine songs, including the Velvets-style stomper, "It's A Rainy Day, Sunshine Girl."

    After two albums on Polydor, Faust followed many of its krautrock contemporaries to Virgin, releasing *The Faust Tapes* and *Faust IV* before disbanding in 1974. The former is a scattered collage of twenty-six pieces recorded between 1971 and 1973. The band members considered it their best effort, but Virgin disagreed and started to pressure the group. "They wanted us to sell records and to tour," Peron told Jason Ferguson of *Alternative Press*. "That was not the situation we wanted to be in, so we split" (though not before a final incarnation that included Peter Blegvad and other members of the experimental English pop group Slapp Happy). Cult appreciation prompted Peron and fellow veteran Werner Dermaier to form a new version of the group in 1990. Faust picked up where it left off, scrounging instruments from the junk yard and incorporating a bleating goat in its sets.

Looking back in 1994, Peron offered what may be the most succinct summation of the krautrock philosophy. "We're German, we're not afraid of it, we're not ashamed of it, and we make different music," he told *The Wire* magazine. That he meant "German" in a new cultural sense rather than the old nationalistic sense was underscored by the fact that, in 1993 as in 1970, he was a French national transplanted in the Fatherland, "living naked and growing dope and tomatoes."

THEN I SAW MUSHROOM HEAD

> Any music without energy I throw to my tape machine's
> starving eraser heads.
>
> —Holger Czukay,
> *The Can Book*

WHEN THEY CAME TOGETHER in Cologne in 1968, the members of Can had little experience with rock 'n' roll. Czukay played the French horn and studied composition under Stockhausen. His goal in forming a band was to merge free jazz, contemporary classical music, and "ethnic music"/worldbeat. His first recruit, Irmin Schmidt, studied classical piano and composition, and Jaki Liebezeit was an accomplished jazz drummer. Only Czukay's student, guitarist Michael Karoli, was a full-blown rock fan. It was Karoli who suggested that the Beatles were more interesting than Stockhausen. "I Am the Walrus" indicated that he might be right, but the Velvets proved even more inspirational.

The musicians jammed in a castle called Schloss Norvenich, and improvisation was key from the beginning. "We began without any concept," Schmidt said in Pascal Bussy and Andy Hall's *The Can Book*. "Our only idea was to find a concept in making music all together spontaneously, in a collective way without any leader." Can's method of reworking songs at each performance came to be called "instant composition," and the group's fans frequently used the word "telepathic" to characterize the members' playing. What set Can's improvisations apart from free jazz, the space jams of the

Grateful Dead, or the virtuosic meanderings of Cream was a devotion to rock simplicity. Czukay was the master of one- and two-note bass lines. Karoli played in what's been described as a spidery, chip-chop style, and Schmidt attacked his keyboards with rapid-fire karate chops. "Inability is often the mother of restriction, and restriction is the great mother of inventive performance," Czukay told Bussy and Hall. As for Liebezeit, even when he played in unusual time signatures, he had a way of locking into a powerful and hypnotic pulse. It was rumored that he learned several "forbidden rhythms" from a Cuban musician who practiced Santeria. Supposedly, the Cuban was executed onstage because he had dared to play the rhythms outside sacred ceremonies. "It is something that I heard, I did not witness the actual execution," is all Liebezeit would say.

Two months after their initial jams, the members of Can were joined by vocalist Malcolm Mooney, an eccentric African-American sculptor from New York who was bumming around Europe.

The Ultimate Psychedelic Rock Library: The influence of the Velvets is obvious on Can's Monster Movie *(Mute), but the band takes the psychedelic drone to a whole new level.*

Mooney had never played music, but he was a jazz and blues fan who dreamed of being a singer. The Germans were drawn to his manic energy, and he was soon improvising rhythmic torrents of words over the band's churning music. The rehearsal room at Schloss Norvenich was converted into a studio with the addition of a two-track recorder and some old U.S. Army mattresses, and there Can recorded its first album. *Monster Movie* was initially released in a batch of five hundred copies on a small Munich label, but United Artists signed the band and re-released the album in August 1969. The disc was credited to "the Can," but the article was dropped a short time later. In the spirit of 1968, Schmidt told journalists that the letters stood for "Communism, Anarchism, and Nihilism," and the original liner notes introduced the musicians as "talented young people who want to stay in line but can't."

As the title indicates, *Monster Movie* is a cinematic album whose ominous tones summon images of lurking predators. It opens with "Father Cannot Yell," recorded in the second take of Mooney's first session with the band. The keyboard, the bass, the frantic rhythm, and the insistent guitar combine to create a feeling of panic as Mooney free-associates in a desperate rap, but the album's most impressive track takes up all of side two. "Yoo Doo Right" is some three minutes longer than the Velvets' "Sister Ray," which was clearly its inspiration. Recorded live during a concert at the castle, one of the band's two amps blew up in the middle of the piece, but the group kept right on playing. Over a primal drum beat, Mooney rants about a love letter from a girlfriend in America. The tension builds throughout the song and it is never resolved, leaving the listener wondering exactly what action the letter prompted.

Even before the release of *Monster Movie*, Mooney's position in the band was undermined by growing psychological problems. During one concert at the castle, he had an episode similar to one of Syd Barrett's onstage freak-outs when he fixated on audience members moving between Can's show and an art exhibit upstairs. He screamed, "Upstairs, downstairs!" for two hours until he finally collapsed. "Malcolm lost his head, which happened sometimes," Karoli explained in *The Can Book*. When a mystic friend told Mooney he was taking the wrong path in life, he began to grow paranoid. On the advice of a psychiatrist, he quit the band in late 1969 and went back to America.

Can spent some time recording soundtracks for art films and porno movies (music that was compiled on the album *Soundtracks*) before releasing its second proper effort in 1971. *Tago Mago* introduced a new vocalist, Damo Suzuki, a twenty-one-year-old Japanese singer whom Liebezeit and Czukay saw busking outside a cafe in Munich. "I saw Damo from far away, and he was screaming

The Ultimate Psychedelic Rock Library: Tago Mago *(Mute) introduced Damo Suzuki and a new ritualistic bent.*

and sort of adoring the sun," Czukay told Bussy and Hall. "I said to Jaki, 'Here comes our vocalist!' and Jaki said, 'No, no, it can't be true!'" Suzuki was invited to that night's performance. He began screaming at the audience and cleared the room in record time, thereby assuring his position in the band.

The group called *Tago Mago* its "magic record." Named after a site that figures in the legend of sorcerer Aleister Crowley, the standout tracks have an air of mystery and forbidden secrets. "Aumgn" features Schmidt chanting ritualistically over a creepy Eastern instrumental, and Suzuki's ranting on the tom-heavy "Hallelujah" is even weirder than Mooney's on "Yoo Doo Right." The trance-inducing "Mushroom" is an obvious tribute to those of the psychedelic variety, and the memorable line, "When I saw mushroom head / I was born and I was dead" neatly encapsulates a psychedelic experience.

In late 1971 Can moved out of Schloss Norvenich and into an old cinema outside Cologne. The new studio was called Inner Space, and it became the band's permanent home. The group was still recording with a simple two-track tape machine, but its live performances were becoming more elaborate. Concerts often featured a juggler and a fire eater as added attractions while the group played for up to four hours in front of as many as ten thousand German fans. Can's third album, *Ege Bamyasi*, took its name and cover art from a can of vegetables found in a Turkish restaurant. The music offers more of the same dark grooves, but it doesn't improve on the first two albums. *Future Days* is another story, expanding the band's sound in an almost symphonic style. "Moonshake" is meant to evoke tugboats chugging down the

The Ultimate Psychedelic Rock Library: Future Days *(Mute) is Can's most idyllic album.*

Rhine, and the side-long "Bel Air" uses echoes and tape loops to create an impressionistic portrait of the wind-swept cliffs on the coast of Portugal.

Suzuki left the group in September 1973 after marrying a German girl and becoming a Jehovah's Witnesses. This time Can abandoned the idea of finding an outside singer, and Karoli and Schmidt divided the vocals. Subsequent albums suffer from this decision, but they have their moments. "Dizzy Dizzy" from 1974's *Soon Over Babaluma* incorporates a reggae beat, and "Chain Reaction" is flavored with African percussion. In 1975 Can signed with Virgin Records, and its albums for that label mix pieces from the "ethnological forgery" series with warped pop tunes such as "Hunters and Collectors" from 1975's *Landed* and "I Want More" from 1976's *Flow Motion.* In 1977 Czukay quit after first retiring to a behind-the-scenes role of mixing and "playing" shortwave radio and telephone. By that time the band included two veterans of Traffic, bassist Rosko Gee and percussionist Reebop Kwaku Baah.

The early experimentation was replaced by rote European dance sounds, and the group offered up a lame disco version of the "Can-Can." A short time later the band wisely called it a day.

Can reunited once in 1986. Mooney, now a remedial reading teacher in New York, flew in to sing, but the resulting album, *Rite Time*, was anti-climactic. The musicians had grown too much during their solo projects, their egos had gotten too big to accept musical accidents, and the lure of fancy technology had become irresistible. It disbanded again and the members went their separate ways. Liebezeit is an in-demand session drummer; Schmidt composes music on his own, and Czukay sometimes tours as a techno DJ. Can's original psychedelic spirit lived on longest in Karoli and Suzuki, who sometimes toured together, continuing to improvise most of what they played on the spot, until Karoli died from cancer in 2000. "He was special," Suzuki said of Karoli when we spoke in 2001. "We were not really best of friends, but we played music much more together. He had really special taste, and he played music in a way you could not really compare to anybody else. He had a really good instinct with my voice, and we played so well together. I don't really know anybody else like him."

Can remains an inspiration to other musicians—in 1997, artists like the Orb, Sonic Youth, and Bruce Gilbert of Wire collaborated for an album called *Sacrilege: The Remixes,* and the New York garage band Mooney Suzuki took its name from Can's two vocalists. Suzuki in particular is a hero (the Fall wrote a song in homage enti-tled "I Am Damo Suzuki"), largely because of the completely free and daring way that he approaches making music. "Comfortable things are the enemy of creative things," he told me. In 2002 he toured with the "intuitive music" band Cul de Sac, but refused to meet them before they got together for the first time on stage. "Damo has three rules: 'No improvisation. No rehearsal. No prepared songs,'" guitarist Glenn Jones said before the start of the tour. Added Suzuki: "We are just going to meet and make music, because that's the way I like to do it. It's much better for me, because you can enjoy the music of the moment. I think it's the best way to make my feelings instinctive. For twenty years, I only make music this way." This, I noted, is what makes him a hero. "Not hero," he said. "I'm much more a shaman or something like this."

THE MAN-MACHINE

> We are playing the machines, the machines play us, it is really the exchange and the friendship we have with the musical machines.
>
> —Ralf Hütter
> in Pascal Bussy's *Kraftwerk: Man, Machine and Music*

WHILE THE MUSICIANS IN CAN were happy to play for their machines, the members of Kraftwerk fantasized about *becoming* machines themselves. Primary auteurs Ralf Hütter and Florian Schneider often talked about the group as if it was a device that generated music at the touch of a button. How many of these statements were for effect and how many were part of a genuine philosophy is open to debate. What can't be disputed is that Hütter and

Schnieder created a perfect pop group, one in which presentation, subject matter, and sound combined to create a timeless archetype. Not for nothing were they called the Beach Boys of Düsseldorf.

Hütter and Schneider would prefer people to think that they surfaced in 1974 as fully formed electronic-pop pioneers but in fact, the two met at the Düsseldorf Conservatory in the late '60s. They were from similar upper-middle-class backgrounds—Hütter's father was a doctor and Schnieder's was an architect—and they were drawn together by an interest in electronic avant-garde music. (They talked about seeing a Stockhausen concert as students while tripping on LSD.) In 1968 the two formed a group called Organisation to play improvised music with organ, flute, and electronics at art galleries and happenings. At one of these gigs they met Conny Plank, a jazz musician and recording engineer who had started his career doing sound for Marlene Dietrich and Duke Ellington. In the late '60s he became fascinated with the Velvets, Jimi Hendrix, and Jamaican dub producer Lee "Scratch" Perry, and he was intrigued by the possibility of working with a rock group that had a distinctive European sound and identity.

Plank recorded Organisation's first album, 1970's *Tone Float*, in a studio set up in a former oil refinery. He released the album on his own Rainbow label in Germany and secured a deal with RCA in England, but the meandering electronic sounds were a flop. Hütter and Schneider regrouped. Inspired by Can, they set up their own studio, located then as now in a rented loft in the center of Düsseldorf. Rather than the cosmic monikers of many krautrock groups, the two wanted a name that evoked images of industry to compliment a new industrial edge in their music, and they chose as

their name the German word for "power plant." Once again recorded by Plank, the self-titled *Kraftwerk* is starker and more rhythmic
than the Organisation album, thanks in part to drummers Andreas
Hohman and Klaus Dinger. The album received favorable reviews,
but the group's progress was soon interrupted by a series of personnel shifts. At one point, Hütter quit. The lineup of Schneider,
Dinger, and guitarist Michael Rother recorded thirty-five minutes of
music at Plank's studio, including an eleven-minute piece called
"Truckstop Gondolero." Before it could be released, Hütter rejoined
and Dinger and Rother left due to what Rother told biographer
Pascal Bussy was "a question of temperament, of character." Dinger
and Rother started a new project called, quite literally, Neu!, and
Hütter and Schneider released the quickly-produced *Kraftwerk 2*.

The band's sophomore album is strikingly similar to its debut,
and since the cover is almost identical, many listeners thought it
was just a repackaging. Released in 1973, *Ralf and Florian* was more
distinctive visually and musically. The cover shows the duo in the
midst of a growing collection of electronic instruments at their studio, which had been christened Kling Klang after the central seventeen-minute composition on *Kraftwerk 2*. The sound is cleaner
and less cluttered on melodic pieces such as "Elektrisches Roulette"
("Electric Roulette") and "Tanzmusik" ("Dance Music"), and for the
first time, Kraftwerk displays a sense of humor. The album ends
with "Ananas Symphonie" ("Pineapple Symphony"), a goofy track
that sounds like *South Pacific* on acid. Hütter and Schneider generally dismiss all of these efforts, and they have yet to sanction their
release on CD. Considering the radical turn their music took with
Autobahn, it's easy to understand why.

In 1974 the duo turned away from the insular world of the avant-garde and made a calculated attempt to go pop. In their new friend, visual artist Emil Schult, they found a guru with a talent for conceptualizing their music and presenting a unified multi-media image, and in the new Mini-Moog synthesizer, they found an electronic instrument that was perfectly suited for rock 'n' roll. It was as if Chuck Berry had just discovered the electric guitar. *Autobahn* was conceived as an aural version of driving on the German-Austrian superhighway. Neu! had made music evocative of this experience in 1971, but Hütter and Schneider made it even more obvious—adding lyrics for the first time—and they did it by using electronic instruments exclusively. The title track starts with the sound of a car revving up, then the pulsating percussion kicks into gear. The song is propelled by an ultra-hummable riff repeated in the rich harmonic overtones of the Moog. The monotone vocals echo the main riff, and it isn't clear whether Hütter is singing in German or English. The lyrics could be "Fahr'n, fahr'n, fahr'n on

The Ultimate Psychedelic Rock Library: Kraftwerk's Autobahn *(Elektra) is a brilliant aural evocation of speeding down the German superhighway.*

der autobahn"—"Riding, riding, riding on the autobahn"—or a very Beach Boys-like "Fun, fun, fun on the autobahn."

The album caught on slowly in Germany, but it was a big success in America. Producer Robin McBride edited the title track into a three-and-a-half-minute single, and it spread from Chicago radio throughout the States. Before making *Autobahn*, Hütter and Schneider expanded to a quartet featuring percussionist Wolfgang Flur and violinist Klaus Roeder, who was soon replaced by a second percussionist, Karl Bartos. These musicians were hired hands, and Hütter and Schneider never shared composing credits, but they helped present a distinctive image of Kraftwerk as a new kind of all-electronic band: Ladies and gentlemen, the robotic Beatles.

After *Autobahn*, Kraftwerk split with Plank. (The engineer went on to work with Eno, Killing Joke, Eurythmics, DAF, and Devo before dying from cancer in 1987, but he never forgave Kraftwerk for abandoning him after what he considered to be key contributions.) Kraftwerk recorded its follow-up, *Radio-Activity*, on its own at Kling Klang. The title was a play on the central theme of invisible forces that could be positive (radio waves) or negative (nuclear fallout). Schult and Hütter drove across Germany in search of the right radio for the cover, finally settling on a short-range model that was used during the war for Nazi propaganda (a swastika between the dials was judiciously removed). Only the title track boasted a strong melody, but the album continued to win fans, including director Rainer Werner Fassbinder, who included passages on the soundtracks to *Chinesiches Roulett* and *Berlin Alexanderplatz*. The cinematic nature of Kraftwerk's music was growing more pronounced. The band's ability to make movies for the mind kept it in the psychedelic tradition even as the musicians adopted the lifestyles of Buddhist monks. "We had certain rules, like we wouldn't get drunk at parties or drunk onstage," Bartos told Bussy. "It is not so easy to turn the knobs of a synthesizer if you are drunk or full of drugs." The musicians referred to themselves as workers, and they followed a very workmanlike routine. "I wake up in the morning, I brush my teeth, I go to the studio, I work, I go back home, I eat, I sleep," is how Hütter described the daily ritual in *Kraftwerk: Man, Machine and Music*.

Released in 1977, *Trans-Europe Express* was the natural successor to *Autobahn*. While the latter duplicates a car trip, the former conjures the sounds of traveling by rail. It was named after the elegant and now-discontinued rail line that once passed through Düsseldorf Station not far from Kling Klang. Kraftwerk was using the most modern technology—including increasingly sophisticated sequencers—to evoke a bygone era. The outdated fashions and stylized tinting of the cover photo only heightened the dichotomy. In addition to several memorable hooks and Kraftwerk's strongest

The Ultimate Psychedelic Rock Library: Trans-Europe Express *(Capitol); this time, Kraftwerk took the train.*

rhythm track yet, the title cut boasts funny lyrics recounting a meeting with Iggy Pop and David Bowie. (Bowie hoped to collaborate with Hütter and Schneider, but he had to settle for dedicating a song to the duo, "V2 Schneider," on *"Heroes."*)

By 1978 the musical landscape had changed. When punk and New Wave arrived, Kraftwerk was recognized as an important influence. Hütter and Schneider had long subscribed to the punk philosophies that less is more and training is overrated. "Our music is rather minimalist," Hütter told Bussy. "If we can convey an idea with one or two notes, it is better to do this than to play a hundred or so notes. With our musical machines, there is no question of playing with a kind of virtuosity, there is all the virtuosity we need in the machines." In turn Hütter and Schneider drew inspiration from the new bands' energy and simplicity to produce their minimalist masterpiece. The songs on *The Man-Machine* are built with streamlined precision from simple repetitive melodies that interconnect like the gears on mechanical rotors. "The Robots" plays with the band's image and pays

The Ultimate Psychedelic Rock Library: The Man-Machine *(Capitol) is evidence for anyone who doubts that machines have a soul.*

tribute to its new alter egos. (At press junkets, specially constructed robots filled in for the absent band members.) Re-released a few years later as a single B side, "The Model" became Kraftwerk's biggest hit; its unbearably catchy riff is perfect accompaniment for a stroll down the runway, while the lyrics satirize the mechanical nature of "too-perfect" high-fashion queens. The album ends with the elliptical title track, and the word "machine" is echoed by a mechanical voice. The tune suggests the Man-Machine being switched off for the evening until it is time to make music again tomorrow.

Kraftwerk spent three years holed up at Kling Klang crafting a follow-up. The themes and melodies on 1981's *Computer World* are stretched thin, and there isn't much behind the concept that the modern world is run by computers (though "Computer Love" has taken on added meaning since the advent of cybersex). In the early '80s, Hütter and Schneider were more interested in pursuing their new passion for bicycling than making new music. This was reflected in 1983 on a single called "Tour De France," notable for a rhythm track based on a bike racer's heavy breathing. Plans to release an album called *Technopop* later in the year were scrapped after Hütter was hurt in a cycling accident, but there were rumors that the band realized that, for the first time, its new music was sounding outdated. Starting in 1982 with Afrika Bambaataa's "Planet Rock," rappers began sampling Kraftwerk to forge some of hip hop's freshest grooves. A few years later Detroit house deejays did the same to craft high-energy dance music.

Kraftwerk finally released a song called "Technopop" on 1986's *Electric Cafe*, and it can be heard as the group passing the baton to a new generation of musicians. Bussy noted that *Electric Cafe* predicted the move in house and techno away from songs and toward the groove as the be-all and end-all, and it brought Hütter and Schneider "full circle back to where they had started—building up atmospheric pieces of music rather than writing conventional songs." The band has performed on rare occasions, essentially packing up

After *Electric Cafe*, Hütter and Schneider launched what would become a five-year project called *The Mix*, reconstructing their old material using new digital technology. Bartos, Flur, and Schult were unhappy after spending four years on the thirty-five minutes of music on *Electric Cafe*, and *The Mix* was the last straw. "Would Leonardo Da Vinci have taken the Mona Lisa back and painted her over?" Schult asked Bussy. One by one, the two percussionists and the conceptual guru defected. In 1991 Bartos and Lothar Manteuffel of the German duo Rheingold formed Elektric Music. Working in collaboration with Schult, who added lyrics and design, they released an album of short, catchy electronic pop songs. Like Kraftwerk's best albums, *Esperanto* is united by a theme: that the tools of modern communications are driving people apart.

When it was finally issued, *The Mix* succeeded neither as a satisfying best-of—too many important tunes were missing—nor as a step forward. "How can we change now?" Hütter asked critic Simon Reynolds in a rare interview in 1991. "We've put twenty years into this kind of thing." The Man-Machine seemed to be stalled, unable to move forward and unable to go back.

Ralf Hütter on the Psychedelic Roots of Kraftwerk

Kraftwerk auteur Ralf Hütter almost never speaks to the press; I tried to interview the electronic music pioneer for the first edition of this book and got as far as reaching a friendly but stern female voice on the phone at Kling Klang: "There are no interviews... Thank you." *Click*. But I finally had the opportunity to talk with the reticent legend in the summer of 2003, shortly before the release of *Tour de France Soundtracks*.

The band's first album of new material in seventeen years picks up where the 1983 single "Tour de France" left off, attempting to evoke the experience of cross-country bicycling the way that *Autobahn* captured a high-speed trip down the superhighway and *Trans-Europe Express* summoned a journey by rail. The twelve long, droning, pulsating cuts have their moments, but the new digital technology lacks the human soul that was always evident through the analog '70s. Hütter lets the computers do most of the singing, and there is a scarcity of truly memorable hooks. On the bright side, though, Hütter promised that this disc would be the first of more frequent offerings from a revitalized Kraftwerk in the new millennium.

J.D.: *I know you're a serious biking aficionado. I'm curious about the connection between this album and the original "Tour de France" single in 1983. What made you go back to the race for the inspiration for this music?*

Hütter: Twenty years ago, in 1983, my friend Florian Schneider and me, we had the whole script for the album. The concept was there, and we started working on it. We ended up finishing the single, and then we went into other projects. Through that time, the script was always there, kind of like sleeping with us, but we did other technical things. Then last year, this came back when we played the concerts in Paris for the very first time with our new, updated Kraftwerk.

J.D.: *I saw the band perform at the Riviera Theatre in Chicago a few years ago and it was one of the most amazing shows I've ever seen. What has changed since then?*

Hütter: That was 1998, when we brought the Kling Klang Studio. It was still kind of like heavy concert equipment. We had transformed everything into the digital format already, but there was still also analog. Now it is all laptops. We played in Paris for the very first time at the Cité de la Musique. We had the screen projections of the images synchronized with the music, and then the Tour de France idea came back with the 100-year anniversary of the Tour de France. It is also the thirty-three-year anniversary of Kraftwerk! [Laughs] So then we started working on this, and over the winter, we went to Japan and then Australia, and just finished the album now.

J.D.: *The goal was to evoke a journey much like "Autobahn" or "Trans-Europe Express," right?*

Hütter: Yes. You can imagine, basically when we were planning, the script was there, but there was still a lot of work to do to actually provide what it sounds like. Basically, it sounds like nothing—silence, silence—because when you're really cycling well, and your bike is functioning well, you don't hear the chain, you don't hear the wheels, you don't hear yourself because you're in good shape and it's running smoothly. That's one of the reasons we like it so much, to get away from the studio—always the musical sounds. The complete silence leaves space for concentration and imagination. When we worked on this album, we tried to incorporate the idea of very smooth, rolling, gliding. That is the sound.

J.D.: *You can almost feel the wind in your face.*

Hütter: Yes! And the breath, and kind of like a humming. In German it's called *"fleischentonal"*—space and soundscapes—landscapes, very open, wide sounds. So we tried to work in this spirit.

J.D.: *Your vocals have changed on this album: They're much more computer-manipulated than the way you used to sing in the old days.*

Hütter: I always used to do the voice, the human voice, the speech—in German, it's called *"sprechsingen."* I don't know the English word. *"Sprechsingen"* means "speech-sing." It's like a form of rap. This started with "Autobahn"—*"Fahr'n, fahr'n, fahr'n on der autobahn"*—and also humming, "Trans-Europe Express," and then incorporating all kinds of electronic voices, synthetic voices. My friend Florian is of course a great specialist in like singing typewriters; they have developed instruments for him. He is very good at getting engineers from computer companies to work after hours and long nights to develop speech synthesis and things like that. So we are using a lot of synthetic voices and all kinds of intonations.

J.D.: *You mentioned Florian's role in developing the electronics. You two have been together since 1968. What is so special about that collaboration?*

Hütter: Well, it's like an electronic marriage. [Laughs] Mr. Kling and Mr. Klang. It's stereo, so it gives the music the overall dimension. Yin Yang, Kling Klang.

J.D.: *So you can't imagine making a Kraftwerk record without Florian?*

Hütter: No, no. This is not possible. That's what Kraftwerk is all about. It's stereo.

J.D.: *Having played a Mini-Moog myself, one of the things that amaze me is the instrument's ability to surprise you. Do you ever miss those old analog synthesizers?*

Hütter: Well, we use them! We have all the Kraftwerk instruments available and working in different areas of our studio, so it's like a little history of Kraftwerk. They are functioning, and we use whatever sound is artistically relevant. We work in the sounds of the bicycle, we work in the sounds of the human heart, the human breath—whatever is available.

J.D.: *I'm curious about Kraftwerk's roots in the psychedelic explosion of the late '60s. The band started as part of what's been called the "krautrock" movement.*

Hütter: It was never called krautrock; the word was invented by the English press, and it was never used in Germany. In Germany it was called *"kosmische musick."* Kraftwerk was closer to some kind of industrial sound from the Rhein-Ruhr area. You can imagine, in the late '60s, we wouldn't even get a spot to perform. So we sneaked into the art world. Within the music world, there were all these rock bands, so we went into some of these happenings situations in the art world, and we would use light shows or projections. The idea was the German word *"gesamtkunst,"* which is like a combination or a fusion of all the arts. Right from the beginning of Kraftwerk, the imagination and the stimulation had always been with us. We were doing little drawings and comics and album covers, we were preparing projections, we worked on the lights, we worked on the tunes, we built speaker cabinets. Everything around Kraftwerk was part of our creative ideas.

J.D.: *There was an effort to create a complete package, a unique world?*

Hütter: Yes! And that has stayed with us until today, I think. Now we have more tools, of course, with computer graphics and synchronization. The equipment has been very helpful—it has developed in our direction, so we are very, very happy. It is always fun to get new toys, but we also keep some of the old ones, because we have the affinity for tuning the motors, tuning the oscillators, finding robotic movements and computer-generated sounds.

J.D.: *For an entire generation of young electronic musicians, Kraftwerk is more influential than the Beatles. Is that ever a burden to carry?*

Hütter: No, not really, because it is giving us all the energy and the encouragement to keep going. Because we started in the late '60s, but we are still looking ahead. When we see the audience and it ranges from the young computer kids to the university electronics or physics professor, we are very, very pleased.

RIDING THROUGH THE NIGHT

> Theirs is music for the present—alive, urgent, bursting with
> energy, and demanding to be played. Neu! are as relevant
> today as they were a decade ago.
>
> —David Elliott,
> liner notes to *Black Forest Gateu*, 1982

IN GERMANY, THERE IS NO SPEED LIMIT. The most culturally
myopic American knows this but tends to envision futuristic super-
highways criss-crossing the country. In fact the autobahns were
built by Hitler to provide a system for quick and easy troop transport, and they have only two lanes running in either direction.
They are simple but efficient blacktops cutting through the countryside, unobtrusive intrusions of modernity in the rolling green
hillsides. Neu! is the sound of driving late at night on these quiet,
empty roads. The white lines move toward the headlights with
mechanical regularity, in time to the steady speed of the car. They
are the only thing you see, but the Fatherland is out there in the
darkness. You can feel it.

Rother and Dinger emerged from Kraftwerk frustrated and
unfulfilled. One suspects that they had been "too rock" for Hütter,
or Hütter had been too staid for them. In any event, they were
determined to make improvised electronic music that retained the
rhythmic drive and harsh edge of the best rock 'n' roll. They recorded with Plank, who had just moved his studio to a farmhouse near
Hamburg. The recording room was in the old pigsty, and the mixing desk was in a former stable. The trio finished Neu!'s self-titled

The Ultimate Psychedelic Rock Library: The cover of Neu!'s debut (Astralwerks) virtually screamed: "Here we are, something new!"

debut in just four days. Dinger handled drums, synthesizers, some guitar, and the album's one vocal, while Rother was responsible for the majority of guitar, piano, bass, and tape manipulations. The two played with a rare empathy, and their improvisations were uncommonly structured and immediate. The key track on Neu!'s first album is the psychedelic opener, "Hallogallo" ("Hullabaloo"). The long, hypnotic instrumental is built around Rother's backwards, echoplexed, or heavily reverbed guitars; simple five- or six-note keyboard patterns, and Dinger's metronomic drumming. The 4/4 rhythm is Neu!'s secret. Dubbed *motorik*, the beat is unrelenting, straightforward, and entrancing—the sound of the white line. Even the fills are dedicated to propelling the song rather than decorating the spartan beat. When I spoke to Rother in 1998, he recalled that the recording had been dominated by a spirit of carefree experimentation. "It's hard to look back twenty-five years, but I think we weren't so very worried about history and the future and being recognized a hundred years after our death," he said. "It was that you did the work you felt like doing and you enjoyed yourself. Basically, when I'm recording, when I'm happy with it, I always expect other people to like it as well."

The rest of the first album—and, indeed, of Neu!'s career—offers subtle variations on the same basic, entrancing hullabaloo. Released in late 1971 on Brain, *Neu!* was a respectable hit in Germany, selling more than thirty-five thousand copies. It was issued in the U.S. on the Chicago label Billingsgate, but aside from influencing a few pockets of freaky music fans—including a fellow in Cleveland named David Thomas—its impact was minimal. "The record is only the beginning," Dinger said in the liner notes. "We are looking for a third member of the group to dig deeper into the trends we introduced in our first album." Neu! recruited Uli Trepte of Guru Guru on bass and played a handful of unsatisfying gigs. The group's true home, it seemed, was the recording studio. The band returned to Plank's barn, but this time, the musicians spent way too much time obsessing over the characteristically Neu! instrumentals on side one. "Für Immer," "Spitzenqualität," and the other songs on the first half of the album are as strong as anything on the debut, but with the budget exhausted, Dinger and Rother simply took both sides of their earlier single, "Super" b/w "Neuschnee," and filled side two with versions at 33, 45, and 78 r.p.m. (With a similarly perverse sense of humor, the covers and titles of all three albums were identical, featuring the word "Neu!" scrawled against different colored backgrounds.)

A few months later, the band was temporarily shelved as Rother joined Moebius and Roedelius of Cluster to record as Harmonia while Dinger worked with his brother, Thomas, and Hans Lampe.

Only Harmonia produced vinyl. The debut, *Musik Von Harmonia,* and a follow-up, *Deluxe,* were both released on Brain. Harmonia's music is more expansive and much less direct than Neu!'s, and it lacks the driving beat. The group disbanded in 1975 because of poor album sales, and Rother rejoined Dinger in Neu!. The pair recorded the first half of their third and final album as a duo, while side two was done as a quartet featuring Lampe and Thomas Dinger. *Neu! 75* predated the punk explosion by a year, but its most exciting tracks have the raw, primal power of the Sex Pistols or the Ramones. "Hero" features the basic Neu! instrumental augmented by Klaus Dinger's frantic shouted vocals. Obscured by the mix, bad diction, or both, the words and even the language are unintelligible, though the English phrase "riding through the night" seems to jump out. Given the intensity of "Hero" and "After Eight," you might assume that Dinger intended the stoned moaning on the lulling "Leb' Wohl" as a joke. Pictured on the album's inner sleeve wearing black clothes, white boots, sunglasses, spiked hair, and a sneer, he could pass for Sid Vicious. In sharp contrast, the bearded, pony-tailed Rother is depicted against a fluffy white background, the model of hippie tranquility.

Perhaps the clash in styles finally proved to be too much. Neu! broke up for good shortly after the release of its third album; the two key members remain estranged, and Dinger has built a reputation as something of a derailed genius along the lines of Arthur Lee. "He's very distant from reality sometimes," Rother told me. "I hesitate to give too much intimate detail about Klaus Dinger, although he's really treated me very badly." After Neu!, the Dinger brothers and Lampe formed La Düsseldorf, and Rother went the solo route, frequently working with Can drummer Jaki Liebezeit; these days, he is more interested in electronics than in playing the guitar. Both men's post-Neu! efforts have moments of inspiration, but the further you get from their collaboration, the less you hear of the rock-'n'-roll edge. The distinctive beat is overpowered by more formal European harmonies and melodies, the guitars and synthesizers grow more symphonic, and the grit of the highway is replaced by the gentle sounds of the idyllic countryside. Late at night on the empty highway, they don't hold a candle to Neu! But then not much does.

TEN

10

AN EVENING OF FUN IN THE METROPOLIS OF YOUR DREAMS
(Psychedelic Punk Return)

> Hopefully, there's going to be a second psychedelic era. People misunderstand what it's all about, because psychedelic music wasn't drug music....It makes you experience different things, and that's essentially where we're at.
> —David Thomas, 1976, in Clinton Heylin's
> *From the Velvets to the Voidoids*

THE PUNK EXPLOSION OF 1976 is often portrayed as a direct reaction to the self-satisfied, pretentious, boring, and bloated groups that had come to dominate rock, especially bands like the Eagles and Fleetwood Mac, but also including art rockers such as Yes and Genesis. Many of the most important punk bands realized that psychedelic rock had lost its way. They were dedicated not only to reassessing rock's musical and philosophical values, but to placing a different set of heroes in the rock pantheon, including some from the first and second waves of psychedelic rock. *Nuggets* compiler Lenny Kaye started a new career as guitarist for the Patti Smith Group. The flowery, extended solos of Television guitarist Tom Verlaine were compared to Jerry Garcia; the band covered "Fire Engine" by the 13th Floor Elevators and "Psychotic Reaction" by the Count Five, and it worked with Brian Eno on a set of legendary demos. It may not have been obvious when they surfaced, but the Ramones shined a light on some of their psychedelic influences years later with their 1994 covers album, *Acid Eaters*. The Damned were devoted fans of the early Pink Floyd and tried to get Syd Barrett to produce their second album. (They had to settle for Nick Mason.) But Pere Ubu was the most vocal in calling its sounds part of the psychedelic tradition.

To Ubu and its peers, psychedelic rock's legacy was an imaginative approach to the recording studio more than it was music inspired by psychedelic drugs. "Pere Ubu has always been concerned with creating a cinema of the imagination," singer David Thomas told me. "If you call that psychedelic, then I suppose so. But we never would endorse the use of drugs as a necessary part of that. There is a basic idea of music as sound having a visual element, and that goes back to the 1800s. We discuss sound visually. When we put together songs, we always see them being in the context of sound as opposed to a melody or a rhythm or something. We see them as being *inside* of something else."

The founding members of the band met in their hometown of Cleveland in 1974. Thomas was a frizzy-haired singer fronting a jokey garage band called Rocket from the Tombs, and Peter

Laughner was its leather-jacketed guitarist. Both men were part-time rock critics who enjoyed discussing music almost as much as they enjoyed playing it. "This was a generation that was interested in seeing rock 'n' roll as a serious musical form—as a true art," Thomas told rock archivist Clinton Heylin. "This was the time that Soft Machine with Kevin Ayers had its greatest day; Can, all that German stuff, the early Eno, *Warm Jets, Tiger Mountain*, the Roxy Music stuff."

Although Rocket from the Tombs lasted barely a year, it produced three of what Heylin called "American punk's most potent anthems"—"Sonic Reducer," "Final Solution," and "Thirty Seconds Over Tokyo"—before splitting into the hell-bent-for-leather Dead Boys and the artier Pere Ubu. The latter was originally intended as a one-off studio project so Laughner and Thomas could record the Rockets' best originals. The new band's name referred to a monstrous character in Alfred Jarry's surrealist play, *Ubu Roi*; uncomfortable with his substantial girth and odd, high-pitched singing, Thomas portrayed the character of Father Ubu, losing himself in a lurking, menacing alter ego that he named Crocus Behemoth. The rest of the group included several residents of an apartment building called the Plaza—guitarist Tom Herman, drummer R. Scott Krauss, and Allen Ravenstine, who coached strange sounds out of a homemade synthesizer—as well as bassist and guitarist Tim Wright. It was Wright who came up with the riff for what would become "Heart of Darkness," and as the band jammed on the sinister, rumbling progression, it became clear that Pere Ubu would have a life beyond one recording.

The Ultimate Psychedelic Rock Library: Terminal Tower: An Archival Collection *(Geffen) charts the birth of psychedelic-punk visionaries Pere Ubu.*

The 1985 compilation, *Terminal Tower: An Archival Collection* (named for the structure that provides the central focus of the Cleveland skyline), offers a compelling overview of early Ubu, tracing the band's development from psychedelic punks wallowing in post-adolescent angst to rock visionaries rejoicing in the power of music. It opens with the group's first single, released on Thomas's own Hearthan Records. "Heart of Darkness" builds in intensity over a monolithic drum beat just as Joseph Conrad's book builds up to the moment when the reader meets Kurtz, the personification of evil. The song climaxes with Thomas's frantic screams in the face of the abyss as the band loses itself in a swirling, chaotic din. Pere Ubu threw Laughner out after its second single, in part because of his drug and alcohol abuse. (He died of an overdose in June 1977, leaving a legacy of scattered recordings.) The second half of *Terminal Tower* sees Pere Ubu moving out of its Laughner-dominated "dark period" and creating more optimistic soundscapes, as on the positively giddy 1977 single, "Heaven." Crocus Behemoth has been replaced by the affable frontman of later years, a loveable eccentric who bears more than a passing resemblance to Oliver Hardy.

Despite its influence on England's post-punk dance bands (especially Joy Division), Pere Ubu's debut album, *The Modern Dance,* has aged more quickly than the singles collected on *Terminal Tower.* Released only a few months later, the band's second album, *Dub Housing,* stands as the best from the first half of its career. Dense and dissonant, it is also filled with undeniably catchy melodies. Hooks are crafted from such unlikely sources as eerie, jagged guitar noise, Ravenstine's unmusical synthesizer squeals and saxophone bleets, and Thomas's adenoidal vocals. The album was inspired by an upbeat period in which Ubu was the house band at a bar on Cleveland's Flats, the industrial wasteland on the banks of the Cuyahoga River. Thomas's lyrics examine the odd juxtapositions of the modern world ("I saw secret scenes in the cracks of the cities / Secret scenes in the seams of the world!"), while upholding the punk ideal of celebrating your individuality, even if you *are* one

The Ultimate Psychedelic Rock Library: Not for nothing was Ubu's second album entitled Dub Housing *(Thirsty Ear). The influence of dub and psychedelic production styles looms large.*

The Ultimate Psychedelic Rock Library: The Tenement Year *(Enigma) finds Pere Ubu returning to the* Nuggets *garage.*

of the most unlikely frontmen in rock history. ("I've got these arms & legs that flip-flop! / Flip-flop! / I have desire / Freedom!")

Subsequent albums are less consistent. *New Picnic Time* (1979) brings the Beefheart influence to the forefront, while the lyrics reflect more of Thomas's religious beliefs. (Raised as a Jehovah's Witness, he left the religion during his early punk days but later returned). Following *The Art of Walking* (1980) and *Song of the Bailing Man* (1982), both less-focused ambient efforts, the group disbanded for what would become a six-year layoff. (One of the last incarnations before the split featured former Red Krayola guitarist Mayo Thompson—the first generation of psychedelic rock linking up with the third.)

Reinvigorated by the break, Pere Ubu relaunched its career in 1988 with *The Tenement Year*. This time the band's heavy rhythms, gurgling synthesizers, and noisy guitars were incorporated into songs that recalled the '60s psychedelic garage bands that the musicians grew up with. "Something's Gotta Give," "George Had a Hat," and "We Have the Technology," are pop tunes—weird, upside-down, and inside-out pop tunes, but pop tunes nonetheless. The group continued to explore a more accessible direction on 1989's *Cloudland*, which yielded an MTV hit with the wonderful trouble-in-clubland video, "Waiting for Mary." *Worlds in Collision* (1991) is more polished and less effective, but 1993's *Story of My Life* features some of Ubu's best songs ever. The opening track, "Wasted," begins as a lulling sea chantey, with Thomas playing melodeon and musing about "throwing time away." It sounds like a melancholy tone poem about wasted youth, until Thomas croaks, "Rock!" and the band kicks in with a chaotic assault that leaves the listener dizzy. The song makes it clear that Pere Ubu continues to uphold the psychedelic ideals of living in the moment and fashioning a personal utopia in the music.

Ubu continues on today, though Thomas is the only one of the original members remaining, and the psychedelic influence surfaces only sporadically. "In the end, we're doomed people," he told me a few years ago. "We were young and came to manhood musically in a time when music was still considered by most people to be important, and when it was the poetry and language of the human experience. It was the idea of it being art, and we happen to believe all that stuff. We're like the people who became Communists in the '30s. They had a powerful vision of the way things should be in an ideal world. And as the years went by, one thing after another, their vision of the world became more and more detached from the reality of the world around them. And it was a tragic, tragic experience."

J FEEL MYSTERIOUS TODAY

> Sometimes they sound like several species of small furry
> animals grooving with a pict, if you get my drift, if not I
> will come right out and say it: Syd Barrett. Early Pink Floyd,
> to be sure....The crucial difference is that whereas Pink
> Floyd wanted (pretended?) to take you into outer space (big
> deal, so go watch Buck Rogers), Wire's saucerful of secrets is
> headed in the opposite direction, down your esophagus
> like a stray carcinogen. Wire wanna isolate and dissect leu-
> cocytes. They're into the micro rather than macrocosm.
>   —Lester Bangs, *The Village Voice*, 1979

ENERGIZED BY THE MUSIC and the D.I.Y. spirit that surrounded
them, the members of Wire came together in London in the summer of 1976, but they were always more than a little different than
the others in England's class of freshman punks. For one thing they
were older: Bruce Gilbert had already passed thirty. They had no
musical training, but like many of the English rockers in the '60s,
they had all attended art school. Their idea of subversion was more
humorous and less direct than shouting, "Anarchy!" Rather than
tearing down rock 'n' roll and starting over, they were fascinated
with what could be built up in the recording studio, and they drew
inspiration from Roxy Music, the Velvet Underground, and Captain
Beefheart.

After garnering some attention for two tracks on the live com-
pilation *The Roxy, London WC2*, Wire was signed to Harvest/EMI by
Nick Mobbs, the man who had signed Pink Floyd years earlier.
"What's interesting is that I hadn't really heard any Syd Barrett

before people made the comparison," singer Colin Newman said in Kevin Eden's, *Wire...Everybody Loves a History*. "I then started listening to his albums, and I quite liked them." As part of its overall aim to thwart expectations and be as perverse as possible, the band members embraced the comparison because it made them stand out. "Any form of misinformation was useful," Gilbert told Eden. Originally a quintet featuring Newman, Gilbert, bassist Graham Lewis, drummer Robert Gotobed, and lead guitarist and songwriter George Gill, the band lurched through angry-young-Englishmen tunes such as "I Just Don't Care" and "Mary Is a Dyke." When Gill was sidelined with a broken ankle, Newman and Lewis figured that they could do better without him. "Graham said, 'Well, I can write lyrics,' and I said, 'Well, I'll write tunes,'" Newman recalled. "So it was, 'There, let's do it!'"

Wire's 1977 debut, *Pink Flag*, is a dense and carefully constructed twenty-one-song suite that intentionally "cocks a snoot at the history of rock 'n' roll." "If the first Ramones album was like Phil Spector, then *Pink Flag* was like all the history of rock mashed up," Newman told Eden. But the vibe was considerably darker; as critic Robert Christgau wrote, "Wire would sooner revamp 'The Fat Lady of Limbourg' or 'Some Kinda Love' than 'Let's Dance' or 'Surfin' Bird.'" Having said all they wanted to say about rock history, the band members were ready to move forward. Released in 1978, their second album takes a sharp turn toward more imaginative and psychedelic sounds. "There was a tremendous sense of excitement, of doing things for the first time," producer Mike Thorne told me. "The synthesizer was very new to us, and it was, 'Let's plug it into

The Ultimate Psychedelic Rock Library: Like The Dark Side of the Moon *and* Wish You Were Here, *Wire's* Chairs Missing *(Restless) is an album evocative of madness; some dubbed the group called "the Punk Floyd."*

a distortion box and see what it does!' On one level, we still didn't know what we were doing, but the results were brilliant."

Undercurrents of isolation and madness run through *Chairs Missing,* starting with the title. "My father-in-law seemed to have a whole bank of phrases about people who weren't all quite there," Gilbert told Eden. "One was...'He's got a few chairs missing in his front room.' It was like a musical joke, and one that stuck." In "Another the Letter," the drums, rhythm guitar, and synthesizer move at a frantic pace that evokes a messenger rushing to his destination. The surreal punch line is that the letter carrier bears the message, "I took my own life." "Mercy" is an ominous guitar epic with impressionistic nightmare lyrics about a ship adrift at sea during a violent storm; "Outdoor Miner" and "I Am the Fly" are deceptively catchy pop songs about insects (the former waxes rhapsodic about a bug called the serpentine miner and the trail of slime left on the leaves it eats), and "I Feel Mysterious Today" is about an out-of-body experience. It ends abruptly after posing the extremely psychedelic question, "Did you ever perceive that you too could leave exactly when you like?"

Although they were praised by critics, *Chairs Missing* and *Pink Flag* didn't really win an audience until the early '80s, when groups as diverse as the Minutemen, Big Black, R.E.M., and Minor Threat extended Wire's ideas in several postpunk directions. Despite the good reviews, EMI was unhappy with Wire's sales at the time, and the company wasn't sure whether it had signed art rockers or punks. After an unpleasant tour supporting *Manifesto*-era Roxy Music, Wire became just as disenchanted with EMI and the promotional merry-go-round. The band recorded one more album for the label before the relationship fell apart.

Released in 1980, *154*, which was issued on Warner Bros. in the States, was named for the number of gigs Wire had played to date. The band continued to show its mastery of the psychedelic vignette, exploring colorful landscapes over longer songs and an even lusher production, but strains were beginning to show. *154*

The Ultimate Psychedelic Rock Library: 154 (Restless) veers wildly from lush psychedelic melodies to grating industrial noise.

divided Wire into a "pop" camp—with Newman, Gotobed, and
Thorne favoring catchy, well-crafted songs such as "The 15th"—
and a "noise camp," with Gilbert and Lewis pushing for more
unstructured experimentation. The battle resulted in failed experiments such as "The Other Window" and "40 Versions," as well as
undeniable highlights like "Map Ref. 41° N 93° W," a sweeping, cinematic tune inspired by Lewis' first flight across the United States,
and "On Returning," a Newman song that ends with the singer in
the role of a travel broker promising a somewhat foreboding
"evening of fun in the metropolis of your dreams."

After splitting with EMI, Wire recorded a single, "Our
Swimmer," and the fractured live album, *Document and Eyewitness*,
both for Rough Trade. Shortly thereafter, the group went on hiatus
for the first time. An avalanche of solo releases followed, with
Newman's being the most enjoyable. Several of the songs on *A–Z*
(1981) and *Not to* (1982) were performed during Wire's final tours,
and a few feature lyrics by Lewis. Both albums continue the cinematic style of *Chairs Missing* and *154*. Newman also recorded an
Eno-inspired ambient album called *provisionally entitled the singing
fish*, and he combined the pop and ambient approaches on
Commercial Suicide (1986) and *It Seems* (1988) before moving into
ambient house music in the '90s.

The activities of Gilbert and Lewis were more scattered and
diverse. Working together as Dome, they released four albums of
industrial experimentation, works-in-progress, and occasional pop
epiphanies ("Rolling Upon My Day"). Duet Emmo was an industrial dance effort with Daniel Miller, the founder of Mute Records;
Cupol and 3R4 were Gilbert and Lewis mixing things up under dif-

ferent names, and Mzui featured Gilbert, Lewis, and artist Russell Mills (who had collaborated with Eno on the book *More Dark Than Shark*). In the years since, Gilbert has released several albums on his own of randomly interesting noise and Lewis has recorded electronic dance music under several different names.

It's no coincidence that the three most influential psychedelic punk bands all reunited a few years after their initial breakups. Several years after Wire, Pere Ubu, and the Feelies called it quits the first time, a new network of college radio stations, fanzines, independent record labels, and rock clubs emerged. In the late '80s that network was happy to hear from the groups that had originally inspired it. Wire initially came together again for a three-day trial run in 1985. "If that hadn't worked out, it would have been over, because after that it would have been a bloody weak excuse to do anything," Lewis told me. "But it worked, and 'Drill' and A 'Serious of Snakes' came out of that."

Both songs appeared in 1986 on the *Snakedrill* EP, which features a stripped-down sound based on rhythmic repetition and noise. *The Ideal Copy* followed in 1987, continuing the rhythmic approach with a sound that owed more than a passing nod to New Order, though it also incorporated more of the old psychedelia on songs such as "Feed Me." The group proceeded to explore electronic dance music with diminishing results on *A Bell Is a Cup Until it Is Struck* (1988), *It's Beginning to and Back Again* (1989), *Manscape* (1990), and *The Drill* (1991). By *The First Letter* in 1992, Gotobed had quit, the band was now calling itself Wir, and Newman, Gilbert, and Lewis were all playing MIDI guitars hooked into a computer controller. Each member added to a continuously evolving digital loop, a system not unlike Kraftwerk's vision of the Man-Machine. Unfortunately, the results were less interesting than the working methods, and the group split up once more.

By reuniting the first time, Wire blew its legendary status, and as the band progressed through its second incarnation, it alienated even its cult following. But the members remained committed to experimentation and forward movement. "When we did *Pink Flag* and came out with *Chairs Missing*, there were a lot of people who just went, 'You guys, you've let us down,'" Lewis told me. "The same thing happened with *154*, and I think that's an inevitability. If you're changing what you're doing and you're committed to that, then that's what happens." Added Gilbert: "Some people would regard that as pure self-indulgence and tell us to go straight to hell. But it's a very spurious, moralistic view, the self-indulgent thing. *I* think it's extremely healthy."

The members all immersed themselves to varying degrees in the techno subculture; Gilbert made a reputation as a DJ under the name the Beekeeper, and Newman started his own label, Swim. But the growth of the so-called "postrock" movement of modern progressive-rock bands such as Tortoise caught the members' attention again in the late '90s, and they began thinking that their still might be some life left in what they'd begun to derisively call "the beat combo." With Gotobed once again coming back to the fold, Wire reunited for its third-go round in 2000. At first, the group performed only old material, but in 2002, it began releasing a scorching series of D.I.Y. EPs that recalled the harsh, abrasive sounds of *Pink Flag*. If the band continues its current creative reincarnation, we can only hope that another psychedelic awakening a la *Chairs Missing* is just around the corner.

THE BOYS WITH THE PERPETUAL NERVOUSNESS

> "Going to the Feelies this evening, Henry?" enquired the
> Assistant Predestinator. "I hear the new one at the
> Alhambra is first-rate. There's a love scene on a bearskin
> rug; they say it's marvelous. Every hair of the beast repro-
> duced. The most amazing tactual effects."
>
> —Aldous Huxley,
> *Brave New World*

LIKE A DROP OF WATER SHATTERING the still surface of a pond,
the Feelies' first album starts with the ringing sound of rosewood
claves: *click, click.* Then silence, until again—*click, click*—this time
higher in pitch and richer in reverb. The scattered drops turn into
a gentle rain as a needle-thin electric guitar repeats a two-note pattern. The song picks up speed, building in intensity, and then a second guitar echoes the first. The guitars combine on the downbeat
to form a chord, but there's no relief in the melody. The raspy
sound of a sand block adds a sharp counter-rhythm, cueing the
uneasy vocals. "There's a boy I know but not too well / He hasn't
got a lot to say / Well this boy lives right next door and he / Has
nothing to say." Without ever visiting Haledon, New Jersey, a quiet,
hilly suburb of blue-collar Patterson, you know the place that the
Feelies are singing about: chipped white paint on the shingles, a
slightly overgrown lawn, a tree-lined street filled with mounds of
autumn leaves. But the Feelies never felt stifled by surburbia. Like
the hero in the tune "The Boy with the Perpetual Nervousness,"

they were into "better things"—namely psychedelic rock and the music of their imaginations.

The Feelies first came together in Haledon in 1972. Guitarist-vocalist Glenn Mercer was playing with drummer Dave Weckerman when Bill Million decided to check them out. In those days a common affinity for the Stooges and the Velvets was all that was needed to forge a friendship and a musical bond. Mercer and Million started writing songs, abandoning their real names in favor of the surnames of a forgotten Tin Pan Alley duo. Million suggested the moniker for the group from a favorite diversion in Huxley's *Brave New World.*

After several years spent honing a sound in the basement, the Feelies started driving east on New Jersey's Route 3 through the Lincoln Tunnel to play at CBGB and Max's Kansas City. Mercer and Million were perfectionists and they were unhappy when they couldn't duplicate the sounds in their heads onstage. Their button-down persona was partly a cultivated image like Talking Heads'—they were fond of telling journalists that they hated to play in New York because driving through the tunnel gave them headaches—but they were also genuinely obsessive, refusing to compromise their ideas about what the Feelies *should* sound like. Their five-hour soundchecks became legendary, and drummer Vinny DeNunzio eventually quit when Mercer and Million told him he couldn't use his cymbals because the frequencies clashed with the guitars. He was replaced by Anton Fier, who moved to New York from Cleveland after playing with the Electric Eels and Pere Ubu.

Although they had similar influences, the Feelies were never really part of New York's punk scene, and they were overlooked in

The Ultimate Psychedelic
Rock Library: The Feelies'
Crazy Rhythms *(A&M) is*
party music for the gang down
at the mad scientist's lab.

the initial major-label feeding frenzy. But as punk became New Wave, several labels started to show interest. The English independent Stiff was the most persistent, and the Feelies became the unlikely label mates of Lene Lovich, Ian Dury, and Wreckless Eric. *Crazy Rhythms* was recorded over four weeks in 1980, a record amount of time for a Stiff band. Former CBGB soundman Mark Abel was credited as producer, but Mercer and Million seized control early in the project. "They are the most obstinate people I've ever met," Abel told *New York Rocker* writer Greg McLean. "They had real set ideas of what they wanted. That record was the culmination of four years of fantasizing about how they were going to record those songs."

"The Boy With the Perpetual Nervousness" and the other tracks on *Crazy Rhythms* display a distinctive vision and a unique set of sonic hallmarks, including layered rhythm guitars that frantically strum simple two- and three-chord progressions; simple gestures such as handclaps and cymbal crashes that become dramatic pop hooks; elaborate fade-ins and fade-outs that lend the songs a sense of endlessness; harmonic, over-driven solos that erupt from the mix, and deceptively banal lyrics that are half spoken and half sung in a Lou Reed monotone. But the most important element is the beat—the Feelies' own crazy rhythm—a kinetic, tom-heavy groove that can be traced through the Velvet Underground, back to Bo Diddley, and all the way to the polyrhythms of tribal Africa.

Crazy Rhythms stands as a brilliant album with its own inimitable ambience. These are after-hours party tunes for the gang down at the mad scientist's lab, and even after hundreds of listens, the mix reveals new surprises. The band's small but devoted following was originally disappointed because the album didn't capture the frantic energy of the Feelies' live shows. (Mercer and Million used to down several cups of coffee laced with chlorophyll and shave with electric razors just before going on stage so that they'd literally be bouncing up and down, and Fier sometimes played so quickly and violently that he vomited behind the drum throne.) But while the drug of choice at Feelies concerts may have been speed, *Crazy Rhythms* is in the end a psychedelic experience. Mercer and Million's approach to the studio came from *Revolver, Their Satanic Majesties Request, Another Green World*, and the Velvets' first album, and they went on to pay homage to all of those albums with cover songs.

Sluggish sales and the Feelies' refusal to take part in a Son of Stiff package tour soured relations with that label, and by 1982 the band was free from its five-album contract. Mercer and Million never considered the Feelies to be officially broken up, but they concentrated on playing with other groups, covering the psychedelic Beatles in a band called Dr. Robert and the Velvets in Foggy

Notion; joining some high school friends in the Trypes (who conjured the orchestrated Beatles of "Flying" and *Magical Mystery Tour*), and backing Weckerman as he sang his own songs with Yung Wu. The main outlet for all of these bands was a Sunday-night series dubbed "Music for Neighbors" at a Haledon bar called the Peanut Gallery, and the Trypes were always the most interesting band on the bill. In addition to George Harrison's Indian drones, their sound drew inspiration from Phillip Glass and Brian Eno, as evidenced on their 1984 EP, *The Explorers Hold* (which is sadly out of print). When the Feelies were reactivated in 1986, the core members of the Trypes continued as Speed the Plough, releasing several strong albums in a similarly trippy vein.

The Feelies played a handful of gigs between 1982 and 1986, almost always on holiday weekends. (Mercer and Million wanted them to be events). Some of these shows featured two drummers—Fier and Stanley Demeski—as well as Weckerman on percussion. The Feelies played only old material, but the band's leaders had begun working on new songs with the Willies, a group they formed with Demeski, Weckerman, and bassist Brenda Sauter. Initially the Willies played textured instrumental drones that recalled Eno's ambient albums; when the band performed, it played completely in the dark. By 1985 the group had turned on the lights and started playing new songs, as well as material from *Crazy Rhythms*. The Willies were becoming the Feelies. The old brute physical force was gone—the classically trained Demeski was a much more mannered and precise drummer than Fier—and the emphasis shifted from crazy rhythms to Million's gorgeous chord progressions and Mercer's dynamic and hummable solos.

the Feelies

the Good Earth

The Ultimate Psychedelic Rock Library: Like Blue Velvet *by David Lynch,* The Good Earth *(Twin/Tone) offers a romantic vision of the heartland, then digs below the surface to find something more unsettling.*

The Feelies re-emerged just as R.E.M.-inspired jangle-mania took hold. When the band agreed to record for the Hoboken-based Coyote Records, R.E.M. guitarist Peter Buck was tapped to produce. Not surprisingly, Mercer and Million grabbed control. Buck spent most of his time sleeping with his feet up on the mixing console (though he did contribute a chorus setting that made the guitars on "Slow Down" sound like bagpipes). While the album was dominated by the shimmering textures and heartland images inspired by the Feelies' first cross-country tour, it also evoked an Eno-esque sense of pregnant expectation on the mostly instrumental "When Company Comes," and it built to a Velvets-style psychedelic climax on the masterful guitar epic, "Slipping (Into Something). The album was a critical and college-radio hit, and it convinced A&M to sign the band. The discs that followed offered subtle variations on the formula of the Feelies' second incarnation, with the polished *Only Life* addressing the topic of maturing and coming to terms with life, and the rawer *Time for a Witness* making a nostalgic return to the garage (including a cover of "Real Cool Time," one of the first songs Million and Mercer learned together).

The band members' perfectionist tendencies always made for uneasy relationships, and the group's lack of commercial acceptance contributed to the strain. The Feelies were a major influence on many of the alternative bands that struck it rich in the '90s, but A&M never had a clue about how to promote them. The group was always ahead of its time, and its time finally ran out in late 1991. Mercer and Weckerman kept playing in a basement in Haledon, forming a new band called Wake Ooloo and continuing the return to the garage started on *Time for a Witness*. Demeski joined former Galaxie 500 leader Dean Wareham in Luna, and Sauter played with Speed the Plough and formed her own band, Wild Carnation.

The Feelies have taken lengthy breaks before. This one seems to be for good, but you never know. "Being in the Feelies is kinda like living in this great pyramid," Weckerman told *Jersey Beat* editor Jim Testa in 1984. "Nothing ever changes, and no one ever grows old."

ELEVEN

11

PASSIONATE FRIENDS:
The English Psychedelic Eccentrics

IN THE WAKE OF PUNK, the English music scene was up for grabs, with minimalist art bands, synthesizer-pop groups, and glam creations all vying for attention. Some of the most interesting groups took punk's energy and reexamined the psychedelic sounds of the '60s and '70s. One band reclaimed the word as part of its name: Revolving around brothers Richard and Tim Butler and wall-of-sound guitarist John Ashton, the Psychedelic Furs debuted in 1980 with a droney, self-titled album derived in part from David Bowie and Brian Eno's Berlin collaborations. *Talk Talk Talk* (1981) boasted stronger songs and more of a Velvet Underground and Bob Dylan influence, while *Forever Now* (1982) expanded the sound in orchestral fashion courtesy of producer Todd Rundgren before the band began to devolve into increasingly less interesting and more glam-oriented mainstream rock.

Sneering at punks for whom the movement had simply become fashion, modern-day mods the Television Personalities drew heavily from the Byrds and the Creation on albums such as ....*And Don't the Kids Just Love It* (1980) and *The Painted Word* (1984). But the group is best remembered for the single "I Know Where Syd Barrett Lives," and the fact that band leader Daniel Treacy once announced the madcap's address onstage while opening a show for Pink Floyd. (The ever-protective David Gilmour was reportedly furious and ripped him a new asshole.)

The driving forces of The Teardrop Explodes, the Soft Boys, and XTC also displayed an abiding fascination with Barrett, and they suffered the inevitable comparisons, partly because they flirted with psychedelic excess or mental breakdown themselves, and partly because they shared similarly whimsical styles. But the tradition of fanciful storytelling is as old as the British Isles themselves, and eccentricity has long been celebrated there, as evidenced by P.G. Wodehouse. Over the course of long and productive careers, Julian Cope, Robyn Hitchcock, and Andy Partridge each perfected their own unique brands of wigginess, in addition to crafting some of the best psychedelic rock of the '80s and '90s.

An ELEGAnT CHAOS

> If you betray one aspect of yourself, you betray all the others. I'd always rather fall on my ass going for it than be scared to.
>
> —Julian Cope

WAITING IN THE WINGS at London's Hammersmith Palais for one of his first solo performances in 1984, Julian Cope seethed in anger as he watched the Woodentops mimic his act. When he finally took to the boards himself, he snapped the mike stand during a frantic version of the story-song "Reynard the Fox" and cut himself repeatedly in the stomach. "Infamy, infamy, they've all got it in for me!" he shouted. Two months later, he appeared naked on the cover of *Fried,* crouching under a giant turtle shell. "Namdam am I, I'm a madman," he wrote in the liner notes.

Few figures in rock history have embodied both the psychedelic and punk impulses as thoroughly as Cope. Through much of his career, he was equal parts Syd Barrett and Iggy Pop. But although he has survived his self-destructive urges to hone his own distinctive method of working, he maintains that "mad," spontaneous, and sometimes dangerous acts are a vital part of creating rock 'n' roll. "I have no desire to sound sensible," he told me. "I don't think wisdom and sensibleness are particularly combined. When you start sounding sensible, that's when you start sounding like Genesis."

Born in 1957 to a middle-class family in Wales, Cope soon moved to Tamworth, a small mining town midway between Liverpool and London. Doing his best to thwart his parents' high expectations, he ignored his studies in favor of krautrock, Captain Beefheart, and Pink Floyd, and he was lucky to be accepted by C.F. Mott, a small college outside Liverpool. Like countless other young musicians, Cope embraced the first wave of punk, but he saw connections between the new sounds and older groups such as the 13th Floor Elevators, the Seeds, and the Doors. Working in a group called the Crucial Three with his mate, Ian McCulloch, he shamelessly recycled riffs from the psychedelic punks of the past. "I just went through all those songs, ripping off as many as I could," he told *Details* magazine in 1993. "But the only people who recognized that were people like you who were thought of as madmen."

Distracted by love, McCulloch lost interest in the band and was given the boot in the summer of 1978. Cope regrouped, choosing the name The Teardrop Explodes from an issue of Marvel Comics' *Daredevil*. (The long moniker was intended as an homage to the 13th Floor Elevators.) Although he had never sung before, Cope insisted on being the singer, and he eventually developed an impressive baritone. By the time the Teardrops were ready to perform, McCulloch had a new band of his own—Echo and the Bunnymen—whom Cope asked to open.

As the bands began to build their respective followings, the music press dubbed their sound "bubblegum trance," and a harsh rivalry developed. Both groups recorded for the small independent Zoo Records, which was run by Bill Drummond and David Balfe, who eventually joined the Teardrops as keyboardist. Cope maintains that the Bunnymen were careerist and happy to be manipulated by Zoo, and that they stole the Teardrops' trademark organ, horns, and mopey paramilitary look. He addressed McCulloch in one of the Teardrops' best singles, the acerbic "Treason." McCulloch wasn't hurt by his old friend's derision, and he proceeded to explore chiming guitars and existential crises (with only occasionally interesting results) for the next two decades.

The Teardrops' first two albums outpower all of the Bunnymen's efforts with more melody and diversity. Drummond re-mortgaged his house to fund the recording of *Kilimanjaro*. He was repaid with the appropriately titled hit "Reward," and a bright, upbeat effort in which Cope liberally applied *Magical Mystery Tour* horns and marimbalike keyboards to emphasize the big New Wave hooks in tunes such as "When I Dream." The second album was a different affair. Before 1980, Cope was a straightedge punk who avoided drugs of any kind, but during the frantic rush of touring before the release of *Kilimanjaro*, his bandmates persuaded him to try marijuana and LSD. He became as extreme in his excesses as he had been in his nonindulgence. "In two short months, I moved from Drug Puritan to Acid King," he wrote in his autobiography, *Head On*. Released at the end of 1981, *Wilder* is a transitional effort that trumpets his expanded psychedelic worldview. "Celebrate the great escape from lunacy dividing / Celebrate the great escape, and carry my soul away," he sings over the kicking horn section, raga guitar, and massive tambourine of "Passionate Friend."

Despite an ever-changing cast of personnel, the Teardrops had made few wrongs moves, but the balance of power was shifting from Cope to Balfe. The keyboardist insisted on sculpting the third album, and he locked Cope and drummer Gary Dwyer out of the studio. They amused themselves by speeding through the country-side, one of them driving and the other clinging spread-eagled to the roof of the car. Convinced that Balfe's album was shit, Cope broke up the group. (The aborted disc was issued in 1990 as *Everybody Wants to Shag...The Teardrop Explodes*, and Cope finally admitted that it "wasn't as crap as it seemed in September '82.") Striking out on his own, he announced, "I regard what I want to do next as an opportunity for gross self-indulgence."

The singer holed up in Tamworth, in need of recovery from the end of his group and his first marriage. Cope purged himself with one of his most productive periods. In 1984 he released both *World Shut Your Mouth,* which continued mining the same vein as late-era Teardrops, and the more introspective *Fried.* Between the two discs, he played his infamous concert at the Hammersmith Palais, providing graphic evidence of his fragile state of mind. But thanks to the influence of his second wife, Dorian, he began to come to terms with his stardom, drug use, and life in general. By 1987 he was healthy enough to poke fun at his position as a cult rock star with the messianic character in the title of *Saint Julian,* but he refused to preach about his earlier behavior. "I always hated people who were considered to be weirdoes straightening their act out. I don't apologize for the way I was," he told *Contrast* magazine in 1987. In another interview with *Details,* he added, "I awoke from a Rip Van Winkle acid haze and, unlike everybody else who awakens from an acid haze, I realized that all those days were not a waste of time. The

The Ultimate Psychedelic Rock Library: Floored Genius: The Best of Julian Cope and the Teardrop Explodes 1979–91 *(Island) provides a great overview of Cope's career through* Peggy Suicide, *from "acid campfire songs" to MTV pop hits.*

problem you get with reformed lunatics is that suddenly their albums are really boring. But my albums are even weirder."

Saint Julian produced two of Cope's biggest hits, the giddy "Trampoline," and the "losers' anthem" and MTV smash, "World Shut Your Mouth." ("I always rip songs off, and most of the songs that I rip off are my old songs," Cope told *Contrast*. "'When I did the album *World Shut Your Mouth*, it never occurred to me that it was a song title.") The album was followed by an equally straightforward effort, *My Nation Underground*, that included more comments on pop-star pomposity ("Charlotte Anne," a pun on "charlatan") and a tribute to old favorites the, 13th Floor Elevators ("Easter Everywhere"). But his masterpiece of pop-rock weirdness came in 1991.

As concept albums go, *Peggy Suicide* makes a lot more sense than the story of a deaf, dumb, and blind pinball wizard. "I had a vision of the world," Cope wrote in the liner notes. "This enormous Mother Earth was standing at the very edge of the highest cliff of Infinity and was about to leap off....I had to make this record about the crazy situation." The plight of Mother Earth/Peggy Suicide is explored in songs about the destructive power of automobiles ("East Easy Rider," "Drive, She Said"), apathy in the face of growing conservatism ("Soldier Blue," "Leperskin"), and life in the age of AIDS ("Safesurfer"). The insistent stomp of earlier work is replaced by a seductive, relaxed groove derived from Sly Stone and Funkadelic, and the sonic canvas is full of bubbling synthesizers, echoed guitar, and tambourine. The instrumental passages carry you along like a pleasant daydream, but the disc is punctuated by

The Ultimate Psychedelic Rock Library: Peggy Suicide *(Island) is Cope's first great concept album, a hypnotic and haunting psychedelic masterpiece.*

sly hooks, and every one of the eighteen songs is strong enough to stand on its own.

Most of the tunes were recorded in one or two takes by Cope and his core collaborators, bassist Donald Ross Skinner and drummer Rooster Cosby. "I think you can make a great pot album and it won't be long and indulgent," Cope told me at the time of the disc's release. "I don't want to bore people. The way I see it, rock'n' roll must have what Lester Bangs used to call that *yorp* that moment where the four musicians in the studio are looking at each other and they all go, 'Well, fucking hell,' and they all play this kind of like sonic *klang!* I could sit down and say to people, 'Look man, you've got to understand where I'm coming from, 'cause it's deadly important.' The greatest artists have to accept that it's deadly important, but it's also got to be top entertainment."

Cope returned to the model of *Peggy Suicide* twice in the years that followed. Released in 1992, *Jehovahkil* ponders the meaning of ancient formations such as Stonehenge and the long tradition of pagan symbols being suppressed by the Church. (The subtitle is *That'll Be the Deicide*—like *Peggy Suicide*, a pun on a Buddy Holly song—but Island Records mangled it in the cover art as *That'll Be the Decide*.) He left Island and moved to Rick Rubin's American Recordings for 1994's *Autogeddon*. Inspired by the freak accident of his car exploding in the driveway on Christmas night, 1992, the album further explores the anti-auto tirades of *Peggy Suicide* while paying tribute to the *motorik* beat and autobahn soundscapes of Neu! and krautrock.

Partly because of their density, and partly because he was reluctant to tour to promote them, Cope's concept albums didn't win the audience they deserved in the States. (The most American-influenced of England's psychedelic postpunks, Cope has always been more popular at home, while the very English Hitchcock and Partridge have bigger followings in the United States.) He proved too strange even for American Recordings, the label that embraced Wesley Willis, and he's been without a Stateside record deal since he was dropped from its roster. Unfazed, the prolific auteur has busied himself with myriad other projects, including two volumes of his autobiography, a scholarly book about England's ancient stone formations (*The Modern Antiquarian: A Pre-Millennial Odyssey through Megalithic Britain*), a fan's guide to krautrock, several volumes of Neu!-like instrumental meditations (*Rite*, *Rite 2*, and *Rite Now*), several volumes of ambient/electronic krautrock (*Queen Elizabeth* and *Queen Elizabeth 2*), a Stooges-style proto-punk side project called Brain Donor, an "ambient metal" side project called L.A.M.F. ("Like a Mother Fucker"), and a label (KAK—English slang for "shit") and

Web site (www.headheritage.co.uk) dedicated to cataloging and selling it all.

In 1996 Cope made a partial return to the more conventional albums of his early solo career with the strong twenty-song collection, *20 Mothers*, a heartfelt homage to incest, in the sense that he believes we're all related and we should all *really* love one another. (At least I *think* that's what he's talking about.) Even better was 1997's *Interpreter*. Like many of his albums, it was divided in the style of old vinyl LP sides. On the first half ("Phase I"), he offers six of his strongest tunes since *Peggy Suicide*, embellishing the massive hooks in songs such as "I Come From Another Planet, Baby" and "The Battle for the Trees" with beautiful Mellotron and real string parts, driving acid guitars, burbling analog synthesizers, and rollicking rhythms. On "Phase II," he delivers a thumbnail history of psychedelic rock, showing his mastery of ornate Beatles-esque pop ("Arthur Drugstore"), krautrock ("S.P.A.C.E.R.O.C.K. With Me"), George Clinton-style freak-funk ("Re-Directed Male"), and progres-

The Ultimate Psychedelic Rock Library: Interpreter *(KAK) is another startling concept disc, as overwhelming for its drive and melody as it is for Cope's mind-boggling philosophizing.*

sive rock ("Maid of Constant Sorrow") before building to a spectacular finale with "The Loveboat" and "Dust," grand anthems built
around the eccentrics' rallying cry, "Celebrate who you are!"

All of Cope's favorite themes are represented—environmental
panic, pagan mysteries, goddess worship, and technological
fascism—but this time he explains how they fit together in liner
notes that quote from Che Guevara, Martin Luther King, and MC5
guru John Sinclair. Apparently aliens visited the earth in ancient
times and gave us the secrets to personal happiness and preserving
the health of our planet. We've turned a deaf ear to them, but the
clues remain if you know where to look—say, Stonehenge, or the
local acid dealer's pad. Salvation is within our grasp, but only if we
tolerate our differences and care for each other and for Mother
Earth. (At least I *think* that's what he's talking about.)

"I was feeling that time was peeling from the twentieth century / And I was given to warmth and healing—the patterns of eternity / The beauty of life force is all over me," Cope sings in one
tune. Then he delivers the chorus, the title of the song, and a
phrase that can stand as the credo for his entire career: "Since I lost
my head, it's awl-right."

THE MAN WHO INVENTED HIMSELF

If you call my music psychedelic, it is. If you say that coffee
cups that have a certain amount of grind on the inside are
psychedelic, people will say they are not. But if you go on
saying it, eventually they will be. Because people will say,
"The mugs were very psychedelic when we came down for
breakfast today," meaning they were full of old coffee grind.
                                    —Robyn Hitchcock

THE FUNNY THING ABOUT INTERVIEWS is that people always
expect me to define myself," Hitchcock said the first time I spoke
with him. He proceeded to launch into the sort of absurdist
monologue that would become very familiar in the coming years.
"It's like saying, 'Good evening, my name is Marsha Lynn. I'm
eighteen and I come from Connecticut. I hope to be a goldfish. My
hobbies are cycling, tennis, and peeling the skin off old people.'"
Hitchcock had come to Maxwell's in Hoboken, New Jersey, on his
first tour with the Egyptians, but he was known primarily as leader
of the late, lamented Soft Boys, a group that was influential in
launching the psychedelic revival in the States. But while the
Paisley Underground bands were so anxious to be linked to the past
that they even dressed the part, Hitchcock was reluctant to be
pigeonholed—unless it was in a role of his own invention.

Hitchcock was born in London in 1953 to upper-middle-class
parents, including a father who was a well-known cartoonist and
painter. He attended an all-male boarding school and arrived in art
college in the early '70s, "indistinguishable from the general

posthippie flotsam." His interests soon shifted to music via a school band called the Beetles, and when they broke up, he decided to move to Cambridge in search of new accomplices. At first he played solo shows at the Portland Arms or busked on the street, singing "Hey Jude" and a handful of originals such as "Wey Wey Hep Uh Hole." He also goofed around with some friends as Maureen and the Meatpackers. "It took about two years for the real musos to unfreeze themselves enough to come sliding up to see what I was doing," he told *Forced Exposure* in 1987. When they did come around, they included bassist Andy Metcalfe and drummer Morris Windsor, who were playing in a band called Dennis and the Experts.

The singer and songwriter borrowed this rhythm section and never returned it. The new group was completed in early 1977 by the addition of guitarist Wang Bo, a.k.a. Alan Davies. A deliberately un-rocking name was chosen from the titles of two books by William S. Burroughs, *The Soft Machine* and *The Wild Boys*. From the start, the Soft Boys were out of touch with the prevailing punk trends. "The Soft Boys were accused of being retrospective or psychedelic or all sorts of words that were unacceptable to the new-wave critical elite because we used guitar solos and harmonies," Hitchcock told me. "Wire covered their tracks better by having short hair; they were basically a psychedelic group in drag. Andy Partridge and XTC managed to get away with it. But we just didn't fit in."

Nevertheless, the group built enough of a following to release an independent EP called *Give It to the Soft Boys*. Hitchcock has said it's his favorite Soft Boys record, and traces of the group's later sound—including the dueling guitar lines, twisted rhythms, and absurdist lyrics—can be heard on "The Yodeling Hoover" and "Hear

My Brane." But the band's leader was ambitious. Prompted by a desire to be "more New Wave," he gave Wang Bo the boot and replaced him with the cute and dexterous lead guitarist of another Cambridge band called the Waves. "It was like if the Stones had kicked out Brian Jones and put Jimi Hendrix in," Hitchcock said. "It was sort of greed. We saw this guy Kimberly Rew and thought, 'What a performer. Let's have him!'"

Hitchcock soon regretted the move. He maintains that the Rew group was top-heavy, too loud, and "too Television." The group's first album was never released because Hitchcock claimed it was too bad, though pieces surfaced on later compilations. Recorded in 1978, *A Can of Bees* was the first effort to actually make it to the stores. "A can of bees was just what it was," Hitchcock told me. "That music is like a load of insects inside a jar just humming and trying to get out—a load of insects that have been drinking paraffin or something pretty lethal, insects that are on fire because they've been soaked in brandy." But though the arrangements are serpentine, the album is full of what one song calls "Human Music," and even the most experimental tunes boast inviting melodies. The psychedelic influence can be heard in echoes of Captain Beefheart and the Incredible String Band (as well as the more obvious Beatles) and in the lyrical imagery.

Dada, surrealism, English folklore, Monty Python, the Goon Show, Bob Dylan, and Syd Barrett are all inspirations for Hitchcock's songwriting, but the biggest factor was and is his fertile imagination. He has only ever had five themes—gender confusion, death, nostalgia, the psychotic side of romance, and sinister doings in the natural world—but he has a thousand metaphors to describe them. Some fans assume that his lyrics and music must be drug-inspired, but the Soft Boys were never as enthusiastic about acid as the bands in Liverpool. "I took a few trips, but I didn't trust it," Hitchcock said. "You certainly don't need to take drugs to make creative music." Like Roxy Music, the group approached a rock song as a pastiche. "The Soft Boys' manifesto was one of taking bits and pieces, a bit like a collage," Hitchcock told *Forced Exposure*. "Like if you gummed a tomato to a squirrel's head and then gaffer-taped a pigeon's wings to a cucumber. I would say that the Soft Boys were about arrangements rather than songs."

This started to change when Metcalfe left and Matthew Seligman joined, shifting the group in a poppier direction and paving the way for its best album. *Underwater Moonlight* (1980) was done primarily on eight tracks, but this time the group and producer Pat Collier indulged in amenities such as echo, reverb, and sitar overdubs. A few songs continue in the style of the early Soft Boys, but most are well-crafted updates of the chiming folk-rock

The Ultimate Psychedelic Rock Library: Underwater Moonlight *(Matador) is the Soft Boys' finest moment, though Robyn Hitchcock has always maintained that he prefers* A Can of Bees.

sounds of Fairport Convention and the Byrds. The single "I Wanna Destroy You" is both an inspiring anti-war song and a cheeky jab at punk, while utopian anthems such as "Positive Vibrations" and "Kingdom of Love" rank among the finest songs Hitchcock has written. His flair for Lennon-esque melodies is in ample evidence, as is the witty, surrealistic cast of lyrics that explore old perverts, jealous madmen, ghosts that emerge from the sea, and all manner of disturbing insect imagery. The Soft Boys weren't looking back toward the psychedelic past but ahead to a free-flowing creative future. "The psychedelic revival was mentioned in 1979—that was actually just when the first things were starting to be revived; up until then everything had been happening for the first time—but as far as we were concerned, what we were doing was very much in the present," Rew told me.

Unfortunately, the album was greeted by general indifference at home in England—over half the sales of *Underwater Moonlight* were as American imports—and the Soft Boys "just sort of petered out" in early 1980, Hitchcock said. (*Invisible Hits* followed, but it was a collection of older material recorded between the first and second albums.) While Windsor remained close to Hitchcock, and Metcalfe soon returned, the mop-topped Rew set out on his own, crafting a strong power-pop album called *The Bible of Bop* before returning to the Waves and new singer Katrina Leskanich to score a major hit with "Walking On Sunshine."

Hitchcock's first solo album, *Black Snake Diamond Röle*, features musical contributions from the former Soft Boys, as well as Psychedelic Furs drummer Vince Ely. It opens with "The Man Who Invented Himself," ostensibly a tribute to Barrett, but just as effective as Hitchcock's own theme song. The album continues the upbeat mood of *Underwater Moonlight*, but the sound is expanded with keyboards and more acoustic instruments, shifting the focus further toward the words and melodies. "They're the first set of songs I developed as a songwriter—he said, leaning on the table in a songwriterly fashion—and they're less novelty but no less a freak-show," Hitchcock told me. "But I'm still not Jackson Browne or anything like that."

One of the few traits that Hitchcock shared with the punk movement was a disdain for rock-star behavior. He lampooned rock excess on several tunes, including the Soft Boys' "Rock 'n' Roll Toilet" and "Trash" from the oddities collection *Invisible Hitchcock*. Nevertheless, he found himself sucked into a disastrous bid at star-dom with 1982's *Groovy Decay*, blindly ceding control as he escaped in an alcoholic daze. Producer Steve Hillage buried Hitchcock's songs under obnoxious horns and disco grooves, inadvertently pre-dicting the Manchester psychedelic dance sound that emerged a few years later. Hitchcock had never been a particular fan of Hillage or Gong, and the idea of the pairing came from his manager at the time. "I think he just thought, 'Oh yeah, *psychedelic*, alright,"' Hitchcock said. "Hillage had justly got into his sort of 1980's Kings' Row suits and was trying to be anything *but* psychedelic. He was into club mixes and all that sort of stuff. I was really lost and get-ting loster in those days."

This spectacular failure prompted Hitchcock to withdraw and reassess. He kept himself afloat by writing lyrics for solo efforts by Captain Sensible of the Damned, but his own songs began to accu-mulate again, and he finally returned to the studio after a three-

The Ultimate Psychedelic Rock Library: Marking his return to music after a three-year retirement, I Often Dream of Trains *is the strongest of Hitchcock's solo albums—a quiet, introspective meditation on his place in the world.*

year break to craft *I Often Dream of Trains.* The best of his solo albums, it's a quiet, introspective effort driven by acoustic guitar, piano, and vocals—Hitchcock's version of Cope's "acid campfire songs" or Barrett's solo albums. "It's like wanting to see what you're like when you take everything else away," he told me. It also comes closer than any other album to merging the styles of his two primary heroes. "Bob Dylan showed me what I wanted to do, and Syd Barrett showed me how I could do it," the singer has often said. (Though he always paid tribute to both men in interviews, the Barrett comparison is the one that took root. Not only was the stylistic resemblance more obvious, but both artists had ties to Cambridge, and Hitchcock eventually signed with former Barrett and Pink Floyd manager Peter Jenner.) Songs such as "This Could Be the Day," "It Sounds Great When You're Dead," and the title track find him contemplating his place in the universe (albeit it in typically surrealistic terms), while "Sometimes I Wish I Was a Pretty Girl," "Uncorrected Personality Traits," and "I Used to Say I Love You" are as close to personal confessionals as he's ever gotten.

Re-energized and reunited with Windsor and Metcalfe in the Egyptians, Hitchcock immediately followed *I Often Dream of Trains* with a new electric pop album, *Fegmania!* During their absence from the scene, the Soft Boys' influence had grown. Peter Buck said the group was more of an inspiration for early R.E.M. than the Byrds. Now the Egyptians were poised to capitalize on their old group's cult status. Embraced by the American rock underground and college radio, the band graduated from indie labels to A&M Records. Between 1986 and 1993, the Egyptians released a string of albums, including *Element of Light*, *Globe of Frogs*, *Queen Elvis*, *Perspex Island*, and *Respect*. (In between, Hitchcock took a break to release another strong solo acoustic effort called *Eye*.) The band's willful quirkiness served as a model for much of the alternative rock that stormed the charts in the '90s, but the Egyptians themselves never expanded beyond a small but loyal following. The group's playing grew increasingly polite and predictable, and Hitchcock's lyrical arsenal of dwarves, lobsters, ghosts, and man-eating vegetables started to sound overly familiar. Yet even the least of his albums have three or four outstanding songs, including brilliant tunes such as "Glass," "Raymond Chandler Evening," "Vibrating," "She Doesn't Exist," and "The Wreck of the Arthur Lee" (a nod to the founder of Love as well anyone else who never realized their potential). A&M dropped Hitchcock after *Respect*, making the title especially ironic, and, once again, the band petered out. "There's only so long you can run a six-legged race," Hitchcock said.

Claiming to be burned out on the band format and loud rock in general, Hitchcock determined to forge ahead in the solo mode of *I Often Dream of Trains* and *Eye*, presenting his songs in the most direct manner possible by touring alone with an acoustic guitar. (Director Jonathan Demme captured one of these performances in the 1998 film, *Storefront Hitchcock*.) The songwriter has never regretted his more whimsical moments, and he maintains that his "serious" songs and his humorous flights of fancy both reflect parts of his personality. But there's no denying that his songs are sometimes drowned out by the persona he invented. "Hitchcock is the kind of English eccentric who becomes impossible to bear when he's taken up by American Anglophiles," critic Robert Christgau charged.

"I've set myself up for that, so if I feel trapped, I've only got myself to blame," Hitchcock told me. "But both the musicianship angle—working with the others—and the 'Robyn Hitchcock unscrews the top of his head and lets it all spring out all over the floor' angle are secondary to what I am, which is a songwriter." In 2001 he once again returned to "working with the others," reuniting the legendary Soft Boys and, in 2002, the band released its first new album in twenty-two years. With its shimmering melodies and gonzo lyrics about fish and Japanese captains, *Nextdoorland* recalls Hitchcock's work with the Egyptians more than Soft Boys classics like *Underwater Moonlight*. But the band also occasionally breaks into the sort of fiery two-guitar duels that characterized *A Can of Bees*. The rhythms are harder and more driving and, once again, Hitchcock has delivered a handful of new tunes ("Pulse of My Heart," "Mr. Kennedy," "My Mind Is Connected to Your Dreams") that add to a catalog of songs that stand with the most impressive in rock history, right up there beside heroes such as Lennon and Dylan.

SENSES WORKING OVERTIME

> Andy's mind was taking him on a terrifying voyage, like a
> bad acid trip. It was a classic Hollywood horror scenario:
> The room began to spin as everyone and everything
> seemed to be drifting further and further away from him.
> He felt more and more nauseous. Finally he thought, quite
> literally, he was going to die.
>
> —Chris Twomey
> describes Andy Partridge's onstage freak-out in 1982

THERE ARE TWO MAJOR DIFFERENCES between Andy Partridge
and the other two psychedelic peers profiled in this chapter. Unlike
Julian Cope, he never really shared the punk appreciation for
spontaneity and immediacy. And unlike Robyn Hitchcock, he came
to despise live performance. Chris Twomey's definitive biography,
XTC: Chalkhills and Children, opens with the central incident in the
band's story. After years of steady touring, the group was playing in
support of its best album to date, 1982's *English Settlement.* Onstage
at Le Palais in Paris, Partridge froze only thirty seconds into the set,
then ran off. In the weeks that followed, he attempted to come to
terms with his paranoia and stage fright, but hours before a sold-out
show at the Hollywood Palladium, he simply decided that he would
never perform live again. After all, the Beatles had done it, and they
had proceeded to do some of their best work.

XTC's guitarist and vocalist was born in Malta in 1953 to Vera
and John Partridge, who was serving in the Royal Navy. When
Andy was three, the family returned to a quiet, working-class life in
Swindon, a small farm community seventy miles west of London.

Andy was exposed to music from early on—his father was a singer who performed in local skiffle groups—but the interest really took hold when he saw *A Hard Day's Night* at age ten. As he entered his teens, he spent hours listening to psychedelic rock singles such as the Small Faces' "Itchycoo Park," the Move's "Fire Brigade," and Pink Floyd's "See Emily Play"—"a three-minute thing of a very memorable tune but with a big dollop of magic injected, either some strange effect or totally nonsensical lyrics that painted great brain pictures," as he told *Musician* magazine in 1987. He eventually bought a guitar and a used reel-to-reel tape recorder, partly with money that he won in a "Draw Your Favorite Monkee" contest, and he began making music himself.

Life wasn't always rosy. Reacting badly to his parents' marital problems, Partridge was put on Valium to control wild mood swings at age twelve, and he didn't stop taking the drug until thirteen years later. He quit Swindon College in 1971 after a year and a half. By 1973 he was playing in a glam band called Star Park—later the Helium Kidz—with hard-drinking drummer Terry Chambers, quiet bassist Colin Moulding, and Dave Cartner, who was soon replaced by keyboardist Barry Andrews. As musical fashions shifted the group moved from glam to pub-rock with science-fiction overtones, and a new name was needed. In late 1975 the Dukes of Stratosphear was passed over as "too psychedelic," and the band became XTC.

Even though its music had little to do with punk, the quartet landed a contract with Virgin Records in the rush of excitement following the Sex Pistols. At Partridge's insistence, early press releases referred to him as a "nuclear-powered Syd Barrett." XTC's first album included a herky-jerk cover of Dylan's "All Along the

Watchtower" (a very unpunk choice) and a hyperenergetic declaration that "This Is Pop." Even the title—*White Music*—could be considered a statement against the punks' "white noise." The album and XTC's tense live shows (which many compared to the Talking Heads') began to win an audience and, by August 1978, the band was ready to record a follow-up. XTC considered working with Brian Eno, who was a fan, but Eno said the band didn't need a producer. Virgin disagreed and paired the group with John Leckie. The resulting album, *Go 2*, is more ambitious and experimental. "Battery Brides" is a mechanical pop song that pays tribute to Eno, and Moulding's "X Wires" shows a serious desire to experiment in the studio.

From the start, Partridge wrote most of XTC's material, with occasional contributions from Moulding. Frustrated by this arrangement, Andrews quit and was replaced by Swindon pal Dave Gregory on guitar and keyboards. (Thomas Dolby lobbied for the spot but was rejected, since he was also an ambitious songwriter. Like Gary Numan, he went on to craft low-rent versions of Eno's and Kraftwerk's synthesizer-pop albums.) XTC toured non-stop through this period in what it called "stupidly hard work," and albums (including the wonderfully poppy and Beatles-esque *Drums and Wires*) were crafted in a rush between commitments. *Black Sea* originally had the protest title *Working Under Pressure*, hence the deep-sea diver suits on the cover. Adding to the edginess, Partridge quit his long-time Valium addiction cold turkey. Ironically, the mounting tensions produced a serene and beautiful double album.

The Ultimate Psychedelic Rock Library: XTC's English Settlement *(Geffen) travels the world and attempts to solve its problems from the serene setting of hometown Swindon.*

English Settlement was crafted in the summer of 1981, the group's first extended down time in four years. It's a subtle and textured effort that makes extensive use of twelve-string guitar, fretless bass, synthesizer, and tom-heavy drum parts that draw on a variety of global rhythms. "Until *English Settlement*, I'd felt like a child in a sweet shop wanting to try a bit of everything, but only being allowed to choose licorice allsorts," Partridge told Twomey. "I'd broken from this moral chastity belt that told me it was wrong to put anything on our records that we couldn't reproduce live." Like the Soft Boys, XTC took a shot at wannabe punks with "No Thugs in Our House," while other songs such as "It's Nearly Africa," "Melt the Guns," and "Jason and the Argonauts" found Partridge exploring distant lands and musing on global politics from the safety of his own comfortable armchair in Swindon. "I felt more English in the face of traveling the world," he said. But the strongest tune is about an inner voyage. If "Senses Working Overtime" wasn't inspired by a pleasurable acid trip—Partridge has never directly addressed the question—its sentiments and expansive sound certainly evoke the feeling. "All the world is biscuit shaped / It's just for me to feed my face," he sings. "I can see, hear, smell, touch, taste / And I've got one, two, three, four, five / Senses working overtime / Trying to take this all in."

The song's title took on a different connotation in the wake of Partridge's onstage breakdown. Returning to Swindon, the band leader, who was now plagued by agoraphobia, decided against straying far from home again any time soon. The group was deeply in debt, and it was left without a drummer when Chambers quit because of the no-touring edict. XTC forged ahead, but the problems contributed to the tentative, stilted sound of *Mummer*, and the album ends with a bitter declaration: "The music business is a hammer to keep you pegs in your holes," Partridge sings in "Funk Pop a Roll." Released in 1984, *The Big Express* has more upbeat moments—including the idyllic "Everyday Story of Smalltown"—but it is often over-produced and leaden. If XTC's earlier albums were limited by time constraints, its work after *English Settlement* suffers from a lack of urgency. The band clearly needed to blow out the cobwebs.

Partridge and Leckie were slated to produce Canadian singer Mary Margaret O'Hara, but she fired them when she discovered they didn't share her strict Roman Catholic beliefs. Virgin owed the pair money, and Leckie convinced the company to give it to XTC for a bit of fun in the studio. The musicians had long been itching to pay tribute to the psychedelic rock they loved as teenagers. Working at a small studio in Hereford, they recorded six songs in two weeks, forcing themselves to use only vintage '60s equipment.

The Ultimate Psychedelic Rock Library: The Dukes of Stratosphear was a side project that helped XTC blow out the cobwebs. Chips from the Chocolate Fireball *(Caroline) combines their debut EP and subsequent album.*

The *25 O'Clock* EP was released on April Fool's Day, 1985, under the guise of the Dukes of Stratosphear. XTC's name didn't appear anywhere in the artwork, but the strong melodies and West Country vocals left little doubt about who the culprits were. Like many of the psychedelic revival bands recording in America at the time, the Dukes' faithfulness to late '60s sounds, styles, and themes produced a classic psychedelic-rock parody and homage. In a lengthy interview with the XTC fanzine, *The Little Express*, the group offered detailed footnotes for each song: "Bike Ride to the Moon" is sung in a sort of "loopy Cambridge" accent over a bass line stolen from the Move, with lyrics that owe a debt to "My White Bicycle" and Syd Barrett's "Bike"; "25 O'Clock" is a cross between the Amboy Dukes and the Electric Prunes, and "The Mole from the Ministry" layers Beatles-style Mellotron over a jaunty "I Am the Walrus" sing-along.

While the EP breaks no ground, it's hard not to enjoy the Dukes' spirited musical forgery. On its release, *25 O'Clock* outsold

The Big Express two-to-one, rekindling enthusiasm at Virgin for what had become a reclusive cult group. The company geared up for another go at making XTC a hit, insisting that the group work with a "name" producer. The band was enthusiastic about the prospect of recording. "With XTC, we'd lost sight of how to enjoy ourselves making a record," Moulding told Twomey. "We spent a lot of time and money on our records and they weren't necessarily any better for it. The Dukes taught us how to have fun again." But Partridge's enthusiasm soon waned as he butted heads with the equally strong-willed producer, Todd Rundgren.

As a member of the Nazz and a quirky solo artist in the '70s, Rundgren had displayed an aesthetic similar to XTC's. He sifted through the group's demos and developed a concept for a song cycle that traced a passing day from dawn to midnight. *Skylarking* returned to the pastoral tranquility of *English Settlement* while adding a new sophistication that represented influences such as the Beach Boys and the Beatles coming even further to the forefront.

The Ultimate Psychedelic Rock Library: The lush and lulling sounds of Skylarking *(Geffen), XTC's last great psychedelic rock album, belie the tensions behind the scenes during its creation.*

Moulding produced two fine pieces of psychedelic rock—"Big Day," which had originally been considered for the Dukes' project, and an homage to making love while lying in and/or high on "Grass"— while Partridge presented an irresistibly catchy three-minute slice of existentialism, "Dear God." This direct and angry letter to the deity became XTC's first major American hit, resurrecting the band's career, generating tons of press by kindling a controversy in the conservative South, and preserving the band's future for some time. But its author hadn't even wanted it on the album, and Rundgren had to insist. (The producer also recruited a ten-year-old girl named Jasmine Veillette over Partridge's objections to play the part of the young Andy who addresses the Almighty and asks the timeless question of why the hell He allows so much pain and suffering down here on earth.)

"The band was at a point in their career where if they didn't get some kind of response to their records, they weren't going to be making any more records," Rundgren told Twomey. "It had to be a record that people would listen to and enjoy. There were times when I was at loggerheads with Andy's natural propensity for excess." Though Partridge bad-mouthed Rundgren in countless interviews after the album's release, in time, even he admitted that the producer had done his job and done it well.

XTC followed *Skylarking* with a second Dukes of Stratosphear release, *Psonic Psunspot*. The album has less of the EP's joy and spontaneity, and XTC really didn't need its alter-egos any more: *Skylarking* had successfully married XTC and the Dukes. "I had always wanted to be in a group that made that kind of music," Partridge told the band's biographer. "There was a split image, and now they're merged." Unfortunately, he never heeded the lesson he should have learned while working with Rundgren, which was that the group needed an editor and mediator. When the band was limited by the time constraints of vinyl LPs, extraneous material was relegated to B sides, EPs, and rarities collections. After *Skylarking*, Partridge simply emptied his notebooks onto bloated and overlong albums. He had often eclipsed Moulding in the past, despite the fact that the bassist wrote many of the band's best songs, and in the absence of a strong producer, he became even more dominant. *Oranges and Lemons* (1989) and *Nonsuch* (1992) are good albums that could have been great if Partridge had accepted some discipline. Too many of the tunes seem like re-writes of earlier material, and Partridge's propensities for wordiness, cloying cuteness, and fussy baroque arrangements go unchecked.

The band lost its British and American recording contracts after *Nonsuch*, and it went on an extended eight-year hiatus. When it returned, the valuable multi-instrumentalist Dave Gregory was no longer in the fold, and 1999's *Apple Venus Volume I* and 2000's *Wasp Star (Apple Venus Volume 2)* failed to measure up to its finest moments in the past. The band's auteur remains unrepentant; in the grand tradition of English eccentrics, he lives by his own rules and makes music today primarily to please himself. XTC is basically "a paying hobby," he has said, a pleasant diversion that ranks up there with arranging his armies of toy soldiers, drinking at the pub, and sitting up nights reading Jules Verne. "People who like XTC like us for precisely the reason we aren't like everyone else," he maintains. "If you like cheesecake, you don't like it because it reminds you of some other form of cake so you'll put up with the cheese element. You like it because it's cheesecake."

TWELVE

RETRODELIC:
The Psychedelic
and Garage Revivals

We belong to the hot generation / Yeah, we belong to the
civilization / We have no responsibility / And people just
can't see / That we need to be free.
                        —The Pandoras, "Hot Generation"

ON THE SUNDAY NIGHT before Labor Day, the crowd was ready to
rock into the early morning hours at the Dive, an aptly named
hellhole on New York's West Twenty-ninth Street. Mod haircuts,
black turtlenecks, tapered trousers, and Beatles boots were the uni-
forms of choice for the men, while the women sported long bangs,
tight miniskirts, Nancy Sinatra go-go boots, and Mary Quant-style
makeup. Strobe lights bounced off a silvery backdrop as a procession of bands took to the tiny stage to raise money for *99th Floor*,
the self-proclaimed "Official Fanzine of Teenage Creeps." The

Creeping Pumpkins started off with their raw, grungy garage rock. The Blacklight Chameleons played psychedelicized surf instrumentals; the Tryfles delivered a collection of snotty protopunk anthems, and the Optic Nerve headlined with a jangly set that would have done the Byrds proud. But the best act of the night was a young trio from New Jersey called the Mod Fun, which had progressed from amped-up R&B a la its original heroes the Who ("I Am With You," "Action Tyme") to inventive psychedelic rockers ("Mary Goes Round," "Open Your Eyes," and a killer cover of "Grounded") driven by the feedback-drenched Rickenbacker of cheekily pseudononymous bandleader Mick London. These witty and unbelievably catchy songs of gender confusion and the adolescent search for identity evoked what the Creation might have sounded like if its career had continued beyond a handful of singles, and the band ended its set with a flurry of chaos by trashing its instruments.

A time traveler might have thought he'd arrived in 1966, but in fact the year was 1985, and the *99th Floor* benefit was evidence of the first American psychedelic and garage revival in full swing. As in England, the American rock underground rediscovered psychedelia as a natural progression from punk. Emerging shortly after the punk scenes that sprang up in Cleveland and New York, Washington, D.C.'s Afrika Korps (later the Slickee Boys) and Boston's DMZ (later the Lyres) were both devoted to faithful organ-driven reproductions of *Nuggets*-era rock. In the early '80s these bands were joined by the like-minded Chesterfield Kings from Rochester, New York, the Unclaimed from Los Angeles, and the Fleshtones from New York City, perhaps the ultimate cave-stomp party band. These groups in turn prompted younger musicians to scour the record racks in search of '60s relics to provide a basis for their own sounds.

Two Dozen Great Psychedelic Rock Records from the First Revival

1. The Lime Spiders, *Nine Miles High 1983–1990* (Raven, 2002, Aus.)

2. Paul Roland, *Danse Macabre* (Bam Caruso, 1987)

3. The Velvet Monkeys, *Rotting Corpse au Go-Go* (Shimmy-Disc, 1989)

4. The Yellow Sunshine Explosion, *The Yellow Sunshine Explosion* (Love's Simple Dreams, 1987, Ger.)

5. The Miracle Workers, *Inside Out* (Voxx, 2000; 1985)

6. The Mod Fun, *Past...Forward* (Get Hip, 2000)

7. Tiny Lights, *The Young Person's Guide to Tiny Lights* (Bar/None, 1995)

8. Absolute Grey, *Green House* (Paisley Pop, 2003; 1986)

9. The 27 Various, *Yes, Indeed* (Susstones, 1989)

10. The Vipers, *Outta the Nest* (Cavestomp, 2000; 1985)

11. The Fleshtones, *Hexbreaker!* (IRS, 1983)

12. The Lyres, *On Fyre* (Ace of Hearts, 1996; 1984)

13. The Fuzztones, *Lysergic Emanations* (Reper, 1996; 1986)

14. The Barracudas, *Drop Out with the Barracudas* (Voxx, 1981)

15. The Bevis Frond, *The Auntie Winnie Album* (Sain, 1997; 1989)

16.   The Hoodoo Gurus, *Stoneage Romeos*
      (Acadia, 2002; 1983)

17.   The Nomads, *Outburst* (Homestead, 1984)

18.   The Hypstrz, *Hypstrization!* (Voxx, 1980)

19.   The Marshmallow Overcoat, *The Marshmallow
      Overcoat: 1986–1990* (Get Hip, 1990)

20.   Plan 9, *Dealing With the Dead* LP (Midnight, 1984)

21.   Yard Trauma, *Must've Been Something I Took Last
      Night* LP (Dionysius, 1985)

22.   The Mad Violets, *World Of...* (Lolita, 1986)

23.   The Chesterfield Kings, *Stop!* (Mirror, 1985)

24.   The Chud, *Silhouettes of Sound*
      (Love's Simple Dreams, 1986, Ger.)

Greg Shaw of the punk label Bomp! formed the subsidiary Voxx Records in 1979 as the home for *Battle of the Garages*, a *Nuggets*-style compilation of modern bands dedicated to "an aesthetic originally formed and perfected in 1966 high school gyms." It took two years and a national competition to round up enough bands for the first volume, but by the time it was released in 1981, Shaw was being besieged with tapes from across the country. "Every city in the country has got some kind of band doing this stuff," Unclaimed veteran Sid Griffin told *Creem* magazine at the peak of the movement in 1986. "Every town has got at least one '60s band."

The revival fascinated editors who had been there the first time, and a host of articles appeared in the national media. Tellingly, *Rolling Stone* covered it as a fashion story. Anti-fashion had been the rule for punk, but style was a prime concern for the '60s revivalists. Bands were extremely conscious of using only period instruments— Vox and Farfisa organs and Vox, Rickenbacker, and Silvertone guitars—and they dressed only in period styles. There was a rigid doctrine, and the rules were spelled out by the albums, films, and magazine articles that documented the original garage and psychedelic movements. By 1986 even Shaw was complaining about the scene's lack of cultural relevance. "It has nothing to do with what's going on today," he said in *Creem*. "I like the sounds, but what made punk important in the '70s was that it was talking about now and handing out answers for now, and that's why it touched so many people."

Defenders of the revival said that its adherents were simply fighting boredom, and they noted the D.I.Y. nature of the scene. "The garage kids were rejecting the corporate, bland, 'modern' music culture," Timothy Gassen wrote in *Echoes in Time: The Garage and Psychedelic Music Explosion 1980–1990*. But unlike the movement in the '60s or the early-'80s punk scene that produced groups such as Hüsker Dü and the Minutemen, the revivalists weren't interested in politics or social change. "Most bands and followers of the '60s sound avoided such personal commitment, many feeling hopelessness in the Reagan and Thatcher years of ever affecting any positive change," Gassen wrote. "Perhaps they didn't equate their rejection of current trends with a return to humanism, or perhaps they couldn't commit themselves to ideas so constantly rejected by their own generation."

Perhaps, like so many people in the '80s and a fair number in the '60s, the revivalists were simply searching for escape. The goal at the Dive in New York or the Cavern Club in Los Angeles was to leave with a sexual partner and as few brain cells as possible after a night of loud music, drink, and drugs. While it's debatable how many of the original psychedelic punks ever had psychedelic experiences, LSD and mushrooms were readily available wherever the revivalists were doing their thing in the '80s. "I remember when [*99th Floor* publisher] Ron Rimsite got up to announce us at that benefit," recalled the Mod Fun's Mick London. "He couldn't even remember the name of the band. He just rambled on about how the world would be so much groovier if Gorbachev and Reagan sat down and took Ecstasy together—and this was years before the rave scene! I'm sure that everybody at the Dive at any given time was on *something*."

Most critics treated releases by the revival groups as novelties, or they dismissed them as insular and inconsequential—souvenirs that the bands put out for their friends. But as with the original *Nuggets* groups, time has revealed memorable songwriting, musical innovation, and an undeniable spirit in the best music from this scene. (And, ironically, many of these albums, which were initially issued on small independent labels, are now harder to find than the '60s originals.) Rochester's Absolute Grey combined chiming guitars and powerful female vocals reminiscent of the Jefferson Airplane. Delaware's Plan 9 represented what the Grateful Dead would have sounded like if it hadn't abandoned the garage rock it played as the Warlocks. Washington, D.C.'s Velvet Monkeys effectively mixed the disparate influences cited in their name, while Portland's Miracle Workers progressed from hyperactive R&B to a psychedelic take on '70s Detroit. Hoboken, New Jersey's Tiny Lights combined Sly Stone's psychedelic soul with elaborate, Beatles-inspired productions and the gutsy vocals of frontwoman Donna Croughn. An even more remarkable frontwoman, Wendy Wild, led New York's rollicking, fuzz-drenched Mad Violets. The hot desert climate of Tucson nurtured the psychedelic pop of the Marshmallow Overcoat and the raunchy garage punk of Yard Trauma, and the frigid temperatures of Minneapolis produced the barn-burning sounds of the Hypstrz (later the Mighty Mofos) and the enigmatic guitar pop of the 27 Various (which started out as a mod band called the Dig).

The first revival wasn't limited to the United States. In Australia, there were the Hoodoo Gurus and the Lime Spiders; in New Zealand, there was the burgeoning "kiwi pop" scene of the Verlaines, the Tall Dwarfs, and the Chills (whose enigmatic productions and complex songwriting evinced an ambition far beyond mere revivalism). Germany had the garagey Chud and the expansive and trippy Yellow Sunshine Explosion, and Sweden gave us the fiery Nomads. While several English groups were having chart success with an updated take on psychedelia, a number of underground artists were devoted to "purer" versions of older sounds, including the Barracudas, the Prisoners, the prolific guitar wizard the Bevis Frond (a.k.a. Nick Saloman), and Paul Roland, who recorded masterful Syd Barrett-style pop tunes orchestrated in the manner of *S.F. Sorrow* by the Pretty Things.

The Chameleons formed in Manchester in 1981 and honed a dense, atmospheric brand of mope rock based on the swirling guitars of Reg Smithies and Dave Fielding. Their first EP was titled

Nostalgia, but at their best—as on *What Does Anything Mean?Basically* (1985) and *Strange Times* (1986)—the musicians looked forward instead of back, crafting memorable and melodic psychedelic rock tunes. Mod and psychedelia were always inextricably linked, and mod revivalist heroes the Jam included many psychedelic touches on albums such as *Setting Sons* (1979) and *Sound Affects* (1980) via songs such as "Private Hell," "Dream Time," and "The Dreams of Children," as well as covers of "And Your Bird Can Sing" and "Rain" by the Beatles. But by far the most influential and enduring efforts by any of the revivalists came from the so-called "Paisley Underground" bands in L.A., and from a group called Plasticland from the unlikely blue-collar, beer-loving burg of Milwaukee, Wisconsin.

THE PAISLEY UNDERGROUND

> Like a kaleidoscope / I turn and I'm turning / What I
> thought was gone / Is now returning / I wonder if it mat-
> ters / As the pattern shifts and shatters.
> —The Rain Parade, "Kaleidoscope"

THE PHRASE WAS COINED by Michael Quercio, founder of the Salvation Army and the Three O'Clock, and it would come to be hated by the bands that it described the way that the word "grunge" would be hated by bands in Seattle a few years later. It referred to the paisley fashions that the groups favored, but most of the California bands had some substance beneath the style, at least in the beginning. Many of the groups had roots in suburban Davis, California, but the scene solidified in Los Angeles. "A lot of the friendships started out of the barbecues that Green On Red would have," Dream Syndicate leader Steve Wynn told *The Bob* in 1985. "They had this house down in Hollywood in 1982, a little two-story apartment for the whole band and their girlfriends. Every Sunday, we'd get together for a barbecue, bring tons of alcohol and whatever drugs—lots of burgers and chicken—and we'd just sit around, play guitar, and talk. That's how the friendships happened, not in nightclubs or recording studios...especially with Green On Red and the Dream Syndicate and the Rain Parade."

Like many of the English psychedelic rockers in the '60s, most of the Paisley Underground musicians were from upper-middle-class backgrounds. They were too young to remember the first wave of psychedelic rock, and they discovered the music by rummaging through their parents' or older siblings' record collections. They were inspired to pick up instruments by punk, and they decided to employ them playing '60s sounds after seeing the Unclaimed. But while the Unclaimed drew its sound almost exclusively from the Seeds and the Music Machine, the younger bands had broader interests and a wider range of emotions, as evidenced by 1983's *Rainy Day* compilation, a revealing moment of unity for a scene that would soon fracture. The album features members of the Rain Parade, the Bangles, the Dream Syndicate, and the Three O'Clock playing in various combinations and paying tribute to the artists who provided the starting points for their own groups, including

Bob Dylan ("I'll Keep It with Mine"), the Beach Boys ("Sloop John B."), the Buffalo Springfield ("Flying on the Ground is Wrong"), Big Star ("Holocaust"), the Velvet Underground ("I'll Be Your Mirror"), and Jimi Hendrix ("Rainy Day, Dream Away").

Like many of the scene's early releases, *Rainy Day* was recorded by Ethan James at Radio Tokyo Studios. Other albums were caught on tape by Earle Mankey in his garage, which was outfitted with the console that had been used to record *Pet Sounds*. In addition to using the same studios, the bands often played on each others' records. Unfortunately, they were also united by the fact that they all took turns for the worse once they were signed to major labels. In the days before Nirvana proved that there was money to be made if bands were left to their own "alternative" ways, it's possible that corporate meddling was to blame. Some bands may have gotten greedy, and some may have lost heart as, with the sole exception of R.E.M., American guitar bands were unable to achieve both critical and commercial success. Or perhaps the charges that they were just nostalgic revivalists were too hard to overcome. "The Paisley Underground tag was simultaneously good and bad," the Rain Parade's Steven Roback told me a decade later. "It was good because it helped a lot of serious musicians get some notoriety and make more good music. It was bad because there were a lot of preconceived notions about this psychedelic trip which really were not accurate."

The man who named the scene was born in 1963 in Carson, California, not far from the Beach Boys' hometown of Hawthorne. Quercio formed the Salvation Army as a pop-punk trio in 1981, and he released his first singles on the Minutemen's New Alliance label. But the band really came into its own when he linked up with gui-

THE THREE O'CLOCK
sixteen tambourines

WITH BAROQUE HOEDOWN AND PREVIOUSLY UNRELEASED SONG

*The Ultimate Psychedelic Rock
Library: A 1993 compilation
(Frontier) combines the Three
O'Clock's sparkling* Baroque
Hoedown *EP with its debut
album,* Sixteen Tambourines.

tarist Greggory Louis Gutierrez. Shortly thereafter the group was forced to change its name because of a threat from the real Salvation Army. The Three O'Clock was chosen from an F. Scott Fitzgerald quote ("In the darkest part of the mind it's always three o'clock in the morning"), and the contention in Tom Wolfe's *The Electric Kool-Aid Acid Test* that people who dropped acid in the early evening would be at the height of their trip at 3:00 a.m.

The influence of the Byrds, the Move, the early Bee Gees, and Syd Barrett's Pink Floyd are obvious on the band's 1982 EP, *Baroque Hoedown*, as well as 1983's *Sixteen Tambourines*. Quercio delivers hook-filled choruses over uplifting rhythms and shifting musical backgrounds based on buzzing keyboards and textured guitar sounds. Like Barrett, the singer projects an ambiguous sexuality, but one of his most memorable tunes is about being "With Cantaloupe Girlfriend." (Despite the obvious mammary inference, Quercio claimed it was a nonsense phrase for an ideal girl.) The band's decline began with its first release on IRS, *Arrive Without Traveling*.

The album boasts two strong tunes in "Her Head's Revolving" and "The Girl With the Guitar" (Quercio penned the latter with Scott Miller, who recorded power-pop with a tinge of psychedelia in Northern California's Game Theory), but these moments are overwhelmed by self-parodying schlock like "Simon in the Park (With Tentacles)." Gutierrez left in 1986, and the band signed to Prince's Paisley Park label for the dreadfully slick *Vermillion*. With its original fans alienated and everyone else indifferent, the Three O'Clock finally broke up in 1989.

The Bangles also slid into glossy commercialism after meeting up with Prince, but they started their career as a spare folk-rock quartet with pristine Mamas and Papas-style interval harmonies. The group changed its name from the Bangs and recorded its self-titled debut in 1982. When the band signed to Columbia, it traded mod fashions for Go-Go's/New Wave-style glamour, but the musicians retained a feisty, independent spirit. *All Over the Place* (1984) succeeds on the strength of guitarist Vicki Peterson's songs,

The Ultimate Psychedelic Rock Library: The Bangles' self-titled debut EP (IRS) remains their finest moment, though 1984's All Over the Place *is also strong. Oh, for a disc that combines them both...*

especially "James" and "Hero Takes a Fall," plus an effective cover of former Soft Boy Kimberly Rew's "Going Down to Liverpool." The balance of power shifted after the group scored hits with the Prince-penned "Manic Monday" and the novelty single, "Walk Like an Egyptian." By 1988's *Everything*, singer Susanna Hoffs was being positioned as the break-out star. The band's original spirit was doused by soggy ballads such as über-hack Dianne Warren's "Eternal Flame," and the group broke up in 1989. Hoffs' solo career stalled after two disappointing efforts, though 1991's *When You're a Boy* was notable for its odd cover of David Bowie and Brian Eno's "Boys Keep Swinging." "The old '60s sounds were safe," Hoffs told me at the time. "They were the old tricks that had come around for me, and I used them, every one in the book." But these were always the sounds that suited her best, and she returned to them when the Bangles reunited in 2000, capitalizing on a wave of '80s nostalgia and the renewed notoriety from an episode of VH1's *Behind the Music*.

Before the Bangles, Hoffs played in a short-lived group called the Unconscious with brothers David and Steven Roback, who went on to form the Rain Parade with guitarist Matt Piucci. The Rain Parade started with a sound that combined Merseybeat and Rolling Stones-style R&B, but it soon developed a moodier and more complex signature. "We started playing with orchestration, instruments, and different types of guitars," Steven Roback told me years later. "We didn't know what the sound was going to be until we heard it. By the time we got into doing the album itself, all the parts were in place and we went in and did it in a fast, commando sort of thing. There was no money to do it any other way."

The Ultimate Psychedelic Rock Library: The Rain Parade's Emergency Third Rail Power Trip *is a hypnotic and enchanting album that stands with the best psychedelic rock of any era. (The Restless CD adds the equally great* Explosions in the Glass Palace *EP.)*

Emergency Third Rail Power Trip is not only the best album from any of the Paisley Underground bands, it ranks with the best psychedelic rock efforts from any era. Recorded in the winter of 1983, it has a startlingly crisp and clear sound achieved at Radio Tokyo. Songs such as "What's She Done to Your Mind," "Kaleidoscope," and "Look at Merri" showcase the Robacks' ethereal vocals, Eddie Kalwa's precise drumming, Will Glenn's colorful sitar, violin, and keyboard accents, and an intricate, chiming, but droney two-guitar attack that picks up where the Byrds left off with "Eight Miles High." But while the melodies are often uplifting, the themes are dark and introspective. "We're psychedelic in a sort of psychoanalytic sense," Piucci told *Matter* magazine at the time. "I think what psychedelic drugs did to people is that it made them reflect on some very internalized parts of their lives." Steven Roback expanded on the vibe of the album when we spoke years later. "The lyrical themes and song content have a sort of punk ethos to them," he said. "The state of mind we were all in was pretty dark, and it was like personal therapy for everybody in the band. We were all feeling kind of hopeless and helpless about things, and the band was this sort of idealistic attempt to create some space where we could all feel really great."

Calling the split a business decision, David Roback quit the Rain Parade in early 1984. "There were just too many cooks, basically," his brother Steven told me. "You had three really strong songwriters, and at some point there was just not enough room." The group continued under the direction of Steven Roback and Piucci, recording the even darker *Explosions in the Glass Palace* EP. But while signing to Island Records should have provided the band with the chance to perfect its sound in the studio, *Crashing Dream* was made under hurried, pressured conditions, and the Rain Parade never got another chance: It split up in late 1985. After dabbling with pickup gigs (Piucci played with Crazy Horse between its stints backing Neil Young) and day jobs (Roback has a degree in architecture), the band's driving forces reunited in the '90s in the low-key but pleasant-sounding Viva Saturn (which also featured contributions from Glenn), and Steven later worked with his wife, Missy, on a charmingly ethereal album called *Just Like Breathing*. Meanwhile, David Roback returned to the model of the Unconscious, forming a series of bands pairing wispy female vocals with gentle, somnambulant sounds. Kendra Smith filled the vocalist roles in Clay Allison and Opal, but she was replaced by the petulant Hope Sandoval in 1990 when Roback formed Mazzy Star (which also featured Glenn's sonic colorings). Though they were more successful commercially, Mazzy Star's recordings fail to match the intensity of Opal's *Happy Nightmare Baby* (1987), or Smith's long-awaited solo bow, *Five Ways of Disappearing* (1995).

The Ultimate Psychedelic Rock Library: The Dream Syndicate's Days of Wine and Roses *(Rhino) is a psychedelic guitar geek's dream. (The Rhino CD adds the* Down There *EP that preceded the album.)*

Once an aspiring rock critic, Steve Wynn formed the Dream Syndicate with bassist Kendra Smith and fiery guitarist Karl Precoda in 1982. The group recorded its self-released EP only three weeks later, following up a short time after that with a powerful album, *The Days of Wine and Roses*. Raw and energetic with extraordinarily potent guitar solos and bursts of controlled feedback, the album was strongly influenced by the Velvet Underground, and tunes such as "Tell Me When It's Over," "Halloween," and "Until Lately" have a psychotic edge unique among the Paisley Underground bands. Smith left after the first album, the band signed to A&M, and Wynn began to come to the forefront as a not always very remarkable singer-songwriter. The best moments on 1984's *The Medicine Show* are the least-structured guitar blow-outs of the title track and "John Coltrane Stereo Blues." Precoda left after this album, and while the Dream Syndicate continued for a few more years, Wynn didn't really hit his stride again until solo efforts such as *Kerosene Man, Dazzling Display,* and *Flourescent* in the '90s, delivering songs full of carefully drawn characters and vivid lyrical images with his familiar Lou Reed-in-Southern-California vocal style and frenetic guitars that recalled his old band at its best.

"You get back to the point of where you were when you started," Wynn told me when he toured in 2001 in support of a strong indie effort called *Here Come the Miracles*. "When you feel like, 'This is the music I'm making, and if you don't like it, you don't have to listen.' It's a real freedom, but it's hard to get back to that. I want to be constantly surprised onstage and in the studio, because then I react to that. The whole thing I love about music—and this is getting back to the psychedelic thing—is the interaction, the call and response, where somebody does one thing and it inspires you to do something else. We were recording in a strange place, experimenting, letting things fly, and going more by instinct than mapping things out. I think that gives the album a sense of time and place, and that's something that most of my favorite records have."

A native of Louisville, Kentucky, Sid Griffin formed the Long Ryders to explore more expansive sounds after tiring of the Unclaimed's rather narrow, garage-centric worldview. Debuting with the *10-5-60* EP in 1983, the group brought a punk attitude to the mix of psychedelic rock and country music that was pioneered by the Gram Parsons-era Byrds. Ex-Byrd Gene Clark made a guest appearance on the beautiful "Ivory Tower" from 1984's *Native Sons*, but the psychedelic intensity of startlingly powerful songs such as "The Trip," "And She Rides," "Wreck of the 809," and "Too Close to the Light" began to wane and the group turned toward more mainstream country after signing to Island in 1985. (The band is best remembered today as a key influence on the burgeoning

The Ultimate Psychedelic Rock Library: A 1992 disc (Frontier) combines the psychedelic country-rock of the Long Ryder's 10-5-60 *EP and* Native Sons *album.*

alternative country movement.) Griffin moved to England in the early '90s, wrote a biography of Parsons, and continued to play with a new combo, the Coal Porters.

Green On Red, the band whose barbecues started it all, are the Paisley Underground's worst case of arrested development. The group formed in L.A. after three of its members relocated from Tucson, Arizona. Its first two EPs get by on garage-rock energy and a swirling keyboard sound, but the group moved toward drunken Dylan and Young imitations with 1983's *Gravity Talks*, and it spiraled downward after that on six more albums for four different labels. (Equally slight is bandleader Dan Stuart's 1985 collaboration with Wynn and the Long Ryders, *Danny & Dusty*.) In retrospect, tough-gal psychedelic garage-rockers the Pandoras predicted the assertive stance of the riot grrrls six years earlier. Finally, at the fringes of the Paisley Underground were two other strong guitar bands from Davis—True West (which did a strong cover of Pink Floyd's "Lucifer Sam" on its debut EP but never delivered on the promise of that disc) and Thin White Rope (which recorded several albums of ominous psychedelic rock and Can-like repetitive drones)—and the Leaving Trains, which were fronted by celebrated transvestite Falling James (who briefly married Courtney Love before she met Kurt Cobain).

COLOR APPRECIATION

> In a moment traveling so far away / Once you're there you'll
> probably want to stay / Wonder wonderful wonderland.
> —Plasticland,
> "Wonder Wonderful Wonderland"

A FEW YEARS OLDER than most of their peers, the key players in Plasticland are actually ringers as revivalists, since they were there the first time around. Childhood friends Glenn Rehse and John Frankovic played together in a mid-'60s garage band, and their musical progression followed the development of psychedelic rock. After playing originals in the style of first-wave British psychedelic bands—the Creation, the Pink Floyd, and the Pretty Things particularly fired their imaginations—they moved to progressive rock in a band called Willie the Conqueror, and then to krautrock in a group called Arousing Polaris. "Then we broke up because Glenn and I had a fight," Frankovic told me. "My mom would always say that Glenn and I fight like a couple of brothers—'You have a big fight, and then two months later, you're inseparable again.' Being as stubborn as we are, a couple of years later, we got back together, but this time, we decided that the band would emphasize recordings rather than live shows."

When Rehse and Frankovic reunited in 1980, they decided to work in the style that inspired them most. The name Plasticland was chosen as what Rehse called "a modernized version of Lewis Carroll's wonderland." Working with different drummers and second guitarists (including future Violent Femme Brian Ritchie), the duo recorded a series of singles starting with the sensual "Mink Dress," which recalls "Arnold Layne" as the male protagonist sees a lady in a mink dress and decides he needs one himself. The group was usually less obvious in its homages, evoking the spirit of London 1967 without being overly derivative. "We were not out to revive the Creation; we were out to write songs as good as those of the bands we'd fallen in love with years ago," Frankovic said. "What attracted us to those sounds was the excitement and the cultural ramifications that went with the music. Psychedelia to us was definitely a state of mind, not a drug. It was an art statement and a fashion statement. Dressing up and not dressing like a slob—pointy shoes, real pants, well-cut Italian-style clothes."

Studying English magazines from the mid-'60s, Frankovic and Rehse put a twist on Carnaby Street fashions by raiding Milwaukee thrift stores, sometimes making their own clothes out of cool fabrics that they found. "This was another thing that Glenn and I had in common: We both loved to dress up," Frankovic said. "We were always in drama club together, and we loved makeup and putting on costumes." Of course, dressing in Edwardian outfits on the streets of Milwaukee could attract unwanted attention. "We ran fast, plus we were punks. We were street-wise, and we knew when it was okay to push people's buttons. In high school, I hung out with the burn-outs because they never cared. Later, I would hang out in gay bars, because that was where the hippest and coolest people were in Milwaukee. These were people who were kindred spirits, and it didn't matter if you were gay or not."

Plasticland's appearance on Greg Shaw's *Battle of the Garages* helped spread the word, and after a wiggy, self-released 1982 EP called *Pop! Op Drops*, the French Lolita label fronted the money for a full album. *Color Appreciation* opens with a crazed version of "Alexander" by the Pretty Things, creating a frame of reference for the Rehse-Frankovic originals that follow. The songs are filled with unforgettable hooks, inventive playing (including Rehse's keyboard parts and Dan Mullen's fuzz guitar leads), and an absurd sense of humor that finds beauty and drama in such seemingly mundane topics as Rehse's overgrown yard ("The Garden in Pain"), Frankovic's

The Ultimate Psychedelic Rock Library: Plasticland made a powerful debut in 1984 with Color Appreciation *(later reissued on Lolita and retitled simply* Plasticland*).*

The Ultimate Psychedelic Rock Library: Wonder Wonderful Wonderland *(Enigma) tours an idyllic dreamscape that's a far cry far from working-class Milwaukee.*

grooming ritual ("Rattail Comb"), and both men's love of flamboyant fashions ("Euphoric Trapdoor Shoes"). The band's enthusiasm virtually flows from the speakers. "It was like, 'It's finally happening, these songs are finally getting recorded,'" Rehse told me. "We had a backlog of songs that was knee-deep." Added Frankovic: "The studio is my playground, and I always have a lot of fun in there. That's what having fun is all about: making a lot of noise."

Supportive of the Paisley Underground bands, California-based Enigma Records signed Plasticland in 1985. Despite the accomplished sound of the first album (which it reissued in the U.S. as *Plasticland*), the label insisted that the band work with producer Paul Cutler, who had replaced Karl Precoda as the guitarist in the Dream Syndicate. Rehse and Frankovic generally ignored his advice and once again followed their own Day-Glo muses. An upbeat travelogue of a Carroll-style fantasyland, *Wonder Wonderful Wonderland* is lusher musically than the debut, with twelve-string guitars, Mellotrons, African percussion, bouzouki, Berimbau, and other textures joining the driving rhythms, fuzz guitar, and Rehse's trademark nasal vocals. Lyrically, the pair are even giddier and more playful, evoking a childlike naïveté and a giddy fascination with the more surreal aspects of everyday life on standout songs such as "Gloria Night," "A Grassland of Reeds and Things," "The Gingerbread House," and the title track.

For 1987's *Salon*, the band pared back and emphasized the grooves of new drummer Victor Demichei, revealing roots in Motown and psychedelic soul. "We didn't want to come out like some syrupy, drippy, hippie kind of bullshit," Rehse said. "John and I were always rockers. We came from the Midwest—rhythm and blues and soul music had a hell of a lot to do with our attitude and life." Added Frankovic: "The whole thing about psychedelia is that it is supposed to take you somewhere. Who says that 'Dancing in the Streets' doesn't take you somewhere?" Unfortunately, the album also took the band off the Enigma roster. The label wanted the group to tour, but Rehse and Frankovic were too old and too

The Ultimate Psychedelic Rock Library: On Salon *(Pink Dust), Plasticland got funky, then more or less retreated from the public realm.*

smart for the '80s indie-rock grind of taking a vacation from their day jobs to drive twelve hours in a van every day and sleep on the floor every night. Although they'd started Plasticland as a studio project, it had developed into a strong live act, but the show was an elaborate affair that required hauling lights, go-go dancers, and Rehse's Mellotron to small, dingy rock clubs with bad sound systems. "Enigma said they wanted a band that was going to be touring at least one hundred fifty nights a year, so they opted not to do a last record with us," Frankovic said. When Rehse talks about the period, a bitter diatribe inevitably follows.

Plasticland basically disbanded, though the group continues to this day to reunite for odd reunion shows and one-off recording projects such as a live album backing Pretty Things-Syd Barrett-Tomorrow drummer Twink. After a tour with Twink fell apart, Rehse and Frankovic were approached by a German label interested in a new recording. Spirits were high as Plasticland started *Dapper Snappings*, but recording dragged on over a two-year period as Repulsion tried to scrape up the money to finish the project. Although it boasts a handful of strong new tunes (including "Let's Play Pollyanna" and "When You Get Subliminal, You Really Get Sublime"), the album doesn't sustain a mood like the earlier efforts. By the time it was released in 1994, the group had split up once again.

Although they've pursued a number of solo projects—including the Fabulon Triptometer, the Gothics, and a Frankovic solo album—anyone who knows Rehse and Frankovic says that sooner or later, they'll probably play together again. "I don't want Plasticland to be a rerun of what we did in the '80s. I have a lot of new ideas," Rehse said, contemplating renewed interest in the group stemming from the 1995 rarities collection, *Mink Dress and Other Cats*. "I don't want to have to stop the creative process and become an old fart."

"Plasticland is a vital part of my life, and it will always be a part of my life," added Frankovic. "Plasticland lives on, whether the band is playing or not."

EVERYTHING OLD IS NEW AGAIN ONCE MORE: THE "NEW GARAGE" REVIVAL

YOU CALL A COUPLE OF FRIENDS, grab a case of beer, a bottle of tequila, a spliff, or some blotter acid (if so inclined), haul out those dusty amps and the old drum set stored in the corner of the garage—a basement will do in the inner city, or a barn if you're out in the sticks—and together you make a god-awful racket until all is once again right with the world. It's the oldest and some would say noblest tradition in rock 'n' roll, a familiar Saturday-night ritual across the United States and in several other countries as well for half a century by the dawn of the new millennium. As long as there's been rock and as long as there have been garages, there has been garage rock, so there's really nothing "new" about the New Garage, the tag some have applied to the second garage revival that was just shifting into high gear when the second edition of this book was completed. (Others would contend that the first garage revival—or, for that matter, the initial garage-band explosion of the

'60s—never really ended, and it's all just been one loud, fuzz-drenched continuum.)

"Just because they haven't been getting attention doesn't mean there haven't been bar bands who've been doing this for a long time," said Derek Mason, lead guitarist with New Garage rockers the Catheters. "Those bands have been out there for quite some time, and people just now have maybe started to notice them a bit more because they're tired of listening to the radio and stuff, and there's nothing else that's really that good. I don't know if it's a new, emerging thing, but people are definitely taking more of notice of it."

Indeed. In the fall of 2002, the Strokes, the White Stripes, and the Hives were three of the most lauded rock bands to burst onto the scene since Nirvana in the early '90s. All three are rooted to some extent in *Nuggets*-era garage rock. New York City's Strokes debuted in early 2001 with a strong EP called *The Modern Age*, which was followed a few months later by an even more potent album, *Is This It*. On songs such as the title track, "Barely Legal," and "Someday," the quintet incorporated unmistakable echoes of New York rock history, from the serpentine guitars of Television and Richard Hell and the Voidoids to the glamorous, sexy swagger of the New York Dolls, but above all there was the insistent pulse, droning melodies, subway-train rhythms, and urgent, monotone vocals of the Velvet Underground. The Hives are a Swedish quintet that calls its sound "punk-rock music avec kaboom!" The group came together in 1993 as teenagers in the small industrial town of Fagersta, Sweden, and started recording its brand of barn-burning garage rock in 1995, gleefully aping the amphetamine overdrive of the early Rolling Stones while building an elaborate mythology that would have us believe that all of its songs are written by a mysterious "Mr. Randy Fitzsimmons," who does not tour or record and has never been seen in public. The White Stripes are a Detroit duo that plays just as fast and loose with the facts—guitarist-vocalist Jack White had been married to drummer Meg White, but he likes to tell the press that they are brother and sister—and its sound combines gritty urban blues and incendiary garage rock.

To date none of these bands have emphasized the psychedelic experimentation of the '60s garage rockers or the '80s revivalists, focusing instead on the raw energy of the *Nuggets* bands and the Stooges. The same is true of most of the best up-and-comers following in their wake and nipping at their heels: Seattle's Catheters; New York City's Mooney Suzuki and Yeah Yeah Yeah's; Sweden's Hellacopters, Backyard Babies, and Soundtrack of Our Lives; L.A.'s Bell Rays and Streetwalkin' Cheetahs, and the Motor City's the Go, the Von Bondies, and the Detroit Cobras. All of these bands insist that they are *not* revivalists, preferring to live in the present rather than recreating the past. "This is the music that people are sort of turning their heads to now," Hives bandleader Nicholaus Arson told me. "But it was always very much alive when it was around. I still think that a lot of the bands back in the old days were a lot more *alive* than a lot of the bands that are around nowadays." Yet this doesn't mean that some of them may not follow the historic progression of the original *Nuggets* bands, whose sonic vistas opened considerably once the influence of psychedelic drugs and the expansive attitude they inspired in the recording studio wafted in amid the gas fumes and the stale air of their original garage getaways.

Ten Great "New Garage" Albums

1.   The Strokes, *Is This It* (RCA)
2.   The White Stripes, *White Blood Cells* (V2)
3.   The Hives, *Veni Vidi Vicious* (Warner Bros.)
4.   The Mooney Suzuki, *Electric Sweat* (Gammon)
5.   The Hellacopters, *Supershitty to the Max* (Sub Pop)
6.   The Catheters, *Static Delusions and Stone-Still Days* (Sub Pop)
7.   The Detroit Cobras, *Life, Love and Leaving* (Sympathy for the Record Industry)
8.   Soundtrack of Our Lives, *Behind the Music* (Universal)
9.   International Noise Conspiracy, *New Morning, Changing Weather* (Epitaph)
10. Streetwalkin' Cheetahs, *Waiting for the Death of My Generation* (Triple X)

THIRTEEN

13

BAD TRIPS AND
ONE-HIT WONDERS

Okay. You've swallowed the magic cube, downed a cup of "organic" tea with filigree leaves, and placed the diamond needle on the appropriate sounds. Now sit back and wait twenty minutes, until twinges of nausea herald the coming of the hereafter. Meanwhile, ponder this: A discotheque called The World advertises "psychedelic beauty contests." Admen chortle: "Don't blow your cool—blow your mind."...Psychedelic shoes. Acid TV commercials. LSD greeting cards. Marijuana brownies. Mandala shopping bags. Tibetan cocktails on the rocks. "Psychedelicize suburbia." Mind-expanding peacock feathers. Buddha himself, gold and grinning, comes embossed on a 100 percent washable cotton sweatshirt in assorted sizes, colors, and cools.

—Richard Goldstein, 1967

AS THE INTRODUCTION to a *Village Voice* feature on Timothy Leary's heavily-hyped "religion," the League for Spiritual Discovery, critic Richard Goldstein's giddy laundry list is evidence that psychedelia was already well established as a pop-culture phenomenon ripe for free-market exploitation at the same time that psychedelic rock was coming into its own as a musical genre. Like other merchants of popular culture, many musicians adopted superficial psychedelic trappings as the influence filtered into the mainstream. By 1967, bands in search of an instant identity needed only to turn to the plethora of studio production tricks, light shows, and fashions that psychedelia ushered in. Notable examples of ersatz "psychedelic rock" hits by faux psychedelic rockers included the Blues Magoos' "(We Ain't Got) Nothin' Yet" (from their 1967 album, *Psychedelic Lollipop*), the Lemon Pipers' "Green Tambourine" (1967), actor Richard Harris's original version of "MacArthur Park" (1968), Kenny Rogers and the First Edition' "Just Dropped In (To See What Condition My Condition Was In)" (1968), Tommy James's "Crimson and Clover" (1968), and Zager and Evans' "In the Year 2525 (Exordius and Terminus)" (1969).

This book has generally dealt with less substantial psychedelic rockers by omission, but several camps of bad-trip artists deserve a closer look, as do some psychedelic rock songs by musicians who weren't really part of the genre. Chief among them is the Doors. Jim Morrison is said to have eaten acid like candy during his days at UCLA Graduate School of Film, and the band's name came from Aldous Huxley's *The Doors of Perception*, but the group never really delivered great psychedelic rock. The band formed in early 1965 after Morrison sat on the beach ponderously reciting his romantic poetry to keyboardist Ray Manzarek ("Let's swim to the moon / Let's climb through the tide / Penetrate the evening / That the city sleeps to hide"). The singer originally viewed the group as a vehicle to literary immortality a la Rimbaud and Baudelaire, but despite the cult that sprang up after his death, Morrison's soggy, sophomoric lyrics were never in that league, and while they may have been pseudo-mystical, they were never especially transcendent. Musically, the jazzy drumming, cocktail-lounge keyboards, and flamenco guitar were very much mired in the mundane, and the Doors only really rocked on rare occasions such as "Break on Through" or "L.A. Woman." The tune that is usually held up as the band's psychedelic masterpiece, "The End," is in fact a plodding Oedipal melodrama. "It was the first major statement of the Doors' perennial themes: dread, violence, guilt without possibility of redemption, the miscarriages of love, and, most of all, death," Lester Bangs wrote. "Nevertheless, the last time I heard 'The End,' it sounded funny."

A generation later the Doors' influence could be heard loud and clear in a subgenre of bands best dubbed "mope rock." These groups embraced some of psychedelia's more obvious stage tricks—enveloping fog, spooky lighting, and a swirling sound mix—and studio sounds, but they were generally too self-obsessed to take their listeners anywhere interesting. Depeche Mode proved the limitations of the synthesizer as a psychedelic rock instrument, while the Cure and the Smiths, who were both capable of crafting hypnotic and otherworldly guitar sounds, were ultimately sabotaged by their maudlin frontmen. Robert Smith and Morrissey could both come across like the guy who takes psychedelic drugs and talks non-stop through the night, ruining the party by trying to convince everyone that they should listen to the Great Truths that he's discovered.

In the mid-'90s an alternative-rock update on this theme was offered by the Smashing Pumpkins, whose lush, well-crafted soundscapes (which early on bore the strong influence of the English shoegazer bands, especially My Bloody Valentine) were marred by the solipsistic and angst-ridden lyrics of bandleader Billy Corgan. (The band's best, most psychedelic, and least commercially successful work came toward the end of its career, on albums such as *Adore* and *Machina: The Machines of God*, when Corgan adopted a less whiny, deeper, and more humanistic approach to his lyrics.)

Throbbing Gristle/Psychic TV, Ministry and its many offshoots, Nine Inch Nails, and other industrial artists often had psychedelic overtones. Genesis P-Orridge and Al Jourgensen (the driving forces behind Psychic TV and Ministry, respectively) were especially vocal about their fondness for psychedelic drugs, while Trent Reznor of Nine Inch Nails enjoyed playing with the acid imagery surrounding the Manson family. But all of these artists dwelled on the dark side of life without ever transcending it; the music was often too cold, mechanical, amelodic, and unappealingly repetitive to function as great rock 'n' roll, and all of that wicked posing just seemed silly in the light of day. (Dishonorable mention must be made, however, of Coil's coyly titled 1991 album, *Love's Secret Domain*—LSD—a merger of industrial and acid house that is one of the most unsettling psychedelic albums ever made.)

Another band with a Manson fixation—as well as myriad other pop-culture obsessions—was New York's long-running noisemongers, Sonic Youth. Surfacing in the indie-rock '80s alongside influential peers such as Hüsker Dü, the Minutemen, and Big Black, the group merged the high-art pretensions of noise composers such as Glenn Branca and Rhys Chatham with the heavy attitude of hardcore punk bands. Unfortunately, too often it replaced the conviction with cheap sarcasm and campy in-jokes. While it may have been a revelation to young fans such as Kurt Cobain that guitars could be played in different tunings or attacked with drum sticks and screw drivers, the free-jazz, white-noise experimentation that Sonic Youth attempted was accomplished with more powerful and psychedelic results by the Velvet Underground, the MC5, Can, Spacemen 3, and others. The band could make great psychedelic rock 'n' roll when it dropped some of the attitude and didn't neglect melody or songcraft, but high points such as "Pacific Coast Highway" and "Halloween" are few and far between in its extensive discography. (In 2002 the group released one of the better, more tuneful albums of its career, *Murray Street*, after incorporating fellow avant-garde noisemaker Jim O'Rourke, whose earlier efforts with Gaster del Sol and myriad other projects represented a different kind of static, pseudo-psychedelic art wankery.)

The transparency of psychedelic poseurs and retro-rockers such as Lenny Kravitz and the Black Crowes is so obvious that it's hardly worth pointing out; much more than any of the bands that critics dismissed as mere revivalists in the '80s, these artists are hopelessly tethered to sounds and styles that were originally progressive but have been transformed into loathsome nostalgia, the worst enemy of great rock 'n' roll. More curious is the tribe of jam-happy "baby Dead" bands that sprouted in the early '90s, delivering varying degrees of psychedelic imagery as they strove to update the hippie utopian ideal. Their styles were often very similar: blues rock mixed with progressive rock (Phish), blues rock mixed with country-rock (the Freddy Jones Band, the Aquarium Rescue Unit), blues rock mixed with pop (Spin Doctors, Hootie and the Blowfish), blues rock mixed with jazz fusion (the Dave Matthews Band), blues rock mixed with Hawkwind (England's Ozric Tentacles), and just plain old blues rock (Big Head Todd and the Monsters, Blues Traveler). Many of these groups built their followings because they offered Deadheads something to do in between Dead tours, and they filled a cultural void once Jerry Garcia was gone. But contrary to what many jam fans seem to think, drinking Bud Lite and doing the awkward white person wiggle dance is not a psychedelic experience. (One jam exception: Gov't Mule, which never loses the garage-rock kick amid its more expansive explorations, and which recorded a killer cover of "She Said, She Said.")

The Dead itself kept on' truckin' until the most efficient and persistent touring corporation in the concert industry was finally stopped by mortality. Before it officially disbanded (only to resurface sans Gerry in the new guises of the Other Ones and the Dead), the mainstream media covered the Grateful Dead's twice-yearly visits with silly features full of tongue-in-cheek '60s drug references, playing into the hands of the stock broker who traded his tie for a night in a tie-dyed T-shirt. Members of the real Deadhead subculture were impressive in their ability to discern every nuance of the band's rambling mixes of country, blues, folk, and space excursions, but the truth is that the music was always a secondary concern for the larger arena crowd. "The phenomenon can partly be understood as a low-risk, low-investment community, almost making community into a commodity," said political philosopher and cultural critic Michael Weinstein. "People could purchase a ticket and be part of a group they felt safe with, that they could express themselves with, and in which they could recreate selective slices of the '60s, like the drugs and the music."

"The band is a time capsule from a Camelot-like era of the 1960s," former keyboardist Tom Constanten told the Reuter's news service after Garcia's death. "It's that magic that people were attracted to." Of course, Camelot never really existed, and the Dead's idealized psychedelic community was sort of like Sixties World at Disneyland. This isn't to say that the concert experience wasn't fun; it was. (In fact, the Dead threw a heck of a party in the parking lot—it's just a shame that they ruined it by performing.) Nor do I mean to imply that groups that are simply *acting* like psychedelic rock bands can't make great psychedelic rock; they can and did, as the *Nuggets* bands first proved.

In the years that followed, many others donned psychedelic trappings for a song or two before returning to their primary styles or moving off in other directions, and the fact that psychedelic rock can be appropriated this way is one of the factors that establishes it as a genre. "To call [a style of music] a genre means to acknowledge it as something more than a marketing category," critic Deena Weinstein wrote in her study of a different genre, *Heavy Metal*. "It has a distinctive sound. It also has a stock of visual and verbal meanings that have been attached to it by the artists, audience members, and mediators who construct it." One way to hone in on these distinctive elements is to look at what was borrowed by bands that weren't psychedelic rock but which waded into the genre pool. What follows are eighteen of my favorite "one-hit wonders."

ONE-HIT WONDERS:
EIGHTEEN GREAT PSYCHEDELIC ROCK SONGS BY ARTISTS THAT WEREN'T (ALWAYS) PSYCHEDELIC ROCK

1. The Monkees, "Porpoise Song" (1968)

Recruited in 1965 as actors to play rockers on TV, the Prefab Four metamorphosed into an actual band by early 1967, though most of their best songs were still written by hired pros. The Monkees were drawn to L.A.'s psychedelic subculture, and they were endorsed by Hollywood hipsters who recognized the potential for some gentle subversion of America's youth. A druggy mindset was firmly in place when they met to discuss their first feature film with Bob Rafelson, the producer and director of their TV show, and actor Jack Nicholson, who somehow landed the gig of writing the script, aptly titled *Head*. "We sat around for days smoking, drinking, and generally having stream-of-consciousness sessions," drummer Mickey Dolenz wrote in his autobiography, *I'm A Believer*. "Jack and Bob took the tapes of the sessions and turned them into one of the strangest films of all time....Basically, it was the story of the Monkees: our birth, life, and death, as metaphors for all of Hollywood and its tinsel-and-fabric manipulations of people, images, and ideas." *Head* opens with a spectacular vignette featuring the Monkees jumping from a bridge to frolic with the mermaids in the water below. Taking her cue from *Sgt. Pepper's*, Carole King wrote the beautiful, undulating "Porpoise Song" to accompany this scene. A gentle, vaguely Eastern melody is paired with a full Western orchestra as the Monkees ponder their place in the universe ("A face, a voice / An overdub has no choice / And it cannot

rejoice"). They also talk to the dolphins years before New Age scientist John Lilly used ketamine, an animal tranquilizer with psychedelic side effects, to do the same in experiments depicted in
another film, *Day of the Dolphin*.

2. Nancy Sinatra and Lee Hazlewood,
"Some Velvet Morning" (1968)

Despite her famous last name, aspiring pop vixen Nancy Sinatra
had produced a series of flops and was on the verge of being
dropped by her father's own label, Reprise Records, when she found
a demo of a catchy little ditty with sado-masochistic undertones
called "These Boots Are Made for Walkin'" in 1966 and began a
long and fruitful collaboration with its author, Lee Hazlewood, a
veteran country and rockabilly producer (he'd worked with Duane
Eddy) whom critic Richie Unterberger described as a combination
of a Nashville cornball and a brooding, desert Leonard Cohen. The
absolute strangest of the pair's many strange offerings was the post-
"Boots" single "Some Velvet Morning." The duet opens with an
incongruous orchestral swell that evokes the enlightened awakening after a surreal psychedelic experience. It goes on to contrast
Hazelwood's earthy, country-tinged commentary about trying to
get his head together (which is delivered in a growl that is lower
and more sandpaper-harsh than Johnny Cash's) with Sinatra's
sweet, idyllic, traipsing-through-the-meadows asides, all while paying homage to a mysterious goddess-like figure named Phaedra (a
character from Greek mythology who appears in Euripides' play of
sexual intrigue and betrayal, the *Hippolytus*). Sings Hazelwood:
"Some velvet morning when I'm straight / I'm gonna open up your

gate / And maybe tell you 'bout Phaedra / And how she gave me life." Coos Sinatra in response: "Flowers growing on the hill / Dragonflies and daffodils / Learn from us very much / Look at us but do not touch / Phaedra is my name." If there has ever been a more sensual psychedelic exchange in the Top 40 (the single peaked at No. 26 on the *Billboard* chart in January 1968), I haven't heard it.

3. The Who, "Armenia City in the Sky" (1968)

Though some critics charged that the rock opera *Tommy* was psychedelic excess at its worst, Pete Townshend always went out of his way to distance himself from psychedelic drugs. "I only used acid a few times and I found it incredibly disturbing," he said in the Syd Barrett biography, *Crazy Diamond*. "I have certain psychotic tendencies and found it extremely dangerous for me." Nevertheless, Townshend appreciated the English psychedelic rock bands, especially the Pretty Things and the Creation, whose guitarist he tried to recruit. Elements of psychedelia crept into several Who songs (including "I Can See for Miles," which has the same on-the-verge-of-takeoff rumble as "Eight Miles High"), but the band's most memorable excursion is the incongruous opening track from *The Who Sell Out*, its paean to rock radio and the pre-hippie lifestyle, as well as a sarcastic and well-ahead-of-its-time commentary on the commercialization of rock (the tune is subtitled "Heinz Baked Beans"). The swooping guitars on "Armenia City in the Sky" recall Eddie Phillips' bowed style, Keith Moon's often excessive drumming is remarkably restrained and tribal, and Roger Daltrey warbles Townshend's lyrics about a fantasy metropolis with the same endearingly silly sincerity that Donovan brought to

"Atlantis." ("If you're troubled and you can't relax / Close your eyes and think of this / If the rumors floating in your head all turn to facts / Close your eyes and think of this / Armenia, city in the sky.")

4. The Kinks, "Wicked Annabella" (1969)

"When everybody else thought that the hip thing to do was to drop acid, do as many drugs as possible, and listen to music in a coma, the Kinks were singing songs about lost friends, draught beer, motorbike riders, wicked witches, and flying cats," Ray Davies wrote in his "unauthorized autobiography," *X-Ray.* But like the Who, the band couldn't resist trying out the psychedelic sounds of 1967 at least once. The tale of the wicked witch Annabella unfolds over distorted vocals, disjointed drums, and a wonderful snaky guitar line. The effect is like a cartoonish nightmare intruding on a tranquil afternoon daydream. (Honorable mention in this vein goes to the Troggs, who shared a producer-svengali with the Kinks in Larry Page. In an effort to broaden the band's sound beyond the three-chord leer of "Wild Thing," Page crafted "Cousin Jane," a creepy, orchestrated, but still leering ballad that appeared in 1966 on the band's second album, *Trogglodynamite.* Incest never sounded so appealing.)

5. Black Sabbath, "Sweet Leaf" (1971)

The best of the English bands that combined blues-rock and psychedelic atmospheres to create heavy metal, Black Sabbath built its own comic-book, horror-film fantasy world from the most basic and primal rock ingredients. Druggy, evocative tunes such as "Tomorrow's Dream," "Am I Going Insane," and "Snowblind" are almost punk in their simple, in-your-face construction and the raw way in which they were recorded, but Sabbath earns its place on this list with a touching and heartfelt homage to *cannabis sativa*. Following an absurdly echoed cough and a typically monolithic guitar riff, Ozzy Osbourne sings, "When I first met you didn't realize / I can't forget you or your surprise / You introduced me to my mind / And left me wanting you and your kind / I love you / Oh you know it!" Ah, sweet romance. (Honorable mention for another psychedelic heavy-metal anthem: Blue Öyster Cult's Byrds-inflected "Don't Fear the Reaper.")

6. Led Zeppelin, "Kashmir" (1975)

Though it wasn't always obvious, the most influential band of the '70s derived its approach in part from what the players learned in the psychedelic '60s. As a member of the Yardbirds, Jimmy Page perfected the echo, slide, and Eastern tunings that gave extended guitar jams such as the one in "Dazed and Confused" their otherworldly feel. He had mastered the essentials of studio craftsmanship as a session player, and Zeppelin bassist John Paul Jones had arranged the impressive psychedelic backings for Donovan's singles and the Rolling Stones' *Their Satanic Majesties Request*. Singer Robert Plant had clearly listened to more than a little Incredible String Band. These influences yielded to the brilliant bastardized blues of the first two albums and the hippie folk of the third, but they came back strong on the untitled fourth effort (in "The Battle of Evermore" and the psychedelic blues, "When the Levee Breaks"), *Houses of the Holy* (via Jones's showcase, "No Quarter"), and best of all, "Kashmir," the hashish-scented travelogue that is the centerpiece of *Physical Graffiti*. "I can't say that drugs didn't play a part in those early days, but the eclecticism [of the British rock scene] played a larger part," Jones told me. "A lot of the psychedelic thing came from that very early world-music movement; it was just interest in other people's music....I used to take drugs and listen to music and it would actually give dimensions to music that simply didn't have that many dimensions. The best psychedelic music achieves the same effect without drugs."

Jimmy Page on the Psychedelic Legacy of Led Zeppelin

"In the Yardbirds, I remember playing at the Fillmore, and I had tapes playing of things like the Staten Island Ferry and all manner of things. It was a whole collage of stuff that was going on, and during that I was playing with the violin bow on top of it. At the time, that was an element of psychedelia, because it was so sort of abstract, and it was kind of disturbing. When you talk about psychedelia, there was the English psychedelia, with the aspect of what Syd Barrett was doing, and it was just amazing—in a class of its own, with the writing and everything.

"What we're talking about, for instance, with 'Kashmir'—when I had that riff, originally I was just running it over with John Bonham, but the importance of that was the whole thing having this totally hypnotic thing. I mean, riff music is a hypnotic thing, that's what it is, and we'd have to start talking about the aspects of music coming from Africa and all the rest of it. Even though I accessed it from the blues, that's what it is—this hypnotic aspect of it. It is very trippy. I remember when William Burroughs was telling me, 'You've got to go! You've got to go to Morocco and hear the musicians there!' I'd sort of heard it on disc, but there they used it for healing and they used it for exorcism, and Burroughs said, 'That's what you're doing!' He'd come to our concerts on a number of occasions, and I was absolutely overwhelmed when he said that, but he could really understand that riff aspect to it.

"Basically, any sound that's out of the norm can be considered 'psychedelic'—like backwards guitar; it's trippy because you can't relate to what it is and what it's doing. I remember taking that one step further, because everyone had used backwards guitar, but I realized that if you applied echo to it and then took the signal out but just used all the backwards echo, you'd have all of this echo sort of sucking you into the source. It was just anything which disturbed the senses somewhat, you know?

"The goal was synaesthesia—creating pictures with sound. Another one of the ones for me that sort of had that intensity was 'When the Levee Breaks.' The thing is that in those days, there were no images to distract you and establish an image for you. Videos have ruined a lot of the psychedelic element. It's like Waldorf Schools over here in England: They don't want children to watch television in the early days because, for example, if you see Snow White, that's your lasting image of *Snow White*. That's exactly how things used to be with our images to those records, wasn't it?"

7. Neil Young, "Cortez the Killer" (1975)

"Everybody gets fucked up sooner or later," Neil Young told *Rolling Stone* interviewer Cameron Crowe in 1975. "You're just pretending if you don't let your music get just as liquid as you are when you're really high." *Zuma* was the follow-up to the cathartic *Tonight's the Night*, which was inspired by the heroin-induced deaths of Crazy Horse guitarist Danny Whitten and roadie Bruce Berry. Young may have preferred tequila to psychedelics at the time, but the standout track lumbers forward in a peyote daze. The extended guitar workout on "Cortez the Killer" fits the mold of the earlier "Down by the River," but it conjures an even stranger and more sinister place. In addition to revising history and enticing the listener into a hot, humid, and erotic dreamscape, the song posed a metaphorical question for members of the Baby Boom as they moved from the idealistic '60s into the materialistic '80s: Were they going to rape and pillage like Cortez, or fight to preserve a doomed but idyllic lifestyle like Montezuma?

8. Donna Summer, "I Feel Love" (1977)

Developed in the gay dance clubs of Manhattan and Fire Island, disco started creeping into the pop mainstream as early as 1974, but it was Donna Summer's 1975 hit, "Love to Love You Baby," that really put it on the map. Born and raised in Boston, Summer made her way to Munich via a touring production of the hippie musical *Hair*. There she linked up with producers and songwriters Giorgio Moroder and Pete Bellotte. This team crafted a bubbly, lighthearted electronic backing track as a demo, and Summer improvised the minimal lyrics and orgasmic moans while lying in the dark on the studio floor, the same way that John Lennon recorded "Tomorrow Never Knows." The song was a strange but wonderful novelty, the sound of a woman making love to a machine, but Summer's next hit was even better. "I Feel Love" almost beats Kraftwerk at its own game with a phased production that gets trippier the louder it's played and vocals that seem to come from another dimension. It's impossible to imagine the acid house and techno of the '90s without this song. (Honorable mention in a similar vein goes to Madonna's "Justify My Love," especially the Book of Revelations remix with Middle Eastern instrumentation and ominous Biblical quotes.)

9. Culture Club, "Karma Chameleon" (1983)

Much-maligned by critics in its day and an admittedly light-weight successor to the punk and New Wave sounds that preceded it, Culture Club was not without its charms, including the soulful singing and confrontational cross-dressing of frontman Boy George. The band's finest moment was its stab at a merger of psychedelic folk and glossy '80s dance pop, an irresistible confection with a sly Moebius strip of a melody and lyrics that are, in great psychedelic fashion, part timeless wisdom and part stoner babble: "Karma karma karma karma karma chameleon / You come and go, you come and go / Loving would be easy if your colors were like my dream / Red gold and green, red gold and green."

10. Prince, "Pop Life" (1985)

After perfecting his own pop-rock-funk synthesis and following in the footsteps of Jimi Hendrix, Sly Stone, and George Clinton on *1999* and the massively successful *Purple Rain*, Prince was rumored to be making his version of *Sgt. Pepper's*. It turned out that he was more interested in Lennon and McCartney-level power and celebrity than Beatles-style sounds. Neither his addled mysticisms nor the clichéd orchestrations succeeded over the course of the entire album, but there are two standout tracks on his muddled concept effort, *Around the World In A Day*. In "Raspberry Beret," he picks up a girl in '60s thrift store clothing (Susanna Hoffs of the Bangles?), puts her on the back of his bike, and has his way with her in a barn over a mechanized dance beat and a sawing string section. Less of a novelty, "Pop Life" is stronger musically, more inventive with its shifting production and musical breakdown, and reminiscent of vintage Sly in its lyrics. Aching to be a role model, Prince preaches against cocaine and advises, "U can't get over if u say u just don't care / Show me a boy who stays in school / And I'll show you a boy aware!"

11. R.E.M., "Feeling Gravity's Pull" (1985)

Peter Buck, the group's resident historian, has long maintained that the favorite sons of Athens, Georgia, were and are a folk-rock band. (He certainly dropped the Byrds' name enough in the early days.) Limiting R.E.M.'s place in this book to a spot on this list may be slighting its psychedelic contributions: Mitch Easter's layered productions on *Chronic Town* and *Murmur* are certainly inspired by albums like *Revolver*; the discs create a waking dream-state vibe, and Michael Stipe's vocals contribute to feelings of mystery and distance. But thumbing through the group's later output, the psyche-delic influences are limited to covers (numerous Velvet Underground B sides, Wire's "Strange," and "Superman" by '60s rockers the Clique), odd instrumentals, and inspired touches such as the echoed guitar that introduces the lead track on *Reconstruction of the Fables*. Produced by Joe Boyd, the album was later dismissed by the band as a failure, but opinion has shifted in recent years, and it stands as the last effort shrouded in mystery and dedicated to creating its own unique soundscape before the group's subsequent move toward more straightforward pop.

12. Tom Petty, "Don't Come Around Here No More" (1985)

A devoted Byrds fan, Petty borrowed the group's chiming, reverbed Rickenbackers many times early in his career, but he first explored the psychedelic implications of "Eight Miles High" on this single. Not that "Don't Come Around Here No More" is that graceful; one of Petty's talents is revisiting uglier or more complex sounds (say, *Exile On Main Street* or "Eight Miles High") and making them palatable for mainstream consumption. He does this with enough wit and melody that only the grumpiest purists can complain. In this case, lest anyone miss the echoed drums, droning sitar, Beatles-inspired cellos, and acid-freaked vocals, he paired the song with a sly and somewhat misogynistic video inspired by *Alice in Wonderland*. (In fact, the clip is one of the first examples of a video being more psychedelic than the song it promotes, which would become increasingly common as MTV endeavored to provide an imagination for music fans who didn't have one of their own.) Petty went on to mine similar turf on "Free Fallin'" and

"Mary Jane's Last Dance," while the 1994 B side "Girl on LSD" was a hokey, folkie drug spoof ("I was in love with a girl on LSD / She'd see things I'd never see / She broadened her perspective / Then I got more selective").

13. Jane's Addiction, "Three Days" (1990)

Jane's Addiction leader, Lollapalooza founder, and alternative-rock godfather Perry Farrell talked a lot about the role psychedelic drugs played in shaping his uniquely warped worldview, but psychedelic rock was always just one of the many influences in his best-known band, which mixed glam-rock gender-bending, Led Zeppelin riff-pilfering, funky guitar wanking, and heroin-chic posing, all delivered by a singer who brought to mind Jon Anderson of Yes with stranger New Age ideas and a bit less of a vocal range. Overall, Farrell's second band, Porno for Pyros, was more effective in evoking the decadent spirit of a psychedelic bacchanal, complete with every imaginable variety of druggy excess and sexual fetish. But Jane's did have one outstanding acid-tinged high point in the eleven-minute centerpiece of its third album, *Ritual de lo Habitual*. On "Three Days," Farrell warbles from some place on the other side as Dave Navarro's guitar carves out a path between Jerry Garcia's fluid leads and classic metal shred, bassist Eric Avery reflects the strong influence of dub reggae, and drummer Stephen Perkins deftly shifts from John Bonham-style hard-rock stomp to complicated worldbeat polyrhythms. The track is like a session of marathon lovemaking, building slowly and gently before finally exploding three-quarters of the way through in a climactic frenzy.

14. Cracker, "Low" (1993)

Before its bitter split in 1989, San Francisco's Camper Van Beethoven nodded at psychedelic rock several times, including the enigmatic "Eye of Fatima" and relatively respectful covers of Pink Floyd's "Interstellar Overdrive" and Status Quo's "Pictures of Matchstick Men." But it was just one of many strains that the band explored while indulging a sometimes stubborn and distracting devotion to eclecticism; the group spent so much time being clever and showing its mastery of different genres that it rarely had time to write good songs. Former bandleader David Lowery took a different route in his solo career, focusing on tight, country-tinged alternative rock, but the old fondness for space-rock surfaced on the lead track of Cracker's second album, *Kerosene Hat*. With a droning melody and languid rhythm that match the lyrical images of floating astronauts and fields of poppies, "Low" creatively nods to Roxy Music's "Love Is the Drug" ("Being with you girl is like being stoned") and David Bowie's "Space Oddity" ("Don't you wanna go down like some junkie cosmonaut?"). It is Lowery's finest moment.

15. Soundgarden, "Black Hole Sun" (1994)

Since grunge mixed punk and early Black Sabbath-style metal, and Sabbath mixed blues-rock and psychedelia, it's surprising how long it took for a good psychedelic grunge tune to break through on modern-rock radio, but "Black Hole Sun" was worth the wait. It comes complete with a grinding riff, eerie, echoed guitar fills, processed vocals, and meaningless but fun brink-of-apocalypse lyrics ("Black hole sun won't you come and wash away the rain"). As in the case of "Don't Come Around Here No More," an effective video spells everything out for fans who might otherwise have missed the point—i.e., things aren't always what they seem.

16. Nick Cave, "Red Right Hand" (1996)

The dark, often gothic ambience of much of the solo output of the former leader of the Birthday Party could well place Nick Cave in the class of too-somber-for-their-own-good mope rockers, but Cave has always been much more adventurous musically and lyrically, working with the Bad Seeds to craft ornate, moody, and elaborately orchestrated settings for his apocalyptic, Old Testament tales of sin and betrayal, which always hold the promise of redemption and spiritual transcendence. The 1996 single "Red Right Hand" is one of his most psychedelic moments, the foreboding story of a mysterious, supernatural figure who's "a ghost, a god, a man, and a guru" with the power to fulfill any of your needs or desires, quite possibly at the Faustian compromise of your soul. "You'll see him in your nightmares, you'll see him in your dreams / He'll appear out of nowhere but he ain't what he seems," Cave sings in an ominous baritone that ranks with those of Hazelwood and Cash as orchestra bells chime, odd metallic percussion clatters, the bass guitar rumbles, and a cheesy funhouse organ offers a surreal interruption and disarming comic relief.

17. Madonna, "Ray of Light" (1998)

While it was heralded as "Madonna goes techno," the Material Girl's first album after 1994's disappointing *Bedtime Stories* and her subsequent foray into the land of Andrew Lloyd Webber was really just a return to typical dance-pop form, with two notable exceptions. On the title track, the hot British DJ and producer William Orbit piled on the burbling synthesizers, cascading electronics, and pulsating beats, taking Madonna's typically limited chirp to a whole new universe, and nicely complimenting her turn toward New Age mysticism. (The lyrics reflect her embrace of Kabbalah, a form of Jewish mysticism then trendy in Hollywood—"She's got herself a little piece of heaven / Waiting for the time when / Earth shall be as one," she sang in the great psychedelic-utopian tradition.) In a similar vein and with an equally intriguing Middle Eastern-tinged melody was "Shanti/Ashtangi," which boasted lyrics adapted from the Yoga Taravali. "Vunde gurunam caranaravinde / Sandarsita svatma sukhavabodhe," Madonna cooed, and really, how could you argue with that? (Honorable mention goes to another aging disco diva who attempted to reinvent herself as a campy raver: Cher, for her 1999 hit, "Believe.")

18. Santana, "Put Your Lights On" (2000)

Many critics derided Carlos Santana's massively successful comeback album, *The Supernatural,* as a contrived music-industry concoction that owed more to the behind-the-scenes machinations of Clive Davis in a corporate boardroom than it did to any magic that the guitarist worked in the studio—and that's certainly true of calculated hits like "Smooth," the easy-listening groove voiced by

Rob Thomas of Matchbox 20. But the album's most striking track worked on a much deeper level, actually delivering on the promise of the colorful piece of folk art that adorned the CD tray, which depicted a meditating individual shooting toward the heavens in a pyramid-shaped rocket ship flanked by two angels and bearing the inscription "Trancedance," a nifty combination of "trance," "dance," and "transcendence." With a moving vocal by the rapper Everlast, "Put Your Lights On" has a deliciously eerie vibe that qualifies it as the at-long-last sequel to "Back Magic Woman." Everlast wrote the lyric while recovering from emergency surgery after a heart attack that nearly took his life. "I used to live in a house on a hill overlooking all of Los Angeles," he told me. "Because of all my surgery, I had to sell my house to pay for a lot of the bills. I was going through a tough time: The house was empty, all the furniture was moved out, and I was spending the last night there and looking out as the sun was going down and all the lights in the city were coming on, and that's pretty much where the song came from: 'All you sinners, put your lights on.' It was just like the city turning its lights on and this sense of being torn up over having to sell my house, but there's also something in that song like, 'This is just wood and cement,' and it helped me let go." Ever the hippie-mystic, Santana told his collaborator that the song would be a hit even before the two had recorded it. "Carlos is a true hippie, man, to the bone, which is a beautiful thing—to see a guy who's so content with who he is and what he is and how he sees things," Everlast said. "When I went to record 'Put Your Lights On' with him, it was a good five months before his record came out, and he was in there telling me, 'An angel came to me in my dreams and told me to make this record.'"

Carlos Santana on Psychedelics and Psychedelic Music

"What people call psychedelic music is basically entering a door—a different door of perception—which brings me to the saying, 'You cannot behave appropriately unless you perceive correctly.' This is why [my 2002 album] *Shaman* is important. When the European people came to America, the first thing they killed was the shamans, because they knew that those guys knew too much and they wanted to make people deaf, dumb, and blind. Same with Africa. This way, they'll indoctrinate you with the Christian thing, but you cannot have access to Christ unless you go through them.

"Psychedelic music liberates you from that kind of thinking. Even Cary Grant took LSD under supervision! I always tell people there's a big difference between drugs, which man makes, and medicine, which Mother Earth makes. There's a big distinction there. I think they should legalize medicine, and they should outlaw drugs. Anheuser-Busch is a drug; cigarettes are a drug. Anything that imprisons you is a drug; anything that liberates you is medicine. But we're just too advanced for a lot of people still!

"I can tell that when I open my mouth people are afraid, because their sense of right and wrong is still in a little box. But I'm comfortable with my existence, and the things that I did learn from mescaline and LSD, I don't regret one trip. I learned so much from each one—as far as all is one, to feel someone else's pain, to feel connectedness. There is something about the terminology 'visit yourself.' In our music, we try to do that even today—to transport people to a place where you're not afraid and you don't have anger or fear. Music remains the most potent psychedelic force, from Beethoven to Jimi Hendrix.

"I equate it with a snake shedding skin: Every time that I took [a trip], I got rid of some luggage that I really didn't need and I got rid of some things that weren't me any more, that didn't fit. I cleaned my closet a lot and got rid of clothes that weren't me any more, and I learned a lot. But the thing that makes the most sense is John Coltrane's music and Bob Marley's music."

The Ongoing Influence of Psychedelic Thought in Pop Culture

absinthe

Kathy Acker

A Clockwork Orange

Charles Addams

A.I.

Altered States

Michelangelo Antonioni

appliquéd tights

Dario Argento

Ralph Bakshi

The Banana Splits

Clive Barker

Batman

Barbarella

Jean-Michel Basquiat

beanbag chairs

Beyond the Valley of the Dolls

birds of paradise

black lights

body paint

Paul Bowles

Roger Brown

Lenny Bruce

bubbles

bungee jumping

William S. Burroughs

butterflies

butterfly chairs

candy corn

caramel

Carlos Castaneda

channel surfing

chaos theory

Cheech and Chong

Christo and Jean-Claude

Arthur C. Clarke

comets

Roger Corman's Edgar Allen Poe movies

Jacques Cousteau

David Cronenberg

crop circles

Aleister Crowley

R. Crumb

crystals

curry

daisies

Salvador Dalí

Day-Glo

Philip K. Dick

digital imaging

the Discovery Channel

Dr. Strange

Doctor Who

Easy Rider

e-mail

Eraserhead

M.C. Escher

Etch-A-Sketch

Fantasia

Fantastic Voyage

Federico Fellini

fireflies

flying

fractals

Freaks

Fruitopia

geodesic domes

geysers

William Gibson

H.R. Giger

Terry Gilliam

Allen Ginsberg

glaciers

gliders

go-go boots

The Golem

Red Grooms

gypsy blouses

gyroscopes

Gumby

Gurdjieff

Keith Haring

Stephen Hawking

Häxan/Witchcraft Through the Ages

Hermann Hesse

Robert Heinlein

hula hoops

the Internet

Jägermeister

Japanese comics

Jim Jarmusch

Jell-O

jellyfish

The Jetsons

Betsey Johnson

Chuck Jones

kaleidoscopes

The Kama Sutra

Andy Kauffman

kites

Ernie Kovacs

Stanley Kubrick

Akira Kurosawa

ladybugs

Laugh-In

lava lamps

Anton LaVey

lobsters

Logan's Run

Lost in Space

H.P. Lovecraft

Malcolm Lowry

Lucite

the luge

the Magic Eightball

Magic Eye pictures

René Magritte

Major Matt Mason

Man Ray

Peter Max

Terence McKenna

meditation

mescal

Rusell Mills

miniskirts

mobiles

Mondo 2000

Monty Python's Flying Circus

mood rings

morphing

Mr. Natural

MRI scans

NASA

the northern lights

Claes Oldenburg

opals

Ouija boards

The Outer Limits

Pac-Man

paganism

paisleys

peacocks

Pee Wee's Playhouse

Pernod

Jackson Pollock

Pogo

polyamory

Harry Potter

the PowerGlove

the Powerpuff Girls

prisms

The Prisoner

Emilio Pucci

H.R. Puffinstuff

Thomas Pynchon

pyramids

Mary Quant

The Red Balloon

Ren and Stimpy

Tom Robbins

Ken Russell

the St. Louis arch

scuba diving

sensory deprivation tanks

Maurice Sendak

Dr. Seuss

Sam Shepard

Silly Putty

The Simpsons

sky diving

smart drinks

smiley faces

Terry Southern

spin art

Spirograf

Sponge Bob Squarepants

Star Trek

static generators

Stonehenge

strobe lights

sunflowers

surfing

Tank Girl

tequila

Tetris

Hunter S. Thompson

tiger balm

J.R.R. Tolkein

tops

Amos Tutuola

The Twilight Zone

Twister

2001: A Space Odyssey

Ulysses

Un Chíen Andalou

FOURTEEN

14

REALITY USED TO BE
A FRIEND OF MINE:
Psychedelic Hip Hop and Trip Hop

> Mirror, mirror on the wall / Tell me, mirror, what is wrong
> / Can it be my de la clothes / Or is it just my de la soul?
> —De La Soul,
> "Me Myself and I"

ARGUABLY THE MOST PSYCHEDELIC INSTRUMENT ever made in that it puts the entire universe of sound at the user's fingertips, the sampler emerged in the late 1970s as a logical progression from analog synthesizers and digital computer technology. Manufactured in Australia, the Fairlight Computer Musical Instrument allowed users to feed in a sound, digitally manipulate it, and replay it in any context he or she chose. It was joined in the '80s by the American-made Emu Emulator and a procession of increasingly less expensive and more user-friendly instruments.

Some enthusiasts say that sampling brings the high-art concept of *musique concrète* to the streets, making it possible to make music out of any sound, but that implies that the technology itself is magical, and that's only the case when it's used by imaginative technicians. Early Fairlight devotees such as Peter Gabriel and Mike Oldfield merely treated the machines like fancier synthesizers. "When the sampler first appeared, few people imagined it would have much effect—another new toy, a nine-days' wonder which would soon be put aside, a Mellotron for the digital age," critic Jeremy Beadle wrote in his history of the instrument and the music it inspired, *Will Pop Eat Itself?* "Except that somewhere in the mid-1980s, the sampler's potential collided with the cutting and scratching techniques popular in the music of New York's hip hop-scene, and a whole range of pop musicians were inspired to create a different kind of music, a music which raided pop's past and put it in a new and modern—and sometimes quite unnerving—context."

Rap began at street parties in the Bronx in the mid-'70s when DJs (many of them Jamaican immigrants) set up their turntables, mixed together the hottest sections of several records, and led the crowds in simple chants and call-and-response rhymes. The Sugar Hill Gang's 1979 novelty, "Rapper's Delight," is generally considered the first rap record, but artists such as Kurtis Blow, Grandmaster Flash, and Afrika Bambaataa followed with music that signaled the birth of not only a genre, but a subculture. Hip hop grew in popularity through the mid '80s as artists focused on harsh tales of life on the streets. Among the biggest innovators was Public Enemy, who constructed dense, sampled white-noise collages that abraded like the wildest free jazz or noise rock. Their political lyrics paved the way for a wave of gangsta rap, but the next big musical innovation came in 1989 when rappers began to sample mellower grooves in the first flowering of psychedelic hip hop.

Robert Christgau called De La Soul "new wave" to Public Enemy's "punk rock." Like Public Enemy's Chuck D., the three rappers in De La Soul were smart, middle-class African-Americans who hailed from suburban Long Island. Posdnuos (Kelvin Mercer) and Trugoy the Dove (David Jolicouer) had been in a more conventional rap group called Easy Street before they linked up with Maseo (Vincent Mason) and producer Prince Paul, a veteran of Stetsasonic. Where Public Enemy urged its listeners to fight the power, De La Soul heralded the start of the Daisy Age, which, in the grand tradition of psychedelic acronyms, stood for "da inner self, y'all." "Many of the B-boys would say that our beats weren't hardcore enough," Maseo told the *New Musical Express* in 1991. "But we're more about a vibe than coming up with hardcore beats…Where we live is very open and mellow. Sure, there are rough neighborhoods. But people don't live one on

The Ultimate Psychedelic Rock Library: De La Soul's amazingly creative debut, 3 Feet High and Rising *(Tommy Boy), ushered in the dawn of hip hop's Daisy Age.*

top of the other. There's room to think about what's going on." Added Trugoy: "If our music reminds you of a hippie, Bohemian vibe, that's okay. We want the music to speak for itself."

Aside from a few scattered marijuana references, De La Soul wasn't vocal about its drug habits on its debut album. The samples on *3 Feet High and Rising* (1989) came from the Jarmels, Steely Dan, Prince, and a French instruction record, and the lyrics were full of good-natured in-jokes and skits inspired by lazy afternoons spent goofing on bad TV. But they combined to make a whole that was joyfully disorienting. "De La Soul create a kind of dance psychedelia, disrupting consciousness by rupturing stylistic integrity," critic Simon Reynolds wrote in *Blissed Out*. "Splicing together grooves, beats and chants, licks and stray murmurings from unconnected pop periods, they create a friction, a rub that's both sensual and uncanny. Different auras, different vibes, different studio atmospheres, and different eras are placed in ghostly adjacence, like some strange composite organism sewn together out of a variety of vivisected limbs, or a Cronenberg dance monster."

De La Soul never bettered the crazy-quilt creativity of its debut. Stung by criticism from hardcore rappers, the members declared that the Daisy Age concept, clothing, and artwork had been forced on them by their label, Tommy Boy Records. Their sophomore effort, *De La Soul Is Dead*, boasted harder beats and more traditional hip hop samples, and the group turned to the sort of gangsta tales it had previously avoided, including "Millie Pulled a Pistol on Santa." (In an effort to thwart bootleggers, Tommy Boy issued advance cassettes of the album to reviewers with a sample of a braying donkey occasionally interrupting the music, and it's telling that many fans preferred this version to the final release.) The trio was more ambitious on its jazzy 1993 effort, *Buhloone Mindstate*, but by then, the frontiers of psychedelic rap were being explored in more adventurous ways by others. The group has returned to form to some extent in recent years; *Art Official Intelligence: Mosaic Thump* (2000) included one of its best tunes ever, "All Good?" with guest vocalist Chaka Khan, and *AOI: Bionix* (2001) featured an updated take on the black astronaut theme so familiar to George Clinton, Lee Perry, and Sun Ra.

Evolving from earlier incarnations as a New York hardcore punk band and snotty white rappers fighting for their right to party, the Beastie Boys produced their best album when they moved west and chilled out with the talented L.A. production team, the Dust Brothers. A mellower and more sophisticated sound emerged on 1989's sprawling double album, *Paul's Boutique*. Curtis Mayfield's psychedelic soul rubbed elbows with the intro to Pink Floyd's "Time" and a thousand other sound bites that contributed to a

The Ultimate Psychedelic Rock Library: The wonderfully scattered and sprawling Paul's Boutique *(Capitol) is the Beastie Boys' trippiest offering, and a high point of psychedelic hip hop.*

funky, surreal collage. Musically and thematically, the album is a channel-flipping blur of junk-culture trivia. "If Raymond Carver wrote K-Mart fiction, than the Beastie Boys create Salvation Army hip hop," critics Havelock Nelson and Michael Gonzales wrote in *Bring the Noise*. The thrill of discovery in the Beasties' bargain bins was never as strong again, though the crew revived some of the ambience of their psychedelic masterpiece on 1998's *Hello Nasty*.

By 1990 hip hop was wide open for experimentation and cross-fertilization. Groups emerged with their own novel twist, caused a splash with a strong debut, then quickly lost inspiration or packed it in. Members of De La Soul's Native Tongues posse, the Jungle Brothers merged hip hop and acid house on "I'll House You," and A Tribe Called Quest used well-chosen jazz and Lou Reed samples and scored a goofy hit with "I Left My Wallet in El Segundo." (The latter was one of the first acts to foreshadow a wave of "acid jazz," a merger of hip hop and jazz that's generally devoid of the psyche-delic influence the name might imply.) Digital Underground one-upped other rappers' use of Funkadelic samples by also updating the vintage P-Funk stage show, complete with sex, science-fiction imagery, and druggy in-jokes. Arrested Development took its inspi-ration from upbeat Sly and the Family Stone; Digable Planets brought a new fluidity to its own merger of jazz and hip hop; a self-styled psychedelic prophet from Brooklyn called the Divine Styler released a wonderfully weird but largely ignored stream-of-con-sciousness effort called *Spiral Walls Containing Autumns of Light*, and Cypress Hill pursued an obsessive devotion to droning melodies and *cannabis sativa*. But it fell to two brothers from Jersey City, New Jersey to make the next great psychedelic hip hop albums and give the subgenre some staying power.

SET ADRIFT ON MEMORY BLISS

> Reality used to be a friend of mine / 'Cause complete con-
> trol I don't take too kind.
>
> —P.M. Dawn,
> "Reality Used to Be A Friend of Mine"

LOCATED JUST ACROSS THE HUDSON RIVER from Manhattan and ten minutes away on the PATH train, Jersey City is a schizophrenic town with all of the problems of its larger neighbor and none of the culture or charm. Run-down ghettoes abut tree-lined neighborhoods of aluminum-sided homes and gentrified historic districts of renovated brownstones. Political corruption, street crime, racism, and drugs are chronic problems, but more soul-shattering is a subtle but pervasive sense of despair and a chronic lack of hope or vision. Growing up as an introverted, overweight misfit, Attrel Cordes Jr. decided that he could see a better way. Rechristening himself Prince Be and forming P.M. Dawn with his brother, Jarrett (a.k.a. DJ Minutemix), he announced that reality was an illusion and that anything could be changed if only one thought hard enough and had enough faith. In doing so, he joined a line of African-American musicians that included Jimi Hendrix and George Clinton, fellow psychedelic visionaries who preached not escapism but optimism and the power of positive thinking.

Infants when their father died of pneumonia in 1967, the Cordes brothers grew up surrounded by music and spirituality. Their mother sang in the church choir and taught them about Catholicism and Edgar Cayce, a Virginia Beach philosopher who wrote about karma, reincarnation, and the lost continent of Atlantis. At sixteen, Prince Be was kicked out of Jersey City's gifted and talented high school for cursing at his gym teacher—"I thought I was a B-boy, and I wasn't," he told Helene Stapinski in *Request* magazine—but he soon focused his adolescent energies on music. In addition to MTV stalwarts such as Prince and Culture Club, he was introduced to older sounds like the Beatles and Stevie Wonder by his stepfather, a sometimes conga player with Kool and the Gang. Prince Be toyed with guitar and DJ Minutemix tried drums and piano, but they abandoned those instruments early on. It was in the sampler that they found their true calling.

Working as a security guard at a homeless shelter for the mentally ill, Prince Be saved up six hundred dollars and recorded a demo that attracted the attention of England's Gee Street Records, the label that launched the Jungle Brothers. P.M. Dawn was flown to London to record its debut, *Of the Heart, Of the Soul and Of the Cross: The Utopian Experience*. Prince Be alternated velvety smooth rapping and high, clear, soulful singing over hook-filled soundscapes that were lush, inviting, and extremely sophisticated. The brothers preferred the terms "sampling artists" or "songwriters" to "rappers." The diverse ingredients in their musical collages included Chick Corea, the Doobie Brothers, Sly Stone, Hugh Masekela, and Spandau Ballet. Prince Be was crushed when he couldn't sample his heroes, the Beatles, but he had musicians duplicate a snatch of "Baby You're a Rich Man" for "The Beautiful." (The original artist's permission is required to sample a song, but not to cover it.)

Although they're aware of the inspiration behind their favorite Beatles tracks, the Cordes brothers say they've never taken psyche-

The Ultimate Psychedelic Rock Library: The only thing awkward about P.M. Dawn's beautiful debut, Of the Heart, Of the Soul and Of the Cross: The Utopian Experience *(Island), was the ponderous title.*

delic drugs, and they aren't interested in trying. "To me, psychedelia is finding something tangible that you can hold on to in the unusual, and that's what any innovator does," Prince Be told me. "That happened with the Beatles; they were trying to find something new, they were tired of just the guitars, drums, and that's that. Then they started using sitars and xylophones and all kinds of stuff. It's just finding innovative ways of making music—to make it different—to make it sound more and more fresh at any point in time." Added his brother: "Whatever we do is just part of us. Prince, when he writes, is always asking questions about things. It's like physical therapy for the soul."

P.M. Dawn doesn't believe in utopia, but it does believe in the "utopian experience," in particular the idea that "heaven is within us all." Prince Be preaches transcending the outside world by accepting that reality is an illusion, and different realities can be created in the mind. ("When you open up your eyes / What's in front of you / Is what's supposed to be there / Really?") His faith in his own hodgepodge of religious ideas is strong, but he isn't seeking converts. When he addresses his "father," it's never clear whether he's writing to Attrel Sr. or penning what Brian Wilson called "teenage symphonies to God." In either case people who aren't interested in his personal philosophy can read the poetic lyrics as simple but moving love songs. Prince Be balances even his weightiest raps with infectious melodies and a playful sense of humor. He was clearly having fun with his image as a dreadlocks-wearing, four-hundred-pound guru in psychedelic pajamas. When he and his brother posed on the album cover atop an Antarctic iceberg, the image was as incongruous as Parliament-Funkadelic's brothers in outer space, and it was just as striking.

The Utopian Experience was an impressive hit in the U.S. and England, where it won support in the mainstream as well as the underground rave culture, but like De La Soul, P.M. Dawn was criticized by hardcore rappers as a sellout. Even worse, Prince Be was called an Uncle Tom because of his talk of a "quest to become color-

The Ultimate Psychedelic Rock Library: The Bliss Album *(Island) proved that the four-hundred-pound Prince Be may have had a sweet temperament, but he wasn't easily pushed around.*

less," and he was subjected to homophobic slurs because of his effeminate mannerisms and high-pitched vocals. The Cordes brothers aren't wimps, and they came back swinging on *The Bliss Album...?* *(Vibrations of Love and Anger and the Ponderance of Life and Existence).* "Plastic" revived a '60s put-down to dis gangsta rappers who are "hard at first but melt in the heat," and Prince Be rightfully claimed that he was doing more to move hip hop forward than his dogmatic peers. "If water can't go any place and it doesn't move, it goes stagnant, and I couldn't see that happening to myself or to hip hop," he told me. But unlike De La Soul, P.M. Dawn didn't allow its anger to distract from its strengths, and the album offers two more beautiful, ethereal ballads, "I'd Die Without You" and "Looking Through Patient Eyes." There's also another tribute to the Beatles, a cover of "Norwegian Wood" that transforms John Lennon's wry tale of infidelity into something much stranger, with noises recalling the backward bird cries of "Tomorrow Never Knows."

P.M. Dawn flirted with touring following the second album's release, performing with a powerful thirteen-piece band as part of Peter Gabriel's first American WOMAD tour. But the ambitious stage show wound up costing the band half a million dollars, and Prince Be said he wasn't really comfortable outside the studio. The group retreated for two and a half years, and Prince Be got married and had a son, Christian. Fans worried that P.M. Dawn had run its course, but in his new Jersey City home studio, Prince Be was crafting his strongest and most psychedelic album. "It's pop, with a slightly experimental edge," he told David Sprague in *Request.* "It's not that far-out, it's just slightly...elevated." Released in 1995, *Jesus Wept* is named for the shortest verse in the Bible, and one that

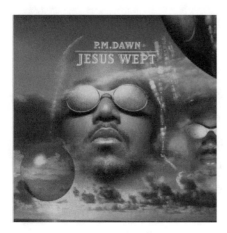

The Ultimate Psychedelic Rock Library: Though it garnered fewer critical hosannas than its predecessors, P.M. Dawn's third effort, Jesus Wept (Island), stands as its psychedelic masterpiece.

Prince Be praises for offering insight into Jesus, the man. The album opens with a snippet from the animated Charlie Brown TV special about the Great Pumpkin—"If you really are a fake, don't tell me; I don't want to know," Linus says—then traces what the singer calls "an individual's spiritual journey through human existence." "We wanted to do an album that was spiritual top-to-bottom without being religious," he told Sprague. "For me, the jury is still out about organized religion. I wanted to evoke the spirituality I feel *inside.*"

Using real instruments instead of samples on most of the tracks, the album climaxes in an unlikely trio of covers dubbed "Fantasia's Confidential Ghetto." The mini-suite starts with a stripped-down version of Prince's "1999," shifts into the layered art-funk of the Talking Heads' "Once in a Lifetime," and ends with a gonzo version of Harry Nilsson's "Coconut" that incorporates the now-obligatory Beatles nod by quoting "Flying." "Put the lime in the coconut and drink it all up," Prince Be sings. His conviction is strong enough to convince any skeptic that this brew —or at least the act of singing about it—is indeed all that is needed to cure life's ills.

The group has largely been missing from the mainstream view ever since, though Prince Be continues to craft his unique sound-scapes, sometimes offering them as free downloads on the Web (www.pmdawn.net), and he has been working on a new album, tentatively titled *Walk On Water*, for several years at this writing.

After the early success of some of the groups in the initial flow-ering of psychedelic hip hop, the mainstream of the music turned toward sounds that were much less creative musically and much crasser lyrically. The multi-platinum triumph of N.W.A in the early '90s marks the start of a trend to pandering, lowest-common-denominator gangsta rap that continues to this day, despite the fact that the style has long been clichéd and artistically bankrupt. Yet in the margins, well-respected as artists if not on the same level as ultra-successful businessmen such as Puff Daddy, Nelly, and Jay-Z, several acts have continued to incorporate a psychedelic influence

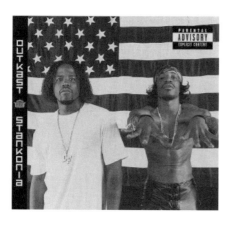

The Ultimate Psychedelic Rock Library: Outkast's Stankonia *(La Face) is a new-millennial update on Parliament-Funkadelic and the psychedelic Temptations.*

as part of their complex and challenging sounds. On its 2000 album, *Stankonia*, the Atlanta duo Outkast explore a broad musical vision that stretches from the interstellar funk of Parliament-Funkadelic and the trippy soul of the Temptations' *Psychedelic Shack* to the streetwise humor of pre-cookie-cutter gangsta rap. One of the factors that marks the group as one of the most important in hip hop today is the willingness of leader Andre "Dre" Benjamin to deal with serious lyrical issues—whether it's familial responsibility in the hit single, "Ms. Jackson", or global political aggression in "B.O.B. (Bombs Over Baghdad)." Dre is thrilled by comparisons to George Clinton, a particular hero. "I think it's the same ideology more than anything," he told me. "When we tried to make this record, we didn't say, 'We're going to do a psychedelic album.' It was more like we wanted a rebellious sound from traditional hip hop. When we went in, the mind frame of doing the album was trippy—we tried all kinds of things that sounded new and fresh to us. It was just kind of like a free and uninhibited approach to the studio. That's what's been pigeonholing hip hop, because you felt like you had to do a certain thing or be a certain way. You had to wear your hat to the back of your head or hold your dick. And the best music doesn't pay attention to those kinds of rules."

An alternate version of southern-fried psychedelia is offered by fellow Atlantan Cee-Lo (a founding member of Goodie Mob and Dungeon Family) on his 2002 album, *Cee-Lo Green and His Perfect Imperfections*, which throws hip hop, gospel, psychedelic rock, and psychedelic soul into a gonzo Cuisinart. Staten Island's extended Wu-Tang Clan family brought the hypnotic surrealism of martial arts films to many of its recordings (the menacing and otherworldly sounds of main musical engine the RZA were nicely matched on film in Jim Jarmusch's 1999 movie, *Ghost Dog: The Way of the Samurai)*, while Philadelphia's Roots, the best live band in hip hop, incorporate some psychedelic undertones on their strongest effort to date, *Things Fall Apart* (1999). Various members of that crew, notably drummer and producer Ahmir "?uestlove" Thompson, also bring their skills to dense, moody, and often otherworldly recordings by so-called "natural R&B" artists such as D'Angelo (whose dense and demanding 2000 effort, *Voodoo,* conjures the surreal, sensual, and slightly threatening sonic landscape of a Santeria ritual) and Erykah Badu (listen to 2000's *Mama's Gun*), as well as to Chicago rapper Common on his masterful *Like Water for Chocolate.*

TRIP HOP

> Please can't you stay a while to share my grief? / It's such a
> lovely day to have to always feel this way.
> —Portishead, "Wandering Star"

SEPARATED GEOGRAPHICALLY AND CULTURALLY from the urban Meccas of American hip hop, English musicians and white suburban sample artists across the United States were inspired by the music's energy and technological advances while being free from constrictions about what constitutes "real" rap music. English artists freely mixed musical elements, as evidenced by the pioneering Justified

Ancients of Mu Mu. Former Liverpool manager, scenester, and Julian Cope nemesis Bill Drummond teamed with Jimmy Cauty and released a series of singles featuring bizarre Scottish rapping and samples of artists ranging from Sly Stone to Petula Clark. Under the pseudonym the Timelords, the duo had an English hit in 1988 with "Doctorin' the Tardis," which was inspired by the *Doctor Who* TV series. As the KLF, they roped Tammy Wynette into a surreal musical and video guest turn. But the pair's interest in hip hop was short-lived—"I ain't no B-boy / I hate that shit," they declared—and they soon shifted their attention to ambient house music.

England's own strain of psychedelic hip hop surfaced several years after the innovations of De La Soul and P.M. Dawn, and it came from the racially-mixed, West Country port city of Bristol. The roots of what the London label Mo' Wax would eventually dub "trip hop" can be traced to a mid-'80s collective of DJs known as the Wild Bunch, who combined dub reggae, jazz, and hip hop influences. Nellee Hooper went on to produce Soul II Soul, Neneh Cherry, and

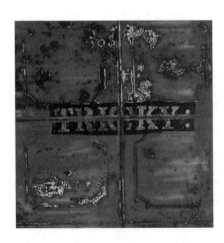

The Ultimate Psychedelic Rock Library: Tricky's Maxinquaye *(Island) is a sinister trip-hop tour de force.*

Sugarcubes singer Björk (who has incorporated enticing elements of trip hop along with the more traditional pop, rock, and classical influences in her complex pastiches), while Daddy G and Mushroom formed Massive Attack and released two brilliant and wide-ranging albums, *Blue Lines* and *Protection*. Massive Attack in turn nurtured Tricky, who rapped on both of its albums, and Geoff Barrow of Portishead, who got his start as the group's studio gofer.

Laid-back, low-key, and claustrophobic, trip hop is steeped in paranoia and melodrama, a musical equivalent to film noir. Critic Simon Reynolds called it "an aural simulation of the urban environment," but it's the sounds of the city as heard through a fever dream. "There's no unifying force to my album except confusion," Tricky said in a 1995 biography for Island Records. "It's totally coming from my mind, so it's filled with contradictions, chaos, paranoia, and happiness—all loosely linked—like a jigsaw with some of the pieces missing." Tricky's '95 solo bow, *Maxinquaye*, blurs the lines between genres, transforming Public Enemy's raging "Black Steel in the Hour of Chaos" into a sinister rock meditation. At the same time, it blurs sexual identities, pairing the gruff vocals of the cross-dressing Tricky with female diva Martina's breathy singing in lusty bisexual fantasies. "Hip hop has always been trippy and weird," Tricky said. "We're just mutating what's been done before."

Stronger melodically and even more cinematic conceptually, Portishead was formed by Barrow after he auditioned twenty vocalists and finally teamed with cover band veteran Beth Gibbons. Gibbons's vocals on spooky, sensual tunes such as "Sour Times" and "Wandering Star" are equal parts Billie Holiday and Nico. The backing tracks on *Dummy* combine the live sounds of a small jazz

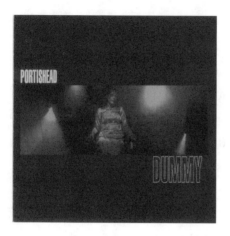

The Ultimate Psychedelic Rock Library: Portishead's Dummy *(London) represents the gentler, more lulling side of trip hop, though it still has menacing undertones.*

combo and samples from soul, lounge music, and soundtrack albums, but while it might not be apparent at first listen, hip hop is the biggest influence, both in the slowed-down rhythms and in the way that the songs are constructed. "Hip hop hit England like a ton of bricks," Barrow told me. "I would never pretend that I know anything about living in America as a black person, because that's disrespectful. But what I've really gotten from that music is the way to use samples and manipulate beats and sounds. You have to take technology by the horns and guide it. The trouble is, a lot of people let it dictate the way they write songs, and all the actual vibe has gone out of music."

The most intriguing trip hop artists in recent years have been all about the vibe. Some of them couldn't rap worth a damn; on his debut album, *Dr. Octagonecologyst*, Dr. Octagon (a.k.a. Kool Keith, formerly of the Ultramagnetic MC's) lurched and stumbled through lyrics that ranged from George Clinton sci-fi stoopidity ("Earth People") to sophomoric sexism ("A Visit to the Gynecologist"). He had nothing much to say, but he said it over some of the wackiest, catchiest, and most inventive grooves since the debut effort by De La Soul (whose pal, Prince Paul, served as the producer). Thankfully, the good doctor simultaneously released *Instrumentalyst*, which offered all of the vocal album's tracks plus a few extras, sans amateurish rapping and gratuitous cussing, putting the spotlight where it belonged: on the innovative mix of live guitars and bass with laid-back rhythm tracks, hooky analog synth lines, hyperactive scratching, and inspired sampling.

Striking out on his own from his position as a backing musician for the Beastie Boys, Keyboard Money Mark (a.k.a. Mark Ramos-Nishita) released several strong solo efforts, including *Mark's Keyboard Repair* (1996) and *Push the Button* (1998). These dish up frosty-cool instrumentals, romantic indie pop tunes, and dusty soul numbers done up in the manner of a bedroom four-track Marvin Gaye. Six years after his acclaimed debut, *Entroducing...*, California turntablist (a fancy word for DJ, producer, and sampling artist) Josh Davis, better known as DJ Shadow, topped that impressive accomplishment with one of the most diverse, imaginative, and creative electronic dance albums since the early '90s. *Private Press* (2002) juggles streetwise hip hop humor with a more subtle suburban sarcasm, dropping in skillfully chosen samples that satirize the plastic ideal of the American advertopolis while crafting some of the most seductive, beguiling, and tuneful rhythm tracks this side of Moby. Equally creative is DJ Spooky (New Yorker Paul D. Miller), who crafts far more disturbing soundscapes, though his nightmares are generally leavened with a wicked sense of humor on his best recording, *Riddim Warfare* (1998). Miller, who has also adopted the handles "That Subliminal Kid" and "the Spatial Engineer of the Invisible City," calls his music "illbient" to differentiate its brand of low-key instrumentals from Eno's ambient music. Where the ambient ideal is to pleasantly enhance the background of everyday life, DJ Spooky strives for sounds that reflect the stresses around him, and his heroes include Xenakis, Steve Reich, John Cage, Sun Ra, and the Aphex Twin. "My music is post-psychedelic," he told me. "To me technology is externalized hallucination—hallucination made concrete. Psychedelic culture is still dealing with internal hallucination. What I do is make equations—rhythms and sound— that allow the externalization of that same mental state. That's why I call it mood sculpture." And his fascination with the dark side? "To me it's a response. Music is always a reflection of our times, and we live in some pretty wild moments. Hopefully, my music points to a new route out of the psychological craziness. "I call it digital exorcism—it's like my dealing with this dark crazy crap opens your mind to another style of thought. What I always say is that bitterness makes you think in loops, and we live in a culture of loops at the moment. Personally, I like broken loops."

Englishman Howie B. (née Bernstein) is probably best known for his contributions to U2's 1997 album, *Pop*, and its Passengers side project, but on his own, the veteran DJ (who got his start in the studio engineering the late '80s releases by Soul II Soul) has released an impressive discography of twisted trip-hop discs, many of them for his own label, Pussyfoot. The best include *Music for Babies* (1996), which was inspired by the birth of his daughter, Chilli, and forwards a psychedelic tradition of musings on parenthood that can be traced back to Pink Floyd's *Atom Heart Mother*, and *Snatch* (1999), a techno update on porno soundtrack music that mixes and matches disparate sounds, hiding musical jokes in the grooves and generally indulging in the joys of the recording studio like the clichéd kid in a candy store. An Eno-esque synth throb gives way to a Mexican mariachi band then to some filling-rattling bass before segueing into an explosion of dissonance—and that's all on *one track* ("Cook for You"). "A lot of people just snub their nose at the term [trip hop] because they immediately relate it to drugs because of the connotations of 'trip,'" the artist told me. "It's the same thing with the connotations of hip hop: A lot of people won't put a tune on because it's called hip hop. I think tags are very dangerous things; they can stifle things before they flower properly. As soon as someone puts a tag on me, then I'll jump into something else. 'If you think that's what I am, then check *this* out.' I always take it as a throw down."

Nicolas Godin and Jean-Benoit Dunckel, the auteurs behind the ambient trip-hop duo Air, have said they've modeled recordings such as *Moon Safari* (1998) and their soundtrack for the Sofia Coppola film *The Virgin Suicides* on the reverb-drenched soundscapes of Pink Floyd's *The Dark Side of the Moon*, and the influence of Rick Wright on their own keyboard parts is obvious. At their best, they've produced subtle, layered, and charmingly bittersweet mood music that is also very sensual and seductive. But the true champions of sexy trip hop are Morcheeba. Formed when guitarist Ross Godfrey and his DJ brother, Paul, linked up with sultry vocalist Skye Edwards, the group debuted with a promising album called *Who Can You Trust?*, though its finest moment was its sophomore offering. *The Big Calm* (1998) specialized in jarring contrasts between light and dark. The trio's R&B-laced trip-hop grooves can

The Ultimate Psychedelic Rock
Library: Morcheeba's Big Calm
(Sire) is makeout music for a
night in a haunted house.

work as lulling makeout music, mixing beautiful string parts with atmospheric keyboards, a jazzy rhythm section, sitar, and pedal steel guitar, and Edwards possesses as smooth and sensual a voice as you'll find anywhere in pop music. At the same time, the lyrics tend toward the dark and obsessive. "I'm so glad to love you and it's getting worse / I'm so mad to love you and your evil curse," she coos on "Blindfold." A few songs later, on "Fear and Love," she adds, "Fear can stop you loving / Love can stop your fear."

"One of the things we like about '60s lounge and soundtrack music is that it has this weird sheen thanks to the way that sweet jazz chords are mixed into very dark sounds," Ross Godfrey told me. "Paul writes bitter and twisted lyrics, but when Skye sings them, they sound beautiful. It's that kind of juxtaposition like when a film soundtrack is nice and melodic, then the movie gets into a nasty situation, and things turn that little bit weird. Something is bubbling beneath the surface." On subsequent efforts, including *Fragments of Freedom* (2000) and *Charango* (2002), the band's outlook brightened considerably. "Our first album was very much on the darker side of things because me and my brother were very poor, sharing one room and just eating beans on toast all day," Ross said. "And then after the first album, when we toured the world and started enjoying ourselves and making a bit of money, we saw the happier side a bit more. But I don't think we'll ever totally get away from the dark, the surreal, and the psychedelic."

FIFTEEN

RAVING AND DROOLING:
Psychedelic Dance Music

What do techno, rave, and Ecstasy have to do with each other? Taken together, are they the basis for an actual youth movement? Is it entertainment? Is it pagan? Is it music? Is it a fad? Is it a drug culture? Is it a religion? Is it a trend? Is it the final decline of Western Civilization? The answer, of course, is yes to all of the above.

—*Reactor* rave zine, 1992

THE EARTH REVERBERATED IN TIME to the throbbing bass as the sweaty twentysomething bodies gyrated directly in front of a twelve-foot-high wall of speakers. The sound drew the dancers in like a powerful magnet, and they undulated in free-form movements that were both awkward and beautiful. Nobody danced in pairs. The crowd was like one giant, bouncing organism, and the sexual tension usually present at discos was missing completely. Blacks and Asians danced beside whites and Hispanics, and that wasn't an issue, either. What some would call infantilism and others a nostalgic yearning for childhood ran rampant. Dancers wore pacifiers around their necks, sucked on lollipops, waved glow-in-the-dark toys, and sported T-shirts with their favorite cartoon characters.

The message was clear: Do your own thing. For some, that was orange hair, multiple piercings, giant Cat in the Hat *chapeaux*, and fuzzy lime-green vests. For others, it was outfits purchased on dad's American Express card at the nearest Gap. The giant tent was almost pitch black, but a light from the DJ booth illuminated a skinny young nude dancing wildly atop the speakers. (He turned out to be Chicago writer David Prince, one of the event's organizers.) Outside, the air was thick with the hazy smoke from two dozen campfires, which could be glimpsed flickering beside smaller tents or next to cars or vans parked in the mud. A powerful argon laser shot a strong green beam into the sky, announcing that for this night, this remote campground on a wooded hillside in rural Wisconsin was the center of the Rave New World.

Located near the Minnesota border, the town of Hixton has a population of 403 or 356, depending on which of the welcome signs you choose to believe. The promoters chose the CMJ Motocross Track because it was roughly equidistant from the Chicago, Milwaukee, Minneapolis, and St. Louis rave scenes that they hoped to unite. Some two thousand dancers descended on the town like a '90s version of the gang in a '60s biker freak-out flick. Freak out they did, but peacefully, dancing all night to the liberating sounds of techno, acid house, and ambient house music. The

May Day, 1994 rave was dubbed "Furthur" in honor of the multi-
colored bus driven by Ken Kesey and his Merry Pranksters. When it
was all over, the promoters faced a giant, muddy mess, legal threats
from an angry sheriff, and arranging bail for a pair English journalists who were the only ravers to get busted. The organizers were
ecstatic nonetheless, partly because the journalists said it was the
closest thing they'd seen in the States to a "real" English rave; partly because guest DJ the Aphex Twin (flown over from Cornwall,
England especially for the event) delivered a transcendent set, and
partly because they couldn't believe that they'd pulled it all off.
"What we vowed to do was bring everybody together to communicate with each other and create more of a family atmosphere similar to Dead shows," said Kurt Eckes of Milwaukee's Drop Bass
Network, primary promoters of the event. "Financially, it wasn't a
success. But everybody that I talked to was having the weekend of
their lives, and hearing that from as many people as I did was exactly what I wanted to happen." Added David Prince: "The idea of people going five hours into the middle of nowhere to dance to cut-
ting-edge electronic music—that's the way it should be."

The music Prince referred to is inextricably intertwined with
the other elements of rave culture as it developed in the late '80s.
First came Ecstasy—or E, or Adam, or X—developed as an appetite
suppressant by the German pharmaceutical company Merck and
patented in 1914 under its proper chemical name, MDMA. The
drug was ignored until 1953, when the U.S. Army began testing its
toxicity on lab animals. Its psychedelic properties weren't noted
until 1976, when biochemist Alexander Shulgin wrote a report that
earned him the title of the "stepfather of Ecstasy." In *Ecstasy: The*

MDMA Story, Bruce Eisner described the experience like this: "You discover a secret doorway into a room in your house that you did not previously know existed. It is a room in which both your inner experience and your relations with others seems magically transformed. You feel really good about yourself and your life. At the same time, everyone who comes into this room seems more lovable. You find your thoughts flowing, turning into words that previously were blocked by fear and inhibition."

While some scientists consider Ecstasy separate from psychedelics, preferring the term "empathogen," most users view the trip as a milder form of the LSD or mescaline experience. "With classic psychedelics, transformations frequently are both extreme and, for the most part, internalized," Peter Stafford said in Eisner's book. "MDMA seems to offer a benign route to many similar consequences." It also allows users to maintain enough of a grip on reality to function responsibly. Unlike people on LSD, Ecstasy trippers can tell that the red light is a red light and the cop is a cop, and they aren't likely to jump off the roof thinking that they can fly. Nevertheless, Ecstasy followed a similar path to LSD in terms of media-fueled paranoia and its eventual outlawing. Shulgin's report was followed by false stories that the drug drained the spinal fluid and caused Parkinson's disease, that it was a potent aphrodisiac (actually, it physically slows amorous adventures), and that it caused drug-crazed partiers to dance until they dropped from heatstroke or exhaustion. As in the '60s, the official clampdown was spurred by Ecstasy's increasing popularity in social settings. A large quantity somehow surfaced in Dallas and Fort Worth in 1984, and it became the rage at yuppie bars after work. It was officially banned in

England and the United States in 1985, just before it collided with a new musical movement and became more popular than ever.

In 1981, DJs in Chicago's gay dance clubs started pumping the bass on mid-tempo disco records and adding melodic snatches ranging from gospel to Kraftwerk. One of the masters at manipulating the crowd's emotions was Frankie Knuckles, who worked at a club called the Warehouse. A shortened version of the club's name gave the music a moniker: house. "The windows of the Warehouse were painted black, the crowd would be high on the music and on drugs"—including the psychedelic MDM, sprinkled on slices of fruit—"I'd pump up the bass, then play this record, which was the soundtrack of an express train," Knuckles told Sue Cummings in *Rolling Stone.* "People would scream—it was mixture of ecstasy and fear—and it sounded like a train was racing through the club."

House music was initially popularized by Chicago labels such as DJ International and Trax. Simultaneously a sound called techno was being developed in Detroit by DJs Derrick May, Kevin Saunderson, and Juan Atkins. The three were influenced by a Motor City radio jock named the Electrifyin' Mojo whose sets mixed Kraftwerk, Gary Numan, disco, and Parliament-Funkadelic. Techno did the same, but all on one track. "We like to say it's tomorrow's soul music for the modern-day black man," May told the Associated Press in 1994. "We took the intellectual technology and ran it through the streets of Detroit." The technology he was referring to was digital samplers and MIDI (musical instrument digital interface), which allowed a single DJ or producer to control any number of synthesizers, drum machines, and samplers in addition to his or her turntables.

Most accounts agree that house, techno, and Ecstasy were first combined in 1986 on the Spanish island of Ibiza, where working-class youth vacation in England's version of spring break. "Somewhere in this sparse technology-based music was a chord that linked the disenfranchised: black American gays and alienated British youth with few job prospects and even fewer expectations of life," Ernest Hardy wrote in *Request*. A harsh critic of the rave scene, Hardy missed the uplifting, addicting, and colorblind physicality of techno, which had an appeal that soon expanded beyond its core devotees. From their Spanish origins, raves moved back to Britain, finding a home in urban warehouses and rural outdoor locales. They spread to Los Angeles, New York, and San Francisco in 1988 and 1989 and by the early '90s they were common throughout the Midwest, as well as in Germany and Belgium.

In the summer of 1988, a hybrid sound called acid house evolved, and critics are still debating what the "acid" refers to. Some DJs say the term came from the distinctive buzzing sound of one of the primary technical components, the Roland TB-303 bass synthesizer. ("Hear that?" Chicago DJs are fond of asking. "*That* is the sound of acid.") Genesis P-Orridge of Psychic TV claimed that he saw the description on a bin in a Chicago record store, was disappointed to find that it meant acid as in "corrosive," and set about making psychedelic music that actually fit the bill. Paul Staines of England's Freedom to Party Campaign admitted that the story he told Parliament—that acid house came from the Chicago street slang "acid burn," meaning to steal or sample another piece of music—was concocted in a public relations effort to separate the phrase from its psychedelic connotation (no one in Chicago that I know has ever heard of the phrase). But anyone who's been to a rave can tell you that the connection between psychedelic drugs and acid house and techno is certainly no fiction.

At any rave a significant portion of the crowd is likely to be tripping, and the rest feels as if it is thanks to the disorienting sounds, overpowering volume, and classic psychedelic light show. LSD is popular, and there have been bursts of enthusiasm for ketamine, or Special K, an anesthetic related to PCP that often prompts hallucinations of a decidedly dark nature. Marijuana is used by dancers who want to come down, but alcohol is rarely in evidence. Ecstasy is still the high of choice, and its effects are often heightened by sucking on balloons filled with nitrous oxide or taking a quick whiff of Vicks Vap-O-Rub, which opens up the bronchial tubes and allows a rush of oxygen. "When MDMA is experienced at raves, it lacks some of the subtle effects experienced in quiet surroundings, but has an extra quality not seen when the drug is taken in private," Nicholas Saunders wrote in *E for Ecstasy*. "The combination of the drug with music and dancing together produces an exhilarating trance-like state, perhaps similar to that experienced in tribal rituals or religious ceremonies."

The difference between raves and ancient rituals or '60s Acid Tests is technology. "Techno-shamanism," some ravers call it, referring to the electronic music-making machines (there is no such thing as acoustic rave music), computer communications (the Internet is the primary avenue for ravers to network and post party announcements), virtual reality (better than LSD, they say), and a general philosophy that technology will improve humanity and preserve the planet. "If ravers lionize anything, it's technology, which offers ways to circumvent the kinds of blockage that derailed countercultures of the past," author Dennis Cooper wrote in a 1995 article for *Spin*. "Rave is not about destroying corrupt power structures; it's about general things like self-belief, open-mindedness, and faith....Ravers have no particular enemies, so they're relatively invisible. And their invisibility is their strength."

Cooper wasn't entirely correct. Ravers are certainly visible to local government officials who take joy in cracking down on a phenomena that means easy headlines and no political fallout. As this book went to press, many major American cities had adopted strict anti-rave ordinances, with the music's birthplace of Chicago having some of the most draconian and onerous in the country. But to a large extent the *artists* who make rave music are indeed invisible, or at least anonymous. The DJ at a rave isn't the focus of the room the way a band is, because the crowd itself is the star of the show. Artists record under different and ever-changing names, most of which don't matter to ravers. The forum of choice is the twelve-inch single, and those are often unavailable to the general public until they're rounded up on compilation discs. "Although it would be exaggerating to suggest that techno records are amelodic at heart, the fact is that most techno singles tend toward short, repetitious phrases— 'tunettes,' if you will—more than fully realized themes," critic J.D. Considine wrote in the *Baltimore Sun*. "Moreover, the dearth of vocals on most of these singles leaves most techno records seemingly indistinguishable from one another."

This belief has led many critics to conclude that techno and acid house can't be judged outside the raves where the music is conceived and played. But there are reasons why certain artists have distinguished themselves from the faceless ranks. The best techno performers succeed because of the same attributes of all of the best psychedelic rock: strong songs, inventive productions, an elemental drive, and distinctive visions.

JAMES BROWN IS BUGGIN'

> The power of sound is almost an archetypal conceit of all theories of magic anywhere in the world. For us, magic means stagecraft and illusion, but for many people, it simply means another way of doing business with reality. Rave culture, to some degree, can be seen ·as a nostalgia for archaic and so-called primitive lifestyles.…Music has to be percussive to address the human physiology. I mean, you wouldn't want to listen to too much Schöenberg on acid.
>
> —Terence McKenna

THE FIRST TECHNO SINGLE TO SCRAPE the U.S. charts and dent the consciousness of mainstream listeners was the grinding novelty tune, "James Brown Is Dead," a 1992 single by a pair of radio DJs. The title was meant not as homage in the style of the Moody Blues' "Legends of a Mind," but as an obnoxious pronouncement signaling the birth of a new dance music with no ties to the past. Of course, this wasn't remotely true. Amid the onslaught of techno, acid house, and the myriad subgenres that followed—including ambient house, intelligent techno, acid, tribal, trance, breakbeat, and jungle—some of the best artists built on the rich legacy of psychedelic rock and extended it into the '90s and the new millennium.

It has been said that Richard James—a.k.a. the Aphex Twin, AFX, Polygon Window, Caustic Window, and too many other aliases to count—makes the techno equivalent of *Nuggets*-style garage rock or the Velvets' "Sister Ray," but he is just in close in spirit to Brian Eno. Born in Cornwall, England, in 1971, he began experimenting with sound as a child, dismantling and rebuilding the piano in his parents' living room. He discovered house music via a tape that a friend brought back from Chicago, but by age thirteen he was already crafting similar tracks using reel to reel tape recorders and old analog synthesizers that he built or customized himself in between performing menial jobs like ditch digging. Tape hiss, crackles, and pops are all part of his music's charm, as are the sounds of improvised instruments. "I'd say to my friends, 'Pick any object in the room and I'll make a track out of it,'" James told *Option* in 1994. "I'd make complete tracks out of Coke cans and carpets. Coke cans are easy because they have a lot of good acoustic characteristics, but with things like carpets, it's very difficult to get a bass drum sound."

Slower and spacier than more hardcore rave music, James's grooves function as well on headphones as they do at raves (if not better), and he has been hailed by many aficionados as techno's one true sonic genius, though he has never achieved the mainstream success of artists like Moby, Fatboy Slim, and the Chemical Brothers. His best known track remains "Didgeridoo," which used electronic sounds to duplicate the drone of the Australian Aboriginal instrument. (The song made didgeridoos as popular in techno as sitars were in the psychedelic rock of the '60s, and it kicked off a wave of DJs incorporating other ethnic instruments, as evidenced by the Wax Trax! compilation, *Ethnotechno*.) Unlike Moby, James doesn't shy away from the subject of psychedelic drugs, though he credits dreams as his major source of inspiration. "I've always had sounds in my dreams," he told David Prince in *Request*. "I can almost always remember melodies. But sounds, you can't get them the same."

James released his first official recording, *Analogue Bubblebath*, in 1991 under the name AFX; his first album, *Selected Ambient Works 85-92*, followed the next year under the more familiar Aphex Twin moniker and included some tracks that he'd recorded a decade earlier while still in his teens. The trancey sounds of both discs were hugely popular on the English club scene, and they spawned a legion of imitators. Troubled by the bland nature of much of the ambient techno that he helped usher in, James turned toward more nightmarish soundscapes on his 1994 Sire Records

The Ultimate Psychedelic Rock Library: The Aphex Twin's first full album, Selected Ambient Works 85–92 *(Pias America), is considered by many to be the ideal entry point into the twisted sonic world of Richard D. James.*

debut, *Selected Ambient Works Volume II*, his first release to be widely distributed in America. Reminiscent at times of Stockhausen, Can, and Eno at his most sinister, the album was also startlingly original at other points, and extremely disturbing throughout.

Befitting his evil scientist image, James bought a British Daimler Ferret Mark 3 tank and took to driving it around his parents' backyard. Naturally, the sound of its engines became part of the mix on 1995's *...I Care Because You Do*, a more diverse but equally dark effort featuring a cover with a self-portrait of its creator grinning demonically. (These wicked portraits would continue on several covers to come, reaching their unsettling peak with the disfigured children of 1997's *Come to Daddy* EP, James's aural evocation of the demonic tykes in *The Children of the Damned*.) With 1997's *Richard D. James*, the electronic auteur offered his take on the burgeoning jungle sound; by this point, he was being widely recruited by the likes of Beck and Nine Inch Nails to work his remix magic, but he was wary of stardom and the hype machine. Shortly after the video for "Come to Daddy" began generating MTV airplay, he announced his retirement, saying he planned to focus on running his independent label, Rephlex, while making music only for himself.

In fact James continued to churn out his distinctive music under a variety of different names—he just didn't play the promotional game the way that the music industry expected him to, preferring to make news of his releases available through the "Aphex Twin community" of his Web site (www.aphextwin.nu). He returned to the spotlight somewhat in 2001 with the powerful double album, *drukqs*. This typically difficult, complex, and extraordinarily creative disc contains thirty oddly named tracks, some brand new, and

The Ultimate Psychedelic Rock Library: Defiantly named in the ongoing era of "just say no," the Aphex Twin came back in grand form on 2001's drukqs *(Sire). Grindingly chaotic (and unpronounceable) tracks such as "jynweythek ylow" and "kladfvbung micshk" abut moments of breathtaking beauty*

others reworking of older pieces, that combine for a listening experience as alien and unsettling as a more tuneful *Trout Mask Replica* or a groovier *Metal Machine Music*. Why had he ended his premature retirement? "The old mind was getting really slow and dull so I thought I'd get a new one," he wrote in a Q&A distributed to the press as compensation for declining all interviews.

Another hugely influential English act was the Shamen, who shifted gears in 1989 from post-punk psychedelic rock to more dance-oriented sounds while breaching the mainstream with the acid house hit, "Move Any Mountain." In 1993 the group started a trend by recording *Boss Drum* with Terence McKenna, the American ethnobotanist who no less an authority than Timothy Leary called "the Timothy Leary of the '90s." The author of poetic pro-psychedelic tracts such as *True Hallucinations*, *The Archaic Revival*, and *Food of the Gods*, McKenna was the closest thing rave culture had to a guru. Although ravers failed to adopt all of his theories, he showed a keen understanding of the rock 'n' roll mindset with his central tenet that going to the grave without having a psychedelic experience is like going to the grave without ever having sex. Samples of such pronouncements delivered in McKenna's lovably nasal voice would soon show up on tracks by Psychic TV, Coil, Youth, and the Orb, among other techno artists. One of the most lucid and enlightened authorities on the subject of drugs in the '90s, he sadly died from brain cancer in April 2000.

London resident Mixmaster Morris—a.k.a. the Irresistible Force—was a psychedelic rock fan whose horizons were broadened by dropping LSD at a Steve Reich concert. Originally a member of the Shamen's sizable posse of DJs, musicians, and lighting technicians, he struck out on his own after founding member Will Sinnott drowned while filming a video. Morris scored a solo hit in 1991 with the Sun Ra-inspired "Space is the Place," and he followed with *Flying High*, a double album with the word "high" in every title but one ("Symphony In E"). One of rave culture's most dedicated egalitarians, he was devoted to the idea of eliminating the artist as star. "I've always been into music that was anti-musician," he told *Option*. "We got rid of musicians and replaced them with DJs. Now I want to get rid of the DJs, too." Sadly he is almost entirely absent from the scene today.

Among the other early avatars of techno were Orbital, English brothers Phil and Paul Hartnoll, whose ambitious soundscapes included *Snivilisation*, a tuneful and danceable concept album about the decline of Western Civilization. Canadian Richie Hawtin, a.k.a. Plastikman, debuted with a crisp, clean techno tribute to LSD, *Sheet One*, and found himself at the center of a controversy when a fan was arrested for carrying the CD jacket, which was made to

resemble a sheet of blotter acid. So-called "intelligent techno" artist
Mark Gage from Rochester, New York recorded beguiling ambient
electronica under the name VapourSpace for England's Swim label,
which was founded by Colin Newman of Wire, before progressing
to several other companies and winning an audience in the new
progressive-rock underground. San Francisco's Jonah Sharp collaborated with McKenna and recorded a strong album of his own as
Space Time Continuum. Chicago DJ Derrick Carter made an influential ambient house disc under the name Symbols and
Instruments and several techno records with a decidedly jazzy bent
under the name Sound Patrol before becoming one of the most in-
demand club DJs in the world. The New York collective Deee-Lite
offered a more old-fashioned brand of house music with delightful
psychedelic overtones and guest bass from former P-Funk member
Bootsy Collins. Vaunted remixers for artists as diverse as Skinny
Puppy and Tortoise, Manchester's Autechre (Sean Booth and Rob
Brown) have also recorded several strong discs of their own,
expanding and further psychedelicizing the Detroit electro sound.

With *Dead Cities* (1996), the followup to 1994's impressive
Lifeforms, samplin' fools and electronic storytellers Garry Cobain
and Brian Dougans, better known as The Future Sound of London,
made an album that could be considered rave noir—close your eyes
as you listen and you're transported to a gray and dreary cityscape
that's part *Brazil* and part *Blade Runner*. Old Bill Burroughs is standing on the corner waiting for the man, the Trans-Europe Express
rushes through headed for Düsseldorf station, and new jack
gangstas struggle to wrest control of the streets from old world
mobsters. "We have explosives," a voice whispers in your ear, and

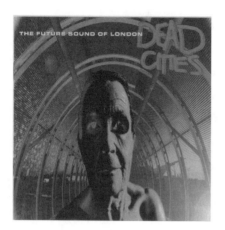

The Ultimate Psychedelic Rock Library: The Future Sound of London's Dead Cities *(Astralwerks) is an electronica concept album.*

the sound of this futuristic terrorist slipping quickly into the shadows sends shivers up your spine. All that and you can dance to it— or most of it. Drawing primarily on "found sounds" from the media, Cobain and Dougans created dense, multi-layered tracks that were both coldly mechanical (thanks to the ubiquitous techno drum machines) and strangely organic in a gritty, urban way ("Quagmire" features a sample from Ennio Morricone's score for *Once Upon a Time in America,* and there are snippets of Run-DMC's *Tougher Than Leather* in "Herd Killing" and "We Have Explosive"), with half an album of rapid-fire dance-floor groovers and half a disc of creepy ambient background music.

Englishmen Paul Hammond and Ian Cooper, better known as Ultramarine, grew up on a steady diet of the Canterbury bands Soft Machine and Caravan, and their music fuses jazzy flutes and guitars with electronic backgrounds. On 1993's *United Kingdom,* they were joined by one of the grand old men of psychedelic rock, Robert Wyatt of the Soft Machine. This wasn't the only example of the first-generation of psychedelic rockers linking up with '90s techno artists. In 1993 Paul McCartney hooked up with DJ and former Killing Joke bassist Youth in a duo called the fireman. Although McCartney reportedly had a blast crafting them in the studio, the resulting albums, *strawberries oceans ships forest* (1993) and *Rushes* (1998) aren't particularly inspired. Former Throbbing Gristle leader, industrial pioneer, and artistic terrorist Genesis P-Orridge turned his attention to acid house with Psychic TV releases such as *Tekno Acid Beat* (1989), *Towards thee Infinite Beat* (1990), and 1996's *Trip Reset,* which featured a cover of Pink Floyd's "Set the Controls for the Heart of the Sun" as well as an original titled "Star Too Far (Lullaby for Syd)." Space-rock veterans Hawkwind dabbled in techno on 1995's *Spirit of the Age*, and Steve Hillage of Gong resurfaced as an unremarkable techno artist under the name 777. (Much more interesting were Hillage's collaborations with Alex Paterson, a.k.a. the Orb.)

Desperately searching for "the next big thing" as alternative rock began to wane in the mid-'90s, the American major labels were briefly convinced that techno would be the new sound that would capture the hearts of young America. It didn't quite happen that way—instead, we got a new wave of bubblegum pop and wretched rap-rock or nü metal—but several artists who watered down the more psychedelic and original sounds of the early innovators did score some impressive pop successes. Reworking the Dust Brothers' moniker and lifting their early '70s B-movie imagery, the Chemical Brothers went for the lowest common denominator with their 1995 debut, *Exit Planet Dust*, penetrating mainstream consciousness with a sound based on strong drum samples and break beats and lots of heavy guitars, the better to woo rock fans and critics. The duo was to true techno avatars what a knock-off like the Strawberry Alarm Clark was to the psychedelic Beatles, and they never really improved over the course of future releases. Fatboy Slim (a.k.a. Norman Cook, formerly a member of undistinguished English popsters the Housemartins) was perfectly suited to craft music for TV commercials, where he found some of his biggest success, while Paul Oakenfold became a dancefloor sensation by reintroducing old-fashioned disco sexism to the previously well-liberated, pro-woman, pro-gay rave scene.

Much as hip hop became enslaved to gangsta pandering after the initial flurry of musical creativity and psychedelic awakening, techno seems to be stalled in 2002 and missing the visionary forces who will take it to the next level (though they will no doubt arrive in time). Meanwhile, two other members of the class of 1990 continue to stretch the boundaries of the music—one primarily on artistic terms, with one of the most consistent discographies the genre has produced, and the other with his ambition and surprising commercial success.

LITTLE FLUFFY CLOUDS OVER BATTERSEA: THE ORB

> The Orb have a little game they play, designed to limit the
> consumption of drugs to those still coherent enough to get
> a spark across a synapse. Having had his fill of a joint,
> Thrash turns to Alex. "What's the capital of Peru?" "Lima,"
> replies Alex with some satisfaction. Thrash surrenders the
> spliff. "The Orb," explains Alex hazily, "has become a very
> geographically conscious band. Mountain ranges in Africa,
> rivers in Russia, cities in South America—we know 'em all.
> Have to. No geography, no drugs."
>
> —Adam Higginbotham,
> *Details*, 1993

BORN IN 1959, the father of ambient house music was raised in the
Battersea section of south London, home of the evil-looking power
station immortalized on the cover of Pink Floyd's *Animals*. Alex
Paterson's interest in outer space took root early on, fueled by his
father's work on the Telstar satellite. He attended Kingham Hill
School in rural Oxfordshire with future Killing Joke bassist Youth
and went on to spend a year and a half in art school before quitting
to work as a roadie for his friend's band. Paterson spent six years
with the industrial punks, occasionally joining Killing Joke onstage
for an encore of Sex Pistols covers. He wound up as an A&R man at
the band's label, EG Records, but by all accounts, he was a lousy talent scout—he thought the music he heard in his head was better
than everything else he encountered. "The Orb is in essence a collaboration of people I would have liked to work with on an A&R

level anyway," he told David Prince in *Option* in 1994. "It's a completely different way of working in a band structure."

Inspired by the sounds of Eno and others in the EG catalog,
Paterson started recording ambient music as a hobby, but Youth
encouraged him to get more serious. In 1988 he began working at
the studio owned by Jimmy Cauty, Bill Drummond's partner in the
KLF. The result was the *Kiss* EP, four songs based on house samples
from New York radio station KISS-FM. It was released on WAU!/Mr.
Modo, a label started by Paterson and Youth. At the same time
Paterson established an ambient/chill-out room at Land of Oz
dance nights in the London club Heaven. Surrounded by billowing
white sheets and spacey slide projections, he played a mix of EG
ambient records, old progressive rock, and other soothing sounds
so that people could relax and re-energize between trips to the
dance floor. One night he was spinning "Rainbow Dome Music" by
Steve Hillage when Hillage walked in. The two struck up a friendship, and the guitarist later appeared on several Orb recordings.

The Paterson-Cauty Orb started to garner more attention with
a 1989 single called "A Huge Evergrowing Pulsating Brain that Rules
from the Centre of the Ultraworld." The melody came from Minnie
Ripperton's 1975 hit, "Lovin' You," and the title was a tip of the hat
to Pink Floyd's "Several Species of Small Furry Animals Gathered
Together in a Cave and Grooving with a Pict." (It wasn't the last
Floyd homage: Another track was called "Back Side of the Moon,"
and the cover of *Live 93* featured a stuffed sheep flying over
Battersea in place of the pig on *Animals*.) Paterson jokingly called
the sound he was developing "ambient house for the E generation."
The name stuck, though he would later say he preferred "ambient
with attitude."

Unlike more static ambient or New Age sounds, you can dance to the Orb, even on tracks where there aren't any drums. Musically, Paterson mixes slowed-down and sometimes subliminal rhythms with melodic samples and the dub production techniques pioneered by producers Lee "Scratch" Perry and Adrian Sherwood. Philosophically, he combines Eno's ambient ideas with a psychedelic approach to the studio and a punkish sense of humor. "People should get into the album for what it is; have a bit of a laugh, and relax," Paterson said of the group's debut in the *New Musical Express*. "The ambient sides you can go off and cook dinner and listen to it, or water the plants or make love. Whether it's the missing link after Pink Floyd, I don't know. Don't ask me, I'm just enjoying myself."

Paterson appeared uncredited on the KLF's two ambient-house forays, *Chill Out* and *Space*, but he and Cauty parted ways after the Orb scored a hit with "Little Fluffy Clouds," a catchy single featuring a melody nicked from Steve Reich and a vocal sample of Rickie Lee Jones longing for the Southwestern skies of her youth. Cauty

The Ultimate Psychedelic Rock Library: This is not your father's Pink Floyd: The Orb's Adventures Beyond the Ultraworld *(Mercury).*

was replaced by the young engineer Kris Weston, a.k.a. Thrash, and the restructured Orb traced a voyage through the cosmos on 1991's ambitious double album, *Adventures Beyond the Ultraworld*. The group also developed into a powerful live unit with the most elaborate light show since Hawkwind. Paterson turned knobs, tweaked dials, and spun records as Thrash played the mixing console like an instrument. A jazzy rhythm section decorated the clock, blurring the lines between electronic and live instrumental sounds. "It's much like I'm a vocalist in a sense, but I don't actually have to have vocals," Paterson told *Option*. "I just *play* what I want to say. If I want to say, 'Back off' or whatever, I have samples on my keyboards, or I just fuck about on top. There's so many ambient noises around."

The Orb continued exploring outer space on the unprecedented forty-minute single, "The Blue Room," which used sound effects, Hillage's guitar, and Jah Wobble's bass to conjure the sounds of an alien abduction. (The track was named for a room at Ohio's Wright-Paterson Air Force Base which is alleged to hold the remains of crashed UFOs.) The album that followed, *U.F.Orb*, entered the English charts at No. 1, but Paterson seemed to be at a crossroads. He retreated to the studio for more than a year, then released an abrasive six-song "little album" called *Pomme Fritz*. Like the Aphex Twin, he was convinced that many new techno artists were noodlers or wankers, and listeners were unthinkingly accepting self-indulgent crap. "We were simply trying to piss off the people who we didn't want to like the Orb," he told me at the time.

Famous for mapping the cosmos, the Orb returned to terra firma in 1995. *Orbus Terrarum* is Paterson's version of *Another Green*

The Ultimate Psychedelic Rock Library: On Orblivion *(Island), Alex Paterson prepared to greet the end of the world and/or the new millennium with a smile on his lips and a song in his heart.*

World, an aural tour of various geographic locales, but what at first seems like a radical departure is actually tied to earlier efforts by the way the artist uses sounds to create images. "From track to track, there may not be any similarity in any of the Orb's material, but the thing that's always connected is the ambiance," he told me. "It's the most obvious link—textural noises and the idea of using natural sounds and turning them into rhythmic sounds." Even stronger was his next effort, *Orblivion* (1997), which found the good doctor proclaiming that it was the end of the world as we know it and he felt fine. In fact, the disc was the cheeriest album about millennial tension and apocalyptic craziness since Prince's *1999*.

The latest version of the Orb found Paterson collaborating with Andy Hughes and Thomas Fehlmann and returning to the conceptual shenanigans of older songs such as "Little Fluffy Clouds" and "The Blue Room," using well-chosen samples to tell a story and set the scenes for his imaginative, hypnotic soundscapes. Over the ominous sounds of "S.A.L.T.," a paranoid Scottish preacher predicts that the number of the Beast described in The Book of Revelations is showing up on our credit cards. Elsewhere a solemn voice intones, "The rocket is waiting," and a perplexed weather girl stumbles when she reads that temperatures tomorrow will be sub-zero, "continued mild." Throw in a snippet from Senator Joseph McCarthy's red-baiting hearings and an hysterical commercial jingle with a bouncy chorus about "the youth of America on LSD," as well as some of the Orb's happiest hooks ever ("Toxygene," "Molten Love") and a set of uniquely fluid and jazzy mid-tempo grooves and you have the perfect party disc for hunkering down in the bomb shelter. Like the ravers who throw roof-top parties to greet the aliens in the awful film *Independence Day*, Paterson was determined to greet the end of the world smiling, dancing, and high as a kite.

Despite the artistic triumph, Paterson followed the Aphex Twin in retreating from the scene for a while to concentrate on his own label and promote new, low-key recordings via his Web site (www.BlackOrb.com). In 2001 he returned with another strong effort, *Cydonia*, though the ever-faddish dance world now seemed to consider him old hat. To his credit Paterson couldn't have cared less. "We've all got our little niche, and nobody's ever really come anywhere close to what the Orb can do in electronic music," he told me. "Every album has been an experiment for us, rather than a need to make cash and cash in on what they call success or whatever. We've never stayed with the same formula."

Considered by many fans to be a paradigm of modern psychedelia, Paterson remains committed more to an open-minded approach to music than to celebrating drugs or trends. "People have to find their own source of psychedelia," he told me. "You could become a deep sea diver in Thailand, and that could become the most psychedelic experience you could ever imagine. And that's just a natural thing as opposed to putting chemicals in your head." He also refuses to invest his music with higher purpose, despite the obvious care he takes in crafting it. "It's pure escapism; that's all psychedelic music is," he said. "That's what we are and that's what we want to be. At the end of the day when you come and see us live or put a record of ours on, that's what you do: Escape."

THE FACE OF TECHNO: MOBY

> When I was very young I wanted to hang out with the cool kids, and the cool kids were smoking pot and smoking hash; this was like when I was ten or eleven years old. I took acid once when I was in college; I didn't like that much. And then I've taken Ecstasy a few times ….It's very bad for your brain. A week or two after I've taken Ecstasy, I've found myself wondering, like, "What are those things you use to tie up your shoes?" But when I was on the Ecstasy, I enjoyed it very much, I have to say. I am in no way endorsing Ecstasy use or condoning it, because I think it can be very dangerous. But obviously it is popular for a reason.
>
> —Moby, 2002

OFTEN CALLED "THE FACE OF TECHNO," Richard Melville Hall was born and raised in Darien, Connecticut, an upper-class bedroom community fifty miles north of Manhattan. He was nicknamed Moby as a baby in a nod to his great-great-granduncle, *Moby-Dick* author Herman Melville. He studied music and classical guitar, dabbled with hardcore punk in the Vatican Commandos, majored in philosophy at the University of Connecticut, and graduated with two abiding fascinations: Christianity and dance music. "Up until college, I had the typical white, suburban attitude towards dance music," he told David Prince in *Request.* "I'd been told I wasn't allowed to like it, so I didn't. It represented everything foreign and threatening about inner-city culture. It was very threatening to me, but I realized it was also very seductive."

Moby became a DJ in New York in the late '80s, and he began crafting imaginative collages that mixed samples of Stockhausen-style industrial noise, pop fluff like Samantha Fox, and James Brown beats. (Moby, for one, knew that the Godfather of Soul was still alive and kicking.) In 1991 he scored a million-selling hit with the catchy single, "Go," which featured him playing (not sampling) Angelo Badalamenti's theme for *Twin Peaks.* Like the TV show, the song has a surreal and vaguely threatening undercurrent. The influence of psychedelic rock was obvious, even if psychedelic drugs weren't a factor. (Moby lives a drug-free vegan lifestyle.) "I've always liked drug music, subversive music," he told Prince. "I love psychedelic stuff. I have strong psychedelic experiences, but they're not drug-related. Dancing for three or four hours with great lights and great music, the body produces its own drugs."

Touring relentlessly, Moby won notice for his energetic stage shows, which featured him hurling his body around like Iggy Pop and standing atop his keyboard drenched in sweat. But even as he was labeled techno's best live performer, he was turning on the rave scene as stagnant, cliquish, and unimaginative. His major label debut, 1995's *Everything Is Wrong*, tried to break down arbitrary genre boundaries by embracing industrial dance music, old-style house music, and alternative rock. The lyrics were preachy and the music was only partially successful, and the disc didn't win any new fans. *Animal Rights* (1996) was an equally spotty affair. More successful was the 1997 collection, *I Like to Score*, which rounded up the artist's movie soundtrack work, including his unforgettable breakbeat version of the James Bond theme. Sales were lackluster, and Moby was dropped by his label. Undaunted, he retreated to his bedroom studio and began recording an album eventually titled *Play*.

The most successful psychedelic dance record ever (and one of the very best), *Play* charts the emotional connections between early

The Ultimate Psychedelic Rock Library: Moby's Play *(V2) connected on a deep emotional level with an audience far beyond the psychedelic subculture of the rave scene.*

blues and African-American folk music and modern hip hop, as well as early disco and techno/rave music, all within the context of Moby's own distinctly melodic and rhythmically gripping ambient stylings. Inspired by the field recordings of folk historian Alan Lomax, the artist crafted tracks such as "Honey" and "Porcelain" by merging samples of forgotten blues musicians with his own seductive keyboard lines and percolating rhythms, playing all of the instruments himself and programming breakbeats that shamed anything by hip hop chart toppers such as Jay-Z or Busta Rhymes. With eighteen hypnotizing, multi-layered tracks, it was the masterpiece that Moby's fans had been waiting for, but it succeeded far beyond the rave scene, eventually selling some ten million copies worldwide and reaching even the suburban soccer moms in their S.U.V.'s and the football fans who usually preferred Dave Matthews. Its success enabled Moby to launch the ambitious Area:1 tour, the most diverse summer concert festival since Lollapalooza, and that somewhat offset the charges of "sellout" from underground music fans who resented the fact that, in an effort to be heard without the support of radio or MTV, he had sold every track on the album to a different TV commercial or movie soundtrack (and some to more than one).

After the success of *Play*, Moby was in as difficult a position as Pink Floyd following *The Dark Side of the Moon*: Almost anything he did next would be considered a disappointment. Released in 2002, *18* was dismissed by some critics and fans as *"Re-Play,"* but it was hard to blame him for going back to the well, especially when the formula remains stunningly effective. In lieu of sampled field recordings, this time Moby lined up some impressive guest singers and vocal samples, including Sinéad O'Connor, Angie Stone, and

The Ultimate Psychedelic Rock Library: More than Re-Play, 18 is another beautiful, melodic album charting the unraveling of a relationship.

Sylvia Robinson (of Mickey and Sylvia and Sugar Hill Records fame). He also delivered a handful of vocals himself in his endearingly flat monotone. The most effective of these was the first single, "We Are All Made of Stars," a wonderfully catchy mood piece in the mold of David Bowie and Brian Eno's "Heroes." (Moby describes it as an uplifting and romantic ditty that also happens to address quantum physics and the notion that, since 98 percent of the matter in the universe is comprised of hydrogen and helium forged in the furnaces of the cosmos, we are literally all made of stars.) The album also boasted haunting ambient house music ("One of These Mornings") and plenty of what can now rightly be called "Moby music" ("In My Heart," "Signs of Love," "At Least We Tried"), so familiar are his signature melancholy melodies.

Talking with Moby

Richard Melville Hall is one of the most cheerful, self-effacing, intelligent, and funny artists I have ever interviewed, and he never fails to illuminate the methods behind his music. Most of the following interview was conducted in the spring of 2002 before the release of *18*, though some questions date from an early chat prior to the Area:1 tour in 2001.

J.D.: More than a decade into the movement, is there a "real" rave culture anymore?

Moby: Yes and no. My cousin who's sixteen years old goes out to parties all the time and listens to the music and has his own fashion style, and he gets made fun of in school because of it. To me, the litmus test of a subculture is if you get made fun of in school.

J.D.: You've been around long enough to be considered the grand old man of techno. Where do you think you fit into the current spectrum of electronic music?

Moby: A friend of mine was the cameraman on [the techno documentary] *Modulations*. Just to test the waters, one of the questions he'd ask of everyone who was interviewed was, "What do you think of Moby?" This was after I'd made *Animal Rights*, and he said that some people would say, "I think he's an interesting musician and an interesting guy and he makes interesting records." But a lot of people didn't know how they were supposed to respond. There was so much confusion attached to me that they didn't know if they were supposed to like me or not. I've never understood the idea of a musician being content or satisfied working within one limited genre of music. All of my heroes have all done lots of different things.

J.D.: *What was your goal in compiling the lineups on the Area:1 and Area:2 festivals?*

Moby: When I go to people's houses and I see their CD collections, I see that most people's tastes are quite eclectic. I'll walk into my best friend's house, and sometimes he's playing an old Bessie Smith record, and sometimes he's playing a Metallica record. It seems there was a period where things were becoming a little more open musically, but then I don't know what happened. Radio has become a lot more narrow in its focus, and on a very selfish level, I just wanted to put together a festival that I guess to some extent reflected my own musical tastes. When I originally went to [promoters] SFX with the idea of doing this festival, their idea was to do something that was almost exclusively dance-oriented. But I felt sort of uncomfortable contributing to the further balkanization of music. My main goal with the festival is just to put on something that is interesting and eclectic and fun. If in the process I actually sort of encourage people to maybe approach music in a little more of an open-minded way, well, that would be wonderful, too.

J.D.: *You were able to do those tours because of the success of* Play. *Do you have any sense of what it was about that album that connected with so many people? Or is that an unfair question to pose to its creator?*

Moby: It's a fair question, I just don't have an answer! [Laughs] I have no idea. I like it as a record, but it's a weird record, and it doesn't really fit in anywhere. Maybe it just came along at the right time. Maybe people felt comfortable with it, where they wanted a record that was challenging, but also warm and emotional. I think a lot of people felt they could buy this record and feel like they were doing something experimental, but it was also emotionally rewarding.

J.D.: *A photographer friend of mine suggested that the album is the musical equivalent of those Matthew Brady Civil War photos, the ones where the eyes seem to be a window to these people's souls. Have you ever considered that there might have been some inherent magic resonating in those samples of field recordings and old blues records?*

Moby: People certainly focused on the field recordings and the samples, which is fine. But if you really look at it, there wasn't really that much of that stuff on there. I think it was just an eclectic, emotional record that didn't bore people. My biggest complaint about most CDs that I've bought or listened to in the last few years is just that stylistically, from the first track to the last track, there isn't much variation. Sometimes that can work, like that Strokes record; they have a very limited palette, but they use it really well. Other times, like the modern-rock/nü-metal stuff, the first couple of songs will be exciting, but then you never feel the need to listen past song three.

J.D.: *You got a lot of crap for being a sellout or a tool of the great marketing machine.* Newsweek *ran a chart showing how you'd sold every song on* Play *to one or more advertisers or film soundtracks.*

Moby: When *Play* came out, nobody was listening to it for the most part; it was a very obscure, underground record. I had worked long and hard on it, and I wanted people to hear it. I didn't use the machine against itself; I just used it for my own purposes. I hope this doesn't sound like I'm justifying it, but with God as my witness, when it comes to making music, I would never compromise what I'm doing. But once a record is made and you put it out into the world, it's bound to have a complicated life regardless of whether you license it to commercials. Once it's out, I'll do anything in my power to get people to listen to it. I won't compromise the integrity of making it, but as far as bringing it to people, I'm happy to do whatever it takes.

J.D.: *But now this music is associated in many people's minds with the advertisers and their messages. I mean, suppose the first time you heard Mission of Burma's "That's When I Reach for My Revolver"—which you covered—it was as the soundtrack for an N.R.A. commercial?*

Moby: When I discovered Mission of Burma, I was sixteen years old and listening to college radio and reading underground music magazines and hanging out at record stores, and that's how I discovered it. When I discovered the Clash, I was eleven years old, listening to AM radio, and I think "Train in Vain" was a Top 40 record for like a minute. If CBS hadn't serviced it to AM radio and the Clash hadn't done interviews with mainstream magazines, I never would have heard about it. It's not difficult to reach people who are obsessed with underground music—and I'm not denigrating them, because I'm one of them. But there are a lot of people who have difficult jobs or live in remote places or are too young or too old to hang out in underground record stores, and I don't want to penalize them. One thing that made me more comfortable licensing music to commercials was that in 1968, the Doors licensed "Light My Fire" to Ford. At the time, every music critic said, "How dare they? They prostituted their art!" But I dare you to find one person now who listens to "Light My Fire" and thinks of a Ford commercial.

J.D.: *At thirty-six, you are now a bona fide pop star and a "career artist." Can you see yourself at forty-six or fifty-six, going out on tour and singing the songs from* Play?

Moby: Oh, yeah, absolutely. I recorded "Go" in 1990, and I haven't done a single concert where we haven't played it since! I'm a populist. If I'm playing a concert, I want people to be happy. I want them to hear songs that they're familiar with.

J.D.: *But as soon as it started to become successful, you famously turned your back on the early techno or rave scene. You've always had this sort of knee-jerk reaction against any scene that starts to prescribe rigid rules for behavior or put boundaries on musicians' creativity.*

Moby: Unfortunately. I don't know where it comes from, but yes I do. At the inception of a genre or a scene, it's usually very creative and very open. One thing I resent is that when a scene develops, it inherently becomes more conservative. It happened with punk rock, it happened with New Wave, and it happened with the rave scene. Suddenly what was once this open-ended genre becomes a little bit formulated. And I don't know what it is about me, I just have to rebel against that. The idea that this spirit of freedom gets compromised bothers me.

J.D.: *Fair enough, and that streak runs through all of your work. But in many ways,* 18 *can be viewed as* Play, *Part Two. I'm surprised you didn't feel the temptation to confound expectations and do something completely different.*

Moby: After the *Animal Rights* record, I think I kind of got that out of my system. A CD is a form of communication, and I am hoping that people will listen to the music that I make. I want to make it a rewarding experience for them. So now I feel like if I want to make self-indulgent, disturbing music, I would rather do that on my own time.

J.D.: *After years of stylistic dabbling, do you feel as if you've developed a signature "Moby sound"?*

Moby: It's funny, I was talking about this yesterday with another journalist who said that if he wanted to create a caricature of a Moby song, it would be something in a minor key where the chorus might be in a major key, and it would be melodic and rhythmic with the focus more on the emotional aspect…[Laughs] I'm a formula now! But you know, if the Zombies could have written "Time of the Season" ten different ways, that would have been great. When I sit down to write music, I don't necessarily think of it as a formula, I just think, "Wow, this is what I really like." I know if I were a musicologist doing a critical examination of my work, I would say, "He's sort of written five or six songs and given hundreds of variations on them." But at the same time, most of my favorite musicians have done similar things. Roxy Music to me are actually the most wonderful and egregious violators. Half of their catalog involves a descending minor-chord figure, like A-minor to G-major to F-major to E-minor. Literally half their catalog has that chord structure, but it works!

J.D.: *18* is a more structured album than Play. *I hear it as a concept album about relationships.*

Moby: Yeah, and it's funny—the last really serious monoga-mous relationship I had was eight years ago!

J.D.: *So you're projecting yourself into a relationship, then dashing it on the rocks?*

Moby: Yeah. Not intentionally, but I definitely think that for someone who is ending a relationship, or for someone who is in the process of breaking up with someone, this will be an important record for them—as modest as that might sound! [Laughs] It does have this weird melancholy streak in it, and it does have this strange subtext of relationships ending. It's odd—maybe I am just being prescient. Maybe I am about to enter a relationship, and then it will end.

J.D.: *Now you're being paranoid! What I'm saying is that* 18 *is a more straight-forward effort than* Play. *I still don't know what* Play *was really about.*

Moby: Neither do I! I like to make records that have a cohesive sense to them, but at the same time, I don't necessarily have one over-arching theme. Ideally, I just respond to it on a more intuitive level, like, "Does this feel right?" But it doesn't necessarily have to have that meta-text.

J.D.: *To date,* 18 *has sold a fraction of the copies* Play *did. I think I know what you'll say, but are you disappointed at all?*

Moby: I really like being able to play concerts that people can come to. I really like being able to meet people and have them tell me that the music I've made is important to them on some level. The mass level of success is something that I can't comprehend, but at the same time, demographics are comprised of individuals. If you sell ten million records or if you sell ten thousand, it's still just a bunch of individuals who are responding to your work. My goal is just to make music that people respond to, which I think is the goal every writer, photographer, or any creative person has. As long as I can continue making music and reaching people with it, I'm going to be just fine, thank you very much.

SIXTEEN

16

PIGFUCKERS AND SHOEGAZERS:
Psychedelic Guitar Bands in the '80s and '90s

"Bliss" and "noise" are the same thing—a rupture/disruption in the signifying system that holds a culture together ....The pleasure of noise lies in the fact that the obliteration of meaning and identity is ecstasy—literally, being out-of-oneself.

—Simon Reynolds,
Blissed Out

FACED WITH THE MUSICAL INNOVATIONS and growing popularity of hip hop and dance music, some critics in the mid-'80s announced that rock had run its course, and that everything that *could* be done with guitars, bass, and drums *had* been done. The *Village Voice* used the term "pigfuckers" to write off a particular strain of aggressive noise bands, but it was equally dismissive of a broad range of inventive groups that struggled to find an audience through fanzines, college radio, and independent labels. The English music weeklies were slightly more encouraging, but the guitar bands of the early '90s were dubbed "shoegazers" or members of "the scene that celebrates itself," branding them with brooding attitudes and superiority complexes that weren't always there. In fact psychedelic rock lived on through this period in dozens of bands on both sides of the Atlantic. The best referenced the past, often through covers and updates of their predecessors' distinctive sounds, while setting their sights on the future, avoiding the self-imposed constraints of the revivalists. Some survived to thrive in the '90s as post-Nirvana alternative rock became a new mainstream specializing in quirkiness and novelty, while others flourished in the margins, leaving discographies that stand with the most inspired and passionate psychedelic rock of any period.

Hardcore punk was generally considered an opposing camp to the psychedelic revival of the '80s, but the hyperactive subgenre produced several groups that evolved into more expansive sounds. California's straightedge-turned-pothead SST Records was at various times home to Arizona's jam-happy psychedelic country-rockers, the Meat Puppets; Dinosaur Jr., whose guitar squalls could be traced back to hardcore punks Deep Wound, and Das Damen, whose high point was a demented cover of "Magical Mystery Tour" that prompted legal action by the begloved owner of much of the Beatles' publishing, Michael Jackson. But SST's most influential band was the Minneapolis trio, Hüsker Dü. Its cover of Donovan's "Sunshine Superman" on *Everything Falls Apart* (1983) should have been the tip-off, but its competing musical impulses—super-melodic psychedelic rock vs. supercharged hardcore punk—became crystal-clear with a version of "Eight Miles High" released as a single in 1984. The Byrds' original is invested with new meaning as Hüsker Dü tears through the song at breakneck speed with a guitar sound evoking a hundred jets at takeoff. Bob Mould's vocal cracks midway through, and by the end of the song, he's reduced to primal screaming. Where the Byrds celebrated the freedom of the '60s, Mould rages against the repression of the Reagan-Thatcher '80s, as well as the stifling cloak of '60s nostalgia.

Heirs to the twisted Texas tradition of the 13th Floor Elevators, the Butthole Surfers came together at Trinity College in San Antonio in 1981. Living a nomadic lifestyle, shifting personnel frequently, and recording prolifically, the Buttholes explored a noisy vision of psychedelia that was overwhelming, disorienting, full of crude humor, and obsessed with the aesthetics of ugliness. Live, the band revived Hawkwind's nude go-go dancers and light show, adding smoke, fire, and autopsy films checked out of the college library. On album, it created sonic collages with tape loops, samples, two drummers, feedback, distorted vocals, and covers of its heroes, including Black Sabbath ("Sweet Leaf") and Donovan ("Hurdy Gurdy Man"). The group eventually settled at a ranch outside Austin and built its own home studio, allowing main men Gibby Haynes and Paul Leary to indulge in solo projects such as the Jack Officers, a dance effort that Haynes dubbed "hick house." Signing to Capitol Records enabled an inspired pairing with producer John Paul Jones, but the band's later releases don't have the insane energy of the early recordings, and the group began pandering to modern rock radio with a more dance-oriented industrial sound. Not that the Buttholes worry about criticism; "Art is just the last three letters of fart," Haynes is fond of saying.

"We just make sounds that appeal to our own retarded needs and limited wants," drummer King Coffee told me in 2001. "We never really had a sound; we never recorded in one genre. On any one of our records, the sound kind of goes from style to style. It's just our own sense of what makes us laugh and what's scary or humorous at the same time. And after this long a time, I'm incredibly grateful to be involved in a band with such funny people and such killer ideas."

In the wake of Wire-inspired art-punks Mission of Burma, the Boston area produced one school of bands dedicated to focused, melodic guitar workouts (including the Neats, Dumptruck, Big Dipper, and the Blake Babies), and another that was more self-conscious in its ambitious eclecticism (including the Pixies, Throwing Muses, and Christmas). In a class of its own was Galaxie 500, a trio of friends who came together while studying at Harvard University. Taking off from the somnambulant, druggy grooves of the Velvet Underground's "Candy Says" and "Here She Comes Now" (which they covered), the group recorded three strong albums, although diversity isn't among their charms. "The whole band has just been like one long jam on the same theme—it's just that you discover a lot of what you can do with it," drummer Damon Krukowski told me. The group split up in 1990, but its influence lives on in bands such as Low and Bedhead. Krukowski and bassist Naomi Yang went on to record several albums on their own, with the Japanese band Ghost, and as part of the Soft Machine-inspired Magic Hour (whose guitar-crazed leader, Wayne Rogers, has also released several intriguing solo albums as well as numerous efforts by a new band, Major Stars), while Galaxie 500 guitarist-vocalist Dean Wareham formed the more accomplished but sometimes sterile-sounding Luna.

Galaxie 500's albums were all produced by Kramer, a New York underground mainstay whose own musical adventures included the psychedelic studio project Bongwater (who did a great cover of "The Porpoise Song," amid a lot of other inspired noise). Former punk Tim Sommer formed Hugo Largo, an ethereal combo dedicated to lilting music that was part ambient, part pop, and part opera. Across the Hudson River in Hoboken, New Jersey, Yo La Tengo progressed from Velvets- and Feelies-inspired jams, to acoustic folkrock, to hypnotic krautrock drones. Formed from the ashes of a band called Beatnik Beach, Jellyfish made two strong albums of Day-Glo psychedelic pop (*Bellybutton* and its follow-up, *Spilt Milk*) before the key members struck out in different directions (the most intriguing of which was keyboardist Roger Manning's analog-synth band, the Moog Cookbook). Long Island's musical prodigy Kurt Ralske forged a sound that merged bubblegum and sinister atmospherics, recording as a one-man band named Ultra Vivid Scene, and in Livonia, Michigan, a studio trio called His Name Is Alive paired two soaring female voices with Eno-style ambient backings. Both of these acts found outlets on the English independent label 4AD, which was also home to Scotland's influential Cocteau Twins.

Formed in 1981, the Cocteaus honed a distinctive sound based on shimmering walls of Robin Guthrie's heavily effected-guitars, hypnotic drum machine patterns, and Elizabeth Fraser's swooping vocals. Melodies unfold leisurely over long musical passages, and Fraser sings in a mix of English, foreign phrases, and nonsense syllables. The effect is of soothing but erotic psychedelic lullabies, with the exact meaning left to be determined by the listener. "I've always assumed that psychedelic music was kind of to do with the hippie culture, drugs, and anything that was slightly left-field that you could sit in your bedroom, crank up to ten, and smoke a pipe to," bassist Simon Raymonde told me. "In that respect, we are quite a psychedelic band, because a lot of people do that with our music, and we used to do that with our music. That's how we actually created half of it."

Echoes of the Cocteau Twins could be heard in the mid-'90s work of the female-led psychedelic pop quartet Lush. The group was also kindred spirits to a class of English bands that critic Simon Reynolds dubbed "oceanic rockers." Guthrie remixed and produced AR Kane, a duo that, after serving as part of the team behind "Pump Up the Volume" by M/A/R/R/S, cut a path between techno and Miles Davis's jazz-rock fusion. Working as Durutti Column, Vini Reilly made ambient instrumental music that updated Mike Oldfield. After starting out as a synth-pop band, Talk Talk moved to ethereal, orchestrated rock, and Dream Academy offered a more accessible take on a similar sound, scoring hits with "Life in a Northern Town" (produced by David Gilmour) and an acid house cover of John Lennon's "Love" that was clearly inspired by the emergence of the so-called Madchester scene. Two shoegazer-related bands benefited from dark, mysterious front women: The Cranes recorded several discs that mixed Velvet Underground drone with shoegazer atmospherics, while Curve's musical stew included guitar noise, dance grooves, dark gothic moodiness, and airy melodies.

At the turn of the decade the gloomy northern town of Manchester became the center for a wave of bands that straddled the line between psychedelic rock and psychedelic dance music. Chosen because of his work with the Dukes of Stratosphear, John Leckie produced the Stone Roses' self-titled 1989 debut, an impressive hit that its creators were unable to follow up. Inspiral Carpets put its twist on the formula of mechanical dance beats and chiming guitars by adding garage-punk organ, while Happy Mondays were distinguished by funkier grooves, a daft sense of humor, plenty of drug imagery, and some of the dopiest lyrics ever written. Only two Madchester groups developed beyond the original sound, and they were marginally connected to the scene in the first place. The Charlatans progressed from "The Only One I Know," a danceable rewrite of Deep Purple's "Hush," to more soulful and psychedelic R&B. More significant and the best of any of these bands was the Essex group Blur.

The dynamic duo at the heart of the band, vocalist Damon Albarn and guitarist Graham Coxon, met at English art school in the mid-'80s. Drama student Albarn was born to be a psychedelic rocker: His father was the road manager of the Soft Machine, and young Damon used to sit around backstage finger-painting. Blur came together with drummer Dave Rowntree and sex symbol bassist Alex James in 1989. It made its debut with *Leisure* at the height of the Madchester craze, and the album spawned two big English dance-pop hits, "She's So High" and "There's No Other Way." From there the band proceeded to evolve and reinvent itself on each new release, reaching a point a decade into its career where its discography stands as one of the most impressive of the '90s. Its second album, *Modern Life Is Rubbish* (1992), positioned the group as England's answer to the Flaming Lips, delivering a weird barrage of strange chord changes, bizarre sound effects, off-kilter beats, and gonzo lyrics shoe-horned into seventeen indelibly catchy pop songs. In 1994 *Parklife* found Albarn honing his lyrical skills, blossoming into a '90s version of Ray Davies as he satirized social mores while painting warm and funny portraits of quintessentially English characters ("Tracy Jacks," "Parklife," "The Debt Collector").

By this point the band members were superstars in England, and the British press created a not entirely fictitious competition with the cheeky bastards in Oasis, making for the most entertaining rivalry since the Beatles and the Stones. Oasis "won" by dominating the British and American charts, but Blur made the better albums. Oasis was content to build a career on the not-unimpressive feat of replicating and reconfiguring *Revolver*, but despite the filigree, there's evidence to suggest that the band never really understood psychedelia. ("I don't know anything about psychedelic, really," Liam Gallagher told me. "Psychedelic is something you can't really structure, you know what I mean? You try to pinpoint psychedelia and you'll never pinpoint it...Oasis is a rock 'n' roll band. We're never gonna write *Sgt. Pepper's*. We're never gonna write psychedelic music because we don't live in that world anymore. Being psychedelic is what—being a fucking hippie, being a loose free cannon, and you can't be that, you've got to be on your fucking toes these days. The world's a harder place these days, and the kids won't take that.") Blur meanwhile gleefully mixed things up in a most psychedelic fashion. *The Great Escape* (1995) was a lushly orchestrated effort that put a postmodern English spin on *Pet*

Sounds; the band's self-titled 1997 disc turned for inspiration to skewed American indie-rock (notably Pavement), vintage krautrock (Neu! and Can), and the bizarre French pop of the mid-'60s (Serge Gainsbourg), and *13* (1999) was a dark and troubling effort that represented Albarn's search for catharsis in the wake of a bitter split with former soul mate Justine Frischmann of Elastica. All of these diverse efforts put the Kinks, Syd Barrett, the Jam, Julian Cope, Wire, XTC, and myriad other influences into a psychedelic Cuisinart, emerging with a sound uniquely the band's own.

"The trick when you go into the studio is to have all that information and all of those reference points stored in your head and then allow your own creativity to modify them," Albarn told me. "It's a case of stealing as much as possible but not borrowing. At the tail end of the century, there's a wonderful opportunity because there's so much in grasp that's still in touch with what's happening now." The turn of the millennium found the group taking an extended break as Coxon went off to craft low-key psychedelic pop solo records while Album scored a surprise hit with Gorillaz, the cartoon simians behind a catchy and disorienting brand of trip hop. In early 2002, Albarn told me Blur had reconvened to complete a new album strongly influenced by Public Image, Ltd., but Coxon was fired shortly thereafter, and 2003's *Think Tank* was a sleepy disappointment.

Critic Rachel Felder noted the contrast between the Madchester bands and what she called the "miasma bands" that followed. "The point of enjoying bands like the Mondays was to get, as the British put it, out of your head—to take so many drugs you escape your reality," she wrote in *Manic Pop Thrill*. "The miasmics aren't so much concerned with getting away from their problems as with somehow articulating them: actualizing angst and bewilderment with grizzled guitars instead of heavy lyrics." Paving the way for miasma bands such as My Bloody Valentine and much of the Creation Records roster were Spacemen 3 and the Jesus and Mary Chain.

Formed by guitarists Peter Kember (a.k.a. Sonic Boom) and Jason Pierce (a.k.a. Jason Spaceman) at Rugby Art College, Spacemen 3 specialized in dark, droning, Velvets-style mantras that sought spiritual transcendence through noise and drugs on efforts such as 1987's brilliant *The Perfect Prescription*, which boasted a warped cover of the Red Krayola's "Transparent Radiation" (co-titled by the Spacemen as "Ecstasy Symphony") as well as self-explanatory tracks such as "Take Me to the Other Side," "Feel So Good," "Things'll Never Be the Same," and "Come Down Easy." *Playing with Fire* (1989) added a stronger gospel influence, while the band's final release, *Recurring* (1991), embraced Kraftwerk-style synthesized rhythms.

A host of Spacemen-related side projects followed. Bassist Pete Bassman led the Darkside, which emphasized the *Nuggets*-Doors elements of his old group's sound. Sonic Boom formed Spectrum, which moved toward techno, and collaborated with Kevin Shields of My Bloody Valentine in Experimental Audio Research, which created atmospheric ambient music; neither matched the brilliance of his former outfit. *Recurring* veteran Mark Refoy formed Slipstream and released a strong debut that added acoustic folk music to the formula, as well as paying tribute to Kraftwerk with a cover of "Computer Love." Tied to the family tree only as kindred spirits, Croydon's Loop mined similar influences and created brooding drones with the stated intention of evoking a nightmarish acid trip. ("It's been said that taking acid is the closest you can come to schizophrenia," bandleader Robert told Reynolds in *Blissed Out*. "But how do the doctors know? How can you find out what being mad is like?") But the most significant spin-off was Pierce's new band, Spiritualized.

Spiritualized's 1992 debut, *Lazer Guided Melodies*, features transcendent rock spirituals that combine the rolling rhythm of the Velvets' "Ocean" with gospel saxophone and a guitar sound somewhere between the Spacemen's drone and Gilmour's echoed slides. Live shows ebbed and flowed like the tides as members performed on fog-drenched stages lit by vertical columns of white light, evoking revival-tent hysteria with the loud passages and Roman Catholic solemnity with the quieter ones. After a four-year delay, *Pure Phase* added a minimalist string section and jazzier interplay. A studio perfectionist—"For us, it's about striving to make an *Electric Ladyland* every time you do a record," Pierce told me—the album was released with two complete mixes done several months apart, one on the right channel and the other on the left. Despite titles such as "Electric Mainline" and "Medication," the songs advocate escape through the beauty of music rather than chemicals. "All the best things in life fuck you up the most, whether it's lovesickness or drug sickness," Pierce said. "I don't think using music as an escape is a bad thing."

Like Blur's *13*, Spiritualized's third album, *Ladies And Gentlemen We Are Floating in Space* (1997), was a work of catharsis after the romantic split between Pierce and keyboardist Kate Radley. "I don't even miss you / But that's cause I'm fucked up / I'm sure when it wears off / Then I will be hurting," Pierce sang midway through the dense and hypnotizing effort. It originally opened with a title track that rewrote (and psychedelicized) the Elvis Presley hit, "Can't Help Falling in Love," but Presley's estate forced Pierce to take it off the album. Nevertheless, the tale of love and love lost comes through loud and clear, culminating in "Cop Shoot Cop," a disc-closing six-teen-minute collaboration with legendary voodoo pianist Dr. John that mixes the Velvet Underground's "Heroin" with "Sister Ray," touches of *Ummagumma*-era Pink Floyd, and John Coltrane at his free-jazz best.

While the group's first three albums all rank with some of the finest psychedelic rock ever made, Spiritualized remained a cult act in America; ironically, the group's fourth effort was its most successful in the States, though it was the least ambitious. *Let It Come Down* (2001) certainly isn't a bad disc, and it introduced what many consider to be the band's best live lineup, including frequent Julian Cope sideman Thighpaulsandra. But it failed to build on or better any of the band's efforts in the '90s. (Released as this book was going to press, 2003's *Amazing Grace* found the band back on track with its loosest, most immediate recording yet.)

Formed in Glasgow by brothers Jim and William Reid, the Jesus and Mary Chain was another Velvets-inspired group, but the drug references and black attitude were underscored by an early Beach Boys-style pop sensibility. The group debuted with a dramatic sin-gle, "Upside Down," that married an indelible melody with some of the most brutal and psychedelic feedback ever recorded. (It was backed by a twisted cover of Syd Barrett's "Vegetable Man.") The group varied this formula from album to album, sometimes taking a quiet, acoustic approach, and at other times stressing a mechanized dance beat. But although it created dozens of memorable tunes, it never topped that first violent explosion.

The Jesus and Mary Chain left Creation Records after "Upside Down," but the single put the label on the map, and it became one of England's biggest indie success stories (as well as one of the biggest busts). Most Creation releases reflect the psychedelic aesthetic of founder Alan McGee. Born in the Glasgow suburb of East Kilbride, McGee told me that he relocated to London in 1981 "because of the drugs." He booked a club called the Living Room and started Creation as a hobby, taking the name from his favorite '60s rockers. (He also played in a modish combo called Biff Bang Pow!, named for the Creation song.) "It's a totally selfish label," McGee said in his thick brogue. "The whole thing is just my taste." Not every Creation band was worth bragging about; at times the roster included lightweights such as Swervedriver, House of Love, and the Telescopes. But the label was also the English home for the Big Star-inspired Teenage Fanclub and Velvet Crush; Bob Mould's new band, Sugar; genre-hopping, nitrous-inhaling New Jersey brothers Gene and Dean Ween (who created a brilliant, noisy, psychedelic masterpiece with *God Ween Satan*); mod-dressing, venom-spewing Irish brothers Noel and Liam Gallagher (a.k.a. the Beatles tribute band, Oasis); Eugenius, the psychedelic guitar band started by former Vaselines leader Eugene Kelly, and Primal Scream, the '60s-flavored dance group led by former Mary Chain drummer Bobby Gillespie. (The latter's finest moment came with its sixth album, 2000's *EXTRMNTR*, when the group was re-energized by an immersion in the sinister funk of Sly and the Family Stone's *There's a Riot Goin' On*, ticked off by what Gillespie called "America's habit of dropping bombs everywhere and fucking doing what it fucking likes," and goosed by the guest shred-guitar of My Bloody Valentine's Kevin Shields.)

Creation was not without its detractors. "The whole Creation aesthetic seems based in the sad conviction that rock is over, it's been and gone, and that all that's left is to uphold the legacy through the Dark Ages of Plastic Pop," Reynolds contends in *Blissed Out*. "The result is bands like Primal Scream: a living, breathing archive of rock gesture, a mere footnote." But while the best Creation bands lovingly referenced their influences, their music succeeded because it crackled with the energy of the present. The Boo Radleys were a charming Liverpool pop group whose swaggering trumpets and swirling guitars recalled the *Revolver*-era Beatles and The Teardrop Explodes. The band's albums are powered by the smart, droll lyrics, unflagging enthusiasm, and an unerring way with a hook. Its best moment is 1997's *C'mon Kids*, a spirited invitation to join in a truly modern vision of psychedelic rock, one that recognizes that there are no boundaries of any kind in the recording studio, and that a geeky Englishman like vocalist Sice can rap his heart out on a tune like "Fortunate Sons" while chaotic noise guitars can be effectively paired with hip hop rhythms. In "Get on the Bus," Sice sings, "Come on kids / Don't put yourself down / Throw out your arms for a new sound," issuing an invitation not unlike the one proffered by Ken Kesey and the Merry Pranksters three decades earlier.

Slowdive's elegant "cathedrals of sound" were modeled on the Cocteau Twins and Brian Eno (whom they worked with as a producer), but songs such as "Spanish Air" and "Alison" are as strong as anything written by their mentors, and a case can be made that no one has ever made better use of chorused and flanged guitar sounds. Meanwhile the introspective but supremely self-confident Ride came together at Oxford in 1988 with a sound based on moody, atmospheric tunes that were also rhythmically compelling, and which showcased the fiery twin guitars of singers and song-writers Andy Bell and Mark Gardener. From the masterful 1990 album *Nowhere*, the band progressed to more structured and con-cisely tuneful homages to its heroes (including the Byrds, the Who, Kraftwerk, the Incredible String Band, and the Creation via a cover of "How Does It Feel to Feel") on 1994's *Carnival of Light*.

The group split up after its disappointing fourth album, *Tarantula* (1996). Bell returned with a strong self-titled release by a new group called Hurricane #1 as well as helping to craft a strong psychedelic folk album by his beloved Idha (1994's *Melody Inn*) before accepting a new, subservient role as the bassist in Oasis. Gardener briefly fronted a new band called the Animal House with former Ride drummer Colbert, then dropped out of the music scene to travel, spending several months in India. He recently returned with backing from a young band called Goldrush and an alternate incarnation as a solo acoustic act.

"I thought it was a great album, but it's funny because a lot of people who were attached to the earlier Ride noise thing didn't take to that album at all," Gardener told me during a conversation about Ride's psychedelic masterpiece, *Carnival of Light*. "If you like the more psychedelic angle, that was definitely a psychedelic thing—we were in a very psychedelic frame of mind in the studio. [Laughs] It was a psychedelic time for all of us, really. I've always been looking for transcendence. I think certain things in life happen, and you want to be able to feel like that. Obviously, I was experimenting with drugs at that time, but now there are other ways that I can achieve that—yoga and the mantra. But more than that, music has always been the ultimate vehicle for me, my ultimate drug. Wherever I am, I can always put some sort of music on that will help me transcend."

Creation served as a model for England's second great psychedelic indie, Too Pure, founded in 1990 by Richard Roberts and Paul Cox. With the exception of the bluesy P.J. Harvey, the Too Pure bands were inspired by artier psychedelic sounds. Moonshake and th' faith healers were both influenced by Can's monster grooves— the former took its name from a Can song—but they were quick to rail against nostalgia. "It's more the openings that groups like that created that no one's followed up since," Moonshake guitarist David Callahan told Eric Gladstone in *Alternative Press*. th' faith healers split up after two strong albums, and half of Moonshake left to form the jazzy techno unit, Laika, named for the first dog in outer space, but Too Pure's catalog continued to grow with strong releases by the poppy ambient group, See Feel, jazz-rock impressionists Pram, and the prolific Stereolab before the quality finally tapered off.

Like Fritz Lang's 1926 film, *Metropolis*, Stereolab has a vision that's both antiquated and futuristic. The group was formed in 1990 by guitarist Tim Gane and French vocalist Laetitia Sadier after the demise of Gane's indie-pop band, McCarthy. Gane embraces old analog synthesizers, the trademark *motorik* beat of Neu!, and the hi-fi production tricks of '50s "space-age bachelor pad" records, while Sadier sings lyrics that, like the Cocteau Twins', mix real words with nonsense syllables. As with the Feelies' *Crazy Rhythms*, another big influence, Stereolab's songs seem to exist before the group starts playing, and they continue after it finishes. "Sometimes I feel like it's a big block of music and we just chip bits off and record them," Gane told me. In recent years, the band has formed an alliance with Chicago post-rockers Tortoise and taken detours toward funk and trip hop, all while retaining a unique overall sound and identity.

Neither the shoegazer movement nor many of the other inventive sounds that followed in England ever succeeded in capturing the imagination of the American rock mainstream, possibly because, as some critics contended, these sounds were too cerebral, but more likely because the grunge explosion of the early '90s (and the alternative marketing craze that it helped to usher in) was simply too distracting. While none of the Seattle bands were ever entirely devoted to psychedelia, several incorporated the influence along with reclaiming the power and melody of early heavy metal. The Melvins were one of the first, most influential, and noisiest of any of the grunge bands, and the psychedelic spirit could be found in their disorienting productions and leader King Buzzo's gonzo guitar work. Soundgarden nodded at psychedelia on its last album, *Superunknown*, as did the Screaming Trees on theirs, *Dust*, which stands as one of the best psychedelic rock albums of the '90s. Meanwhile, on the fringes of the scene was the Olympia, Washington band Earth, whose mix of psychedelia and metal foreshadowed a wave of stoner rock to come.

Books could be written about many of the modern psychedelic rock groups namechecked so quickly above, but two bands in particular deserve a closer look here. Both are led by auteurs who are products not of privileged art-school backgrounds, but of ordinary middle-class upbringings. They honed their sounds over long periods spent working in relative obscurity in the rock underground, recording quickly and cheaply in the punk D.I.Y. spirit. Both experimented with psychedelic drugs, but they have always been more impressed with the power of imagination, and they prefer a laidback style of living and creating to more fast-paced "rock star" lives. Their stories are indicative of the experiences of psychedelic rock bands in the '90s striving to sustain the "no rules" ideals of a genre that is now four decades old. But most importantly, their music shows just how much can still be done with guitars, bass, and drums.

TO HERE KNOWS WHEN

> Ultimately, where we're all heading in music is a sort of integration of the reality of what it's all about in the end, and that's extremely psychedelic in its purest sense. Music can remind you of what else is out there. It's a guidepost or a stepping stone.
>
> —Kevin Shields, 1995

BECAUSE SEVERAL OF THE SHIELDS CHILDREN wound up in the arts, fans often assume that My Bloody Valentine's founder grew up in privilege. In fact Kevin Shields had an ordinary upbringing remarkable only for its uprooting when he was eleven. Reversing the common trend in immigration, the family relocated from an Irish enclave of Queens, New York, to Dublin, and their father worked for the A&P grocery store chain. "We moved over to Ireland and were completely broke," Shields told me. "We lived in a rented house in a row of rented houses with all the other employees from the store. We lived beside the car-park, and that was our playground." School took a back seat to rock 'n' roll—Shields learned to play guitar by mimicking the down strokes on the Ramones' *It's Alive*—but his parents were supportive enough to let the band rehearse in the living room on Sunday afternoons.

My Bloody Valentine formed in 1983 as a gloomy, mascarawearing goth band enamored of the Cramps, the Doors, and the Birthday Party. Dublin was unreceptive, so the group took the advice of Gavin Friday of the Virgin Prunes and lined up some shows in Europe. The band settled in Germany in 1985 and recorded the *This Is Your Bloody Valentine* EP in Berlin. "The first one was crap," Shields said frankly. Over the course of several more EPs, the group began to construct a wall of noise to rival the Jesus and Mary Chain's, but it was dragged down by David Conway's basso profundo crooning and posing. "The whole thing became a kind of intellectual project around '86, and by '87, it died," Shields said.

Relocating to England, Shields regrouped with veteran drummer Colm O'Ciosoig and new member Bilinda Butcher on guitar and vocals. The band started over with a pair of 1987 EPs, *Strawberry Wine* and *Ecstasy*. These ushered in a new, optimistic vibe reminiscent of Love's sunny psychedelia, but Shields was "still in this apologetic frame of mind, not just going for it, wherever your imagination takes you." In 1988 the band signed to Creation and finally went for it. *You Made Me Realise* was the first time Shields felt totally in control. The EP introduced what he called "glide guitar" (strumming the guitar while holding the tremolo arm, or whammy bar, a relic of the surf era, so that the tuning is shifting slightly all the time). "In '88 a lot of elements came together at the same time, and a lot of extreme things happened," Shields said. "What I did then was virtually invent my own way of playing. It didn't come about in any conscious way; it just came about from messing around on borrowed equipment. It felt playful, but on a much stronger level. Everything was adding up, and I was twenty-five then....Everything starts to come in and you go, 'God, what was I messing around with before?'"

This approach solidified on a second EP and a 1988 album, *Isn't Anything*, engineered by Hawkwind and Amon Düül II veteran Dave Anderson. Critic Rachel Felder proclaimed the group king of the miasma bands, while Simon Reynolds credited it with developing "a new and private lexicon of sounds and effects—shapeless surges, swathes, precipices, vortices, wraiths, and detonations." Shields was happy to explain his tools, including glide guitar and the backwards reverb setting of his Yamaha digital effects machine, but he wasn't above a little impressionism himself. "The thing is, the sound literally isn't all there," he told Reynolds in *Blissed Out*. "It's actually the opposite of rock 'n' roll. It's taking all the guts out of it; there's no guts, just the remnants, the outline. It's like—did you ever walk around in the city on a Sunday, somewhere like the East End or the Angel?—and there's this dead, where-is-everybody feel....That kind of deserted feel. Not spooky; you are not made uncomfortable. But you're not comfortable either."

*The Ultimate Psychedelic Rock
Library: My Bloody Valentine's
Isn't Anything (Warner Bros.)
is the album where sonic architect
Kevin Shields felt that it finally
"all came together." But the
band's ultimate masterpiece
was yet to come.*

Like the Cocteau Twins, the Valentines rarely write songs that
are "about" anything. The words are often inaudible, and the vocals
are placed behind the wall of guitars. Adding to the mystery is the
lazy way that they're sung. "Often when we do vocals, it's seven-
thirty in the morning; I've usually just fallen asleep and have to be
woken up to sing," Butcher told Reynolds. "I'm usually trying to
remember what I've been dreaming about when I'm singing." Song
titles such as "Feed Me with Your Kiss," "Soft as Snow (But Warm
Inside)," and "To Here Knows When" combine with the mood of
the music to offer clues about the band's recurring themes: lustful
yearning, the longing for blissful escape, and feelings of overwhelming alienation.

Repeating the pattern they had just established, the Valentines
recorded two more work-in-progress EPs—1989's *Glider* and 1990's
Tremolo—paving the way for the next full album. Released in 1991,
Loveless was the culmination of everything the group had attempted. Writing in *Request*, critic David Sprague called it "part *Metal*

*The Ultimate Psychedelic Rock
Library:* Loveless *(Warner Bros.)
is quite simply one of the most
unique, imaginative, and
otherworldly rock albums ever
made. It's a vocal record whose
influence grows by leaps and
bounds with the passing of time.*

Machine Music and part *Pet Sounds.*" Shields abandoned the near-
mono mix of *Isn't Anything* in favor of a shifting and thoroughly disorienting stereo soundscape. It's the sound of bed spins—or a psychedelic rush. "I think it was influenced a little bit too much by
Ecstasy culture," Shields told me. "A lot of the melodies and the kind
of hook lines that come from the instruments are extremely dinky
and toy-like. For me, that was the after-effects of experiencing too
much Ecstasy....I love dance music; that was when De La Soul came
out, and it was all such a happy sound." But not everybody was
happy. The album was crafted over a three-year period, requiring the
services of sixteen engineers and costing Creation 250,000 pounds.
"I don't cry, but it drove me to tears, just drove me insane," label
head Alan McGee told the *New Musical Express* in 1995.

Three months after *Loveless* was released, the Valentines and
Creation parted ways. The group spent a year on the road, touring
in support of *Loveless* and earning a reputation as the loudest band
anyone had ever seen. "A lot of what we've done is perceived by

people as coming from somebody who's not quite sane, or a bit woozy or dreamy," Shields said. "That's why when we play live, it's quite aggressive or confrontational....What I do is about consciousness, being conscious of a feeling in my whole body. The trouble with the attitude toward psychedelic music is that it's about your head only. And to me, all non-Western people when they get into altered states of mind, it's the whole body that's involved."

When the Valentines finally returned to London, they signed to Island in England and invested their advance in building a home studio. The group ran into equipment problems, and time dragged on. There were rumors that Shields was making a jungle record, that bassist Debbie Googe had been seen driving a cab around London, and that the band would never finish whatever it was that it was working on. "That's one of the great misconceptions about this band, that everything is intellectual and there's an awful lot of time spent in the studio perfecting things," Shields told me in the summer of 1995. "Everything you ever hear on our records, virtually all the overdubs are first-take stuff, and all the guitar parts are first or second take. It's more like capturing the moment. For me, everything hinges on one critical thing, and that's being in an inspired state of mind."

During that conversation, Shields promised a new My Bloody Valentine album by the end of the year, and a long career thereafter. "Too often when people make good records, there's an aftershock effect, and they collapse psychologically and emotionally, " he said. "Brian Wilson is a classic case of that. I'm trying to prove that you can make genuinely interesting music and come out with new ideas without an emotional drain to the point where you break down. I

could make another record that would top the others we've made—
I've been ready to for a while now—but to me it's extremely important to make that record in such a way that I'll be able to make
another one. For lots of small, petty, human reasons that I won't go
into, I'd like to be around in five years' time, making better and better records."

Unfortunately, the followup has yet to arrive more than seven
years after those comments and eleven years after the release of
Loveless. With the exception of a handful of cameo appearances
over the last decade (most notably a cover of Wire's "Map Ref. 41°N
93°W" on the Wire tribute album, *Whore*), My Bloody Valentine has
been completely absent from the music scene, though as with the
music of Syd Barrett or Roky Erickson, the influence of *Loveless* has
only grown with the passing of time. Musicians ranging from Brian
Eno to Billy Corgan and from Radiohead to Trey Anastasio of Phish
have hailed it as a masterpiece, and it is no exaggeration to say that
the forward-looking sounds of this unique disc have positioned the
band as one of the most influential and inspiring rock groups since
the Velvet Underground.

TURN IT ON

> When people say psychedelia, it's been tainted by tie-dye
> shirts and people smoking dope. We think of it as cine-
> matic music; it gives you something to think about, and
> there's all this imagery within in it. People who record
> Christmas music have all this imagery: You hear bells and
> the swishing of sleighs and horse hooves and angels. These
> are visual references you can turn into sound because
> you're trying to get a mood across. That's us. We're the
> band that's always making a Christmas record.
>
> —Wayne Coyne

IN EARLY APRIL 1995, the Flaming Lips had been hunkered down
for six weeks at Studio 7, a big, squat building located on the wrong
side of the tracks dividing Oklahoma City's north and south sides.
(The Murrah Federal Building, which would be torn apart be
Timothy McVeigh's fertilizer bomb two weeks later, was only about
a mile away.) Guitars, percussion toys, a pedal steel, orchestra bells,
some old analog synthesizers, a Fender Rhodes piano, a Hammond
organ, and even a hurdy-gurdy were all piled about the main
recording room. Steven Drozd's drums were set up in another brick-
walled room in front of a giant, tacky mural that looked like something from a hippie day-care center, and two dozen broken sticks
littered the floor. (A monster drummer, Drozd has to duct-tape his
headphones to his head so they won't fly off when he plays.) In a
separate vocal booth were an impressive pile of cigarette butts, a big
collection of Bob Dylan lyrics, and William Joyce's children's book,

Santa Calls. ("For inspiration," Coyne said.) In the cluttered lounge, Jean-Luc Godard's in-studio film about the Rolling Stones, *Sympathy for the Devil*, played on the VCR.

The night before I arrived, Coyne recorded vocals and acoustic guitar for "Brainville University, Tuition One Dollar," which started as a hokey tune that sounded a bit like Rick Nelson's "Garden Party." Over the course of the next sixteen-hour day, a dozen guitar and vocal overdubs turned the song into a two-minute, seventeen-second minisymphony. Time and again, band members stopped to ask, "That's not another song, is it?" or "This hasn't been done before, has it?" (They don't mind borrowing from rock history, but only as long as it fits into something that's entirely their own.) At one point everyone in the studio (including me) was pressed into recording some handclaps for the end of the tune. A passionate debate followed about how engineer Dave Fridmann should make the clapping sound. Lead guitarist Ronald Jones favored the giant handclaps of Queen and the Cars. Coyne preferred the loose clapping on the first Stooges album. Finally, Drozd pulled out a CD of David Bowie's *Hunky Dory* and played "Andy Warhol." Everyone agreed that *that* was the way handclaps should sound, and work moved on. "The best part about working the way we do is that you can never do anything wrong," Coyne said in his charming Will Rogers drawl.

The youngest of six children, the driving force of the Flaming Lips grew up in a lower-middle-class Catholic family surrounded by Baptists in what's often called the buckle of the Bible Belt. He didn't go to college, but he was drawn to the University of Oklahoma in neighboring Norman when some enterprising rock fans began hosting hardcore punk shows in the early '80s. He started the band with his brother, Mark, and bassist Michael Ivins. They bought a PA that had been stolen from a cowboy bar, and they hauled it to gigs by touring groups like the Meat Puppets. In return they got into shows for free and learned about the indie-rock ritual of making your own album and selling it at gigs while touring the country in a van. They chose the name Flaming Lips for its random weirdness and decided to join in the fun by trying to be a band themselves.

In 1985 Coyne's dad was selling office products, and he had accumulated credit under the barter system from a studio specializing in Christian jingles. Wayne, Mark, Ivins, and drummer Richard English went into the studio in the middle of the night and recorded a self-titled six-song EP released on the band's own Lovely Sorts of Death Records. The name was borrowed from the poster for the '60s acid-exploitation flick, *The Trip*, and though the initials spelled "L-S-D," Coyne was never indulgent in his use of psychedelic drugs. "I've done acid probably three or four times, and one of them I don't think counted because it was shitty," he told me with characteristic frankness. "I think that's the great misconception about our music. People think, 'The only way you could do that is to be on drugs.' If you look for the influence of drugs on our music, it's like looking for a UFO. You'll probably find it. But it has always been more about propelling the ideas away from what's boring."

Early on none of the band members was a virtuoso, but that didn't bother them. "We've always figured that, if we can't play our instruments, at least we can come up with some weird ideas no one's done before," Coyne said. The Lips toured for a while, Mark quit, and eventually the independent Restless Records offered the band a contract. The three-man Lips released three albums: *Hear It Is* (1986), *Oh My Gawd!!!…The Flaming Lips* (1987), and *Telepathic Surgery* (1989). The company never gave the Lips much money, so they never had a choice besides making records in intense two- or three-day bursts. "We never called it punk rock, that was just all the money and all the time we had," Coyne said. For the most part, the Lips came across as a druggier version of the Replacements, but the albums had hints that the band was capable of much more, including the Pink Floyd-inspired "One Million Billionth of a Millisecond on a Sunday Morning," the lulling "Jesus Shootin' Heroin," and the crushing "Godzilla Flick."

English quit midway through the tour supporting *Telepathic Surgery*, and Coyne and Ivins finished the remaining gigs as a duo. They considered packing it in, but Coyne had just signed a publishing deal and gotten a ten-thousand-dollar advance. They decided to spend it by going out in a blaze of glory. Jonathan Donahue, a Lips fan from Buffalo, New York, had hopped in the van during that last ill-fated tour, joining the group as soundman. When Coyne and Ivins reassembled the Lips, Donahue became the second guitarist and Nathan Roberts joined on drums. "We did *In a Priest Driven Ambulance* thinking it was the last record we were ever gonna do," Coyne said. "There'd been a bad accident, and the priest was on his way, but there was also a slight glimmer of hope, so the ambulance had been called as well. We wanted to make one album that really sounded like we wanted it to sound, and we really liked the idea of breaking free of that whole thing where independent bands spend fifty dollars making shitty-sounding records." The group worked at a studio in Buffalo staffed by students, including their producer,

Fridmann. "These were guys who wanted to be engineers. They liked us giving them challenges. It wasn't like dreading going into the recording studio. We'd wake up every day and ideas would be flying out of everybody's heads. We could set up an amp and put a mike sixty feet down the hall just to see how it sounded. After that, we didn't want to make a record ever again if we had to do it the old way."

In a Priest Driven Ambulance is the Lips' first masterpiece. It takes familiar influences such as the Stooges, the Velvets, and Pink Floyd and twists and contorts them like images in a funhouse mirror in tunes such as "Shine on Sweet Jesus," "Unconsciously Screamin'," and "Five Stop Mother Superior Rain," gonzo psychedelic noise fests that are also insanely catchy. Unfortunately, Restless nearly folded just as the album was released, and it was impossible to find it in stores. Around the same time, longtime manager and booking agent Michele Vlasimsky threw up her hands and quit. Managing the band fell by default to Scott Booker, a fan who was running Oklahoma City's one cool record store.("Basically, the Lips liked me

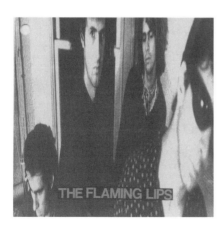

The Ultimate Psychedelic Rock Library: After nine tracks of psychedelic fury, the Flaming Lips ended In a Priest Driven Ambulance *(Restless) with a beautiful, tender cover of Louis Armstrong's "What A Wonderful World."*

'cause I had a phone," he said.) Just when things were looking bleakest, Booker got a call from Warner Bros. executive Roberta Peterson, the woman who signed Jane's Addiction. Other staffers had been raving about the Lips' indie releases and wild stage shows featuring smoke and bubble machines and thousands of blinking Christmas lights. Peterson offered the group a contract.

"We were like, 'We're glad you like us and all that, but we just wanna make records like the last one,'" Coyne said. "They said, 'Sure!' But we kept thinking there had to be some catch." There was, and it came in the sort of corporate red tape that the Lips had never dealt with before. Working with Fridmann, they recorded another strong and twisted album, *Hit to Death in the Future Head*. They delivered it to Warners, and then—nothing. The band waited for the better part of a year as lawyers tried to get copyright approval from conductor Michael Kamen. It seems the group was watching a videotape of Terry Gilliam's 1985 film *Brazil* during the recording, and a bit of the soundtrack made its way onto "You Have to Be Joking (Autopsy of the Devil's Brain)." The Lips liked this happy accident too much to fix it, but it took forever to get the sample cleared. (The band got their revenge on the company by tacking on a thirty-minute "bonus track" of grating noise and following the album with an EP titled *Wastin' Pigs Is Still Radical*—this at the height of the Warners Bros.-Ice-T "Cop Killer" controversy.)

By the time *Hit to Death in the Future Head* was released in mid-1992, Roberts had quit the band and Donahue had returned to Buffalo to form Mercury Rev. Slightly derivative of the Lips and initially suffering from an über-indie, too-cool-for-the-room attitude, Mercury Rev's first three albums, *Yerself Is Steam* (1992), *Boces*

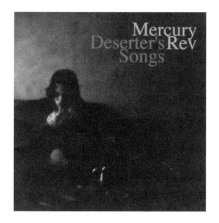

The Ultimate Psychedelic Rock Library: Deserters' Songs *(V2) is the finest offering from Flaming Lips offshoot Mercury Rev. "People tend to look at both bands as competing with each other," Jonathan Donohue told me. "For the most part, we're just different branches off the same tree."*

(1993), and *See You on the Other Side* (1995) were psychedelic fun, but certainly not earth-shaking, with the most distinctive element being David Baker's slightly deranged vocals. The fourth time out, the group crafted its own masterpiece. *Deserter's Songs* (1998) found Donohue taking over as vocalist, seeking catharsis from his romantic woes, and enhancing the group's sound with everything from orchestral instruments to bowed saws. The result was not unlike Phil Spector's "Leader of the Pack" reimagined on DMT. "Leading up to this record for three years we went through some tough times, [guitarist] Grasshopper and I, just the way old friends sort of fall in and out of love over and over again," Donahue told me. But despite the troubles that inspired it, the record is oddly uplifting, and supremely psychedelic. "A lot of people tend to use the word psychedelic as a direct comparison to some of the late '60s wah-wah-toting, mumbo-jumbo drug reference, but for us, in a positive light, psychedelic means something that stimulates more of the senses than just the aural ones," Donahue said. "Maybe you're seeing something in your mind when you're listening to our record that has nothing to do with our music. That's the music that generally we love; music you can listen to without thinking of the music itself. It reminds you of something else."

Meanwhile, back in Oklahoma, the Flaming Lips were in need of a new guitarist and drummer, and Jones and Drozd came onboard. Born in Hawaii to African-American and Filipino parents, Jones wound up in Oklahoma when his father was transferred by the Air Force. He taught himself to play guitar in his bedroom, developing a swirling calliope sound by using racks of effects and ingenious tricks such as placing a small speaker next to his pick-ups to create a roar like a million electric razors. (His role in the Lips was similar to Brian Eno's in Roxy Music or Allen Ravenstine's in Pere Ubu, transforming the ordinary into art by injecting the unexpected, and Steve Hackett of Genesis was a particular hero.) Drozd attacked his kit with the bombastic ferocity of vintage John Bonham or Bill Ward, but he was also an accomplished piano and guitar player. "Those guys are both such amazing musicians, I feel sorry that they're stuck with a singer like me," Coyne said, referring to his plaintive Neil Young whine. But the combination worked, resulting in the band's best live lineup, and another studio triumph.

The reconfigured Lips produced *Transmissions from the Satellite Heart*, the band's most accessible collection. At their core, songs such as "She Don't Use Jelly" and "Pilot Can at the Queer of God" are simple, catchy rock tunes, albeit ones with highly impressionistic lyrics. The magic comes from the twists and turns and the band's dense wall of sound, which can hold surprises even after dozens of listens. "Moth In the Incubator" is a perfect example. It starts as a

The Ultimate Psychedelic Rock Library: The Flaming Lips scored a most unlikely hit with "She Don't Use Jelly" from Transmissions from the Satellite Heart *(Warner Bros.).*

lonely acoustic number with Coyne singing, "Something in you / It titters like a moth." Soon the band kicks into a grinding T. Rex-style riff full of sexual bravado. "Your incubator is so tight / Your incubator is alright," Coyne sings. "Been born before / I'm gettin' used to it / Brain-dead is how it always ends." The song launches into a wonderful hum-along instrumental that builds in intensity as Coyne and Jones pile on layers of harmonics with guitars that buzz like an army of insects on the move, until it finally climaxes in an explosion of dissonance, an epic evocation of nature's cycle of birth, death, and rebirth.

Transmissions was released in mid-1993, and when alternative-rock radio passed on the single, "Turn It On," Warners shifted its attention to the next piece of product in the pipeline. "This was a dead, dead, dead record," one executive said. Coyne, then thirty-four, and Ivins, thirty-two, knew that this was probably their last shot at making a major-label album. *Hit to Death* had sold only sixteen-thousand copies, which was dismal by indie standards, let alone a major's. The Lips were determined to convert fans one gig at a time, so they toured relentlessly. The work began to pay off in the fall of '94 when novelty-starved modern-rock radio started playing "She Don't Use Jelly," finally realizing the potential of an irresistibly catchy ditty about tangerines, toast, Vaseline, and Cher. The video that Warners scoffed at because it was directed by Coyne for a mere $12,000 wound up in MTV's Buzz Bin. The band was soon appearing on *The Late Show with David Letterman*, contributing a song to the *Batman Forever* soundtrack, and even guesting as the band performing at the Peach Pit on *Beverly Hills 90210*, a move roughly comparable to Amon Düül II appearing on *The Brady Bunch*.

Coyne had spent eleven years working as a fry cook at Long John Silver's before the Flaming Lips became successful enough circa *Transmissions* for him to finally quit his day job. The band was in an enviable position when they started recording *Clouds Taste Metallic*. "We're lucky in the regard that this time, if it flops, it's the record company's fault," Coyne said. "We can't lose now. If

The Ultimate Psychedelic Rock Library: Clouds Taste Metallic *was less successful than* Transmissions, *but it was still an ambitious, upbeat, and typically fabulous Flaming Lips effort.*

we sell a million records, fine. If we sell fifty-thousand, it just looks they fucked up. But it doesn't make doing records any easier, because all that shit really doesn't matter."

True enough. At Studio 7, no one ever mentioned Warner Bros. or MTV or modern-rock radio. The band concentrated on having fun with the business at hand, crafting thirteen more brilliant and diverse songs for the alien hit parade. Less in-your-face than *Transmissions*, *Clouds* was a sprawling work full of different moods and atmospheres but never lacking strong melodies or rock 'n' roll drive. "The Flaming Lips' music, if it's done right, can reach some guy who walks in off the street liking Lynyrd Skynyrd, Led Zeppelin, and the Stone Temple Pilots," Coyne has always said. "He can hear Flaming Lips music and not understand that it's being subversive or weird and just think it's good rock 'n' roll. Whereas it's a stretch to be a normal guy and listen to some Sonic Youth or Pavement records."

This attitude may come from where the band lives: There's simply no room for pretensions in Oklahoma City, and Coyne doesn't plan on moving. He and his girlfriend, J. Michelle Martin, are the proud owners of a sprawling two-level brick building that's vaguely in the style of Frank Lloyd Wright. It stands out in the somewhat grim Classen Ten Penn neighborhood—with its rows of ramshackle ranch houses with cars on cinder blocks and babies playing in the dirt in their diapers in the front yards—even before you notice the gargoyles on the roof, the stained glass windows, and the giant flower sculptures on the balcony. Most people call the house "the compound," but Coyne prefers "stately Wayne manor." When I visited him there for the second time, in the spring of 2002, the place had gotten even stranger: This time, Coyne had built a space station in the backyard.

Clouds failed to match the success of *Transmissions*, and the band foundered for a time after its release, uncertain of where to go next. Jones quit the band to pursue a career in aromatherapy. Sensing that it would be impossible to replace him, Coyne took the Lips in a strange and very different direction. A few years earlier, he was walking through a stadium parking lot before a big-time rock concert and he noticed the strange effect that came from different speakers in different cars blasting the same tune at the same time. He began conducting what he called "parking lot experiments," rounding up as many as forty cars at a time, arranging them in covered parking ramps (the acoustics were better indoors), and distributing a different numbered cassette to each car. The drivers would roll down their windows, turn their stereos up full blast, and hit "play" on Coyne's cue as he stood in the center of the garage on a stepladder, shouting instructions through a bullhorn while wearing a ratty yellow raincoat. Songs such as "The March of the Rotting Vegetables" came together in a surreal swirl as a different instrument blared from each car, and listeners were encouraged to walk around to experience the sound from different perspectives, letting the songs envelop them.

From there the Lips took the experiments indoors with the "boom box symphonies," recruiting as many as a hundred members of the audience to sit onstage with boom boxes on their knees. The recorded result of all this lunacy came in 1997 with *Zaireeka*—the title combined "Zaire" and "eureeka"—a four-CD set in which all four discs were intended to be played simultaneously. It was essentially a '90s update of a '60s happening in a handy box set. "The idea that you got your friends over there all pressing CD players all at the same time—that in itself has an element of entertainment about it," Coyne told me. "To say, 'O.K., we're doing this, and I don't know why.' If people perceive this as something that you participate in, and it's different and unique and it *does* take a bit of a hassle—well, instead of looking at that as being bad, if people think that's cool, then maybe they'll like it."

When the Lips returned with their next proper album, the band was still a trio, with Drozd taking over on most of the instruments. ("Steven's somebody who's really of the caliber of a Stevie Wonder," Coyne says.) *The Soft Bulletin* (2000) introduced a new, complex sound; on tunes such as "The Spiderbite Song" and "The Spark That Bled," swarms of insects buzzed stately grand pianos, mysterious voices echoed in the ether, and a string section sawed away from the bottom of a pool filled with Jell-O. Meanwhile Coyne abandoned the old surrealistic approach to the lyrics in favor of much

The Ultimate Psychedelic Rock Library: The Lips went ork-pop and turned from surrealism to straightforward statements from the heart on The Soft Bulletin *(Warner Bros.).*

more direct commentary on love and the human condition. The album's key line: "Looking into space, it surrounds you / Love is the place that you're drawn to."

"I felt that after *Zaireeka, The Soft Bulletin* really would be our last record," Coyne told me. "I thought, 'Well, you've really painted yourself into a corner this time, you may as well go out with something to say.'" He poured his heart out and people responded, but he wasn't content with creating a studio masterpiece or a cult favorite; the psychedelic populist set about the challenge of bringing his strange new music to the masses. He wound up with a multi-media extravaganza that found the Lips taking the stage as more of a performance troupe than a rock band. Live instruments joined digital backing tracks, roadies and friends dressed as giant furry cartoon characters danced on the sides of the stage, a giant video screen flashed images of Leonard Bernstein "conducting" the band, confetti flew everywhere, and Coyne stood front and center amid the jolly chaos, cheerfully pouring his heart out. From there it was only a short leap for the Flaming Lips to make their first feature film.

When I arrived at Coyne's house for my second visit, a dozen young artists and aspiring filmmakers had turned out on a windy spring evening to help the band film a scene for *Christmas on Mars*. They gathered around a ten-thousand-gallon white plastic tank some twenty feet long and eight feet in diameter. The giant cylinder was intended to be buried beneath a gas pump, but Coyne had drilled holes in it, rigged it with tubing, wiring, and discarded computer parts, and paired it with some upended acrylic hot tubs and a revolving darkroom door. He had effectively transformed a pile of junk into something out of *2001: A Space Odyssey* as re-envisioned by David Lynch.

Among those waiting to begin filming was Steve Burns, an ambitious young actor from Brooklyn best known as the wide-eyed guy in the striped polo shirt from *Blues Clues*, the enormously popular Nickelodeon kids' show where he helped a big blue cartoon canine solve puzzles and riddles. He was at a party on the Lower East Side when he first heard *The Soft Bulletin*, and he left, ran to the record store, and bought a copy on the spot. He didn't hesitate for a second when Coyne asked him to drive half way across country to make a movie in his backyard. "It's not that I drove across country to be in a guy's gas tank; I drove across country to be in the *Flaming Lips'* gas tank-pod-space-shuttle-thing," he told me. "I had an opportunity to do it, and I'd have driven all the way to California to be in this film."

Coyne has that sort of effect on people. From a certain carpenter and his twelve disciples to Ken Kesey and his Merry Pranksters, history is full of enthusiastic kooks who convinced people to drop everything to help them pursue their whims. The word "charisma" derives from a Greek term meaning "a gift that flows from God's benevolent love." To his credit, the charismatic Coyne will truck no mystical theorizing. He doesn't want to be anybody's guru. "I'm glad people believe in me, but I earn their belief by working hard," he said. "I think they get here and they go, 'You know, this isn't magic. This guy is the first one up, he's the last one to leave, and if he's gonna do it, I can do it.'" But to hear his bandmates tell it, Coyne's appeal is a bit more complicated than that. "I could never do anything on my own that would be as good as what I can do with Wayne," Drozd told me. "He's just really good at selling an idea—so good that you don't even know you're being sold." Added Ivins: "Wayne has just always been, 'I have this idea...' and it's like magic, where he thinks of something and it becomes real. Who knows what he could have been three hundred years ago? He could have been a Napoleon or the guy in charge of building the pyramids. We're in the entertainment industry, so we don't get sphinxes or pyramids or Waterloos. But that same sort of drive and the constructive channeling of energy is what it's all about."

Hence the movie in progress in the backyard. Even before the Lips completed their tenth album, *Yoshimi Battles the Pink Robots*— which augments the orchestrations of *The Soft Bulletin* by adding more electronics while ironically standing as a concept album about the triumph of the human spirit over techno-fascism— Coyne was angling to convince Warner Bros. to pony up a hundred grand to fund the full-length feature film, which he hopes the company will release on DVD in 2004. He was shooting *Christmas on*

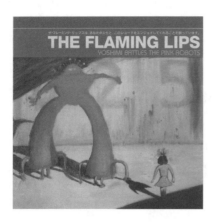

The Ultimate Psychedelic Rock Library: Yoshimi Battles the Pink Robots *(Warner Bros.) is the most eloquent voicing of Wayne Coyne's philosophy yet. "Do you realize that everyone you know someday will die / And instead of saying all of your goodbyes / Let them know you realize that life goes fast; it's hard to make the good things last,"* Coyne sings.

Mars without a script, but he did have a two-page outline. In it, a depressed crewman (Drozd) may or may not be loosing his mind when he encounters an alien (Coyne in greenface and antennae), who helps celebrate the first Martian Yule after the astronaut who was to have played Santa (Ivins) commits suicide. Coyne doesn't read science fiction, and he isn't particularly obsessed with sci-fi films. It just seemed like the right vehicle to convey a particular feeling that he calls "the benevolent joyous moment." "Movies are such a powerful medium because you can elevate a moment beyond actual emotion to super-emotion," he said. "Even if it's badly done, you see *My Dog Skip*, and he dies, and you know it's a movie, but you still cry because it's that powerful. I think this movie is about the idea of belief—that if people around you believe in you, it influences what you do."

This, of course, sounds like the Wayne Coyne story, and the auteur doesn't disagree. More than drug use or cosmic concerns, it is this philosophy that positions the Flaming Lips as one of the prime modern inheritors of the storied forty-year legacy of psychedelic rock. The group continues to pursue its own unique path, whether that involves a forty-car symphony or touring as the inspired backing band (like Neil Young and Crazy Horse or Bob Dylan and the Band) for reformed alternative-rock loser Beck. "Success is living a good life," Coyne told me. "This is how we wanna live our lives. I don't think people have to agree with it or anything. We just do our trip. Hopefully, the main thing the Flaming Lips stand for is individuality in a sea of conformity—even if conformity isn't what it used to be."

Thirty Great Psychedelic Rock Albums from the '80s and '90s

1. Blur's **Modern Life is Rubbish** (EMI) may have been a stylistic mess, but it was valuable psychedelic garbage nonetheless.

2. The self-titled **Blur** (EMI) introduced elements of American indie rock and krautrock to the band's veddy English sound.

3. The Boo Radleys' **Everything's Alright Forever** (Capitol) is classic shoegazer rock: danceable, driving, disorienting, but melodic.

4. On ***C'mon Kids*** (Polygram), the
   Boo Radleys issue a call to a new
   generation to hop onboard the
   psychedelic bus.

5. The Butthole Surfers were angry,
   subversive, and ***Pioughd*** (Capitol),
   but charmingly psychedelic
   nonetheless.

6. John Paul Jones was at the helm for
   the Butthole Surfers' ***Independent
   Worm Saloon*** (Capitol), but that
   didn't make things any less freaky.

7. ***Treasure*** (Capitol) was the strongest
   of the Cocteau Twins' early releases,
   a perfectly realized dreamscape.

8. The Cocteau Twins gave us their last truly great album on **Heaven or Las Vegas** (Capitol), which included their best song ever, the typically lulling and enigmatic "Iceblink Luck."

9. The debut album by the Darkside, **All That Noise** (RCA), merged Sapcemen 3 drone with *Nuggets*-style garage-rock drive.

10. Kurt Cobain's hero, Eugene Kelly, offered a psychedelic mantra with **Oomalama** (Atlantic), the debut by his post-Vaselines group, Eugenius.

11. Galaxie 500 made its impressive debut with **Today** (Rykodisc). The band never altered its trippy, somnambulistic formula, but what a splendid formula it was.

12. With ***This Is Our Music*** (Rykodisc), Galaxie 500 bowed out in style.

13. The posthumous collection ***Double Easy: The U.S. Singles*** (Elektra) offers a solid overview of the Happy Mondays' trippy, danceable career and explains why they were the premier group in the Madchester scene.

14. ***Best of Lush—Ciao!*** (4AD) is another powerful compilation providing a solid retrospective of the band that mixed Cocteau Twins ambience and shoegazer swirl.

15. Yes, Oasis is derivative and hopelessly retro, and sure, it panders to the mainstream. But ***(What's the Story) Morning Glory?*** (Sony) is an irresistible psychedelic pop confection nonetheless.

16. The best effort from Primal Scream came late in the game with *XTRMNTR* (Astralwerks), an abrasive, political, and forward-looking psychedelic gem.

17. As with Lester Bangs, the drug of choice for Chicago's Red Red Meat was cough syrup, but *Jimmywine Majestic* (Sub Pop) was a sterling example of modern psychedelic blues-rock.

18. Rarely has a cover painting evoked the sounds of the album as well as on Ride's debut, *Nowhere* (Reprise). The band's psychedelic guitar rock ebbs and flows with oceanic power.

19. Ride pilfers joyfully from psychedelic rock history throughout *Carnival of Light* (Reprise), but it emerges as much more than the sum of its influences.

20. The Screaming Trees' *Dust* (Epic) was the Seattle grunge-rockers' best album, a brilliant psychedelic effort that added sitars, tabla, harmonium, and Mellotron to the group's bluesy, metal-edged rock.

21. Slowdive's debut, *Just for a Day* (Capitol), introduces one of the lushest and most layered sounds of the shoegazer movement.

22. Calling Dr. Dream: Spacemen 3 offer *The Perfect Prescription* (Taang!).

23. Spiritualized debuted with *Lazer Guided Melodies* (RCA), one of the most enchanting psychedelic rock albums ever made.

24. Early editions of Spiritualized's third album, *Ladies and Gentlemen We Are Floating in Space* (RCA), came packaged in a mock pillbox.

25. Psychedelic folk meets the Madchester groove via the Stone Roses, who benefit from a career overview on *The Complete Stone Roses* (Silvertone).

26. The early compilation, *Switched On* (Slumberland), opens with a track called "Super—Electric," an apt description of the band's music.

27. Stereolab's ***Transient Random-Noise Bursts with Announcements*** (Elektra) climaxes with the epic "Jenny Ondioline," its version of the Velvets' psychedelic-noise epic, "Sister Ray."

28. Ween's ***God Ween Satan*** (Restless) is one of the most complicated and twisted genre-hopping pastiches since ***Trout Mask Replica.***

29. Yo La Tengo came into its psychedelic own with the frenetic ***Electr-O-Pura*** (Matador).

30. Tracks such as "Big Day Coming" and "Sudden Organ" on Yo La Tengo's ***Painful*** (Matador) are pregnant with psychedelic expectations.

SEVENTEEN

SEVENTEEN

PSYCHEDELIC ROCK LIVES ON:
Ork Pop, Intuitive Music, Elephant 6, Stoner Rock, and Fifteen Albums to Turn on Your Mind in the New Millennium

BY THE TIME THEY GOT TO TERRASTOCK, they were about six-hundred strong. The small but passionate crowd that gathered in Providence, Rhode Island (the final resting place of H.P. Lovecraft) in the spring of 1996 for three days of peace, love, and modern psychedelic rock certainly couldn't be considered part of a major cultural shift, a burgeoning youth movement, or any of that other "come on people now, smile on your brother" '60s hoo-ha that springs to mind whenever you call something "anything"-stock. These were just indie-rock geeks—think of Anthony Michael Hall in *Sixteen Candles*, all grown up but just as dweebie as ever—gathered in a makeshift club called the Rogue Lounge to see some thirty bands, compare notes with like-minded fans, try to bail out the fanzine that united them, and celebrate a particular fringe aesthetic, but they illustrated something in the rock zeitgeist nonetheless.

Dubbed the Ptolemaic Providence Perambulation, the second annual festival, like the Terrastock that preceded it and all of the festivals since, was intended to benefit *The Ptolemaic Terrascope*, the English fanzine dedicated to covering a particular strain of underground artists new (Azusa Plane, Wayne Rogers, Bardo Pond) and old (Silver Apples, the Deviants, Guru Guru). That none of these gatherings has ever raised a cent for the zine doesn't seem to bother the magazine's driving forces, publisher Nick Saloman (a.k.a. the Bevis Frond) and editor Phil McMullen. Instead the shows have become an annual reunion of fellow travelers joining together to fly their freak flags high.

The bands and the fans were all loathe to use the word "psychedelic" to characterize the sounds or the philosophy in evidence. Thirty years after the much-ballyhooed Summer of Love, many felt unjustly limited by the term, tainted as it's been by '60s nostalgia. A week after Terrastock II, the Rock and Roll Hall of Fame and Museum in Cleveland hosted an exhibit called "I Want to Take You Higher: The Psychedelic Era, 1965–1969." In addition to the Grateful Dead, it celebrated the Jefferson Airplane, Janis Joplin, Traffic, Country Joe and the Fish, Donovan, and the Quicksilver Messenger Service. The performers and the fans at Terrastock had a very different set of heroes, and one much closer to the pantheon cited in this book.

At the tail end of the age of postmodern irony and alternative-rock careerism, it wasn't hip to talk about striving to transcend the everyday and connect with something deeper and more spiritual, but that's exactly what Terrastock was about. The bands' wildly varying approaches could generally be linked to one of two broad categories: hypnotic, droning, and often improvised walls of sound ("intuitive music") and ornate, emotional, and introspective "ork pop" (short for "orchestral pop"). The festival had good and bad examples of each. It kicked off with a performance by the reunited Silver Apples, whose legend loomed larger than the reality. The Michigan duo Windy & Carl delivered two sets of ethereal, ambient drones, and it was the surprise hit of the weekend, easily outshining Bristol, England's prolific Flying Saucer Attack, whose Dave Pearce collaborated with Chicago's sonic terrorist, Jim O'Rourke. Boston's Cul de Sac peppered its trance grooves with Asian and Indian seasonings, while Hovercraft offered an intriguing set of Cluster-like drone and space rock. Hoboken, New Jersey's Tadpoles successfully crossed Pink Floyd and My Bloody Valentine, while the Bevis Frond indulged in sub-Jimi Hendrix or Carlos Santana lead-guitar wankery—exactly the sort of thing that gave psychedelia a bad name in the first place.

On the pop tip, the core quartet of the Olivia Tremor Control was augmented by six members of the Elephant 6 Orchestra for a set of tunes from the ambitious concept album, *Music from the Unrealized Film Script, "Dusk at Cubist Castle."* The Massachusetts trio Papas Fritas delivered flawless three-part harmonies and enthusiastic versions of the tunes from *Helioself*, its stellar second album, and Galaxie 500 veterans Damon Krukowski and Naomi Yang played their "faux folk" for a rapt audience that included genuine folkie Tom Rapp of Pearls Before Swine, who joined them for a Bob Dylan cover. Former Moles and Cardinal songwriter Richard Davies wrapped it all up, backed by former Flaming Lips guitarist Ronald Jones for a closing set of warped but wonderful balladry.

What was it that united these bands and the readers of *The Ptolemaic Terrascope*? "What we all have in common I think is a shared love of the music," McMullen told me. "When we talk to bands, they understand that we're genuinely interested in what they're doing and not just what they're wearing or smoking that week. We've accidentally tapped into a 'spirit of the underground,' wherein genuinely independent bands and record labels all pull together for the common good." Like the goal of transporting listeners some place new and full of wonder, this sense of community never goes out of style, and it never completely disappears—it just goes deeper underground from time to time. Otherwise, it's as vital today as it was in the '60s, and it continues to mutate and evolve.

As this book draws to a close, there are still myriad names on my list of "topics for further research," still hundreds of records that I am desperately eager to hear, and still dozens of people I'd like to interview to better understand this slippery, chameleonlike beast called psychedelic rock. I've added a hundred pages of new material and I still I haven't come to terms with ethereal chanteuse Kate Bush, voodoo pianist Dr. John, worldbeat trip-hoppers Dead Can Dance, alien guitarist John Fahey, gonzo collage artists Fantomas, post rock progenitors Slint, or drunken rock historians Guided By Voices, to name a few. But as I noted at the outset, neither this book nor any other could ever be definitive on the subject. It is simply the companion to my own sonic journey.

Before this trip concludes, it's worth considering four more psychedelic subgenres that blossomed in the time between the first edition and this one. And because the most exciting psychedelic rock may be yet to come, I'll end with a nod to fifteen recent albums that point to new directions for the psychedelic sound and philosophy in the future.

ORK POP

> And I know that words will fail me but I don't mind /
> Because she's so intoxicating, I'll take my time.
> —Yum-Yum, "Words Will Fail"

FLOURISHING FOR A YEAR OR TWO in the mid-'90s just as alternative rock was starting to wane, ork pop can be heard as a reaction to several years of more abrasive, fuzz-driven sounds, though it also represents a school of creative young musicians rediscovering the elaborate soundscapes of psychedelic and folk-rock masterpieces such as *Pet Sounds*, *Forever Changes*, and *Five Leaves Left*. These discs represent an approach to the studio and a style of arranging that never really goes out of style—even at the height of the grunge era, there were a handful of musicians who continued to incorporate lusher production values, among them Billy Corgan of the Smashing Pumpkins.

In the psychedelic underground, the turn toward the baroque was prompted in large part by a duo called Cardinal formed by Eric Matthews, a native of the blue-collar suburb of Gresham, Oregon, who studied trumpet at the San Francisco Conservatory of Music,

The Ultimate Psychedelic Rock Library: The elaborately orchestrated Cardinal (Flydaddy) inspired a host of ork-rock followers.

and Richard Davies, who first made his mark as the leader of psychedelic garage rockers the Moles in his native Sydney, Australia. The Moles won a small but devoted following in England after a strong debut album, *Untune the Sky* (1991), but a move to London didn't work out as planned, and the band fell apart a short time later. Davies relocated to Boston, where he linked up with Matthews, who had abandoned his original goal of joining the symphony orchestra there when he was distracted by the city's vibrant rock scene. In Matthews, Davies found the ideal partner to help him realize his goal of making a cross between *The Piper at the Gates of Dawn* and *Forever Changes*. Cardinal's eponymous debut (1994) was comprised mostly of fragile, soul-searching tunes that Davies had been saving since his early days in London. Matthews added elaborate and moving scores and his smoky baritone vocals, but dissonance was simmering beneath the lovely, melodious sounds. "There was an intense relationship," Davies said. "There's good and bad about that." Added Matthews: "It was fruitful, but

Richard and I pretty much intended on making only one record together. He's more comfortable being his own boss, really."

Cardinal disbanded, and both men went on to pursue similar sounds on their own. Matthews recorded the excellent albums *It's Heavy in Here* (1995) and *The Lateness of the Hour* (1997) with help from former Jellyfish guitarist Jason Falkner (who also recorded several ork pop efforts of his own), layering guitars, strings, harpsichord, marimba, trumpet, and grand piano. Meanwhile, Davies stripped down to a more bare-bones though still psychedelic sound on albums such as *There's Never Been a Crowd Like This* (1995) and *Telegraph* (1998).

Strongly influenced by Cardinal, Chicago songwriter Chris Holmes turned from his Hawkwind-style space-rock band, Sabalon Glitz, to beautiful and heartfelt ork pop on *Dan Loves Patti* (1996), the debut album by a new group called Yum-Yum. Holmes incorporated a wide array of sounds (including strings, horns, Moog, and the Moody Blues' old Chamberlin, a tape-driven keyboard similar

The Ultimate Psychedelic Rock Library: Pretension isn't always a dirty word, as Yum-Yum proved with its ork-pop debut, Dan Loves Patti *(TAG).*

to the Mellotron) to enhance what were essentially simple love songs. The album title came from an old acoustic that Holmes found in a used-instruments store; the previous owner had carved the names of his ex-girlfriends in the back of the guitar, "So it was 'Dan Loves Marla,' then 'Judy,' 'Heide,' 'Susan,' 'Kimme,' and then 'Patti,'" he said.)

"Putting strings on a simple pop record is a pretty pretentious concept," Holmes granted. "There are weird connotations with the word, but I certainly had pretensions in what I wanted to do with the music, and I wasn't afraid to work with those." Yum-Yum fell apart after this promising debut, and Holmes went off to craft his answer to *The Dark Side of the Moon* with yet another group, Ashtar Command, though it has yet to release a full album.

Adopting a similar aesthetic on the other side of the Atlantic was Sean O'Hagan, a mad scientist with a shaggy Beatles haircut, and the most *Pet Sounds*-obsessed of any of the ork-pop auteurs. "On the early records, it was obvious to the point of being derivative," he said. "I'm just a habitual pop songwriter. I try to purge myself of it sometimes, but I love harmony. I love chords. I have fairly eclectic listening tastes, but at the end of the day, I dream of Henry Mancini and Ennio Morricone. When a chord progression happens that I would not have envisaged—that I did not expect but which really brought me home—that's the greatest thrill in music as far as I'm concerned. I just love affecting people emotionally and physically with chord progressions."

O'Hagan first surfaced as the leader of the Irish punk-pop group Microdisney, which had the distinction of being thrown off a U2 tour for making sarcastic cracks about religion. (This was before

The Ultimate Psychedelic Rock Library: The High Llamas' Hawaii *(V2) does Brian Wilson proud.*

U2's postmodern irony phase.) That group split up in 1987, but O'Hagan re-emerged in two capacities, as a sometimes member of Stereolab (he plays on four of the band's albums and collaborates with Tim Gane in various side projects), and as the leader of the High Llamas. The band crafted its masterpiece with 1996's *Hawaii,* a seventy-four-minute collection of beautiful, lushly orchestrated instrumentals, musical vignettes, and impressionistic mood pieces that bring to mind what *Smile* might have been if Brian Wilson hadn't cracked up. "What we wanted to do is venture the idea that you can create an accessible instrumental avant-garde music," O'Hagan told me. "The avant garde is always regarded as being anti-populist, which I understand, but I'd love to challenge that. It came from my interest in soundtrack music—in not having to go to the chorus—to develop a melodic cycle that subliminally works on the listener." On subsequent efforts such as *Cold and Bouncy* (1998), O'Hagan followed his old mates in Stereolab in turning toward more electronic

The Ultimate Psychedelic Rock Library: Paul McCartney crunching celery and an orchestra's worth of strange and lovely sounds; the Super Furry Animals' Rings Around the World *(Beggars Banquet) offers all of this and more.*

sounds, drawing particular inspiration from the pioneering electronic composer Morton Subotnick.

When the Super Furry Animals toured the United States in support of their sixth album, a sprawling double effort called *Rings Around the World*, they ended their set with a video loop of Arnold Schwarzenegger heralding "the best mind-fuck yet." That wasn't quite true—the group could easily be written off as the Welsh answer to the Flaming Lips—but you certainly can't fault it for a lack of ambition. Onstage the quintet employs a surround-sound PA system thet likes of which hasn't been heard since Pink Floyd, and it flashes a non-stop barrage of impressionistic videos to enhance the grand, orchestral waves of sound. Coming together around lead singer and songwriter Gruff Rhys, the Animals are unique among modern ork-pop bands (as well as many new psychedelic rock groups) for including biting political commentary among more mundane romantic concerns. Like the High Llamas, the band is obsessed with *Pet Sounds* and *Smile*, and it won an influential fan in Paul McCartney, who asked the group to remix several vintage

Beatles tracks on *Liverpool Sound Collage* (2000). McCartney returned the favor by crunching some celery on "Receptacle," a tune from *Rings Around the World*, reprising a sound he added to "Vegetables" on Wilson's aborted *Smile* project more than three decades earlier.

Named after a French children's television series about a boy and his dog and hailing from Glasgow, Scotland, the eight-piece ork pop band Belle and Sebastian explores the common ground between *Pet Sounds* and early '60s lounge music/easy-listening kitsch. In addition to the undeniable craftsmanship—think of the Fifth Dimension as produced by George Martin—the group's driving forces, Stuart Murdoch and Isobel Campbell, show flashes of Morrissey-like lyrical wit, though they can sometimes sink under the weight of their own archness. Chicago's Aluminum Group mines similar territory, adding a dose of Tortoise-derived post rock; the Chamber Strings favors more traditional indie pop adorned with orchestral instruments; Stereo Total mixes Stereolab and *Pet Sounds*, and Beulah uses the sounds of the symphony to enhance its brand of alternative country. By the time these bands appeared on the scene, the ork-pop movement was already in decline, but the Flaming Lips injected fresh energy with *The Soft Bulletin* in 2000, and that album clearly inspired the most promising new group to emerge in this subgenre.

In the alternative '90s, Dallas singer and songwriter Tim DeLaughter fronted a gleefully goofy band called Tripping Daisy whose debt to the early Lips was so obvious it was embarrassing. The Polyphonic Spree is less derivative and much more ambitious, crossing *Pet Sounds*-style psychedelic pop with vintage "God rock" (think *Godspell* and *Jesus Christ Superstar*) to create an uplifting, feel-good genre that well could be called "Wellbutrin rock." Fronting a

The Ultimate Psychedelic Rock Library: The Beginning Stages of...The Polyphonic Spree *(Good) may usher in a new genre that could be called "Wellubtrin rock."*

ten-piece choir and a thirteen-piece band that includes keyboards, guitars, synthesizers, theremin, violin, cello, tuba, trumpet, and French horn—all played by musicians sporting angelic white robes—DeLaughter sings uplifting odes to sunshine and smiles, and the most jaded rock 'n' roll hipster can help but grin as joyfully as an Up With People cheerleader.

"I certainly didn't put this band together to send out a message," DeLaughter told me. "But once it got together and people started reacting to the music, it turned into something I had never even thought about. I was more or less thinking on a sonic level, and then it turned into this kind of spirited celebration that caught me off guard. I was like, 'O.K., what is going on here? Hell, I really don't know!' I know that it makes me feel really good, and I really feel like I'm part of a celebration when this band cranks up and gets going on all fours. It's really hard for me to describe and talk about, but the effect that I see that people are having from this group is like nothing I've ever experienced."

INTUITIVE MUSIC

> There are certain abilities required now in order to play this
> sort of music that I call intuitive music. Musicians must
> learn to become the opposite of egocentric....When you
> become like what I call a radio receiver, you are no longer
> satisfied with expressing yourself; you are not interested in
> yourself at all. You will be amazed at what happens to you
> when this state is achieved: You become a medium.
> —Karlheinz Stockhausen

AMBIENT MUSIC IS MUSIC that rewards close attention," Brian
Eno said, "but it does not demand it." Starting in the mid-'90s the
lines began to blur between one branch of the indie-rock underground and the ambient end of the electronic dance world, and listeners have been awash in sounds that fit Eno's description while
retaining a sometimes subliminal rock 'n' roll edge. The practitioners of this sound scoff at names such as "space rock," "drone rock,"
and "post rock," just as they recoil from the words "progressive"
and "psychedelic." *"Strum und drone"* was a phrase offered by an
editor at *Option* when I covered the movement for that magazine,
but the most fitting moniker was suggested by Jessamine guitarist
Rex Ritter from the comments quoted above, which Karlheinz
Stockhausen delivered at a lecture in London in 1971. It is this
notion of transcending your surroundings to tap into something
deeper and more spiritual that places intuitive music firmly in the
continuum of psychedelic rock.

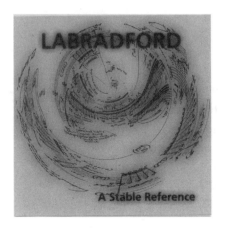

The Ultimate Psychedelic Rock Library: Labradford's second album, A Stable Reference *(Kranky), stands as the best introduction to this influential intuitive group.*

One of the most influential of the intuitive bands is the Richmond, Virginia, trio Labradford. The group first appeared as a duo with keyboardist Carter Brown and guitarist Mark Nelson, but bassist and sample artist Bobby Donne joined the fold as the band progressed from the spare, dub-influenced *Prazision LP* (1993) to the darker and more complex soundscapes of *A Stable Reference* (1995) and the self-titled *Labradford* (1996). "It's interesting that you're only the second journalist who's ever mentioned that we have songs," Brown told me. "It's always two-hundred adjectives and metaphors—everything but the word 'songs.'" But songs is exactly what Labradford plays, complete with effective if unconventional hooks. Witness the sinister creepy-crawl of "Mid-Range," the Pink Floyd-meets-Phillip Glass classicism of "Lake Speed," or the lulling waves and whispering breezes of "The Cipher."

The most mysterious of the intuitive musicians, Flying Saucer Attack not only borrowed Wire's "Outdoor Miner" for a 1995 EP, it adopted the influential art punks' theory that "any form of disin-

The Ultimate Psychedelic Rock Library: Flying Saucer Attack's Further *(Drag City) is the strongest of its many ambient instrumental offerings.*

formation is useful." As a result much of what fans think they know about the act is wrong. Often described as a full band centering on the duo of Dave Pearce and Rachel Brook, it was actually a one-man show pretty much from the beginning in 1992, when Pearce began recording his distinctive brand of "rural psychedelia" in his bedroom. As with Labradford fans often think they're hearing synthesizers that aren't really there. (*"Achtung! Diese platte ist Moog-frei!"* Pearce announced on 1996's *Tele:Funken* EP.) Pearce is a guitarist, not a keyboardist, and his sound veers between the extremes of introspective acoustic picking (his heroes include John Fahey, Nick Drake, and Tim Buckley) and full-throttle feedback skronk.

"There's really very little other instrumentation on the records," Pearce told me. "One of the things about using so-called 'low-quality' recording equipment is that you can put down two distorted guitars and they will start melting into each other, so you get this thickening, which almost needs a certain amount of dex-

The Ultimate Psychedelic Rock Library: The spirit of Popol Vuh lives on in Cul de Sac's China Gate *(Thirsty Ear).*

terity to control so you don't just turn it into sludge. You get harmonics, and a lot of times people will hear things that aren't there."

In the spirit of Can's spontaneous composition, the Seattle quartet Jessamine prefers to jam with the tape recorder rolling, then listen back to see what emerged as a possible song. In compiling *Long Arm of Coincidence* (1996), Ritter and his bandmates sorted through twelve hours of material. Resulting tunes such as "Periwinkle" and "It's Cold in Space" are so good they make you wonder about the stuff that *didn't* make the cut. It's an extremely psychedelic methodology, but of all the intuitive musicians, Cul de Sac guitarist Glenn Jones and synthesist Robin Amos are the most willing to embrace that word. "I've always loved psychedelic music," Jones said. "It wasn't a conscious effort to imitate any one thing, except the manner of getting out of yourselves and going somewhere else." You could argue that Cul de Sac is sometimes a bit *too* free, especially during Jones's more indulgent solos. But the best moments on *I don't want to go to bed* (1995) and *China Gate* (1996) bring to mind an atmospheric travelogue that recalls Popol Vuh's early soundtrack work for Werner Herzog. "We like to think of almost all of our songs as vehicles to get somewhere else," Jones said.

The cozy Dearborn, Michigan duo Windy & Carl (who never use their last names) get something of a bad rap from intuitive enthusiasts. It may be because they're working from a more instinctual, less intellectual place—they're really just home four-track nerds—or it may be because their music is the most blissful of any of these sounds, infused with happy thoughts of gentle ripples on still, quiet ponds. "When we started writing songs together in 1993, we would go to the park and hang out and take our acoustic guitars," said guitarist Carl. Added bassist Wendy: "Our music is spacey and dreamy, but it's not rock in any form."

Indeed, after the artists cited above, the rest of the intuitive groups get further and further away from the essential rock pulse. These include Microstoria, the collaboration between Berliners Jan St. Werner of Mouse On Mars and Markus Popp of Oval; Main, the

The Ultimate Psychedelic Rock Library: Windy & Carl's Antarctica *(Darla) conducts an ambient instrumental tour of those icy landscapes.*

group started by Loop veteran Robert Hampson; New Zealand guitarist Roy Montgomery; the Austin, Texas, duo Stars of the Lid; the modern chamber group Rachel's (the middle ground between ork pop and intuitive music); Bowery Electric; Azusa Plane; Monaural, and the Third Eye Foundation. But though it doesn't really fit neatly into this or any other genre, no discussion of intuitive sounds or modern psychedelic rock would be complete without consideration of Chicago's Tortoise.

Four of the six members of the band were seated around a makeshift plywood table in the loft that they shared in the industrial no man's land west of the Chicago Loop when I interviewed them shortly before the release of *TNT* (1998). In between fielding calls, mainlining extra-large coffees, and playing with Billy, the resident pooch, John Herndon, Doug McCombs, John McEntire, and Jeff Parker listened intently to a CD of rough mixes from the album. Two giant paintings of John Coltrane looked down on the area where the instrumental combo's gear would normally be set up; at the time, there were only a few stray congas, snare drums, and floor toms, as well as a vibraphone that sat below a shelf holding an impressive collection of old thermoses. It's difficult to describe the scene without giving it an air of serious self-importance that didn't really exist. Most of the journalists who visit the Tortoise loft play up the industrial setting and the musicians' shy, soft-spoken demeanors, working some grand metaphor about a group that intellectualizes its every move, forging a distinctive music from elements of dub reggae, jazz, krautrock, the Canterbury sound, hip hop, and electronica. But things aren't nearly that clinical or serious.

"I was just on tour with Eleventh Dream Day in Germany, and there were actually posters at one club advertising us as 'Chicago's pre-post-rock legends,'" McCombs told me. "Doesn't that mean we're just 'rock'?" His band mates all laughed heartily, and it was clear that journalists' failed attempts to hang a label on them has become a big inside joke. They were quick to respond when asked about the biggest misconceptions about Tortoise. "There's this idea that has been propagated that we are all very serious and we spend hours and hours in the studio," McEntire said. "And that when we're on stage, we all just stare at our instruments." He paused for a beat. "Well, *we* do do that. But there's a big misconception about us being super-serious, because we have a lot of fun with what we do." Added Parker once the laughter had died down once more: "I don't think there's anything I'd rather do than play in this band. I think it can still be serious *and* be fun."

There was no master plan when neighbors McCombs and Herndon conceived of the band in 1990, inspired in part by a shared passion for David Byrne and Brian Eno's *My Life in the Bush of Ghosts*. McCombs was the bassist for sometimes psychedelic-leaning alternative-country heroes Eleventh Dream Day, and Herndon was the drummer in the industrial-flavored Precious Wax Drippings. One by one other members joined the fold; friends stopped by to jam, and they never left. The moniker Tortoise was chosen from the name of John Fahey's publishing company. No one in the band ever has a defined role—everyone is best described as a multi-instrumentalist—and they all trade off on bass, guitar, Farfisa, Moog, vibes, marimba, melodica, timbales, percussion, lap steel, and whatever other instruments happen to be handy.

The Ultimate Psychedelic Rock Library: Tortoise took the title of Millions Now Living Will Never Die *(Thrill Jockey) from a famous apocalyptic tract by the Jehovah's Witnesses.*

The group's self-titled debut (1994) was a rather static effort, but *Millions Now Living Will Never Die* (1996) was a significant step forward, with an extraordinary twenty-one-minute opening suite called "Djed" and five other multi-layered tracks comprising a sort of "ambient with attitude." Here was invigorating hipster party music somewhere between the kitsch of space-age bachelor pad exotica, the joyless precision of latter-day progressive-rock, and the snooze-inducing quality of new age music. Like many of the intuitive groups, Tortoise rarely gets credit for writing catchy tunes, but that's exactly what "The Taut and the Tame," "Along the Banks of Rivers," and even "Djed" are. "In the most general sense, I tend to think of things in a verse-chorus-bridge way, even if it's only a slight difference in texture," McCombs said. "It's there just in terms of the way I build a song. But it's kind of a weird area for me to think about, because while I think most of our stuff is 'crowd rock,' the melodies aren't always super-recognizable....My mom tells me she likes Tortoise and listens to it a lot, and I always wonder what she's responding to."

No doubt Mrs. McCombs is grooving on the same things that excite many listeners: a certain visceral power inherent in the music (it moves you) and a sense of fun that comes through even in the more dense and complicated pieces. These are the factor that keeps Tortoise firmly in the rock tradition, and which make the group kindred spirits with the best psychedelic explorers of any era.

ELEPHANT 6

> In the moonlight I see my memories / In a new light, they seem so real to me.
> —The Apples In Stereo, "Baroque"

IF RUSTON, LOUISIANA, isn't officially the middle of nowhere, it's the first exit before it. Five or six hours north of New Orleans, the only reason it even makes the tourist guidebooks is because it's home to Louisiana Tech University. The college is an engineering school—not exactly an artistic hotbed or a center of cultural thought—but it does have a radio station. Jeff Mangum, Robert Schneider, William Cullen Hart, and Bill Doss all started assaulting the airwaves there as volunteer DJs while they were still in high school and the college kids were home for the summer. The station's library gave them access to all of the hippest indie rock—Guided By

The Ultimate Psychedelic Rock
Library: Neutral Milk Hotel's
On Avery Island *(Merge)*
introduced Jeff Mangum's uneasy
psychedelic folk songs about
religion, family, and the stickier
aspects of sex.

Voices, Pavement, and Sebadoh—but they also discovered
krautrock, Eno's pop efforts, and albums such as *Revolver, Pet
Sounds*, and *The Piper at the Gates of Dawn*. Duly inspired, they started making music themselves in various combinations in their parents' basements and garages. They traded four-track cassettes with
each other and—with the sense of drama inherent to all teenagers
but especially amplified in those who live one exit before the middle of nowhere—they marked all of their recordings as products of
the Elephant 6 Recording Co. "I look up to and respect those guys
so much," Doss told me in 1998. "Every time they give me a tape
of their news songs, I'm like 'Wow! Wait 'til I give you a tape of my
new stuff!' It's a competition, but not in a bad way at all."

In time the guerrilla DJs left Ruston—Mangum moved to New
York, Schneider to Denver, Colorado, and Hart and Doss to Athens,
Georgia—but they continued playing and recording together (generally with Schneider behind the board), maintaining their friendships and a similar psychedelic aesthetic. Recording as Neutral Milk

Hotel, Mangum made his full-length debut after a series of promising singles with *On Avery Island* (1996), a charmingly melancholy
disc that evokes the post-Soft Machine efforts of Robert Wyatt. It
kicks off with the rollicking "Song Against Sex," a driving ditty
punctuated by off-kilter trombone lines and boasting torrents of
words that paint an impressionistic picture of what may or may not
be the weird rush of feelings following a virgin same-sex experience: "And the first one tore a picture of a dead and hanging man
/ Who was kissing foreign fishes that flew right out from his hands
/ And when I put my arms around him I felt the blushing blood run
through my cheeks / And an eeriness surrounded when his tongue
began to speak." A nearly morbid fear of intercourse permeates
Mangum's work. "I'm grossed out about sex being used as a tool for
power; about people not giving a shit about who they're putting
their dick into," he told *Puncture's* Mike McGonigal. "I've known a
lot of people who have been badly damaged by some asshole's
drunken hard-on. That really upsets me."

*The Ultimate Psychedelic Rock
Library: If the words "psychedelic
rock masterpiece" have been
overused in this book, they
should rightly have been saved
for Neutral Milk Hotel's* In the
Aeroplane Over the Sea *(Merge).*

Mangum sang and played most of the key instruments on his debut, while childhood friend Schneider produced and added organ, fuzz bass, xylophone, and horn arrangements. By the time Neutral Milk Hotel got to its sophomore offering, *In the Aeroplane Over the Sea* (1998), it had become an actual band, but the disc was even more intensely personal lyrically and complex and otherworldly musically. It stands not only as the most extraordinary record by any of the Elephant 6 bands, but as one of the most strikingly original psychedelic rock albums ever, a hypnotic tour through the twisted psyche of a songwriter with a vision of the world that brings to mind Dr. Seuss illustrating William S. Burroughs, or perhaps Sigmund Freud collaborating on lyrics with Syd Barrett. Songs such as "Two-Headed Boy," "King of Carrot Flowers, Pt. 1," and the title track build from spartan acoustic guitar to a bizarro-world orchestra of theremin, horns, and bowed saws before ratcheting back down to simple strumming and Mangum's plaintive vocals. The singer evokes the naiveté and wonder of childhood, as well as the sense of dread and foreboding that comes from wondering if there really *are* monsters under the bed (or in the closet).

"Some of the songs really scared me when I first wrote them," Mangum told Jud Cost of *Magnet*. "They were so intense I wasn't sure I even wanted them on the album until I got to [Schneider's studio in] Denver. I let my subconscious take over." Mangum's music is almost all id. "I had the typical drug experiences in high school, but I don't do anything now," he told McGonigal. "I have all kinds of crazy hallucinations. I open my eyes and see things. I've seen, like, spirits moving through the walls. I've seen a vortex coming through the wall. I've seen amorphous balls of light bouncing around the front yard. I've seen giant bugs on the floor." Whether his fantasies eventually became too daunting to record or he simply ran out of musical ideas, he disappeared from the music scene after *Aeroplane*, joining the ranks of missing-in-action psychedelic giants like Syd Barrett and Kevin Shields. "Jeff has been working on a collection of short stories," his Web site informs us. "He also just joined the circus and wants to make a movie about snails."

"Nothing can be done without the willingness to succeed," Hart and Doss sing on "The Opera House," the opening track on 1996's startling *Music from the Unrealized Film Script, "Dusk at Cubist Castle,"* an absurdly ambitious triple-album debut. Recorded with able assistance from Mangum and Schneider, among other pals, it features two discs of elaborately orchestrated psychedelic pop, plus a bonus ambient record. In the manner of Eno's *Music for Films*, the duo conceived of the disc as the soundtrack for a movie that didn't exist. They also view it as a concept album, though the story (which has something to do with two women named Olivia and Jacqueline

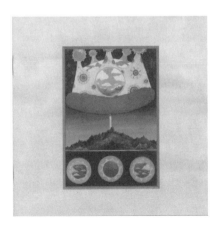

The Ultimate Psychedelic Rock Library: The Olivia Tremor Control's Music from the Unrealized Film Script, "Dusk at Cubist Castle" *(V2) marks one of the few times a band debuted with a triple album.*

The Ultimate Psychedelic Rock Library: On Black Foliage: Animation Music by the Olivia Tremor Control *(Flydaddy),* Hart and Doss switched from making music for an imaginary film to crafting soundtracks for imaginary cartoons.

1906 and a big earthquake called the California Demise) is harder to follow than *The Lamb Lies Down on Broadway.* "We want to do the movie, but it's really not a tangible story that I can say," Hart told me. "It's just life happening all the time. To really explain it out wouldn't be beneficial to you or your readers. There's definitely a story in there, but we're still looking up clues ourselves."

For their second album, *Black Foliage,* Hart and Doss turned for inspiration to *Soft Machine Volume 2,* the United States of America, and the music of Carl Stalling and Raymond Scott, who composed the wildly visual soundtracks for the classic Warner Bros. cartoons. "The first album was subtitled 'music from the unrealized film script,'" Doss said. "We call the new one 'animation music.' Like a movie score, we wanted you to be able to visualize things happening on *Dusk.* When we started doing *Black Foliage,* it seemed like it got way more animated, so we focused on that. Rather than music for a film, it was like it was music for a cartoon, where anything can hap-

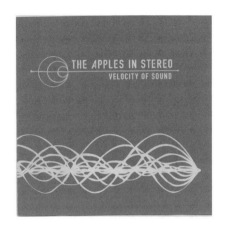

The Ultimate Psychedelic Rock Library: The sixth album by the Apples In Stereo, Velocity of Sound *(Spin Art), is the group's best, and the one where it finally matched the accomplishments of its Elephant 6 peers.*

pen and the laws of nature don't apply: You can fall off a cliff, get up, and brush yourself off. You can drop an anvil on your head..."

Shortly after the release of *Black Foliage*, the Olivia Tremor Control went on hiatus as its driving forces went off to pursue individual projects, Hart with the Circulatory System and Doss as the Sunshine Fix. These groups join other marginal Elephant 6 acts such as Chocolate USA, Elf Power, the Gerbils, the Minders, and the Music Tapes, but the last major band in this extended family is Schneider's own outfit, the Apples In Stereo. As the master technician of the Ruston crowd, Schneider is more interested in craftsmanship, and he's less intrigued by surreal wordplay (though science-fiction themes have a way of infiltrating his otherwise straightforward love songs). Early albums such as *Fun Trick Noisemaker* (1995) and *Tone Soul Evolution* (1997) cribbed a bit too freely from the common influences of *Pet Sounds* and *Revolver*, though the band dug a bit deeper in concert to cover the Creation's "Making Time". But with 2002's *Velocity of Sound*, the quartet finally made a disc strong enough to stand with the best of the Olivia Tremor Control and Neutral Milk Hotel. Tunes such as "Please," "Rainfall," and the wonderfully bouncy garage-rocker "She's Telling Lies" explode from the speakers in gleeful bursts of chiming guitars, layered harmonies, and jangling tambourines, and as with much of the Elephant 6 catalog, it's simply impossible to suppress a smile or resist humming along.

STONER ROCK

> This is how we go about it / To make our heads explode
> all night.
>   —Monster Magnet, "Heads Explode"

CALL IT THE REVENGE OF SPICOLI. Sean Penn's perpetually zonked Southern California surfer dude is everyone's favorite character from *Fast Times at Ridgemont High*. But in real life, Spicoli and his kind—the unrepentant stoners—are most often shunned, cast off to their own table in a corner of the high school cafeteria, and doomed to four-year sentences of detentions, demerits, and warnings sent home to their parents. It turns out that those superior mall rats, jocks, and cheerleaders don't know what they're missing—the key factor that unites the Spicolis of the world even more than the coveted toke of the sweet leaf. It's the music, man. *The music.*

"When I was growing up, if you were into Black Sabbath, you were on the other side of the room, man," said Scott "Wino" Weinrich, leader of the legendary bands Obsessed and Spirit Caravan. "Back in the day when I first started getting stoned, we were really, really put through the mill; if you were known to smoke pot, then you were called a junkie—that kind of stuff." Stoner rock is a name that none of the musicians in the subgenre is crazy about. "I might use the word 'stoner' in my lyrics, but I think we're really metal, dude, or just plain rock 'n' roll," said Matt Pike, the driving force behind Sleep and High On Fire. Meanwhile, another camp persists in slicing and dicing the burgeoning movement into ever-finer and more exclusive sub-genres, breaking stoner rock down into categories like dirt rock, desert rock, biker rock (the Steppenwolf sound), and beard rock (a la ZZ Top). The Europeans refer to it as "doom," but that name is even less popular than stoner rock, redolent as it is of gothic trappings like black nail polish and bat wings. Call it what you will, it's hard to deny the kindred spirit and unifying vibe shared by these hard-rocking, uncompromising, but never less than ultra-melodic bands, the best of which draw heavily from the psychedelic tradition.

One of the most influential bands in the stoner movement, Kyuss burst out of Palm Desert, California, in 1991. Taking its name from some monsters called "the Sons of Kyuss" in the Dungeons & Dragons book, *Deities and Demigods*, the quartet unleashed a pounding, fuzz-laden sound that fell somewhere between punk, metal, and grunge. The group toured relentlessly and delivered four albums that were beloved by fans, but it never rose much above cult status. Determined to reach a larger audience, guitarist Josh

The Ultimate Psychedelic Rock Library: Krautrock drive meets stoner intensity and psychedelic trippiness on Queens of the Stone Age *(Loose Groove).*

Homme formed the Queens of the Stone Age, a vehicle for his songs that is essentially a revolving crew of talented backing musicians with only one other steady cohort, bassist-vocalist Nick Oliveri. The Queens' searing self-titled debut (1998) mixes classic-rock melodies, headbanging intensity, and elements of trippy krautrock, notably the driving, metronomic beat of Neu! The follow-up, *Rated R* (2000), simplifies the sound a bit, emphasizing the massively catchy riffs. (It boasts an unforgettable stoner anthem in the aptly titled "Feel Good Hit of the Summer," which features the irresistible chorus, "Nicotine, Valium, Vicodan, marijuana, Ecstasy, and alcohol!"). Released in 2002, the band's third album, *Songs for the Deaf,* finds a middle ground between the two approaches and benefits from the propulsive drumming of Nirvana veteran Dave Grohl.

Another giant of the scene was San Jose, California's Sleep. The trio came together in the late '80s when Pike dropped out of military school, moved to the desert, and hooked up with bassist-vocalist Al Cisneros and drummer Chris Hakius. Their goal was the now

*The Ultimate Psychedelic Rock
Library: Sleep's stoner classic
Jerusalem (The Music Cartel) is
quite simply one of the heaviest
and trippiest albums ever made.*

familiar one of mixing Sabbath and punk rock; for a while, the
vehicle was a quartet, but the nascent band's second guitarist quit
to become a priest in Alaska, and the lineup settled in as a trio. Its
debut, *Holy Mountain* (1993), updated Hawkwind-style space rock
with a new punk energy, and the band toured with Nik Turner, but
it was the sophomore effort that really set heads reeling. *Jerusalem*
is quite simply one of the heaviest psychedelic rock records ever
made. Released in 1998, it consists of one fifty-two-minute track—
massive, monolithic, and lumbering like a brontosaurus stomping
through the bog. "Earache [Records] sat on *Holy Mountain* forever,
and that fucked with us real bad," Pike recalled. "It took us about
four years to get out of that, and during those four years we wrote
the song 'Jerusalem.' Al had said, 'Gee, don't you think it would be
awesome just to cut through the bullshit and do one huge gigantic
piece—like Beethoven, but make it different?' Our influences were
real monotone, real Indian-sounding, real dub-reggae. It's pot

music, you know what I mean? We were smoking like…God, dude, two to four ounces a day!"

Not for nothing does the back cover depict one of the funkiest homemade bongs ever photographed. But *Jerusalem* isn't merely stoned self-indulgence or a particularly inspired jam preserved for posterity. After its four-year genesis, it was painstakingly recorded during two months of intense studio sessions. "Man, it took a long time," Pike told me. "When I was playing that slow intro, that was a bitch to play the whole thing through and keep the time perfect. And then once the drums and bass come in…there were like fucking math charts on the wall, everything. There was so much to remember." This includes mystical lyrics that would do the Cult of the Illuminatis proud. "It was a real spiritual, holy thing for all of us. All of us are very unorthodox Christians and amateur theologists; we like to study different religions but kind of believe in one God. I give a lot of that album's doing to Him. Without a lot of prayer and without a lot of marijuana and our past psychedelic experiences, that album wouldn't have happened."

The problem with an epic effort like *Jerusalem* is that it's almost impossible to top, and Sleep came to an end shortly after the disc's release. Pike has continued on with a simpler, less psychedelic, but no less powerful trio called High On Fire, but Cisneros is yet another psychedelic rock explorer who has sadly been lost in the wilderness.

The final group in stoner rock's holy trinity is Monster Magnet. Formed in the shore town of Red Bank, New Jersey, in 1989, guitarist-vocalist Dave Wyndorf paired the punk-rock humor and attitude of his first band Shrapnel with a love for the pseudo-psyche-delic early-'70s metal of Black Sabbath, Deep Purple, and Hawkwind.

The Ultimate Psychedelic Rock Library: Hardcore fans favor earlier Monster Magnet efforts such as Spine of God *and* Dopes to Infinity, *but 2001's* God Says No *(A&M) hits the perfect balance between psychedelic genius and stoner stoopidity.*

Over the course of its first three albums—*Spine of God* (1992), *Superjudge* (1993), and *Dopes to Infinity* (1995)—the band emerged as one of the most formidable forces in the burgeoning stoner genre. With 1998's gold-selling *Powertrip*, it reached its biggest audience, scoring a radio and MTV hit with the memorable single, "Spacelord." This proved that the band had well learned the vintage Sabbath formula of Heavy + Hooky = Anthemic, but some longtime fans missed the psychedelic edge of the earlier material. Wyndorf and company recovered a measure of trippiness on their monumental fifth effort, *God Says No* (2001), a virtual tour of different stoner-rock styles, ranging from the garage-band rave-up of "Melt" to the massive Stooges groove of "Doomsday" and from the twisted psychedelic blues of "Gravity Well" to the Middle-Eastern drone of "Cry."

"I love garage rock, I love psychedelic hard rock, I love blues," Wyndorf told me. "Monster Magnet's music is like the music of England—British rock and American psych—all filtered through a New Jersey native, so it doesn't come out the same way." Indeed, when Wyndorf portrays a randy sex-god-satyr in "Kiss of the Scorpion," you can't help but laugh at lines like, "You'll swim in the sweat of a million orgies / You'll live in the fire of the sweetest hell / A pit of souls who raise a mortal sun / Give your lips to the kiss of the scorpion"—especially when he follows that anthemic chorus by growling, "It's time to suck the cock of the fire god!" as the guitarists launch into an orgasmic solo. To paraphrase Spinal Tap's Nigel Tufnel, it's a fine line between clever and *stoopid*, and Monster Magnet strikes the perfect balance.

Other stoner rock bands that fall at the more psychedelic end of the spectrum include Newfoundland's Sheavy (pronounced "Chevy"), which mixes Ozzy Osbourne-style vocals with Kyuss-like rhythmic drive; England's Orange Goblin, which combines American biker rock and interstellar overdrive, and Electric Wizard, which released a massively heavy and trippy album called *Dopethrone*; desert rockers Nebula (who are famous for their flaming gong and druggy tunes like "Fields of Psilocybin") and Fu Manchu; the Atomic Bitchwax, formerly the power-trio side project of Monster Magnet guitarist Ed Mundell, and Acid King, one of the rare female-led stoner-rock bands. For stoner fans, none of these bands has recorded a bad note. Lay your hands on any of their discs, fire up the bong, and judge for yourself.

Fifteen Albums to Turn on Your Mind in the New Millennium

1. **Bardo Pond,** *Amanita*
    (Matador, 1996)

    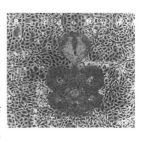

    Named after an obscure and toxic
    hallucinogenic mushroom said to
    instill the user with the power of
    telepathy, this album boasts a crude
    sketch on the back cover depicting a disembodied cerebel-
    lum being held aloft by a couple of buzzing flies, spoon-
    feeding an indie-rock fan who smiles blissfully. It's hard to
    come up with any words that more accurately convey the
    spirit of this Philadelphia quintet's mind-melting music,
    which falls somewhere in a netherworld between intuitive
    music, stoner rock, and classic psychedelic skronk. The
    group contrasts the miasmic noise guitars of brothers
    Michael and John Gibbons with the fragile, beautiful
    vocals and flute of Isobel Sollenberger and the insistent
    drive of a forceful rhythm section. "For us, [the concept of
    psychedelia] has always been an inspiration, but it's more
    in the sense of a religious experience than drugs," Michael
    Gibbons told me. "It signifies some kind of a gateway to
    another forum where your senses are changed, altered, and
    you're able to experience 'the real thing.' We've always
    embraced psychedelic rock because of that, but when I say
    that, I don't think of the Grateful Dead—more like the
    13th Floor Elevators or Syd Barrett or the more visionary
    John Lennon stuff."

2.   **The Beta Band, *The Three E.P.'s*
(Astralwerks, 1999)**

The only thing unimaginative about the first American release by this Scottish quartet is the title. It is indeed a compilation of three indie EPs (*Champion Sounds, The Patty Patty Sound,* and *Los Amigos Del Beta Banditos*) released between July 1997 and July 1998. The group's lineup of guitar, bass, drums, and samples and its relaxed, trip-hop grooves bring to mind a European version of Soul Coughing, but the Beta Band is far more ambitious, melodic, and psychedelic. Songs such as "Dry the Rain" and "Needles in My Eyes" build to grand orchestral climaxes, other tunes detour into space-rock explorations, and everything is infused with killer hooks in the tradition of indie pop maestros and fellow country-men Teenage Fan Club and Eugenius.

3.   **Clinic, *Walking With Thee*
(Domino, 2002)**

Indie-rock hipsters hail this Liverpool quartet as the second com-ing of Radiohead, but the group's second album actually has a lot more venom and vinegar in the manner of early Public Image, Ltd., Wire, or Gang of Four. There is also a devotion to the monotonous trance grooves of the Velvet Underground or Can, but without neglecting the melodies.

Songs such as the disc-opening "Harmony," the rollicking "Pet Eunoch," and the gleefully obtuse "Sunlight Bathes Our Home" worm their way into your subconscious, evoking myriad cool influences (from the bands listed above to surf music and spaghetti western soundtracks) while sounding fresh, vital, and mysterious all at once. "We want a hook, but we also want something that's got an edge to it," bandleader Ade Blackburn told me. "There's always a sort of punk basis to the guitars—which you could say is rooted in things like Captain Beefheart or the Velvets—but we're trying to use that in an inventive way that isn't sort of a clichéd indie sound."

4.   **Common,** *Electric Circus*
     (MCA, 2002)

For the Chicago native Common, the Electric Circus is a place of infinite possibilities. The smart and extremely musical rapper's fifth album embraces a broad spectrum of inventive psychedelic sounds—from Pink Floyd and Jimi Hendrix to psychedelic soul to trippy New Orleans jazz—bringing them all into the realm of hip hop or neo-soul with seductive, laidback grooves and free-flowing rhymes that emphasize positivity, acceptance, and the quest for peace, both personal and political.

5. **Cornershop, *When I Was Born for***
    ***the 7th Time* (Warner Bros., 1997)**

    Led by singer, songwriter, guitarist,
    and dholki player Tjinder Singh,
    this British group scored a hit sin-
    gle with the bouncy "Brimful of
    Asha" from this forward-looking album. The disc com-
    bines Eastern drones, world rhythms, and Beatles-style
    psychedelic pop, at long last following up (and bettering)
    George Harrison's Indian experiments. It also points the
    way to new horizons for psychedelic rock and trip hop
    incorporating more global influences.

6. **The Doves, *The Last Broadcast***
    (Capitol, 2002)

    The Doves' second album is even
    stronger than its acclaimed 2000
    debut, *Lost Souls*. Singer Jimi
    Goodwin and multi-instrumentalist
    brothers Andy and Jez Williams chart a new path between
    the guitar-crazed assaults of the best shoegazer bands (espe-
    cially Ride) while matching the bombast of Pink Floyd at
    its heaviest and capturing the sensual fluidity of acid-house
    and trip-hop rhythms. And it's all delivered with a unique
    brand of ethereal ambience.

7. **Granddaddy,** *Sumday* **(V2, 2003)**

With its incongruous mix of charac-
terless strip malls and rebellious
skateboard parks, serene nature
reserves, and ugly suburban sprawl,
Northern California is an organically
surreal place, and few bands have captured its weird
vibe as well as the Modesto quintet Grandaddy. The
delightfully idiosyncratic group spent three years crafting
the follow-up to 2000's inspired and wonderfully skewed
concept album, *The Sophtware Slump*, but it was worth the
wait. The melodies on these twelve tracks are even more
effervescent and more memorable, while the dense, layered
production hones a brand of modern psychedelic pop that
has less in common with the legions of Deadheads in near-
by San Francisco than it does with cosmonaut peers such as
the Flaming Lips and Mercury Rev. "Paint the words a
simple wish / For peace of mind and happiness," bandleader Jason Lytle sings on "El Caminos in the West" as a
gently propulsive groove, droning analogue synthesizer,
and sinewy guitar line decorate his typically impressionistic lyrics. Those lines could well be the band's mantra, as
each tune sketches another unique soundscape, and it all
adds up to one of the trippiest, most soulful, and most
enticing summer soundtracks since the Beach Boys' "pocket symphony to God," "Good Vibrations."

8. Incubus, *Morning View*
   (Epic, 2001)

Rising head and shoulders above
their nü-metal peers (with whom
they actually have very little in
common), this California quintet
takes its post-alternative sound to a new level with this
effort, shedding its earlier Primus and Red Hot Chili
Peppers obsessions and merging hard rock, ethnic percussion, DJ scratching, string sections, analog synthesizers,
and a dramatic use of dynamics. The album is named for
the beachfront mansion in Malibu where it was recorded,
a most psychedelic setting. "We never set out to create
psychedelic rock per se," singer Brandon Boyd told me.
"We're just trying to write music that we feel speaks
accurately of us as musicians and artists."

9. **The Negro Problem,** *Post Minstrel*
   Syndrome **(Aerial Flipout, 1997)**

Following in L.A.'s tradition of
swirling psychedelic pop, from the
Byrds and Love to the Bangles and
the Three O'Clock, this confronta-
tionally-named quartet is fronted by Stew (the linebacker-
sized Mark Stewart), an African-American singer and songwriter with ebullient personality to spare. The group's
debut overflows with strange sounds, indelible melodies,
and sharp-eyed lyrics critiquing society, race relations, and

pop culture. (Inspirational verse: "She want a man straight out of that *Ebony* magazine / Newscaster nightmare, she don't want no dreadlocks / She want a man who has that Sting thing happening.") With the band, Stew's songs tend to be freer, more imagistic, and more surreal, but equally worthy are his solo psychedelic folk efforts, perfect music for the gonzo coffeehouse or cabaret.

10. **Porcupine Tree, *In Absentia* (Atlantic, 2002)**

Hailed by progressive rock fans as well as the psychedelic rock under-ground, Porcupine Tree mainstay Steve Wilson has spent his career crafting seductive rock music that takes as its starting point *The Dark Side of the Moon* then attempts to venture beyond. Wilson is no revivalist; his vision of psychedelia incorporates everything from Radiohead to industrial noise to pure imagination. "I think that what most people tend to get wrong is the correlation between psychedelic music and drugs," he told me. "I've never taken drugs, but for me, if you look at some of the most bizarre and creative music that's been made in the history of rock music, it's been made by people like Frank Zappa and Robert Fripp, who are famous for their abstinence. The drugs are like a facilitator for achieving that, but I would say that an even more powerful facilitator is dreams."

11. **Radiohead, *Kid A* (Capitol, 2000)**

With 1997's widely acclaimed but somewhat overrated *OK Computer*, these English art rockers blended elements of post rock or intuitive music with the psychedelic lunacy of bands like the Flaming Lips and Mercury Rev, to say nothing of those progenitors in Pink Floyd. But that alleged masterpiece was an at-times dense, sluggish, and self-consciously heavy concept album about the dehumanizing effects of technology. On the follow-up, the group learned to stop worrying and love the machine, and though it's a more atmospheric, understated, and ambient disc, it's actually much more engaging. The lyrics here are sparer and more impressionistic, and singer Thom Yorke is often buried in the mix—a good move, since a little of his slippery, plaintive whine goes a long way. All manner of percolating electronic percussion, buzzing synthesizers, and droning electronic loops decorate the band's alien soundscapes, showing that the group has internalized (if not imitated) Brian Eno albums like *Another Green World* and *Before and After Science*. The group is certainly not the savior of modern music that some devotees proclaim, but it is a creative psychedelic force nonetheless.

12. **Sigur Ros, *Agaetis Byrjun***
     (Pias America, 2001)

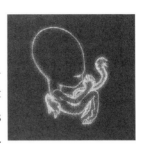

This Icelandic group (the name can
be translated as "Victory Rose") first
came together in the mid-'90s
around singer, guitarist, and then-
teenage wunderkind Jonsi Birgisson, but it first made an
impact in the United States in 2000 when fans began trading its second album over the Net. The centerpiece of
Agaetis Byrjun ("A New Beginning") is the epic "Svefn-G-
Englar" ("Sleepwalkers"), which draws inspiration from the
Cocteau Twins and Slowdive while conjuring a strange
lunar landscape, or perhaps the barren expanses of the
Antarctic. The guitars swell like a string-section, the
rhythms range from a barely perceptible pulse to a
Bonhamesque pounding, and the weird, asexual, and dis-
embodied vocals sound like nothing else you've ever heard.

13. **Mary Timony, *The Golden Dove***
     (Matador, 2002)

On her second solo album, the former leader of Boston's Helium continues to weave her haunting, wonderfully creepy spells via a mix of
'60s psychedelic folk in the style of the Incredible String
Band or Nick Drake and modern electronica, with hints of
gothic ambience and Renaissance Fair minstrelsy thrown in
for good measure. Amid these dark purple vibes, it's easy to

give short shrift to Timony's flair for melodic songcraft and wryly humorous lyrics, but both are in ample evidence. As on 2000's more conceptual *Mountains*, the singer plays most of the instruments herself, and while "14 Horses" stands as a potent musical evocation of the Apocalypse, "Musik and Charming Melodee" gives us the catchiest overdriven guitar line since David Bowie's "Heroes." Sings the witchy chanteuse: "Music sets us free...Music of the spheres / Recovers the ghost of ancient years."

14. **Tool, *Lateralus* (Volcano, 2001)**

Tool is another band combining ele-ments of progressive rock, industrial music, and psychedelia. More than four years in the making, this dense, sprawling epic of a third album is an undeniably impressive sonic collage where alien machine sounds collide with driving hard-rock riffs, crunching metallic guitars yield to passages of whisper-quiet intensity, and all manner of ethnic percussion decorates the otherwise mechanical pile-driver rhythms. Singer Maynard James Keenan's histrionic take on Jim Morrison can grow tire-some, but the band's musical imagination carries the day.

15. **Wilco,** *Yankee Hotel Foxtrot*
    (Nonesuch, 2002)

With 2000's *Summer Teeth*, Wilco
turned away from the alternative
country sounds that made band-
leader Jeff Tweedy's reputation (first as a member of Uncle
Tupelo, then on the albums *A.M.* and *Being There*) in favor
of beautiful ork pop. But *Yankee Hotel Foxtrot* was even
more of a departure, and it stands as one of the first psychedelic rock masterpieces of the new millennium. Alien
synthesizers, unsettling strings, and the fractured, Captain
Beefheart-style rhythms of drummer Glenn Kotche combine with the familiar jangling acoustic guitars and plaintive vocals to open broad new vistas for the band, as well
as for rock in general. Tweedy is one of the most poignant
lyricists of his generation, and haunting songs such as
"War on War" and "Ashes of American Flags" took on
even more resonance in the wake of Sept. 11th. "I feel like
this is a really hopeful album," the songwriter told me a
few months before that fateful day and the album's
release. "There are some dismal lyrics and ugly sounds, but
every song to me has a positive element. In 'War on War,'
the line, 'You have to learn how to die if you want to be
alive'—that's something I believe is pretty much a blanket
statement for the whole record. You're not going to experience life unless you completely surrender to failure."
These are words to live by—and they are a psychedelic
philosophy if ever there was one.

THE ULTIMATE PSYCHEDELIC ROCK LIBRARY:
One-Hundred Eighty-Nine Albums You Can't Live Without

THE ALBUMS LISTED BELOW, more or less in order of preference, comprise my version of the ultimate psychedelic rock record collection. In most cases the label listed is the one which has issued the current American version of the album; the original release date follows in the case of significant CD reissues.

1. The Beatles, *Revolver* (Capitol, 1966)
2. The Beach Boys, *Pet Sounds* (Capitol, 1966)
3. The Velvet Underground, *The Velvet Underground and Nico* (Verve/Polygram, 1985; 1967)
4. My Bloody Valentine, *Loveless* (Warner Bros., 1991)
5. Pink Floyd, *Wish You Were Here* (Columbia, 1975)
6. The 13th Floor Elevators, *The Psychedelic Sounds of the 13th Floor Elevators/Live* (Collectables, 1993; 1966)

7. The Flaming Lips, *Transmissions from the Satellite Heart* (Warner Bros., 1993)
8. Neutral Milk Hotel, *In the Aeroplane Over the Sea* (Merge, 1998)
9. Captain Beefheart, *Trout Mask Replica* (Reprise, 1970)
10. Brian Eno, *Another Green World* (EG, 1975)
11. Pink Floyd, *The Piper at the Gates of Dawn* (Capitol, 1967)
12. Jimi Hendrix, *Are You Experienced* (MCA, 1993; 1967)
13. Sleep, *Jerusalem* (The Music Cartel, 1998)
14. Wilco, *Yankee Hotel Foxtrot* (Nonesuch, 2002)
15. Brian Eno, *Here Come the Warm Jets* (EG, 1973)
16. Various artists, *Nuggets: Original Artyfacts from the First Psychedelic Era, 1965–1968* box set (Rhino, 1998)
17. Neu!, *Neu!* (Astralwerks, 2001; 1972)
18. P.M. Dawn, *Jesus Wept* (Island, 1995)
19. The Soft Boys, *Underwater Moonlight* (Matador, 2001; 1980)
20. The Rain Parade, *Emergency Third Rail Power Trip/Explosions in the Glass Palace* (Restless, 1994; 1983, 1984)
21. Robyn Hitchcock, *I Often Dream of Trains* (Rhino, 1995; 1984)
22. Julian Cope, *Peggy Suicide* (Island, 1991)
23. Pink Floyd, *Animals* (Columbia, 1977)
24. The Rolling Stones, *Their Satanic Majesties Request* (Abkco, 1967)
25. Spiritualized, *Lazer Guided Melodies* (RCA, 1992)
26. The Screaming Trees, *Dust* (Epic, 1996)
27. The Dream Syndicate, *The Days of Wine and Roses* (Rhino, 2001; 1982)
28. The Aphex Twin, *Selected Ambient Works Volume II* (Pias America, 2002; 1992)

29. Moby, *Play* (V2, 2000)

30. P.M. Dawn, *Of the Heart, Of the Soul and Of the Cross: The Utopian Experience* (Island, 1991)

31. De La Soul, *3 Feet High and Rising* (Tommy Boy, 1989)

32. Ride, *Nowhere* (Reprise, 1990)

33. Spiritualized, *Ladies and Gentlemen We Are Floating in Space* (RCA, 1997)

34. The Flaming Lips, *Yoshimi Battles the Pink Robots* (Warner Bros., 2002)

35. The Beatles, *Rubber Soul* (Capitol, 1965)

36. The Orb, *The Orb's Adventures Beyond the Ultraworld* (Mercury, 1991)

37. Love, *Forever Changes* (Elektra, 1968)

38. Roxy Music, *Roxy Music* (Island, 1972)

39. Wire, *Chairs Missing* (Restless, 1989; 1977)

40. The Feelies, *Crazy Rhythms* (A&M, 1991; 1980)

41. Can, *Monster Movie* (Mute, 1998; 1969)

42. Pere Ubu, *Terminal Tower: An Archival Collection* (Geffen, 1998; 1985)

43. Sly and the Family Stone, *There's a Riot Goin' On* (Sony, 1971)

44. The Olivia Tremor Control, *Music from the Unrealized Film Script, "Dusk At Cubist Castle"* (V2, 1997; 1996)

45. Jimi Hendrix, *Electric Ladyland* (MCA, 1993; 1968)

46. The Temptations, *Psychedelic Shack* (Motown, 1970)

47. XTC, *English Settlement* (Geffen, 1984; 1982)

48. Hawkwind, *In Search of Space* (One Way, 1992; 1971)

49. Genesis, *The Lamb Lies Down on Broadway* (Atlantic, 1974)

50. Pink Floyd, *Atom Heart Mother* (Capitol, 1970)

51. Kraftwerk, *Autobahn* (Elektra, 1974)

52. The Creation, *Our music is red—with purple flashes* (Diablo, 1998, Eng.)

53. Brian Eno, *Taking Tiger Mountain (By Strategy)* (EG, 1974)

54. The Jefferson Airplane, *Surrealistic Pillow* (RCA, 1967)

55. The Byrds, *Fifth Dimension* (Columbia, 1966)

56. Cardinal, *Cardinal* (Flydaddy, 1994)

57. Pink Floyd, *The Dark Side of the Moon* (Capitol, 1973)

58. The Rolling Stones, *Between the Buttons* (Abkco, 1967)

59. Brian Eno, *Before and After Science* (EG, 1977)

60. Julian Cope, *Interpreter* (KAK, 1997, Eng.)

61. Ride, *Carnival of Light* (Reprise, 1994)

62. The Orb, *Orblivion* (Island, 1997)

63. The Incredible String Band, *The Hangman's Beautiful Daughter* (Hannibal/Rykodisc, 1994; 1967)

64. Syd Barrett, *The Madcap Laughs* (Capitol, 1990; 1970)

65. Roky Erickson, *You're Gonna Miss Me: The Best of Roky Erickson* (Restless, 1991)

66. Syd Barrett, *Barrett* (Capitol/EMI, 1990; 1970)

67. Mike Oldfield, *Tubular Bells* (Virgin, 1992; 1973)

68. Plasticland, *Wonder Wonderful Wonderland* (Pink Dust/Enigma, 1985)

69. Peter Gabriel, *Peter Gabriel* (Mercury, 1980)

70. Jimi Hendrix, *Axis: Bold As Love* (MCA, 1993; 1968)

71. Hawkwind, *Space Ritual* (Cleopatra, 2002; 1973)

72. The Pretty Things, *S.F. Sorrow* (Snapper, 2000, Eng.; 1968)

73. David Bowie, *"Heroes"* (Rykodisc, 1991; 1977)

74. Pere Ubu, *Dub Housing* (Thirty Ear, 1999; 1977)

75. The Seeds, *The Seeds* (GNP/Crescendo, 1987; 1966)

76. The 13th Floor Elevators, *Easter Everywhere* (Collectables, 1993; 1967)

77. U2, *Achtung Baby* (Island, 1991)

78. John Cale and Brian Eno, *Wrong Way Up*
     (Opal/Warner Bros., 1990)

79. Roxy Music, *For Your Pleasure* (Island, 1973)

80. Amon Düül II, *Phallus Dei* (Mantra, 1993, Fr.; 1969)

81. Ween, *God Ween Satan* (Restless, 2001; 1990)

82. Galaxie 500, *This Is Our Music* (Rykodisc, 1997; 1990)

83. Red Red Meat, *Jimmywine Majestic* (Sub Pop, 1993)

84. The Cocteau Twins, *Treasure* (Capitol, 1984)

85. Blur, *Modern Life is Rubbish* (EMI, 1993)

86. Spacemen 3, *The Perfect Prescription* (Taang!, 1994; 1987)

87. Tortoise, *Millions Now Living Will Never Die*
     (Thrill Jockey, 1996)

88. Stereolab, *Switched On* (Slumberland, 1992)

89. The Flaming Lips, *In a Priest Driven Ambulance*
     (Restless, 1990)

90. Amon Düül II, *Yeti* (Mantra, 1993, Fr.; 1971)

91. Can, *Tago Mago* (Mute, 1998; 1971)

92. Kraftwerk, *Trans-Europe Express* (Capitol, 1977)

93. Lee "Scratch" Perry, *Open the Gate* (Trojan, 1994)

94. Beastie Boys, *Paul's Boutique* (Capitol, 1989)

95. P.M. Dawn, *The Bliss Album...? (Vibrations of Love and Anger and the Ponderance of Life and Existence)* (Island, 1993)

96. Wire, *154* (Restless Retro, 1989; 1979)

97. Kraftwerk, *The Man-Machine* (Capitol, 1978)

98. Pere Ubu, *The Tenement Year* (Enigma, 1988)

99. The Feelies, *The Good Earth* (Twin/Tone, 1986)

100. Julian Cope, *Floored Genius* (Island, 1992)

101. XTC, *Skylarking* (Geffen, 1986)

102. The Dukes of Stratosphear, *Chips from the Chocolate Fireball (An Anthology)* (Geffen, 1988)

103. Plasticland, *Plasticland* (Pink Dust/Enigma, 1985)

104. Morcheeba, *Big Calm* (Sire, 1998)

105. The Aphex Twin, *drukqs* (Sire, 2001)

106. Can, *Future Days* (Mute, 1998; 1972)

107. Moby, *18* (V2, 2002)

108. Genesis, *Foxtrot* (Atlantic, 1972)

109. Blur, *Blur* (EMI, 1997)

110. The Boo Radleys, *C'mon Kids* (Polygram, 1996)

111. The Cocteau Twins, *Heaven or Las Vegas* (Capitol, 1990)

112. Galaxie 500, *Today* (Rykodisc, 1997; 1988)

113. Stereolab, Transient *Random-Noise Bursts with Announcements* (Elektra, 1993)

114. Yo La Tengo, *Painful* (Matador, 1997)

115. My Bloody Valentine, *Isn't Anything* (Warner Bros., 1989)

116. Mercury Rev, *Deserters' Songs* (V2, 1998)

117. Plasticland, *Salon* (Pink Dust/Enigma, 1987)

118. The Flaming Lips, *The Soft Bulletin* (Warner Bros., 2000)

119. The Polyphonic Spree, *The Beginning Stages of... The Polyphonic Spree* (Good, 2002)

120. Neutral Milk Hotel, *On Avery Island* (Merge, 1995)

121. The Olivia Tremor Control, *Black Foliage: Animation Music by the Olivia Tremor Control* (Flydaddy, 1999)

122. Yo La Tengo, *Electr-O-Pura* (Matador, 1995)

123. Monster Magnet, *God Says No* (Interscope, 2001)

124. Screamin' Jay Hawkins, *Voodoo Jive: The Best of Screamin' Jay Hawkins* (Rhino, 1990)

125. The Beta Band, *The Three E.P.'s* (Astralwerks, 1999)

126. Mary Timony, *The Golden Dove* (Matador, 2002)

127.   Radiohead, *Kid A* (Capitol, 2000)

128.   Sigur Ros, *Agaetis Byrjun* (Pias America, 2001)

129.   Wilco, *Summer Teeth* (Reprise, 2000)

130.   The Flaming Lips, *Clouds Taste Metallic* (Warner Bros., 1995)

131.   The Beach Boys, *Smiley Smile* (Capitol, 1968)

132.   The Beatles, *Sgt. Pepper's Lonely Hearts Club Band* (Capitol, 1967)

133.   Funkadelic, *Free Your Mind and Your Ass Will Follow* (Westbound, 1970)

134.   The Beatles, *Magical Mystery Tour* (Capitol, 1967)

135.   The Amboy Dukes, *Journey to the Center of the Mind* (Repertoire, 1995; 1968)

136.   The Zombies, *Odyssey and Oracle* (Big Beat, 1998, Eng.; 1968)

137.   Tomorrow, *Tomorrow* (See for Miles, 1991, Eng.; 1968)

138.   Funkadelic, *Maggot Brain* (Westbound, 1971)

139.   Love, *Da Capo* (Elektra, 1967)

140.   Donovan, *Donovan—Troubadour: The Definitive Collection / 1964–1976* (Epic/Legacy, 1992)

141.   The Soft Machine, *Volumes One and Two* (Big Beat, 1995, Eng.; 1968)

142.   The Moody Blues, *Days of Future Passed* (Polygram, 1997; 1968)

143.   Mike Oldfield, *Ommadawn* (Virgin, 2000; 1975)

144.   The Deviants, *Ptoof!* (Alive, 1995; 1967)

145.   The United States of America, *The United States of America* (Sony, 1992; 1967)

146.   Silver Apples, *Silver Apples/Contact* (MCA, 1997; 1968, 1969)

147.   Os Mutantes, *Everything Is Possible!: The Best of Os Mutantes* (Luaka Bop, 1999)

148. Brian Eno and David Byrne, *My Life in the Bush of Ghosts* (Sire, 1981)

149. Ash Ra Tempel, *Schwingungen/Seven Up* (Cleopatra, 1998; 1971, 1972)

150. Popol Vuh, *Affenstunde* (Spalax, 1993, Fr.; 1971)

151. Faust, *Faust/So Far* (Collector's Choice, 2000; 1971, 1972)

152. The Three O'Clock, *Sixteen Tambourines/Baroque Hoedown* (Frontier, 1993; 1982, 1983)

153. The Bangles, *Bangles* EP (IRS, 1982)

154. Outkast, *Stankonia* (La Face, 2000)

155. Tricky, *Maxinquaye* (Island, 1995)

156. Portishead, *Dummy* (London, 1994)

157. Love, *Love* (Elektra, 1966)

158. The Future Sound of London, *Dead Cities* (Astralwerks, 1996)

159. Primal Scream, *XTRMNTR* (Astralwerks, 2000)

160. The Boo Radleys, *Everything's Alright Forever* (Capitol, 1992)

161. The Butthole Surfers, *Pioughd* (Capitol, 1992; 1991)

162. Frank Zappa and the Mothers of Invention, *We're Only In It for the Money* (Rykodisc, 1995; 1968)

163. The Darkside, *All That Noise* (RCA, 1990)

164. Eugenius, *Oomalama* (Atlantic, 1992)

165. The Happy Mondays, *Double Easy: The U.S. Singles* (Elektra, 1993)

166. Lush, *Best of Lush—Ciao!* (4AD, 2001)

167. Oasis, *(What's the Story) Morning Glory?* (Sony, 1995)

168. Slowdive, *Just for a Day* (Capitol, 1992)

169. The Stone Roses, *The Complete Stone Roses* (Silvertone, 1995)

170. Yum-Yum, *Dan Loves Patti* (TAG, 1996)

171. The High Llamas, *Hawaii* (V2, 1996)

172. The Super Furry Animals, *Rings Around the World* (Beggars Banquet, 2002)

173. Labradford, *A Stable Reference* (Kranky, 1995)

174. Flying Saucer Attack, *Further* (Drag City, 1995)

175. Cul de Sac, *China Gate* (Thirsty Ear, 1996)

176. Windy & Carl, *Antarctica* (Darla)

177. The Apples In Stereo, *Velocity of Sound* (Spin Art, 2002)

178. Queens of the Stone Age, *Queens of the Stone Age* (Loose Groove, 1998)

179. Clinic, Walking With Thee (Domino, 2002)

180. Cornershop, *When I Was Born for the 7th Time* (Warner Bros., 1997)

181. Incubus, *Morning View* (Epic, 2001)

182. The Negro Problem, *Post Minstrel Syndrome* (Aerial Flipout, 1997)

183. The Butthole Surfers, *Independent Worm Saloon* (Capitol, 1993)

184. Porcupine Tree, *In Absentia* (Atlantic, 2002)

185. Tool, *Lateralus* (Volcano, 2001)

186. Various artists, *Where the Pyramid Meets the Eye: A Tribute to Roky Erickson* (Sire/Warner Bros., 1991)

187. Grandaddy, *Sumday* (V2, 2003)

188. Grandaddy, *The Sophtware Slump* (V2, 2000)

189. Common, *Electric Circus* (MCA, 2002)

FURTHER PSYCHEDELIC EXPLORATIONS

Absolute Grey
Green House (Paisley Pop, 2003; 1986)

Acid King
Zoraster (Sympathy for the Record Industry, 1995)
Busse Woods (Man's Ruin, 1999)

Acid Mothers Temple
Acid Mothers Temple & The Melting Paraiso U.F.O. (PSF, 1997, Jap.)
Wild Gals a Go-Go (Acid Mothers Temple, 1999, Jap.)
Troubadours from Another Heavenly World (PSF, 2000, Jap.)
In C (Squealer, 2002, Jap.)

The Action
Rolled Gold (Reaction/Parasol, 2002)

Air
Moon Safari (Caroline, 1998)
The Virgin Suicides: Original Motion Picture Score (Astralwerks, 2000)
10,000 Hz Legend (Astralwerks, 2001)

Damon Albarn
Mali Music (Astralwerks, 2002)

The Aluminum Group
Pedals (Minty Fresh, 1999)
Happyness (Wishing Tree, 2002)

Amon Düül I
Airs on a Shoe String (Best Of...) (Thunderbolt, 1994, Eng.)

Amon Düül II
Tanz der Lemmings (Mantra, Fr., 1993; 1972)
Wolf City (Mantra, Fr., 1993; 1972)
Carnival in Babylon (Mantra, 1993, Fr.; 1973)

The Aphex Twin
Analogue Bubblebath EP (as AFX; Wax Trax!/TVT, 1994; 1991)
Surfing on Sine Waves (as Polygon Window; Wax Trax!/TVT, 1993)
Selected Ambient Works Volume II (Sire, 1994)
...I Care Because You Do (Sire, 1995)
Richard D. James (Elektra, 1997)
Come to Daddy (Sire, 1997)

The Apples In Stereo
Fun Trick Noisemaker (Spin Art, 1995)
Tone Soul Evolution (Sire, 1998)
Her Wallpaper Reverie EP (Spin Art, 1999)
The Discovery of a World Inside the Moone (Spin Art, 2000)

A. R. Kane
Sixty Nine (Rough Trade, 1988, Eng.)
"i" (Rough Trade, 1989, Eng.)

Arrested Development
3 Years, 5 Months & 2 Days in the Life of... (Chrysalis, 1992)
Zingalamaduni (Chrysalis, 1994)

Atomic Bitchwax
Atomic Bitchwax (MIA, 1999)
Atomic Bitchwax II (Tee Pee, 2000)

A Tribe Called Quest
People's Instinctive Travels and the Paths of Rhythm (Jive, 1990)
The Low End Theory (Jive, 1991)

Autechre
Incunabula (TVT, 1994)
Amber (TVT, 1995)
Tri Repetae + + (TVT, 1996)

Kevin Ayers
Joy of a Toy (Harvest, 1969)
The Confessions of Dr. Dream and Other Stories (Harvest, 1970)

Azusa Plane
Tycho Magnetic Anomaly and the Full Consciousness Hidden
(Camera Obscura, 1997)

Howie B.
Music for Babies (Island, 1996)
Snatch (Palm Pictures, 1999)

Erykah Badu
Baduizm (Universal, 1997)
Mama's Gun (Universal, 2000)

The Bangles
All Over the Place (Columbia, 1984)

Bardo Pond
Bufo Alvarius Amen 29:15 (Drunken Fish, 1995)
Lapsed (Matador, 1997)
Set and Setting (Matador, 1999)
Dilate (Matador, 2001)

The Barracudas
Drop Out With the Barracudas LP (Voxx, 1981)

Syd Barrett
The Peel Sessions (Strange Fruit, 1988)
Opel (Capitol/EMI, 1989)
Crazy Diamond box set (Capitol/EMI, 1994)

The Beach Boys
Good Vibrations box set (Capitol, 1993)

The Beastie Boys
Hello Nasty (Capitol, 1998)

The Beatles
The Beatles (Apple, 1968)
Yellow Submarine (Apple, 1969)
Abbey Road (Apple, 1969)

Beaver and Krause
In a Wild Sanctuary/Gandharva (Warner Bros., 1994; 1970, 1971)

Beck
Mellow Gold (Geffen, 1994)
Odelay (Geffen, 1996)
Mutations (Geffen, 1998)
Sea Change (Interscope, 2002)

Bedhead
   WhatFunLifeWas (Touch & Go, 2001; 1993)
   Transaction De Novo (Touch & Go, 2001; 1998)

Captain Beefheart
   Safe As Milk / Mirror Man (Castle, 1988, Eng.; 1967)
   Lick My Decals Off, Baby (Enigma Retro, 1989; 1970)
   The Spotlight Kid / Clear Spot (Reprise, 1991; 1970)
   Shiny Beast (Bat Chain Puller) (Rhino, 1991; 1978)
   Doc at the Radar Station (Virgin, 1980)
   Ice Cream for Crow (Blue Plate/Caroline, 1990; 1982)

Chris Bell
   I Am the Cosmos (Rykodisc, 1992)

Belle and Sebastian
   Tiger Milk (Matador, 1996)
   The Boy with the Arab Strap (Matador, 1998)
   If You're Feeling Sinister (Matador, 1999)
   Fold Your Hands Child, You Walk Like a Peasant (Matador, 2000)

The Beta Band
   The Beta Band (Astralwerks, 1999)
   Hot Shots II (Astralwerks, 2001)

Beulah
   When Your Heartstrings Break (Elas, 2000)
   The Coast Is Never Clear (Velocette, 2001)

The Bevis Frond
   Inner Marshland (Rubric, 2001, Eng.; 1987)
   Triptych (Reckless, 1988)

Big Star
   Third (Rykodisc, 1992; 1978)

Björk
   Debut (Elektra, 1993)
   Post (Elektra, 1995)
   Homogenic (Elektra, 1997)
   Vespertine (Elektra, 2001)

Black Sabbath
   Black Sabbath (Warner Bros., 1970)
   Paranoid (Warner Bros., 1970)
   Master of Reality (Warner Bros., 1971)
   We Sold Our Soul for Rock 'n' Roll (Warner Bros., 1976)

Tim Blake
New Jerusalem (Mantra, 1992, Fr.; 1978)

Blue Cheer
Vincebus Eruptum (Polygram, 1968)
Good Times Are So Hard to Find: The History of Blue Cheer
(Polygram, 1990)

Blue Öyster Cult
Agents of Fortune (Columbia, 2001; 1976)
Workshop of the Telescopes (Columbia, 1995)

Blur
Leisure (Capitol, 1991)
Parklife (Capitol, 1994)
The Great Escape (Virgin, 1995)
13 (Virgin, 1999)
Think Tank (Virgin, 2003)

Bongwater
Double Bummer + box set (Shimmy Disc, 1989)

The Boo Radleys
Giant Steps (Columbia, 1993)
Wake Up! (Columbia, 1995)

Bowery Electric
Lushlife (Beggars Banquet, 2000)

David Bowie
Low (Rykodisc, 1991; 1977)
Lodger (Rykodisc, 1991; 1979)

The Buffalo Springfield
Retrospective: The Best of the Buffalo Springfield (Atco, 1969)

The Butthole Surfers
Another Man's Sac/Cream Corn from the Socket of Davis
(Touch and Go, 1985)
Rembrandt Pussyhorse (Touch and Go, 1986)
Locust Abortion Technician (Touch and Go, 1987)
Hairway to Steven (Touch and Go, 1988)
The Hole Truth...And Nothing Butt! (Trance Syndicate, 1995)
Oklahoma! (Capitol, 1996)

The Byrds
Younger Than Yesterday (Columbia, 1967)
The Byrds box set (Columbia, 1990)

John Cale
Paris 1919 (Reprise, 1973)
Fear (Island, 1974)
Slow Dazzle (Island, 1975)
Helen of Troy (Island, 1975)
Fragments of a Rainy Season (Hannibal/Rykodisc, 1992)
Seducing Down the Door: A Collection 1970–1990 (Rhino, 1994)

Robert Calvert
Captain Lockheed and the Starfighters (BGO, 1987, Fr.; 1974)
Lucky Lief and the Longships (BGO, 1987, Fr.; 1975)

Can
Soundtracks (Mute, 1998; 1970)
Ege Bamyasi (Mute, 1998; 1972)
Soon Over Babaluma (Mute, 1998; 1974)
Landed (Mute, 1998; 1975)
Unlimited Edition (Mute, 1998; 1976)
Saw Delight (Mute, 1998; 1977)
Sacrilege: The Remixes (Mute, 1997)

Derrick Carter
Mood EP (as Symbols & Instruments; KMS, 1988)
Sweetened—No Lemon (as Sound Patrol; Organico, 1995)
About Now (611, 2001)

The Catheters
Static Delusions and Stone-Still Days (Sub Pop, 2002)

Nick Cave and the Bad Seeds
The Best of Nick Cave and the Bad Seeds (Mute, 1998)

Cee-Lo
Cee-Lo Green and His Perfect Imperfections (Arista, 2002)

The Chambers Brothers
Goin' Uptown (Sony Music Special Products, 1991)

The Chameleons U.K.
What Does Anything Mean? Basically (Static, 1985)
Strange Times (Geffen, 1986)

The Charlatans U.K.
Some Friendly (RCA, 1990)
Between 10th and 11th (RCA, 1992)
Up to Our Hips (Atlantic, 1994)
The Charlatans U.K. (Atlantic, 1995)

The Chesterfield Kings
Stop! (Mirror, 1985)

The Chills
Kaleidoscope World (Homestead, 1986)
Brave Words (Homestead, 1988)
Submarine Bells (Warner Bros., 1990)

The Chocolate Watchband
Forty-Four (Big Beat, 1985, Eng.)

The Chud
Silhouettes of Sound LP (Love's Simple Dreams, 1986, Ger.)

Circulatory System
Circulatory System (Cloud, 2001)

Cluster
Cluster & Eno (Gyroscope, 1996; 1977)
After the Heat (Gyroscope, 1996; 1978)

The Cocteau Twins
Head Over Heels (4AD, 1983, Eng.)
Victorialand (4AD, 1986, Eng.)
Blue Bell Knoll (Capitol, 1988)
Four-Calendar Café (Capitol, 1993)

Coil
Love's Secret Domain (Loci, 2001; 1991)

Common
Like Water for Chocolate (MCA, 2000)

Julian Cope
World Shut Your Mouth (Mercury, 1983)
Fried (Mercury, 1984)
Saint Julian (Island, 1987)
My Nation Underground (Island, 1988)
Jehovahkill (Island, 1992)
Rite (KAK, 1993, Eng.)
Autogeddon (American, 1994)
Queen Elizabeth (KAK, 1994, Eng.)
20 Mothers (American, 1995)
Queen Elizabeth 2 (Elizabeth Vagina) (KAK, 1997, Eng.)
Rite 2 (KAK, 1997, Eng.)
Ambient Metal (as L.A.M.F.; KAK, 2001)
Love Peace & Fuck (as Brain Donor; KAK, 2001, Eng.)
Rite Now (KAK, 2002, Eng.)

Cornershop
Handcream for a Generation (V2, 2002)

The Count Five
Psychotic Reaction: The Very Best of Count Five (Collectables, 1999)

Graham Coxon
The Sky Is Too High (Caroline, 1998)
Golden D (Caroline, 2000)

Cracker
Kerosene Hat (Virgin, 1993)

Cranes
Wings of Joy (Dedicated, 1998; 1991)

The Crazy World of Arthur Brown
The Crazy World of Arthur Brown (Polydor, 1991)
Strangelands (Reckless, 1988)

Cream
Disraeli Gears (Polygram, 1967)
The Very Beat of Cream (Polygram, 1995)

Cul de Sac
I don't want to go to bed (Thirsty Ear, 1997)
Crashes to Light, Minutes to its Fall (Thirsty Ear, 1999)
Immortality Lessons (Strange Attractors, 2002)

Culture Club
At Worst...The Best of Boy George and Culture Club (SBK, 1993)

Curve
Doppelganger (Virgin, 1992)
Cuckoo (Virgin, 1993)

Cypress Hill
Black Sunday (Columbia, 1993)

Damon and Naomi
More Sad Hits (Shimmy Disc, 1992)
The Wondrous World of Damon & Naomi (Sub Pop, 1995)
Playback Singers (Sub Pop, 1998)
Damon and Naomi with Ghost (Sub Pop, 2000)

The Darkside
All That Noise (RCA, 1991)

Das Damen
Jupiter Eye (SST, 1987)
Triskaidekaphobe (SST, 1988)
Marshmellow Conspiracy EP (SST, 1988)

D'Angelo
Black Sunday (Columbia, 1993)
Voodoo (Virgin, 2000)

Richard Davies
There's Never Been a Crowd Like This (Flydaddy, 1996)
Telegraph (Flydaddy, 1998)
Barbarians (Kindercore, 2000)

De La Soul
De La Soul Is Dead (Tommy Boy, 1991)
Buhloone Mindstate (Tommy Boy, 1993)
Art Official Intelligence: Mosaic Thump (Tommy Boy, 2000)
AOI: Bionix (Tommy Boy, 2001)

Deee-Lite
World Clique (Elektra, 1990)
Infinity Within (Elektra, 1992)
Sampladelic Relics & Dancefloor Oddities (Elektra, 1996)

Deep Purple
Shades of Deep Purple (Spitfire, 2000, Eng.; 1968)
The Very Best of Deep Purple (Rhino, 2000)

The Detroit Cobras
Life, Love and Leaving (Sympathy for the Record Industry, 2001)

The Deviants
*This CD Is Condemned: Black Tracks of Mick Farren & the
Deviants   1967–96* (Total Energy, 2000)

Digable Planets
Reachin' (a new refutation of time and space) (Elektra, 1993)
Blowout Comb (Elektra, 1994)

Digital Underground
Sex Packets (Tommy Boy, 1990)

Dinosaur Jr.
You're Living All Over Me (SST, 1987)
Bug (SST, 1988)

The Divine Styler

Spiral Walls Containing Autumns of Light (Giant, 1992)

DJ Shadow
Entroducing... (Full Frequency, 1996)
Private Press (MCA, 2002)

DJ Spooky
Songs of a Dead Dreamer (Asphodel, 1996)
Riddim Warfare (Uni/Outpost, 1998)
Under the Influence (Six Degrees, 2001)
Optometry (Thirsty Ear, 2002)

DMZ
Live at the Rat (Bomp, 2001)

Dr. Octagon
Dr. Octagonecologyst (Dreamworks, 1996)
Instrumentalyst (Dreamworks, 1996)

Dome
Dome 1. 2. (Mute, 1992; 1980, 1981)
Dome 3. 4. (Mute, 1992; 1981, 1982)

The Doors
The Best of the Doors (Elektra, 1985)

The Doves
Lost Souls (Astralwerks, 2000)

Nick Drake
Fruit Tree box set (Hannibal, 1991)

The Dream Academy
The Dream Academy (Warner Bros., 1985)
Remembrance Days (Reprise, 1987)
A Different Kind of Weather (Reprise, 1991)

The Dream Syndicate
The Medicine Show (A&M, 1984)
The Day Before Wine and Roses: Live at KPFK, September 5, 1982
    (Atavistic, 1995)

Dumptruck
D Is for Dumptruck (Big Time, 1985)
Positively Dumptruck (Big Time, 1986)

Durutti Column
The First Four Albums box set (Factory, 1988, Eng.)

Earth
Bureaucratic Desire (Sub Pop, 1991)
Earth 2 (Sub Pop, 1993)
Phase 3: Thrones and Dominions (Sub Pop, 1995)

Echo and the Bunnymen
Crocodiles (Sire, 1980)

Electric Wizard
Dopethrone (The Music Cartel, 2001)
Let Us Prey (The Music Cartel, 2002)

Elektric Music
Esperanto (Atlantic, 1994)

Eleventh Dream Day
Beet (Collector's Choice, 2001; 1989)
Prairie School Freakout (Amoeba, 1991)
Eighth (Thrill Jockey, 1997)
Stalled Parade (Thrill Jockey, 2000)

Emerson, Lake and Palmer
Pictures at an Exhibition (Rhino, 1996; 1972)
Brain Salad Surgery (Rhino, 1996; 1973)

Brian Eno
Discreet Music (EG, 1975)
Music for Films (EG, 1978)
Music for Airports (EG, 1978)
On Land (EG, 1978)
Thursday Afternoon (EG, 1985)
Nerve Net (Opal/Warner Bros., 1992)
The Shutov Assembly (Opal/Warner Bros., 1992)

Roky Erickson
Roky Erickson and the Aliens (CBS International, 1980, Eng.)
Don't Slander Me (Pink Dust/Enigma, 1986)
All That May Do My Rhyme (Trance Syndicate, 1995)
Never Say Goodbye (Emperor Jones, 1998)

Eugenius
Mary Queen of Scots (Atlantic, 1994)

Experimental Audio Research
Mesmerised (Sympathy for the Record Industry, 1994)
Beyond the Pale (Big Cat, 1996)

Fairport Convention
Meet on the Ledge: The Classic Years (1967–1975) (Polygram, 1999)

th' faith healers
Lido (Too Pure/Elektra, 1992)
Imaginary Friend (Too Pure/Elektra, 1994)

Jason Falkner
Presents Author Unknown (Elektra, 1996)
Can You Still Feel? (Elektra, 1999)
Everyone Says It's On (Cool, 2001)

Faust
The Faust Tapes (Recommended, 1995; 1973)
Faust IV (Caroline, 1993; 1973)

The Feelies
Only Life (A&M, 1988)
Time for a Witness (A&M, 1991)

the fireman
strawberries oceans ships forest (Capitol, 1993)
Rushes (Capitol, 1998)

The Flaming Lips
Hear It Is (Restless, 1986)
Oh My Gawd!!!...The Flaming Lips (Restless, 1987)
Telepathic Surgery (Restless, 1989)
Hit to Death in the Future Head (Warner Bros., 1992)
Zaireeka (Warner Bros., 1997)

The Fleshtones
Hexbreaker! (IRS, 1983)

Flying Saucer Attack
Flying Saucer Attack (Vhf, 1994)
Chorus (Drag City, 1995)
Mirror (Drag City, 2000)

John Frankovic
Under the Water Lilly (Midnight, 1994)

Robert Fripp and Brian Eno
The Essential Fripp and Eno (Caroline, 1994)

Fu Manchu
Daredevil (Bongload, 1995)
In Search Of (Mammoth, 1996)
Action Is Go (Mammoth, 1997)
California Crossing (Mammoth, 2001)

Funkadelic
Funkadelic (Westbound, 1970)
America Eats Its Young (Westbound, 1972)
Cosmic Slop (Westbound, 1973)
Standing on the Verge of Getting it On (Westbound, 1974)
Tales of Kidd Funkadelic (Warner Bros., 1976)
Hardcore Jollies (Warner Bros., 1976)
One Nation Under a Groove (Warner Bros., 1978)
Uncle Jam Wants You (Warner Bros., 1979)
The Electric Spanking of War Babies (Warner Bros., 1981)

The Future Sound of London
Lifeforms (Astralwerks, 1994)

The Fuzztones
Lysergic Emanations (Reper, 1996; 1986)

Peter Gabriel
Peter Gabriel (Atco, 1977)
Peter Gabriel (Atlantic, 1978)
Security (Geffen, 1982)
Up (Universal, 2002)

Galaxie 500
On Fire (Rykodisc, 1997; 1989)

Game Theory
The Big Shot Chronicles (Enigma, 1986)

Genesis
Trespass (MCA, 1970)
Nursery Cryme (MCA, 1971)
Selling England by the Pound (Atlantic, 1973)
Genesis Live (Atlantic, 1973)
The Lamb Lies Down on Broadway (Atco, 1974)
A Trick of the Tail (Atlantic, 1976)
Wind & Wuthering (Atlantic, 1977)

Gentle Giant
Giant for a Day (One Way, 1995; 1974)

David Gilmour
David Gilmour (Columbia, 1978)

The Godz
Contact High with the Godz (ESP, 2000; 1966)
Godz 2 (ESP, 2001; 1966)

Gong
    Camembert Electrique (Snapper, 2000, Eng.; 1971)
    Flying Teapot (JVC, 2000, Jap.; 1972)
    Angels Egg (Caroline, 1990; 1973)
    You (Caroline, 1990; 1975)

Gorillaz
    Gorillaz (Virgin, 2001)

Gov't Mule
    Dose (Volcano, 1998)

The Grateful Dead
    Grateful Dead (Warner Bros., 1967)
    Anthem of the Sun (Warner Bros., 1968)
    Aoxomoxoa (Warner Bros., 1969)
    Live Dead (Warner Bros., 1970)
    The Golden Road (1965–1973) box set (Warner Bros./Rhino, 2001)

Guru Guru
    The Very Best of Guru Guru (Cleopatra, 1999)

Harmonia
    Music Von Harmonia (Germanofon, 1994)
    Harmonia Deluxe (Germanofon, 1994)

George Harrison
    Wonderwall Music (Capitol, 1968)

Hawkwind
    Spirit of the Age (Griffin, 1995)
    25 Years On, Vol. I (Griffin Music, 1995)
    25 Years On, Vol. II (Griffin Music, 1995)
    25 Years On, Vol. III (Griffin Music, 1997)

Helium
    Pirate Prude (Matador, 1994)
    The Dirt of Luck (Matador, 1995)
    Magic City (Matador, 1997)

The Hellacopters
    Supershitty to the Max (Sub Pop, 1996)
    Payin' the Dues (Sub Pop, 1999)
    Grande Rock (Sub Pop, 1999)
    High Visibility (Gearhead, 2002)

Jimi Hendrix
    Band of Gypsys (MCA, 1995; 1970)

His Name Is Alive
Livonia (4AD, 1990, Eng.)

Robin Hitchcock
Black Snake Diamond Röle (Rhino, 1995; 1981)
Groovy Decay (Rhino, 1995; 1982)
Fegmania! (with the Egyptians; Rhino, 1995; 1985)
Element of Light (with the Egyptians; Rhino, 1995; 1986)
Invisible Hitchcock (Rhino, 1995; 1986)
Eye (Rhino, 1995; 1990)
Globe of Frogs (with the Egyptians; A&M, 1988)
Queen Elvis (with the Egyptians; A&M, 1989)
Perspex Island (with the Egyptians; A&M, 1991)
Respect (with the Egyptians; A&M, 1993)
You & Oblivion (Rhino, 1995)
Moss Elixir (Warner Bros., 1996)
Storefront Hitchcock: Music from the Film (Warner Bros., 1998)
Jewels for Sophia (Warner Bros., 1999)

The High Llamas
Santa Barbara (V2, 1998; 1992)
Gideon Gaye (V2, 1998; 1994)
Cold and Bouncy (V2, 1998)
Snowbug (V2, 1999)
Buzzle Bee (Drag City, 2000)

High On Fire
Art of Self Defense (Man's Ruin, 2000)
Surrounded by Thieves (Relapse, 2002)

The Hives
Barely Legal (Gearhead, 1998)
Veni Vidi Vicious (Warner Bros., 2002; 2000)

The Hoodoo Gurus
Stoneage Romeos (Acadia, 2002; 1983)

Hovercraft
Akathisia (Mute, 1997)
Experiment Below (Mute, 1998)

Hugo Largo
Drum (Opal/Warner Bros., 1987)
Mettle (Opal/Warner Bros., 1989)

Hurricane #1

Hurricane #1 (Warner Bros., 1997)

Hüsker Dü
Everything Falls Apart and More (Rhino, 1982)
Metal Circus (Reflex/SST, 1983)
Zen Arcade (SST, 1984)
New Day Rising (SST, 1985)
Flip Your Wig (SST, 1985)
Candy Apple Grey (Warner Bros., 1986)
Warehouse: Songs and Stories (Warner Bros., 1987)

The Hypstrz
Hypstrization! (Voxx, 1980)

Idha
Melody Inn (Creation, 1994)

The Incredible String Band
The Incredible String Band (Hannibal/Rykodisc, 1994; 1966)
The 5000 Spirits or The Layers of the Onion
   (Hannibal/Rykodisc, 1994; 1967)
Wee Tam and the Big Huge (Hannibal/Rykodisc, 1994; 1968)

International Noise Conspiracy
New Morning, Changing Weather (Epitaph, 2001)

The Irresistible Force
Dream Fish (Big High Productions, 1993)
Chill Out or Die! (Big High Productions, 1993)
Flying High (Rising High/Instinct, 1993)

Iron Butterfly
In-A-Gadda-Da-Vida (Rhino, 1995; 1968)
Light & Heavy—Best of Iron Butterfly (Rhino, 1993)

The Jam
All Mod Cons/Sound Affects (Ultradisc, 1996; 1978, 1980)
Setting Sons (Collector's Choice, 2001; 1979)

Jane's Addiction
Ritual de lo Habitual (Warner Bros., 1990)

The Jefferson Airplane
Volunteers (RCA, 1969)
Jefferson Airplane Loves You box set (RCA, 1992)

Jellyfish
Bellybutton (Virgin, 1990)
Spilt Milk (Virgin, 1993)

Jessamine
Jessamine (Kranky, 1994)
Long Arm of Coincidence (Kranky, 1996)
Don't Stay Too Long (Kranky, 1998)

The Jesus and Mary Chain
Psychocandy (Reprise, 1985)
Darklands (Warner Bros., 1987)
Barbed Wire Kisses (Warner Bros., 1988)
Stoned and Dethroned (American, 1994)
The Jesus and Mary Chain Hate Rock 'n' Roll (American, 1995)

Jethro Tull
Aqualung (Capitol, 1991; 1971)
Thick As a Brick (Capitol, 1999; 1972)

Janis Joplin
18 Essential Songs (Legacy/Columbia, 1995)

Judas Priest
Rocka Rolla (Koch, 2000; 1974)

The Jungle Brothers
Straight Out the Jungle (Warlock, 1988)

Kaleidoscope
Egyptian Candy (A Collection) (Epic/Legacy, 1991)

Keyboard Money Mark
Mark's Keyboard Repair (Full Frequency, 1996)
Push the Button (Mo' Wax, 1998)

King Crimson
In the Court of the Crimson King (Caroline, 1999; 1969)
Discipline (Caroline, 2001; 1981)
Sleepless / The Concise King Crimson (Caroline, 1993)

The Kinks
The Kinks Are the Village Green Preservation Society (Reprise, 1969)

The KLF
Chill Out (TVT, 1993)
The History of the JAMS a.k.a. The Timelords (TVT, 1988)

Kraftwerk
Tone Float (as Organisation; Phantom, 1999, Eng.; 1970)
Kraftwerk (Phantom, 1999, Eng.; 1972)
Kraftwerk 2 (Phantom, 1999, Eng.; 1972)
Ralf and Florian (Phantom, 1999, Eng.; 1973)
Radio-Activity (Capitol, 1975)
Computer World (Elektra, 1981)
Electric Café (Elektra, 1986)
Tour de France Soundtracks (Astralwerks, 2003)

Kyuss
Wretch (Chameleon, 1991)
Blues for the Red Sun (Chameleon, 1992)
Welcome to Sky Valley (Elektra, 1994)
...And the Circus Leaves Town (Elektra, 1995)

Labradford
Prazision LP (Kranky, 1993)
Labradford (Kranky, 1996)
Mi Media Naranja (Kranky, 1997)
E Luxo So (Kranky, 1999)
Fixed::Context (Kranky, 2001)

La Düsseldorf
La Düsseldorf (Nova, 1976)

Laika
Silver Apples of the Moon (American, 1995)

Led Zeppelin
Untitled (IV) (Atlantic, 1971)
Houses of the Holy (Atlantic, 1973)
Physical Graffiti (Atlantic, 1975)

The Lime Spiders
Nine Miles High 1983—1990 (Raven, 2002, Aus.)

The Long Ryders
10-5-60/Native Sons (Frontier, 1992)

Loop
Heaven's End (Head, 1987, Eng.)
The World in Your Eyes (Head, 1988, Eng.)
Fade Out (Rough Trade, 1989)
A Gilded Eternity (RCA, 1990)

Lothar and the Hand People
Presenting…Lothar and the Hand People
(CEMA Special Markets, 1994; 1968)

Low
I Could Live In Hope (Vernon Yard, 1994)
Long Division (Vernon Yard, 1995)
Songs for a Dead Pilot (Kranky, 1997)
Secret Name (Kranky, 1999)
Things We Lost in the Fire (Kranky, 2001)
Trust (Kranky, 2002)

Luna
Lunapark (Elektra, 1992)
Bewitched (Elektra, 1994)
Penthouse (Elektra, 1995)
Pup Tent (Elektra, 1997)
Close Cover Before Striking (Jet Set, 2002)

The Lyres
On Fyre (Ace of Hearts, 1996; 1984)

The Mad Violets
World Of… (Lolita, 1986)

Madonna
The Immaculate Collection (Warner Bros., 1990)
Ray of Light (Maverick, 1998)

Magic Hour
No Excess Is Absurd (Twisted Village, 1994)
Will They Turn You on or Will They Turn on You (Twisted Village, 1995)

Magma
Mekanik Destruktiw Kommandoh (Phantom, 1974, Ger.)

Major Stars
Space/Time (Twisted Village, 1999)
The Rock Revival (Twisted Village, 1997)
Distant Effects (Squealer, 2002)

Phil Manzanera
The Manzanera Collection (Caroline, 1995)

Mercury Rev
  Yerself Is Steam (Columbia, 1992)
  Boces (Columbia, 1993)
  See You on the Other Side (Columbia, 1995)
  Paralyzed Mind of the Archangel Void (as Harmony Rockets; Excelsior, 1995)

The Minders
  Hooray for Tuesday (Spin Art, 1998)
  Cul-De-Sacs & Dead Ends (Spin Art, 1999)
  Golden Street (Spin Art, 2001)

Roy Montgomery
  Scenes from the South Island (Drunken Fish, 1995)
  And Now the Rain Sounds Like Life Is Falling Through It (Drunken Fish, 1998)
  Allegory of Hearing (Drunken Fish, 2000)

Mouse on Mars
  Autoditacker (Thrill Jockey, 1997)
  Idiology (Thrill Jockey, 2001)

My Bloody Valentine
  This Is Your Bloody Valentine (Dossier, 1990, Eng.; 1985)
  Ecstasy and Wine (Lazy, 1989, Eng.; 1987)
  Untitled (You Made Me Realise) (Creation, 1988)
  Glider EP (Sire, 1989)
  Tremolo EP (Sire, 1990)

Marillion
  Misplaced Childhood (Sanctuary, 2001; 1985)

The Marshmallow Overcoat
  The Marshmallow Overcoat: 1986–1990 (Get Hip, 1990)

Nick Mason
  Fictitious Sports (Columbia, 1981)

Massive Attack
  Blue Lines (Virgin, 1992)
  Protection (Virgin, 1995)

The Master Musicians of Jojouka
  Brian Jones Presents: The Pipes of Pan at Jajouka (Virgin, 1971)

Matching Mole
  Matching Mole (BGO, 1972, Fr.)
  Matching Mole's Little Red Record (BGO, 1972, Fr.)

Eric Matthews
It's Heavy in Here (Sub Pop, 1995)
The Lateness of the Hour (Sub Pop, 1997)

Mazzy Star
She Hangs Brightly (Capitol, 1991)
So Tonight That I Might See (Capitol, 1993)
Among My Swan (Capitol, 1996)

Paul McCartney
Liverpool Sound Collage (Capitol, 2000)

The MC5
Kick Out the Jams (Elektra, 1969)

The Meat Puppets
Up on the Sun (Rykodisc, 1999; 1985)
Mirage (Rykodisc, 1999; 1987)
Huevos (Rykodisc, 1999; 1987)

The Melvins
Houdini (Atlantic, 1993)
Stoner Witch (Atlantic, 1994)
Stag (Atlantic, 1996)
The Maggot (Ipecac, 1999)
Bootlicker (Ipecac, 1999)
The Crybaby (Ipecac, 2000)
Electroretard (Man's Ruin, 2001)

Microstoria
—snd (Thrill Jockey, 1996)
Reprovisers (Thrill Jockey, 1997)
Model 3, Step 2 (Thrill Jockey, 2000)

The Mighty Mofos
Sho' Hard! (Treehouse, 1988)

The Miracle Workers
Inside Out (Voxx, 2000; 1985)
Moxie's Revenge (Get Hip, 1990)
Primary Domain (Glitterhouse, 1990, Ger.)

Mission of Burma
Mission of Burma (Rykodisc, 1988)

Moby
Go Remixes EP (Instinct, 1991)
Moby (Instinct, 1992)
Move EP (Elektra, 1993)
Early Underground (Instinct, 1993)
Everything Is Wrong (Elektra, 1995)
Animal Rights (Elektra, 1997)
I Like to Score (Elektra, 1997)

Moby Grape
Vintage: The Very Best of Moby Grape (Columbia/Legacy, 1993)

The Mod Fun
Past...Forward (Get Hip, 1995)

The Moles
Untune the Sky (Flydaddy, 1991)
Instinct (Flydaddy, 1994)

Monaural
Monitor Interference (Ba Da Bing, 1999)

The Monkees
Greatest Hits (Rhino, 1995)

The Monks
Black Monk Time (Infinite Zero, 1997; 1966)

Monster Magnet
Spine of God (Primo Scree, 1992)
Superjudge (A&M, 1993)
Dopes to Infinity (A&M, 1995)
Powertrip (A&M, 1998)

The Moog Cookbook
The Moog Cookbook (Restless, 1996)
Ye Olde Space Band (Restless, 1997)

The Mooney Suzuki
Electric Sweat (Gammon, 2002)

Moonshake
Eva Luna (Too Pure/Matador/Atlantic, 1993)
Big Good Angel (Too Pure/Matador, 1994)
The Sound Your Eyes Can Follow (Too Pure/American, 1994)

Morcheeba
Who Can You Trust? (Discovery, 1996)
Fragments of Freedom (Sire, 2000)
Charango (Warner Bros., 2002)

The Move
Great Move! The Best of the Move (EMI, 1994)

Nebula
To the Center (Sub Pop, 1999)
Charged (Sub Pop, 2001)

The Negro Problem
Joys & Concerns (Aerial Flipout, 1997)
Welcome Black (Image, 2002)

Neu!
Neu! (Astralwerks, 2001; 1972)
Neu! 75 (Astralwerks, 2001; 1975)

Colin Newman
A–Z (Beggars Banquet, 1980)
provisionally entitled the singing fish (4AD, 1981)
Not to (4AD, 1982)
Commercial Suicide (Restless, 1986)
It Seems (Restless, 1988)
Bastard (Swim, 1997)

Nico
Chelsea Girl (Verve, 1967)
The Marble Index (Elektra, 1969)
Desert Shore (Reprise, 1969)

The Nomads
Outburst (Homestead, 1984)

Oasis
Definitely Maybe (Sony, 1994)
Be Here Now (Sony, 1997)
The Masterplan (Sony, 1998)
Standing on the Shoulder of Giants (Sony, 2000)
Heathen Chemistry (Sony, 2002)

The Obsessed
Obsessed (Tolotta, 2000; 1990)

Mike Oldfield
Hergest Ridge (Virgin, 2000; 1974)
Exposed (Virgin, 2000; 1979)
Elements box set (Virgin, 1994)

Opal
Happy Nightmare Baby LP (SST, 1987)

Orange Goblin
Time Traveling Blues (The Music Cartel, 1999)
The Big Black (The Music Cartel, 2000)

The Orb
U.F.Orb (Mercury, 1992)
Live 93 (Island, 1993)
Pomme Fritz (Island, 1994)
Orbus Terrarum (Island, 1995)
Cydonia (MCA, 2001)

Orbital
Orbital I (ffrr, 1992)
Orbital II (ffrr, 1993)
Snivilisation (ffrr, 1994)
The Middle of Nowhere (ffrr, 1999)

Outkast
Aquemini (La Face, 1998)

Oval
Systemische (Thrill Jockey, 1996)
Ovalcommers (Thrill Jockey, 2001)

The Pandoras
It's About Time (Voxx, 1986)

Papas Fritas
Papas Fritas (Minty Fresh, 1995)
Helioself (Minty Fresh, 1997)
Buildings and Grounds (Minty Fresh, 2000)

Parliament

Up for the Down Stroke (Casablanca, 1974)
Chocolate City (Casablanca, 1975)
Mothership Connection (Casablanca, 1976)
The Clones of Dr. Funkenstein (Casablanca, 1976)
Funkentelechy vs. the Placebo Syndrome (Casablanca, 1977)
Motor Booty Affair (Casablanca, 1978)
Gloryhallastoopid—Or Pin the Tail on the Funky (Casablanca, 1979)
Trombipulation (Casablanca, 1981)

The Peanut Butter Conspiracy
The Great Peanut Butter Conspiracy
    (Sony Music Special Products, 1992)

Pere Ubu
The Modern Dance (Geffen, 1998; 1978)
Cloudland (Mercury/Fontana, 1989)
Story of My Life (Imago, 1993)
Raygun Suitcase (Tim/Kerr, 1995)

Tom Petty and the Heartbreakers
Greatest Hits (MCA, 1993)

Pink Faeries
Golden Years 1969–1971 (Cleopatra, 1998)

Pink Floyd
A Saucerful of Secrets (Capitol, 1968)
Ummagumma (Capitol, 1969)
More (Capitol, 1969)
Meddle (Capitol, 1971)
The Wall (Columbia, 1979)
Shine On box set (Columbia, 1992)

Plan 9
Dealing with the Dead (Midnight, 1984)

Plastic People of the Universe
Plastic People of the Universe 1997
    (Globus International, 1997)

Plasticland
Dapper Snappings (Repulsion, 1994, Ger.)
Mink Dress and Other Cats (Timothy's Brain, 1995)

Plastikman
Sheet One (Novamute, 1994)
Musik (Novamute, 1995)

Polara
   Polara (Restless, 1995)
   C'est La Vie (Interscope, 1997)
   Formless/Functional (Interscope, 1998)
   Jetpack Blues (Susstones, 2002)

Popol Vuh
   In Den Gärten Pharaos/Aguirre (Spalax, 1992, Fr.; 1972, 1975)
   Best of Popol Vuh from the Films of Werner Herzog (Milan, 1993)

Porcupine Tree
   Stupid Dream (Madfish, 1999)
   Signify (Ark 21, 2000)

Porno for Pyros
   Porno for Pyros (Warner Bros., 1993)
   Good God's Urge (Warner Bros., 1996)

Portishead
   Portishead (London, 1997)

The Pretty Things
   Emotions (Snapper, 2000, Eng.; 1967)
   Parachute (Snapper, 2000, Eng.; 1968)

Prince
   Purple Rain (Warner Bros., 1984)
   Around the World in a Day (Warner Bros., 1985)

The Prisoners
   Revenge of the Prisoners (Pink Dust, 1984)

Procul Harum
   Chapter One: Turning Back the Page 1967–1991 (Zoo, 1991)

Pram
   The Stars Are So Big, the Earth Is So Small...Stay as You Are
(Too Pure, 1993, Eng.)
   Helium (Too Pure/American, 1995)
   Sargasso Sea (Too Pure/American, 1995)

The Psychedelic Furs
   The Psychedelic Furs (Columbia, 1980)
   Talk Talk Talk (Columbia, 1981)
   Forever Now (Columbia, 1982)

Psychic TV
Towards Thee Infinite Beat (Cherry Red, 1999; 1990)
Trip Reset (Cleopatra, 1996)
Best Ov Psychic TV: Time's Up (Cleopatra, 1999)

Pulnoc
City of Hysteria (Arista, 1991)

Queens of the Stone Age
Rated R (Interscope, 2000)
Songs for the Deaf (Interscope, 2002)

Rachel's
Music for Egon Schiele (Quarter Stick, 1996)

Radiohead
Pablo Honey (Capitol, 1993)
The Bends (Capitol, 1995)
OK Computer (Capitol, 1997)
Amnesiac (Capitol, 2001)
Hail to the Thief (Capitol, 2003)

The Rain Parade
Crashing Dream (Island, 1985)

The Ramones
Acid Eaters (Radioactive, 1994)

The Red Crayola
The Parable of Arable Land /God Bless the Red Crayola and All Who Sail With It (Decal, 1990, Fr.; 1967, 1968)

Red Red Meat
Jimmywine Majestic (Sub Pop, 1994)
Bunny Gets Paid (Sub Pop, 1995)
There's a Star Above the Manger Tonight (Sub Pop, 1997)

Lou Reed
Berlin (RCA, 1973)
Metal Machine Music (RCA, 1975)
The Blue Mask (RCA, 1982)

R.E.M.
Chronic Town EP (IRS, 1982)
Murmur (IRS, 1983)
Reconstruction of the Fables (IRS, 1985)

Kimberly Rew
   The Bible of Bop (Press, 1982)
   Anthology (with Katrina and the Waves; One Way, 1995)
   Tunnel Into Summer (Gadfly, 2000)
   Great Central (Bongo Beat, 2002)

Ride
   Going Blank Again (Reprise, 1992)
   Tarantula (Reprise, 1996)

Missy Roback
   Just Like Breathing (Hear Kitty, 2002)

Paul Roland
   Danse Macabre (Bam Caruso, 1987, Eng.)

The Rolling Stones
   Aftermath (Abkco, 1966)
   Exile on Main Street (Abkco, 1972)
   Hot Rocks 1964–71 (Abkco, 1972)
   More Hot Rocks: Big Hits and Fazed Cookies (Abcko, 1973)

The Roots
   Things Fall Apart (MCA, 1999)

Michael Rother
   Flammende Herzen (Sky, 1976)
   Fernwarme (Polydor, 1981)

Roxy Music
   Stranded (Island, 1973)
   Country Life (Island, 1974)
   Siren (Island, 1975)

Sabalon Glitz
   Ufonic (Trixie, 1994)

Santana
   Dance of the Rainbow Serpent box set (Legacy/Columbia, 1995)
   The Supernatural (Arista, 2000)

Klaus Schulze
   Klaus Schulze: The Essential '72–'93 (Caroline, 1993)

The Screaming Trees
   Uncle Anesthesia (Sony, 1991)
   Sweet Oblivion (Sony, 1992)

See Feel
   Quique (Too Pure/Caroline, 1994)

The Shamen
What's Going Down? EP (Communion, 1988)
In Gorbachev We Trust (Demon, 1989)
En-Tact (Epic, 1991)
Boss Drum (Epic, 1993)

Sheavy
Electric Sleep (The Music Cartel, 1999)
Celestial Hi-Fi (The Music Cartel, 2000)

Sigur Ros
( ) (MCA, 2002)

Nancy Sinatra
Lightning's Girl: Greatest Hits 1965–1971 (Raven, 2002)

Sleep
Holy Mountain (Earache, 1993)

Slipstream
Slipstream (Carrot Top, 1995)
Side Effects (Che, 1996)

Slowdive
Souvlaki (Capitol, 1994)

Sly and the Family Stone
Anthology (Epic, 1973)

Small Faces
There Are But Four Small Faces (Sony, 1991)
Ogden's Nut Gone Flake (Sony, 1991)

The Smashing Pumpkins
Adore (Virgin, 1998)
Machina: The Machines of God (Virgin, 2000)

Kendra Smith
Five Ways of Disappearing (4AD, 1995)

The Soft Boys
A Can of Bees (Rykodisc, 1992; 1979)
Invisible Hits (Rykodisc, 1992; 1983)
1976–81 (Rykodisc, 1993)
Nextdoorland (Matador, 2002)

Sonic Youth
Bad Moon Rising (Geffen, 1995; 1985)
EVOL (Geffen, 1994; 1986)
Sister (Geffen, 1994; 1987)
Daydream Nation (Geffen, 1993; 1988)
Murray Street (DGC, 2002)

Soundgarden
Superunknown (A&M, 1994)

Soundtrack of Our Lives
Extended Revelation (Hidden Agenda, 2001)
Welcome to the Infant Freebase (Hidden Agenda, 2001)
Behind the Music (Universal, 2002)

Spacemen 3
Sound of Confusion (Taang!, 1994; 1986)
Performance (Taang!, 1994; 1988)
Playing With Fire (Taang!, 1994; 1989)
Recurring (Dedicated/RCA, 1991)
Taking Drugs to Make Music to Take Drugs To (Bomp, 1994)

Space Time Continuum
Sea Biscuit (Caroline, 1994)
Alien Dreamtime (Caroline, 1994)

Spectrum
Spectrum (Silvertone, 1990)
Soul Kiss (Glide Divine) (Silvertone, 1994)

Speed the Plough
Speed the Plough (East Side Digital, 1991; 1989)
Wonder Wheel (East Side Digital, 1991)
Mason's Box (East Side Digital, 1993)
Marina (East Side Digital, 1995)

Skip Spence
Oar (Sony Music Special Products, 1991)

Spirit Caravan
Jug Fulla Sun (Tolotta, 2000)
Elusive Truth (Tolotta, 2001)

Spiritualized
Let It Come Down (Arista, 2001)
Amazing Grace (Sanctuary, 2003)

Stars of the Lid
The Ballasted Orchestra (Kranky, 1997)
Tired Sounds of Stars of the Lid (Kranky, 2001)
Avec Laudenum (Kranky, 2002)

Steppenwolf
Steppenwolf the Second (MCA, 1968)

Stereolab
Peng! (Too Pure, 1992)
The Groop Played Space Age Batchelor Pad Music (Too Pure, 1993)
Mars Audiac Quintet (Elektra, 1994)
Refried Ectoplasm (Switched On Volume 2) (Drag City, 1995)
Emperor Tomato Ketchup (Elektra, 1996)
Dots and Loops (Elektra, 1997)
Cobra and Phases Group Play Voltage in the Milky Night (Elektra, 1999)
Sound-Dust (Elektra, 2001)

Stereo Total
Stereo Total (Bobsled, 1998)
Total Pop (Analog, 2000)
Musique Automatique (Kill Rock Stars, 2002)

Stew
Guest Host (Telegraph 2000)
The Naked Dutch Painter (Image 2002)

The Stooges
The Stooges (Elektra, 1969)
Funhouse (Elektra, 1970)

Streetwalkin' Cheetahs
Waiting for the Death of My Generation (Triple X, 2001)

The Strokes
The Modern Age EP (RCA, 2001)
Is This It (RCA, 2001)

Donna Summer
The Donna Summer Anthology (Polygram, 1993)

Sun Ra
The Heliocentric Worlds of Sun Ra, I (ESP, 1965)
The Heliocentric Worlds of Sun Ra, II (ESP, 1966)

The Sunshine Fix
Age of the Sun (Emperor Norton, 2002)

The Super Furry Animals
Fuzzy Logic (Sony, 1996)
Mwng (Flydaddy, 2000)
Phantom Power (Beggars Banquet, 2003)

The Tadpoles
He Fell Into the Sky (Bakery, 1994)
Far Out (Bakery, 1996)
Smoke Ghost (Bakery, 1998)

Talk Talk
Spirit of Eden (EMI, 1988)
Natural History: The Very Best of Talk Talk (EMI, 1990)

Talking Heads
More Songs About Buildings and Food (Sire, 1978)
Fear of Music (Sire, 1979)
Remain in Light (Sire, 1980)

Tangerine Dream
In the Beginning box set (Relativity, 1985)

The Teardrop Explodes
Kilimanjaro/Wilder (Collector's Choice, 2001; 1988, 1989)
Everybody Wants to Shag…The Teardrop Explodes (Fontana, 1990)

Teenage Fanclub
A Catholic Education (Matador, 1990)
The King (Creation, 1991, Eng.)
Bandwagonesque (DGC, 1991)

Television
Marquee Moon (Elektra, 1977)

The Television Personalities
…And Don't the Kids Just Love It (Razor & Tie, 1995; 1980)
Yes Darling, But Is It Art? (Early Singles and Rarities) (Atlantic, 1995)

The Temptations
Cloud Nine/Puzzle People (Universal International, 2000; Eng.)

Thin White Rope
Exploring the Axis (Frontier, 1985)
Moonhead (Frontier, 1987)

Third Eye Foundation
Ghost (Merge, 1997)
You Guys Kill Me (Merge, 1998)
Little Lost Soul (Merge, 2000)
I Poo Poo on Your Juju (Merge, 2001)

The 13th Floor Elevators
Bull of the Woods (Collectables, 1993; 1968)

The Three O'Clock
Befour Three O'Clock (as the Salvation Army; Frontier, 1985)
Arrive Without Traveling (IRS, 1985)

Mary Timony
Mountains (Matador, 2000)

Tiny Lights
The Young Person's Guide to Tiny Lights (Bar/None, 1995)

Tonto's Expanding Headband
Zero Time (Atlantic, 1975; 1972)

Tortoise
TNT (Thrill Jockey, 1998)
Standards (Thrill Jockey, 2001)

Tricky
Nearly God (Island, 1996)
BlowBack (Island, 2001)

Tripping Daisy
Bill (Mercury, 1993)
I Am an Elastic Firecracker (Polygram, 1995)
Tripping Daisy (Sugar Fix, 2000)

The Troggs
Archeology (1966–1976) (Fontana, 1992)

The Trypes
The Explorers Hold EP (Coyote, 1984)

The 27 Various
Hi. (Susstones, 1987)
Yes, Indeed (Susstones, 1989)
Approximately (Clean 1990)
Up (Clean, 1992)
Fine (Clean, 1992)

Tyrannosaurus Rex
Definitive Tyrannosaurus Rex (Sequel, 1999, Eng.)

UFO
Unidentified Flying Object (Disky, 1998, Eng.; 1971)

Ultramarine
Every Man and Woman Is A Star (Rough Trade, 1992)
United Kingdom (Sire/Giant, 1993)

Ultra Vivid Scene
Ultra Vivid Scene (4AD/Rough Trade, 1988)
Joy 1967–1990 (4AD/Columbia, 1990)

U2
The Joshua Tree (Island, 1990)
Zooropa (Island, 1993)

VapourSpace
Gravitational Arch of 10 (ffrr, 1993)
*Space + Time * Liquids + Metals* (Swim, 1995, Eng.)
Sweep (Uni, 1997)
Sonic Residue from Vapourspace (Magna Carta, 2002)

Various artists
Battle of the Garages 1 & 2 (Voxx, 1994; 1981, 1982)
Best of Techno Volumes 1–3 (Profile, 1993)
Ethnotechno (Wax Trax!/TVT, 1994)
Excursions in Ambience (Caroline, 1993)
Excursions in Ambience: The Second Orbit (Caroline, 1993)
Excursions in Ambience: The Third Dimension (Caroline, 1994)
Excursions in Ambience: The Fourth Frontier (Caroline, 1995)
Love, Peace & Poetry, Vol. 4: Japanese Psychedelic (QDK, 2001, Jap.)
Nuggets II: Original Artyfacts from the British Empire and Beyond box
set   (Rhino, 2001)
Ohm: The Early Gurus of Electronic Music box set (Ellipsis Arts…,
2000)
Rainy Day (Rough Trade, 1989)
Vol. 1–2 Desert Sessions (Man's Ruin, 1998)
Vol. 3–4 Desert Sessions (Man's Ruin, 1998)
Vol. 5–6 Desert Sessions (Man's Ruin, 1999)
Vol. 7–8 Desert Sessions (Southern Lord, 2001)
Whore: Various Artists Play Wire (WMO, 1996)

Velvet Crush
In the Presence of Greatness (Ringers Lactate, 1991)
Teenage Symphonies to God (Creation/Epic, 1994)

The Velvet Monkeys
Future (Fountain of Youth, 1983)
Rotting Corpse au Go-Go (Shimmy-Disc, 1989)

The Velvet Underground
White Light/White Heat (Verve/Polygram, 1985; 1967)
The Velvet Underground (Verve/Polygram, 1985; 1969)
Loaded (Cotillion, 1970)
V.U. (Polygram, 1985)
Another View (Polygram, 1986)

The Vipers
Outta the Nest (Cavestomp, 2000; 1985)

Viva Saturn
Viva Saturn (Hey Day, 1990)
Brightside (Restless, 1995)

Wake Ooloo
Hear No Evil (Pravda, 1994)
What About It (Pravda, 1995)
Stop the Ride (Pravda, 1996)

Ween
The Pod (Elektra, 1991)
Pure Guava (Elektra, 1992)
The Mollusk (Elektra, 1997)
White Pepper (Elektra, 2000)

The White Stripes
The White Stripes (V2, 2002; 1999)
De Stijl (V2, 2002; 2000)
White Blood Cells (V2, 2002)

The Who
The Who Sell Out (MCA, 1967)

Wild Carnation
Tricycle (Delmore, 1995)

Windy & Carl
Portal (Ba Da Bing, 1995)
Depths (Kranky, 1998)
Consciousness (Kranky, 2001)

Wire
Pink Flag (Restless, 1989; 1977)
The Ideal Copy (Mute, 2000; 1987)

Stevie Wonder
Music of My Mind (Motown, 1972)
Talking Book (Tamla, 1972)
Innervisions (Motown, 1973)
Songs in the Key of Life (Tamla, 1976)

Rick Wright
Wet Dreams (Columbia, 1978)

The Wu-Tang Clan
Enter the Wu-Tang (36 Chambers) (RCA, 1993)
Wu-Tang Forever (Relativity, 1999)
Wu Tang Iron Flag (Sony, 2001)

Robert Wyatt
Rock Bottom (Virgin, 1974)
Ruth Is Stranger Than Richard (Virgin, 1975)

Steve Wynn
Kerosene Man (Rhino, 1990)
Dazzling Display (Rhino, 1992)
Take Your Flunky and Dangle (Innerstate, 1994)
Melting in the Dark (Zero Hour, 1996)
Sweetness and Light (Zero Hour, 1997)
Here Come the Miracles (Innerstate, 2001)
Flourescent (Innerstate, 2002)

XTC
Drums and Wires (Geffen, 1984; 1979)
Black Sea (Geffen, 1984; 1980)
Mummer (Geffen, 1984)
The Big Express (Geffen, 1984)
Oranges & Lemons (Geffen, 1989)
Nonsuch (Geffen, 1991)

The Yardbirds
Roger the Engineer (Diablo, 1999, Eng.)
The Yardbirds, Vol. 2: Blues, Backtracks and Shapes of Things
    (Sony, 1991)

Yard Trauma
Must've Been Something I Took Last Night (Dionysius, 1985)

The Yellow Sunshine Explosion
The Yellow Sunshine Explosion (Love's Simple Dreams, 1987, Ger.)

Yes
The Yes Album (Atlantic, 1994; 1971)
Fragile (Atlantic, 1994; 1971)
Close to the Edge (Atlantic, 1994; 1972)
Going for the One (Atlantic, 1994; 1978)

Neil Young
Decade (Reprise, 1976)

Yo La Tengo
New Wave Hot Dogs/President Yo La Tengo
    (Coyote-Twin/Tone, 1989)
May I Sing With Me (Alias, 1992)
Painful (Matador/Atlantic, 1993)
Electr-O-Pura (Matador/Atlantic, 1995)
I Can Hear the Heart Beating As One (Matador, 1997)
And Then Nothing Turned Itself Inside-Out (Matador, 2000)

Yung Wu
Shore Leave (Coyote-Twin/Tone, 1987)

Frank Zappa and the Mothers of Invention
Freak Out! (Rykodisc, 1995; 1966)
Absolutely Free (Rykodisc, 1995; 1967)

A nOTE On SOURCES

THROUGHOUT THE BOOK, quotations that are not otherwise cited have been taken from interviews I conducted in the '80s, the '90s, and as recently as the summer of 2003 for publications including the *Chicago Sun-Times, Request, Spin, Penthouse, Guitar World, Modern Drummer, New Times Los Angeles*, and *The Bob*. The sources for other quotes have been indicated in the text, and complete citations follow in the Bibliography.

Interview subjects included Damon Albarn, Nicholaus Arson, Howie B., Tony Banks, Geoff Barrow, Andre Benjamin, Ade Blackburn, Scott Booker, Joe Boyd, Vratislav Brabenec, Carter Brown, Steve Burns, John Cale, George Clinton, Phil Collins, King Coffee, Stu Cook, Julian Cope, Wayne Coyne, Richard Davies, Tim DeLaughter, DJ Spooky, Jonathan Donahue, Bill Doss, John Drake, Steven Drozd, the Edge, Brian Eno, Roky Erickson, Everlast, Bryan Ferry, John Frankovic, Peter Gabriel, Liam Gallagher, Tim Gane, Mark Gardener, Michael Gibbons, Bruce Gilbert, David Gilmour,

Ross Godfrey, Robert Gotobed, Mickey Hart, William Cullen Hart, John Herndon, Robyn Hitchcock, Susanna Hoffs, Chris Holmes, Josh Homme, Steve Howe, Ralf Hütter, Michael Ivins, Bruce Johnston, Glenn Jones, John Paul Jones, Ronald Jones, Lenny Kaye, Wayne Kramer, Damon Krukowski, Graham Lewis, Mick London, Kawabata Makoto, Phil Manzanera, Derek Mason, Nick Mason, Eric Matthews, Doug McCombs, John McEntire, Alan McGee, Terence McKenna, Phil McMullen, Dennis McNally, Glenn Mercer, Bill Million, Moby, Colin Newman, Sean O'Hagan, Mike Oldfield, Jimmy Page, Jeff Parker, Andy Partridge, Alex Paterson, Dave Pearce, Eddie Phillips, Jason Pierce, Matt Pike, Prince Be, Simon Raymonde, Lou Reed, Glenn Rehse, Kimberly Rew, Keith Richards, Rex Ritter, Steven Roback, Michael Rother, Mike Rutherford, Laetitia Sadier, Carlos Santana, Robert Schneider, Kevin Shields, Simeon, Damo Suzuki, Chris Squire, David Thomas, Mike Thorne, Jeff Tweedy, Maureen Tucker, Nik Turner, Dean Wareham, Dave Weckerman, Scott Weinrich, Steve Wilson, and Steve Wynn.

I am thankful for the insights gleaned from each and every one of them.

BIBLIOGRAPHY

Books

Andersen, Christopher. *Jagger Unauthorized*. New York: Delacorte, 1993.

Arnold, Gina. Route 666: *On the Road to Nirvana*. New York: St. Martin's, 1993.

Bangs, Lester. *Psychotic Reactions and Carburetor Dung*. New York: Knopf, 1987.

Barr, Tim. *Kraftwerk: From Düsseldorf to the Future (with Love)*. London: Ebury Press, 1998.

Beadle, Jeremy J. *Will Pop Eat Itself? Pop Music in the Soundbite Era*. London: Faber and Faber, 1993.

Bockris, Victor, and Gerard Malanga. *Up-Tight: The Velvet Underground Story*. New York: Omnibus Press, 1983.

Booth, Stanley. *The True Adventures of The Rolling Stones*. New York: Vintage, 1985.

Bromell, Nick. *Tomorrow Never Knows: Rock and Psychedelics in the 1960s*. Chicago: University of Chicago Press, 2000.

Brown, Peter, and Steven Gaines. *The Love You Make: An Insider's Story of the Beatles*. New York: Signet, 1984.

Bussy, Pascal, and Andy Hall. *The Can Book*. London: S.A.F., 1989.

Bussy, Pascal. *Kraftwerk: Man, Machine and Music*. London: S.A.F., 1993.

Cavanagh, David. *The Creation Records Story: My Magpie Eyes are Hungry for the Prize*. London: Virgin Books, 2000.

Carducci, Joe. *Rock and the Pop Narcotic*. San Francisco: Redoubt Press, 1990.

Clapton, Diana. *Lou Reed & The Velvet Underground*. New York: Proteus, 1982.

Christgau, Robert. *Christgau's Record Guide: Rock Albums of the '70s.* New Haven and New York: Ticknor & Fields, 1981.

———. *Christgau's Record Guide: The '80s.* New York: Pantheon, 1990.

Cohen, Scott. *Yakety Yak: The Midnight Confessions and Revelations of Thirty-Seven Rock Stars and Legends.* New York: Fireside, 1994.

Cope, Julian. *Head-On: Memories of the Liverpool Punk Scene and the Story of the Teardrop Explodes, 1976–82.* London: Ma-Gog Books, 1994.

———. *Krautrocksampler.* London: Head Heritage, 1995.

Corbett, John. *Extended Play: Sounding Off from John Cage to Dr. Funkenstein.* Chapel Hill, N.C.: Duke University Press, 1994.

Covach, John, and Graeme M. Boone, editors. *Understanding Rock: Essays in Musical Analysis.* London: Oxford University Press, 1997.

Crosby, David, and Carl Gottlieb. *Long Time Gone: The Autobiography of David Crosby.* New York: Dell, 1988.

Dallas, Karl. *Pink Floyd: Bricks in the Wall.* New York: S.P.I., 1994.

Davies, Ray. *X-Ray: The Unauthorized Autobiography.* Woodstock, N.Y.: Overlook Press, 1994.

DeCurtis, Anthony, and James Henke and Holly George-Warren, editors. *The Rolling Stone Album Guide.* New York: Straight Arrow Publishers, 1992.

Dolenz, Mickey, and Mark Bego. *I'm a Believer: My Life of Monkees,* Music and Madness. New York: Hyperion, 1993.

Durr, R.A. *Poetic Vision and the Psychedelic Experience.* Syracuse, N.Y.: Syracuse University Press, 1970.

Eden, Kevin S. *Wire...Everybody Loves A History.* London: S.A.F., 1991.

The Editors of Rolling Stone. *Neil Young: The Rolling Stone Files.* New York: Hyperion, 1994.

———. *The Rolling Stone Record Review.* New York: Pocket Books, 1971.

———. *The Rolling Stone Record Review Volume II.* New York: Pocket Books, 1974.

Eisner, Bruce. *Ecstasy: The MDMA Story.* Berkeley, Calif.: Ronin, 1994.

Eno, Brian. *A Year With Swollen Appendices.* London: Faber & Faber, 1996.

Eno, Brian, and Russell Mills with Rick Poynor. *More Dark Than Shark.* London: Faber and Faber, 1986.

Eno, Brian, and Peter Schmidt. *Oblique Strategies.* London: Opal Information, Ltd., 1992.

Erickson, Roky. *Openers II: The Lyrics of Roky Erickson.* Los Angeles: 2.13.61, 1995.

Felder, Rachel. *Manic Pop Thrill.* Hopewell, N.J.: Ecco Press, 1993.

Flür, Wolfgang. *Kraftwerk: I Was a Robot.* London: Sanctuary, 2000.

Gaines, Steven. *Heroes & Villains: The True Story of the Beach Boys.* New York: NAL, 1986.

Gallo, Armando. *Genesis: I Know What I Like.* London: D.I.Y., 1980.

Gans, David. *Conversations with the Grateful Dead.* Secaucus, N.J.: Citadel Underground, 1993.

Gassen, Timothy. *Echoes in Time: The Garage and Psychedelic Music Explosion 1980-1990.* Telford, England: Borderline, 1991.

George, Leonard. *Alternative Realities: The Paranormal, the Mystic and the Transcendent in Human Experience.* New York: Facts on File, 1995.

Godwin, Robert. *The Illustrated Collector's Guide to Hawkwind.* Burlington, Ontario: Collector's Guide Publishing, 1993.

Goldstein, Richard. *Goldstein's Greatest Hits: A Book Mostly About Rock 'n' Roll.* New York: Prentice-Hall, 1970.

Goldman, Albert. *The Lives of John Lennon.* New York: William Morrow, 1988.

Grahame, Kenneth. *The Wind in the Willows.* New York: Bantam Classic, 1982.

Henderson, David. *'Scuse Me While I Kiss the Sky: The Life of Jimi Hendrix.* New York: Bantam, 1983.

Henderson, Leigh A., and William J. Glass. *LSD: Still with Us After All These Years.* New York: Lexington Books, 1994.

Heylin, Clinton. *From the Velvets to the Voidoids: A Pre-Punk History for a Post-Punk World.* New York: Penguin, 1993.

Hofmann, Albert. *LSD, My Problem Child: Reflections on Sacred Drugs, Mysticism, and Science.* Los Angeles: J.P. Tarcher, 1983.

Howe, Steve, with Tony Bacon. *The Steve Howe Guitar Collection.* New York: GPI, 1993.

Huxley, Aldous. *The Doors of Perception and Heaven and Hell.* New York: Harper Perennial, 1990.

———. *Brave New World.* New York: Harper & Row, 1969.

Jonnes, Jill. *Hep-Cats, Narcs, and Pipe Dreams: A History of America's Romance with Ilegal Drugs.* New York: Scribner, 1996.

Joynson, Vernon. *The Flashback: The Ultimate Psychedelic Music Guide.* Telford, England: Borderline, 1993.

———. *Fuzz, Acid And Flowers: A Comprehensive Guide to American Garage, Psychedelic and Hippie Rock 1964–1975.* Telford, England: Borderline, 1993.

Kadrey, Richard. *Covert Culture Sourcebook.* New York: St. Martin's, 1993.

Lazell, Barry, and Dafydd Rees. *Bryan Ferry & Roxy Music.* New York: Proteus Books, 1982.

Leary, Timothy, and Ralph Metzner and Richard Alpert. *The Psychedelic Experience: A Manual Based on the Tibetan Book of the Dead.* Secaucus, N.J.: Citadel Press, 1990.

Leary, Timothy. *Flashbacks: An Autobiography.* Los Angeles: J.P. Tarcher, 1983.

———. *Chaos & Cyber Culture.* Berkeley, Calif.: Ronin, 1994.

Lee, Martin A., and Bruce Shlain. *The Complete Social History of LSD: The CIA, the Sixties, and Beyond.* San Francisco: Grove Weidenfeld, 1985.

Lewisohn, Mark. *The Beatles Recording Sessions: The Official Abbey Road Studio Session Notes, 1962–1970.* New York: Harmony Books, 1988.

Mackay, Andy. *Electronic Music: The Instruments, the Music & the Musicians.* London: Harrow House, 1981.

MacDonald, Ian. *Revolution in the Head: The Beatles' Records and the Sixties.* New York: Henry Holt, 1994.

Maconie, Stuart. Blur: *3862 Days, The Official History.* London: Virgin Books, 1999.

Martin, Bill. *Music of Yes: Structure and Vision in Progressive Rock.* Chicago: Open Court, 1996.

———. *Listening to the Future: The Time of Progressive Rock 1968-1978.* Chicago: Open Court, 1997.

McKenna, Terence. *The Archaic Revival.* New York: Harper Collins, 1991.

———. *The Food of the Gods: The Search for the Original Tree of Knowledge.* New York: Bantam, 1992.

———. *True Hallucinations.* New York: Harper Collins, 1993.

McNally, Dennis. *A Long Strange Trip: The Inside History of the Grateful Dead.* New York: Broadway Books, 2001.

Miles. *Pink Floyd: A Visual Documentary.* New York: Quick Fox, 1980.

Miller, Jim, editor. *The Rolling Stone Illustrated History of Rock & Roll.* New York: Random House, 1980.

Murray, Charles Shaar. *Crosstown Traffic: Jimi Hendrix and the Rock 'n' Roll Revolution.* New York: St. Martin's, 1989.

Nelson, Havelock, and Michael A. Gozales. *Bring the Noise: A Guide to Rap* Music and Hip-Hop Culture. New York: Harmony Books, 1991.

Paglia, Camille. *Vamps & Tramps.* New York: Vintage, 1994.

Palacios, Julian. *Lost in the Woods—Syd Barrett & the Pink Floyd.* London: Boxtree Ltd., 2001.

Perry, Charles. *The Haight-Ashbury, A History.* New York: Vintage, 1985.

Pinchbeck, Daniel. *Breaking Open the Head: A Psychedelic Journey into the Heart of Contemporary Shamanism.* New York: Broadway Books, 2002.

Priore, Domenic. *Look, Listen, Vibrate, Smile—The Beach Boys.* St. Paul, MN: Small Press Distribution, 1997.

Reynolds, Simon. *Blissed Out: The Raptures of Rock.* New York: Serpent's Tail, 1990.

Reynolds, Simon, and Joy Press. *The Sex Revolts: Gender, Rebellion, and Rock 'n' Roll.* Cambridge, Mass.: Harvard University Press, 1995.

Riley, Tim. *Tell Me Why, The Beatles: Album by Album, Song by Song, The Sixties and After.* New York: Vintage, 1989.

Robbins, Ira, editor. *The Trouser Press Record Guide*. New York: Collier Books, 1991.

Romanowski, Patricia, and Holly George-Warren with Jon Pareles, editors. *The New Rolling Stone Encyclopedia of Rock & Roll*. New York: Fireside, 1995.

Rose, Cynthia. *Design After Dark: The Story of Dancefloor Style*. London: Thames and Hudson Ltd., 1991.

Roxon, Lillian. *Rock Encyclopedia*. New York: Grosset & Dunlap, 1969.

Rushkoff, Douglas. Cyberia: *Life in the Trenches of Hyperspace*. San Francisco: Harper San Francisco, 1994.

Saunders, Nicholas. *E for Ecstasy*. London: Nicholas Saunders, 1993.

Schaffner, Nicholas. *Saucerful of Secrets*. New York: Harmony Books, 1991.

Scoppa, Bud. *The Byrds*. New York: Scholastic Book Services, 1971.

Selvin, Joel. *Summer of Love: The Inside Story of LSD, Rock & Roll, Free love and High Times in the Wild West*. New York: Dutton, 1994.

Stafford, Peter. *Psychedelics Encyclopedia*. Berkeley, Calif.: Ronin, 1992.

Stevens, Jay. *Storming Heaven: LSD and the American Dream*. New York: Harper & Row, 1988.

Tamm, Eric. *Brian Eno: His Music and the Vertical Color of Sound*. London: Faber and Faber, 1989.

Thompson, Dave. *Space Daze: The History & Mystery of Electronic Ambient Space Rock*. Los Angeles: Cleopatra, 1994.

Tosches, Nick. *Unsung Heroes of Rock 'n' Roll: The Birth of Rock in the Wild Years Before Elvis*. New York: Harmony Books, 1991.

Troy, Sandy. *One More Saturday Night: Reflections with the Grateful Dead, Dead Family, and Dead Heads*. New York: St. Martin's, 1991.

Twomey, Chris. *XTC: Chalkhills and Children*. London: Omnibus Press, 1992.

Unterberger, Richie. *Unknown Legends of Rock 'n' Roll: Psychedelic Unknowns, Mad Geniuses, Punk Pioneers, Lo-Fi Mavericks & More*. San Francisco: Miller Freeman, 1998.

———. *Urban Spacemen and Wayfaring Strangers: Overlooked Innovators and Eccentric Visionaries of '60s Rock*. San Francisco: Miller Freeman, 2000.

Vassal, Jacques. *Electric Children: Roots and Branches of Modern Folk Rock*. New York: Taplinger, 1976.

Vorda, Alan. *Psychedelic Psounds: Interviews from A to Z with '60s Psychedelic and Garage Bands*. Telford, England: Borderline Productions, 1994.

Ward, Ed, and Geoffrey Stokes and Ken Tucker, *Rock of Ages: The Rolling Stone History of Rock & Roll*. New York: Rolling Stone Press/Summit Books, 1986.

Watkinson, Mike, and Pete Anderson. *Crazy Diamond: Syd Barrett and the Dawn of Pink Floyd*. London: Omnibus Press, 1991.

Watson, Ben. *Frank Zappa: The Negative Dialectics of Poodle Play*. New York: St. Martin's, 1995.

Weinstein, Deena. *Heavy Metal: A Cultural Sociology.* New York: Lexington Books, 1991.

————. *Serious Rock:* Bruce Springsteen/Rush/Pink Floyd. Montreal: Culture Texts, 1985.

Whitburn, Joel. *The Billboard Book of Top 40 Hits.* New York: Billboard, 1989.

White, Timothy. *The Nearest Faraway Place: Brian Wilson, the Beach Boys, and the Southern California Experience.* New York: Henry Holt 1994.

Wilson, Brian, with Todd Gold. *Wouldn't It Be Nice: My Own Story.* New York: Harper Collins, 1991.

Wolfe, Tom. *The Electric Kool-Aid Acid Test.* New York: Quality Paperback, 1990.

Wyman, Bill, with Ray Coleman. *Stone Alone: The Story of a Rock 'n' Roll Band.* New York: Viking, 1990.

Articles

Author unknown. "Brian Eno: Taking the Recording Studio by Strategy." *Musician,* November 1993.

————. "First Things Faust," *The Wire,* February 1994.

————. "XTC Talk to The Little Express." *The Little Express,* June 1985.

Bangs, Lester. "The History of Garage Rock, Part 1." *New Wave* magazine No. 2, 1977.

Becker, Howard. "History, Culture, and Subjective Experience." *Journal of Health & Social Behavior,* Vol. 8, 1967.

Beeson, Frank. "Arthur Lee Loves You." *The Bob,* No. 49.

Bentley, Bill. "Tommy Hall's Trip Through the Revolving Doors of Perception." *The Austin Chronicle,* Oct. 24, 1990.

Bookasta, Randy. "Julian Cope: The Saint Came Marching In." *Contrast* #3, fall 1987.

Cameron, Keith. "(No) Sign of the Valentines." *The New Musical Express,* April 15, 1995.

Considine, J.D. "When Techno Music Pulsates, There is Just No Sitting Still." *The Baltimore Sun,* Sept. 20, 1992.

Cooper, Dennis. "A Raver Runs Through It." *Spin,* March 1995.

Cost, Jud. "Through the Looking Glass." *Magnet,* May/June 1998.

Cross, Nigel. "A Boring Midday Chat with Robyn Hitchcock." *Forced Exposure* #13, 1987.

Cummings, Sue. "Welcome to the Machine." *Rolling Stone,* April 7, 1994.

DiMartino, Dave. "Love Through the Ages (Of Prophets, Seers and Sages): Arthur Lee's Legend Lingers." *Creem*, April 1981.

Ferguson, Jason. "White Flags Over Georgia" [Faust]. *Alternative Press*, August 1994.

Fox, Marisa. "Others from a Brother Planet." *New Musical Express*, April 13, 1991.

Gladstone, Eric. "Moonshake: Standing Naked in This Back of the Woods." *Alternative Press*, December 1993.

Hanners, Doug, Joe Nick Patoski, and Kirby McDaniel. "Roky '75." *Third Coast* magazine, November 1984.

Hardy, Ernest. "Why I Hate Techno." *Request*, July 1994.

Hibbert, Tom. "Mad Dog and Englishman" [Julian Cope]. *Details*, March 1993.

Higginbotham, Adam. "Music for Spaceports." *Details*, April, 1993.

Himes, Geoffrey. "Williamson's Celtic Connection." *The Washington Post*, April 9, 1987.

Isler, Scott. "The Dukes of Swindon." *Musician*, January 1987.

Kot, Greg. "The Experiment Continues." *The Chicago Tribune*, May 1, 1994.

———. "Amazon Grace: Brazil's Inventive Musical Genius Is Finally Infiltrating U.S. Scene." *The Chicago Tribune*, May 16, 1999.

Lieby, Richard. "The Elevator Doesn't Stop Here Anymore." *The Washington Post*, June 23, 1991.

McGonigal, Mike. "Dropping in at the Neutral Milk Hotel." *Puncture*, Spring 1998.

McLean, Greg. "Up & Down with the Feelies." *New York Rocker*, June 1980.

Morton, Roger. "Cloud Cuckoo Man." *New Musical Express*, Jan. 5, 1991.

———. "The Correct Use of Soup." *New Musical Express*, Jan. 21, 1995.

Phillip, Elizabeth. "Rain Parade: Flashback or Stand Still?" *Matter*, February 1984.

Prince, David. "Head Music." *Request*, July 1994.

———. "Interstellar Overdrive: Reaching Escape Velocity with the Orb." *Option*, January 1994.

———. "Moby Feature." *Request*, April 1995.

———. "Moby In Chicago." *Reactor*, September 1992.

Sprague, David. "Soul Brothers." *Request*, December 1995.

———. "Don't Write Him Off." *Request*, May 1991.

———. "Pop Shredded Through the Looking Glass." *Request*, February 1992.

Stapinski, Helene. "Nothing Is Real." *Request*, April 1992.

Strauss, Neil. "Beat Generation." *Option*, January 1994.

Strychn, Angus. "The Return of Hellfire: An Interview with Arthur Brown." *Your Flesh* No. 29, 1993.

Thomas, Pat. "Dream On: Steve Wynn Gets Down & Dirty...Er, Dusty." *The Bob,* 1985.

Turner, Gregg. "Cavern Club Psych-Out: The '60s are Alive and Well (Sort Of)." *Creem,* March 1986.

———. "Roky: On the Line With God and His Mom." *Forced Exposure* No. 9, 1986.

Whitworth, Armstrong. "Deutsch Nepal." *Strange Things Are Happening,* September-October 1988.

Witter, Simon. "Robopop!" [Kraftwerk]. *New Musical Express,* June 8, 1991.

Kageyama, Yuri. "Soul Meets Technology in New Detroit Dance Music." The Associated Press, Oct. 31, 1994.

INDEX

About the Author

Jim DeRogatis (left) with Wayne Coyne of the Flaming Lips in the Martian
space station in Coyne's backyard, Oklahoma City, Oklahoma, spring 2002.
(Photo by Scott Booker)

BORN IN JERSEY CITY, NEW JERSEY, the year the Beatles arrived in
America, Jim DeRogatis began voicing his opinions about rock 'n' roll
shortly thereafter. As a high-school senior, he spent a long and fascinating
day interviewing Lester Bangs two weeks before that legendary rock writer's
untimely demise. The experience fostered a lifelong obsession with
rock criticism, and he is currently the pop music critic at the *Chicago
Sun-Times*, as well as a freelance contributor to publications such as *Spin,*

Harp, Guitar World, Modern Drummer, and *Playboy.com.* Together with *Chicago Tribune* rock critic Greg Kot (Siskel to his Ebert), he is the host of *Sound Opinions,* "the world's only rock 'n' roll talk show," now in its fifth year on Chicago radio (check it out on the Web at www.soundopinions.net), and a televised version of the show recently debuted on WTTW, Chicago's PBS affiliate. The first edition of *Turn On Your Mind* was published in the summer of 1996 as *Kaleidoscope Eyes;* this edition has been fully updated and adds nearly 50,000 words. (And the author *still* isn't certain he's fully come to grips with this slippery but fascinating subject!) His other books are *Let It Blurt: The Life and Times of Lester Bangs, America's Greatest Rock Critic,* and the recent anthology, *Milk It! Collected Musings on the Alternative Music Explosion of the '90s.* He jokes that he is not a musician, but he *is* a drummer, and an account of his adventures in various groups over the last two decades is in the works. He can be reached through the Web at www.jimdero.com.